General History of Africa · IV

Africa from the Twelfth to the Sixteenth Century

Abridged Edition

UNESCO General History of Africa

Volume I *Methodology and African Prehistory*
Editor **J. Ki-Zerbo**

Volume II *Ancient Civilizations of Africa*
Editor **G. Mokhtar**

Volume III *Africa from the Seventh to the Eleventh Century*
Editor **I. Hrbek**

Volume IV *Africa from the Twelfth to Sixteenth Century*
Editors **J. Ki-Zerbo and D. T. Niane**

Volume V *Africa from the Sixteenth to Eighteenth Century**
Editor **B. A. Ogot**

Volume VI *Africa in the Nineteenth Century until the 1880s**
Editor **J. F. Ade Ajayi**

Volume VII *Africa under Foreign Domination* 1880–1935
Editor **A. Adu Boahen**

Volume VIII *Africa since* 1935*
Editor **A. A. Mazrui**

***forthcoming**

The abridged edition of
THE UNESCO GENERAL HISTORY OF AFRICA
is published by the following publishers

In Ghana, Sierra Leone,
the Gambia and Cameroon by
Readwide Bookshop
P.O. Box 0600
Accra, Ghana
In Kenya by
EAEP
P.O. Box 45314
Nairobi, Kenya
In Nigeria by
Heinemann Nigeria
P.O. Box 6205
Ibadan, Nigeria
In South Africa, Namibia, Botswana,
Lesotho and Swaziland by
David Philip Publishers
P.O. Box 23408
Claremont 7735, South Africa
In Tanzania by
Tanzania Publishing House
P.O. Box 2138
Dar es Salaam, Tanzania
In Uganda by
Fountain Publishers
P.O. Box 488
Kampala, Uganda
In Zambia by
UNZA Press
P.O. Box 32379
Lusaka, Zambia
In Zimbabwe,
Botswana, Swaziland and Malawi by
Baobab Books
P.O. Box 1559
Harare, Zimbabwe
In the United States of America
and Canada by
The University of California Press
2120 Berkeley Way
Berkeley, California 94720
And in the United Kingdom, Europe
and the rest of the world by
James Currey Publishers
73 Botley Road
Oxford OX2 0BS

and
UNESCO Publishing
7 Place de Fontenoy, 75700, Paris

International Scientific Committee for the Drafting of a General History of Africa (UNESCO)

General History of Africa · IV

Africa from the Twelfth to the Sixteenth Century

EDITORS JOSEPH KI-ZERBO and DJIBRIL TAMSIR NIANE

Abridged Edition

JAMES CURREY · CALIFORNIA · UNESCO

First published 1997 by the
United Nations Educational, Scientific
and Cultural Organization
7 Place de Fontenoy, 75700, Paris

James Currey Ltd
73 Botley Road
Oxford OX2 0BS

and

University of California Press
2120 Berkeley Way, Berkeley
California 94720

ISBN (UNESCO): 92-3-102496-5
ISBN (UC Press): 0-520-06699-5

British Library Cataloguing in Publication Data
UNESCO general history of Africa. – Abridged ed.
4: Africa from the twelfth to the sixteenth century.
1. Africa – History – To 1884
I. Ki-Zerbo, J. II. Niane, D.T. (Djibril Tamsir) III. UNESCO
IV. General history of Africa
960.2'1
ISBN 0-85255-094-4

Typeset in Bembo by Exe Valley Dataset Ltd, Exeter, UK,
and printed in Britain by Villiers Publications, London N3

Contents

Preface

AMADOU-MAHTAR M'BOW
Former Director-General of UNESCO (1974–87)

For a long time, all kinds of myths and prejudices concealed the true history of Africa from the world at large. African societies were looked upon as societies that could have no history. In spite of important work done by such pioneers as Leo Frobenius, Maurice Delafosse and Arturo Labriola, as early as the first decades of this century, a great many non-African experts could not rid themselves of certain preconceptions and argued that the lack of written sources and documents made it impossible to engage in any scientific study of such sciences.

Although the *Iliad* and *Odyssey* were rightly regarded as essential sources for the history of ancient Greece, African oral tradition, the collective memory of peoples that holds the thread of many events marking their lives, was rejected as worthless. In writing the history of a large part of Africa, the only sources used were from outside the continent, and the final product gave a picture not so much of the paths actually taken by the African peoples as of those that the authors thought they must have taken. Since the European Middle Ages were often used as a yardstick, modes of production, social relations and political institutions were visualized only by reference to the European past.

In fact, there was a refusal to see Africans as the creators of original cultures which flowered and survived over the centuries in patterns of their own making and which historians are unable to grasp unless they forgo their prejudices and rethink their approach.

Furthermore, the continent of Africa was hardly ever looked upon as a historical entity. On the contrary, emphasis was laid on everything likely to lend credence to the idea that a split had existed, from time immemorial, between a 'white Africa' and a 'black Africa', each unaware of the other's existence. The Sahara was often presented as an impenetrable space preventing any intermingling of ethnic groups and peoples or any exchange of goods, beliefs, customs and ideas between the societies that had grown up on either side of the desert. Hermetic frontiers were drawn between the civilizations of Ancient Egypt and Nubia and those of the people of the Sahara.

It is true that the history of Africa north of the Sahara has been more closely linked with that of the Mediterranean basin than has the history of sub-Saharan Africa, but it is now widely recognized that the various civilizations of the African continent, for all their differing languages and cultures, represent, to a greater or lesser degree, the historical offshoots of a set of peoples and societies united by bonds centuries old.

Another phenomenon that did great disservice to the objective study of the African past was the appearance, with the slave trade and colonization, of racial stereotypes that bred contempt and lack of understanding and became so deep-rooted that they distorted even the basic concepts of historiography. From the time when the notions of 'white' and 'black' were used as generic labels by the colonialists, who were regarded as superior, the colonized Africans had to struggle against both economic and psychological enslavement. Africans were identifiable by the colour of their skin, they had become a kind of merchandise, they were earmarked for hard labour and eventually, in the minds of those dominating them, they came to symbolize an imaginary and allegedly inferior *Negro* race. This pattern of spurious identification relegated the history of the African peoples in many minds to the rank of ethno-history, in which appreciation of the historical and cultural facts was bound to be warped.

The situation has changed significantly since the end of the Second World War and in particular since the African countries became independent and began to take an active part in the life of the international community and in the mutual exchanges that are its *raison d'être*. An increasing number of historians have endeavoured to tackle the study of Africa with a more rigorous, objective and open-minded outlook by using – with all due precautions – actual African sources. In exercising their right to take the historical initiative, Africans themselves have felt a deep-seated need to re-establish the historical authenticity of their societies on solid foundations.

In this context, the importance of the eight-volume *General History of Africa*, which UNESCO is publishing, speaks for itself.

The experts from many countries working on this project began by laying down the theoretical and methodological basis for the *History*. They have been at pains to call into question the over-simplification arising from a linear and restrictive conception of world history and to re-establish the true facts wherever necessary and possible. They have endeavoured to highlight the historical data that give a clearer picture of the evolution of the different peoples of Africa in their specific socio-cultural setting.

To tackle this huge task, made all the more complex and difficult by the vast range of sources and the fact that documents were widely scattered, UNESCO has had to proceed by stages. The first stage, from 1965 to 1969, was devoted to gathering documentation and planning the work. Operational assignments were conducted in the field and included campaigns to collect oral traditions, the creation of regional documentation centres for oral traditions, the collection of unpublished manuscripts in Arabic and Ajami (African languages written in Arabic script), the compilation of archival inventories and the preparation of a *Guide to the Sources of the History of Africa*, culled from the archives and libraries of the countries of Europe and later published in eleven volumes. In addition, meetings were organized to enable experts from Africa and other continents to discuss questions of methodology and lay down the broad lines for the project after careful examination of the available sources.

The second stage, which lasted from 1969 to 1971, was devoted to shaping the *History* and linking its different parts. The purpose of the international meetings of experts held in Paris in 1969 and Addis Ababa in 1970 was to study and define the problems involved in drafting and publishing the *History*; presentation in eight volumes, the principal edition in English, French and Arabic, translation into African languages such as Kiswahili, Hausa, Fulfulde, Yoruba or Lingala, prospective versions in German, Russian, Portuguese, Spanish and Chinese, as well as abridged editions designed for a wide African and international public.

The third stage has involved actual drafting and publication. This began with the appointment of the 39-member International Scientific Committee, two-thirds African and one-third non-African, which assumes intellectual responsibility for the *History*.

The method used is interdisciplinary and is based on a multi-faceted approach and a wide variety of sources. The first among these is archaeology, which holds many of the keys to the history of African cultures and civilizations. Thanks to archaeology, it is now acknowledged that Africa was very probably the cradle of humankind and the scene – in the neolithic period – of one of the first technological revolutions in history. Archaeology has also shown that Egypt was the setting for one of the most brilliant ancient civilizations of the world. But another very important source is oral tradition, which, after being long despised, has now emerged as an invaluable instrument for discovering the history of Africa, making it possible to follow the movements of its different peoples in both space and time, to understand the African vision of the world from the inside and to grasp the original features of the values on which the cultures and institutions of the continent are based.

We are indebted to the International Scientific Committee in charge of this *General History of Africa*, and to its Rapporteur and the editors and authors of the various volumes and chapters, for having shed a new light on the African past in its authentic and all-encompassing form and for having avoided any dogmatism in the study of essential issues. Among these issues we might cite: the slave trade, that 'endlessly bleeding wound', which was responsible for one of the cruellest mass deportations in the history of mankind, which sapped the African continent of its life-blood while contributing significantly to the economic and commercial expansion of Europe; colonization, with all the effects it had on population, economics, psychology and culture; relations between Africa south of the Sahara and the Arab world; and, finally, the process of decolonization and nation-building which mobilized the intelligence and passion of people still alive and sometimes still active today. All these issues have been broached with a concern for honesty and rigour which is not the least of the *History*'s merits. By taking stock of our knowledge of Africa, putting forward a variety of viewpoints on African cultures and offering a new reading of history, the *History* has the signal advantage of showing up the light and shade and of openly portraying the differences of opinion that may exist between scholars.

By demonstrating the inadequacy of the methodological approaches which have long been used in research on Africa, this *History* calls for a new and careful study of the twofold problem areas of historiography and cultural identity, which are united by links of reciprocity. Like any historical work of value, the *History* paves the way for a great deal of further research on a variety of topics.

It is for this reason that the International Scientific Committee, in close collaboration with UNESCO, decided to embark on additional studies in an attempt to go deeper into a number of issues that will permit a clearer understanding of certain aspects of the African past. The findings being published in the series 'UNESCO Studies and

Documents – General History of Africa'[1] will prove a useful supplement to the *History*, as will the works planned on aspects of national or subregional history.

The *General History* sheds light both on the historical unity of Africa and also its relations with the other continents, particularly the Americas and the Caribbean. For a long time, the creative manifestations of the descendants of Africans in the Americas were lumped together by some historians as a heterogeneous collection of *Africanisms*. Needless to say, this is not the attitude of the authors of the *History*, in which the resistance of the slaves shipped to America, the constant and massive participation of the descendants of Africans in the struggles for the initial independence of America and in national liberation movements, are rightly perceived for what they were: vigorous assertions of identity, which helped forge the universal concept of humankind. Although the phenomenon may vary in different places, it is now quite clear that ways of feeling, thinking, dreaming and acting in certain nations of the western hemisphere have been marked by their African heritage. The cultural inheritance of Africa is visible everywhere, from the southern United States to northern Brazil, across the Caribbean and on the Pacific seaboard. In certain places it even underpins the cultural identity of some of the most important elements of the population.

The *History* also clearly brings out Africa's relations with southern Asia across the Indian Ocean and the African contributions to other civilizations through mutual exchanges.

I am convinced that the efforts of the peoples of Africa to conquer or strengthen their independence, secure their development and assert their cultural characteristics must be rooted in historical awareness renewed, keenly felt and taken up by each succeeding generation.

My own background, the experience I gained as a teacher and as chairperson, from the early days of independence, of the first commission set up to reform history and geography curricula in some of the countries of West and Central Africa, taught me how necessary it was for the education of young people and for the information of the public at large to have a history book produced by scholars with inside knowledge of the problems and hopes of Africa and with the ability to apprehend the continent in its entirety.

For all these reasons, UNESCO's goal will be to ensure that this *General History of Africa* is widely disseminated in a large number of languages and is used as a basis for producing children's books, school textbooks and radio and television programmes. Young people, whether schoolchildren or students and adults in Africa and elsewhere will thus be able to form a truer picture of the African continent's past and the factors that explain it, as well as a fairer understanding of its cultural heritage and its

1. The following 12 volumes have already been published in this series: *The peopling of ancient Egypt and the deciphering of Meroitic script; The African slave trade from the fifteenth to the nineteenth century; Historical relations across the Indian Ocean; The historiography of Southern Africa; The decolonization of Africa; Southern Africa and the Horn of Africa; African ethnonyms and toponyms; Historical and socio-cultural relations between black Africa and the Arab world from 1935 to the present; The methodology of contemporary African history; Africa and the Second World War; The educational process and historiography in Africa; Libya Antiqua; The role of African Student Movements in the political and social evolution of Africa from 1900 to 1975.*

contribution to the general progress of humankind. The *History* should thus contribute to improved international co-operation and stronger solidarity among peoples in their aspirations to justice, progress and peace. This is, at least, my most cherished hope.

It remains for me to express my deep gratitude to the members of the International Scientific Committee, the Rapporteur, the different volume editors, the authors and all those who have collaborated in this tremendous undertaking. The work they have accomplished and the contribution they have made plainly go to show how people from different backgrounds, but all imbued with the same spirit of goodwill and enthusiasm in the service of universal truth can, within the international framework provided by UNESCO, bring to fruition a project of considerable scientific and cultural import. My thanks also go to the organizations and governments whose generosity has made it possible for UNESCO to publish this *History* in different languages and thus ensure that it will have the worldwide impact it deserves and thereby serve the international community as a whole.

Description of the Project

B. A. OGOT[1]
Former President, International Scientific Committee for the Drafting of a General History of Africa

The General Conference of UNESCO at its 16th Session instructed the Director-General to undertake the drafting of a *General History of Africa*. The enormous task of implementing the project was entrusted to an International Scientific Committee which was established by the Executive Board in 1970. This Committee, under the Statutes adopted by the Executive Board of UNESCO in 1971, is composed of 39 members (two-thirds of whom are African and one-third non-African) serving in their personal capacity and appointed by the Director-General of UNESCO for the duration of the Committee's mandate.

The first task of the Committee was to define the principal characteristics of the work. These were defined at the first session of the Committee as follows:

(a) Although aiming at the highest possible scientific level, the history does not seek to be exhaustive and is a work of synthesis avoiding dogmatism. In many respects, it is a statement of problems showing the present state of knowledge and the main trends in research, and it does not hesitate to show divergencies of views where these exist. In this way, it prepares the ground for future work.

(b) Africa is considered in this work as a totality. The aim is to show the historical relationships between the various parts of the continent, too frequently sub-divided in works published to date. Africa's historical connections with the other continents receive due attention, these connections being analysed in terms of mutual exchanges and multilateral influences, bringing out, in its appropriate light, Africa's contribution to the history of mankind.

(c) The *General History of Africa* is, in particular, a history of ideas and civilizations, societies and institutions. It is based on a wide variety of sources, including oral tradition and art forms.

(d) The *History* is viewed essentially from the inside. Although a scholarly work, it is also, in large measure, a faithful reflection of the way in which African authors view their own civilization. While prepared in an international framework and drawing to the full on the present stock of scientific knowledge, it should also be a vitally important element in the recognition of the African heritage and should bring out the factors making for unity in the continent. This effort to view things

1. During the Sixth Plenary Session of the International Scientific Committee for the Drafting of a General History of Africa (Brazzaville, August 1983), an election of the new Bureau was held and Professor Ogot was replaced by Professor Albert Adu Boahen.

> from within is the novel feature of the project and should, in addition to its scientific quality, give it great topical significance. By showing the true face of Africa, the *History* could, in an era absorbed in economic and technical struggles, offer a particular conception of human values.

The Committee has decided to present the work covering over three million years of African history in eight volumes, each containing about 800 pages of text with illustrations, photographs, maps and line drawings.

A chief editor, assisted if necessary by one or two assistant editors, is responsible for the preparation of each volume. The editors are elected by the Committee either from among its members or from outside by a two-thirds majority. They are responsible for preparing the volume in accordance with the decisions and plans adopted by the Committee. On scientific matters, they are accountable to the Committee or, between two sessions of the Committee, to its Bureau for the contents of the volumes, the final version of the texts, the illustrations and, in general, for all scientific and technical aspects of the *History*. The Bureau ultimately approves the final manuscript. When it considers the manuscript ready for publication, it transmits it to the Director-General of UNESCO. Thus the Committee, or the Bureau between committee sessions, remains fully in charge of the project.

Each volume consists of some 30 chapters. Each chapter is the work of a principal author assisted, if necessary, by one or two collaborators. The authors are selected by the Committee on the basis of their *curricula vitae*. Preferences is given to African authors, provided they have requisite qualifications. Special effort is made to ensure, as far as possible, that all regions of the continent, as well as other regions having historical or cultural ties with Africa, are equitably represented among the authors.

When the editor of a volume has approved texts of chapters, they are then sent to all members of the Committee for criticism. In addition, the text of the volume editor is submitted for examination to a Reading Committee, set up within the International Scientific Committee on the basis of the members' fields of competence. The Reading Committee analyses the chapters from the standpoint of both substance and form. The Bureau then gives final approval to the manuscripts.

Such a seemingly long and involved procedure has proved necessary, since it provides the best possible guarantee of the scientific objectivity of the *General History of Africa*. There have, in fact, been instances when the Bureau has rejected manuscripts or insisted on major revisions or even reassigned the drafting of a chapter to another author. Occasionally, specialists in a particular period of history or in a particular question are consulted to put the finishing touches to a volume.

The work will be published first in a hard-cover edition in English, French and Arabic, and later in paperback editions in the same languages. An abridged version in English and French will serve as a basis for translation into African languages. The Committee has chosen Kiswahili and Hausa as the first African languages into which the work will be translated.

Also, every effort will be made to ensure publication of the *General History of Africa* in other languages of wide international currency such as Chinese, Portuguese, Russian, German, Italian, Spanish, Japanese, etc.

It is thus evident that this is a gigantic task which constitutes an immense challenge to African historians and to the scholarly community at large, as well as to UNESCO under whose auspices the work is being done. For the writing of a continental history of Africa, covering the last three million years, using the highest canons of scholarship and involving, as it must do, scholars drawn from diverse countries, cultures, ideologies and historical traditions, is surely a complex undertaking. It constitutes a continental, international and interdisciplinary project of great proportions.

In conclusion, I would like to underline the significance of this work for Africa and for the world. At a time when the peoples of Africa are striving towards unity and greater co-operation in shaping their individual destinies, a proper understanding of Africa's past, with an awareness of common ties among Africans and between Africa and other continents, should not only be a major contribution towards mutual understanding among the people of the earth, but also a source of knowledge of a cultural heritage that belongs to all humankind.

Note on chronology

It has been agreed to adopt the following method for writing dates. With regard to prehistory, dates may be written in two different ways.

One way is by reference to the present era, that is, dates BP (before present), the reference year being +1950; all dates are negative in relation to +1950.

The other way is by reference to the beginning of the Christian era. Dates are represented in relation to the Christian era by a simple + or − sign before the date. When referring to centuries, the terms BC and AD are replaced by 'before the Christian era' and 'of the Christian era'.

Some examples are as follows:

(i) 2300 BP = −350

(ii) 2900 BC = −2900
AD 1800 = +1800

(iii) Fifth century BC = Fifth century before the Christian era
Third century AD = Third century of the Christian era.

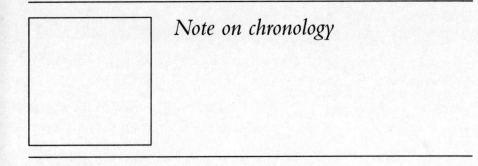

Members of the International Scientific Committee for the Drafting of a General History of Africa

The dates cited below refer to dates of membership.

Professor J. F. Ade Ajayi
(Nigeria), from 1971
Editor Volume VI

Professor F. A. Albuquerque Mourão
(Brazil), from 1975

Professor D. Birmingham
(UK), from 1985

Professor A. Adu Boahen
(Ghana), from 1971
Editor Volume VII

The late H. E. Boubou Hama
(Niger), 1971–8 (resigned in 1978);
deceased 1982

Dr (Mrs) Mutumba M. Bull
(Zambia), from 1971

The late Professor D. Chanaiwa
(Zimbabwe), from 1975;
deceased 1993

Professor P. D. Curtin
(USA), from 1975

Professor J. Devisse
(France), from 1971

Professor M. Difuila
(Angola), from 1978

The late Professor Cheikh Anta Diop
(Senegal), 1971–86; deceased 1986

Professor H. Djait
(Tunisia), from 1975

The late H. E. M. El Fasi
(Morocco), from 1971; deceased 1991
Editor Volume III

Professor J. D. Fage
(UK), 1971–81 (resigned)

The late Professor J. L. Franco
(Cuba), from 1971; deceased 1989

The late Mr M. H. I. Galaal
(Somalia), 1971–81; deceased 1981

Professor Dr V. L. Grottanelli
(Italy), from 1971

The late Professor E. Haberland
(Germany), from 1971;
deceased 1992

Dr Aklilu Habte
(Ethiopia), from 1971

The late H. E. A. Hampâté Bâ
(Mali), 1971–8 (resigned); deceased 1991

Dr I. S. El-Hareir
(Libya), from 1978

The late Dr I. Hrbek
(Czech Republic), from 1971;
deceased 1993
Assistant Editor Volume III

Dr (Mrs) A. Jones
(Liberia), from 1971

The late Abbé Alexis Kagame
(Rwanda), 1971–81; deceased 1981

Professor I. N. Kimambo
(Tanzania), from 1971

Professor J. Ki-Zerbo
(Burkina Faso), from 1971
Editor Volume I and IV

Mr D. Laya
(Niger), from 1979

Dr A. Letnev
(USSR), from 1971

Dr G. Mokhtar
(Egypt), from 1971
Editor Volume II

Professor P. Mutibwa
(Uganda), from 1975

Professor L. D. Ngcongco
(Botswana), from 1971

Professor D. T. Niane
(Guinea), from 1971
Editor Volume IV

Professor T. Obenga
(People's Republic of the Congo),
from 1975

Professor Bethwell A. Ogot
(Kenya), from 1971
Editor Volume V

Professor C. Ravoajanahary
(Madagascar), from 1971

The late Professor W. Rodney
(Guyana), 1979–80; deceased 1980

The late Professor M. Shibeika
(Sudan), 1971–80; deceased 1980

Professor Y. A. Talib
(Singapore), from 1975

The late Professor A. Teixeira da Mota
(Portugal), 1978–82; deceased 1982

Mgr T. Tshibangu
(Zaire), from 1971

Professor J. Vansina
(Belgium), from 1971

The late Rt Hon. Dr E. Williams
(Trinidad and Tobago), 1976–8;
resigned 1978; deceased 1980

Professor Ali A. Mazrui
(Kenya)
Editor Volume VIII,
not a member of the Committee

Professor C. Wondji
(Côte d'Ivoire)
Assistant Editor Volume VIII,
not a member of the Committee

Secretariat of the International Scientific Committee
Division of International Cultural
Co-operation, Preservation and Enrichment
of Cultural Identities
UNESCO
1, rue Miollis, 75015 Paris

Biographies of the authors who contributed to the main edition

The abridged version was prepared from the texts of the main version written by the following authors:

INTRODUCTION	D. T. Niane (Guinea); specialist in the Mandingo world; has published a number of works on West Africa at the time of the great empires, from the eleventh to the sixteenth century; former Director of the Fondation L. S. Senghor, Dakar; researcher.
CHAPTER 2	O. Saidi (Tunisia); specialist in the history of the Almohads; has published various works on the classical history of the Maghrib, of Tunisia in particular; teaches history at the Faculty of Arts and the Ecole Normale Supérieure of the University of Tunis.
CHAPTER 3	M. Talbi (Tunisia); Islamologist; has published many works and articles on the various aspects of Islamic religion and culture; teaches at the Faculty of Arts, Tunis.
CHAPTER 4	I. Hrbek (Czech Republic); specialist in the Arab sources of the history of Africa, particularly West Africa, as well as specialist in Islam; has published many works and articles in these fields; researcher at the Oriental Institute, Prague.
CHAPTER 5	R. Idris (France); specialist in Arabic language and literature; taught the history of the Muslim West; deceased.
CHAPTER 6	D. T. Niane.
CHAPTER 7	M. Ly-Tall (Mali); specialist in the history of Mali; has published works on the Mali empire; teaches at the Ecole Normale Supérieure, Bamako; researcher.
CHAPTER 8	S. M. Cissoko (Senegal); specialist in the history of medieval Timbuktu; has published various works on the history of West Africa; Assistant Lecturer at the Faculty of Arts, Dakar.
CHAPTER 9	M. Izard (France); specialist in the history of the Volta basin and particularly that of the Mossi kingdoms; has published many works on the pre-colonial, colonial and modern history of this region; Senior Researcher at the Centre National de la Recherche Scientifique, Paris.
CHAPTER 10	D. Lange (Germany); specialist in the pre-colonial history of the central Sudan; has published various works on this period; teaches at the University of Niamey.
CHAPTER 11	M. Adamu (Nigeria); specialist in the history of the Hausa; has published works on this subject; Director of the Centre for Nigerian Cultural Studies of Ahmadu Bello University, Zaria.
	A. Salifou (Niger); specialist in the history of the Hausa; has published various works on Niger and Nigeria; teaches in Niger.
CHAPTER 12	Y. Person (France); specialist in the history of Africa, particularly the Mandingo world; has published many works on the history of Africa; Professor at the University of Paris I, Panthéon-Sorbonne; deceased.

CHAPTER 13 P. Kipre (Côte d'Ivoire); specialist in modern and contemporary history of Côte d'Ivoire; has published various articles based on oral tradition; teaches at the Ecole Normale Supérieure, Abidjan.

CHAPTER 14 A. F. C. Ryder (UK); specialist in the history of West Africa; has published many works on the pre-colonial and colonial periods of this region; Professor at the University of Bristol.

CHAPTER 15 J. C. Garcin (France); specialist in the history of Muslim Egypt; has published various studies on the history of Egypt under the Mamluks and on Muslim Upper Egypt; teaches at the University of Provence, Aix-en-Provence.

CHAPTER 16 L. Kropáček (Czech Republic); specialist in the social, political and religious history of the Sudan; has published various works on Darfūr, teaches at the Department of Oriental and African Studies of Charles University, Prague.

CHAPTER 17 T. Tamrat (Ethiopia); specialist in the medieval history of Ethiopia; has published various studies on this period; teaches at the University of Addis Ababa.

CHAPTER 18 V. Matveiev (Federation of Russia); historian and ethnologist; has published many works on the Arab sources of the history of Africa; Senior Researcher at the Institute of Ethnography, Russian Academy of Sciences, St Petersburg.

CHAPTER 19 C. Ehret (USA); linguist and historian of East Africa; has published many works and articles on the pre-colonial and colonial history of East Africa; teaches at the University of California, Los Angeles.

CHAPTER 20 B. A Ogot (Kenya); specialist in African and particularly East African history; has published many works and articles on the history and archaeology of East Africa; teacher, researcher, former Director of the International Louis Leakey Memorial Institute for African Prehistory; Director, Institute of Research and Postgraduate Studies, Maseno University College, Kenya.

CHAPTER 21 B. M. Fagan (UK); anthropologist, archaeologist; has published many works on the Iron Age and Stone Age cultures in East and Southern Africa; Professor of Anthropology at the University of California, Santa Barbara.

CHAPTER 22 J. Vansina (Belgium); specialist in oral tradition; has published many works on the history of Equatorial and Central Africa; teaches at the University of Wisconsin, USA.

CHAPTER 23 L. Ngcongco (Botswana); specialist in the pre-colonial history of Southern Africa; has published various studies on Botswana in pre-colonial times; taught at the University of Botswana; Director of National Institute of Research, Gaborone.
J. Vansina.

CHAPTER 24 F. Esoavelomandroso (Madagascar); specialist in the history of Madagascar; has published various studies on the history of Madagascar from the sixteenth to the eighteenth century; teaches at the Faculty of Arts, Antananarivo.

CHAPTER 25 D. T. Niane.

CHAPTER 26 J. Devisse (France); specialist in the history of North-West Africa from the fourth to the sixteenth century; archaeologist; has published many articles and works on the history of Africa; Professor of African History at the University of Paris I, Panthéon-Sorbonne.
S. Labib (Egypt); specialist in the medieval history of Africa; has published various works on the social and economic history of this period; teaches at the University of Utah (USA) and the University of Kiel (Germany).

CHAPTER 27 D. T. Niane.

1 Introduction

Although it is not equally meaningful for every part of the continent, this subdivision of the period from the twelfth to the sixteenth century may be considered valid since these few centuries present a certain unity for the continent as a whole. It was a crucial period in which Africa developed its original cultures and assimilated outside influences while retaining its own individuality – until the major impact of the Atlantic slave trade which opened a new period (Volume V).

The preceding volume covered a period for which new light is thrown on the continent, principally by Arab writers. It was the period of the discovery of the Land of the Blacks (the Sudan) south of the Sahara, where a number of well-established empires and kingdoms stand out. In the western Sahara there was the Soninke empire of Ghana which dominated the area from the Niger Bend to the Senegal estuary. Al-Bakrī gives a short but valuable description of it. At the other end of the Sudan, in the area of the Chad basin, there were the kingdoms of Kānem-Borno. Between these two regions, other kingdoms such as Songhay had grown up. After the eleventh century, and especially after the fourteenth and fifteenth centuries, written records become more abundant: the number of Arab writings increases; but also, at the end of the period, with the contribution of Portuguese sources on the coastal and inland kingdoms of western, central, southern and eastern Africa.

Three principal themes

Three major themes characterize this period in Africa: the triumph of Islam over vast areas; the expansion of exchanges and especially of trade relations; and, finally, the formation of large empires that were more or less solidly established.

The triumph of Islam

Islam, which had spread on the fringes of the continent, now penetrated it much more deeply and became firmly established. Muslim Arab traders linked into a multi-continental network were replaced by African traders who penetrated deep into the forest zones.

The continent was thus besieged from two sides – the Sudan and the eastern coast.

North Africa had already been profoundly penetrated by Islam during the previous period. In the eleventh century the Almoravid movement had set out from the banks of the Senegal and restored strict Mālikite orthodoxy in the Maghrib and Spain; then in about 1076 it had taken Koumbi Saleh, the capital of Ghana. This important event almost escaped notice by the chroniclers, as the trans-Saharan links between North Africa and the Sudan continued with the empires that succeeded Ghana: Takrūr, Mande, Songhay etc. Islam, adopted and sometimes adapted by the Berbers and the peoples of the Sudan now spread peacefully above all from the cities and courts, mainly through trade, without destroying the traditional structures.

On the eastern side of the continent, starting from Egypt and from the Muslim principalities along the Red Sea, the Gulf of Aden and the Horn of Africa, but also from the Muslim trading settlements or bases on the Indian Ocean (Sofala, Kilwa, Zanzibar, Pate, Mogadishu etc.), Islam penetrated, sometimes imposing itself by force, towards Nubia, the eastern Sudan, the Ethiopian highlands and vast areas of eastern and southern Africa. There the Swahili civilization developed, the child of Africa fertilized by Islam, whose language, Bantu in structure, enriched by Arabic, was to spread all over East and Central Africa as far as the Great Lakes and the mouth of the Congo (Zaire).

The two chief obstacles to this ineluctable expansion were the stronghold of Ethiopia and, at least during this period, the vast Bantu world of the interior.

The Ethiopian kingdom stands out sharply during this period in the resistance to Islam, thanks to a Christianity that was original in its architectural forms, its painting and its monastic structures. Despite, or because of, the fact that this Ethiopian Church was frequently cut off from its 'head', the patriarch of Alexandria, it produced a variety of achievements many of which were due to the monasteries perched in the high plateaux where education was dispensed and the history of the kings and religious reforms were prepared; while the old Cushitic and pre-Christian influences left a clear mark on Christian forms of worship, in festivals, dances and animal sacrifices. Here, as with Islam, the African personality asserted itself. The Swahili language and civilization, with their basically African character enriched by Arab borrowings, were to spread from the east coast to the lower Congo on the Atlantic Ocean by way of the countries around the Great Lakes.

Islam's success is largely to be explained by the similarity between the way of life of its first propagators and that of many black or Berber African peoples. Furthermore, after the warlike episode of the Almoravids, this religion was spread peacefully by city-dwellers, traders or courtiers, flexibly, without destroying traditions, or asking anything but a tribute from any conquered peoples.

The development of trade relations

The expansion of trade relations is closely linked to that of Islam. Islam covered an intercontinental area from the Indus to the Iberian peninsula and from the island of the Mediterranean to Madagascar. The unit of language and religion, as well as the relative but very real security that prevailed within this area, could not fail to promote a high level of exchanges of all sorts. Placed between Asia and Europe, on the one hand, and between the Mediterranean and the Indian Ocean, on the other, Africa could not avoid being affected by these patterns of exchange.

Intra-African relations themselves were on a scale that archaeology, toponymy and linguistics are increasingly revealing to us. The Sahara was constantly being crossed by large caravans with up to 12,000 camels. And this traffic was continued southward to the thick forests and the coast by thousands of pedlars. These exchanges carried food crops (mainly introduced from the Indian Ocean), techniques and sociological traits that explain the fundamental cultural unity of the continent over and beyond local disparities.

South of the Equator, however, the influence of Islam barely penetrated during this period, as the chapters dealing with the countries around the Great Lakes, and the Congo, Zambezi and Limpopo basins as well as southern Africa show.

What products were exchanged? Sub-Saharan Africa exported mainly gold, ivory, craft products and agricultural produce (cereals, leather and cotton goods etc.); it also sent slaves to the Maghrib, Egypt and the Near East: women for the harems and men for domestic duties, princely guards and plantations. The capitals and trading cities south of the Sahara imported mainly luxury goods: richly ornamented weapons and utensils, luxury textiles, horses, iron and copper bars etc. In addition to these, there were also a few slaves skilled in the arts brought back from Cairo by rich Sudanese after their pilgrimage to the Muslim Holy Places.

In any event, the slave trade in this period towards the countries of North Africa and the Middle East cannot be put on the same footing as the Atlantic slave trade which prevailed south of the Sahara from the sixteenth century onwards which will be analysed in Volumes V and VI.

The development of kingdoms and empires

This third feature of the period dealt with here must not be looked upon as a result of the first two, even though in the Sudan-Sahel area Islam and trade obviously had some influence on political development, even if they did not give rise to it. On the other hand, the kingdoms of Kongo, Zimbabwe and Mwenemutapa, for example, owed nothing to the influence of Islam.

The fact is that the trading centres all along the coasts of the Indian Ocean, the Red Sea and the Mediterranean, and on both sides of the Sahara, were, as we have seen, centres where educational and religious acculturation occurred. But on the political, sociological and even cultural levels, the Berbers and Sudanese remained tenaciously attached to their own institutions and accepted Islam without Arabization.

And yet it was during this period that Egypt became the cultural centre of the Muslim world, displacing Baghdad, Damascus and the towns of Arabia, while the Maghrib was diffusing the prestigious literary, technical and scientific heritage built up by Islam to Europe by way of Andalusia and southern Italy. It was at the court of the Christian king Roger of Sicily that al-Idrīsī produced his famous *Geography*, which awakened the interest of the leisured classes in the African continent.

On the political level, after the brilliant victories of Yūsuf Ibn Tās͟hrīn over the Christians in Spain, notably at Zallaca (1086), the Almoravid movement disintegrated into rivalries between the *ḳabīlas* of the Maghrib and the Sahara, and before the resistance of the Ghana provinces after the death of Abū Bakr in 1087.

King Roger II of Sicily took advantage of this decline to risk an incursion into North Africa and impose tribute on certain ports frequented by the Barbary pirates. But before long the whole African coast of the Mediterranean was conquered in the west by the Almohads and in the east by the Ayyubids, and particularly the Mamlūks, in the thirteenth and fourteenth centuries. These latter put a stop to the Christian offensive of the Crusades in the Near East, forcing the Crusaders to take refuge in *kraks* (fortresses) without being able to get hold of Jerusalem.

It was during this period that the states of the western and central Sudan reached their apogee. Although the twelfth century remains rather obscure for this region, al-Idrīsī's writings and oral traditions make it possible to reconstruct the bitter struggle for supremacy fought over the ruins of Ghana in the regions of Wagadu, Takrūr and Mande. After the interlude under the domination of the Soso, a Soninke-Mande splinter group who resisted Islam, the thirteenth century saw the rise of Mali with Sundiata the victor over Sumaoro Kante, king of the Soso, at Kirina in 1235. Sundiata's ancestors had been converted to Islam in the eleventh century and he restored relations with the Muslim traders and men of letters and established the institutions which were to govern the empire of Mali for centuries. Trans-Saharan trade, redirected mainly towards Egypt, now experienced its greatest days, while large numbers of Dyula (Diola, Juula) traders moved down into the forest countries producing kola nuts (*Worodugu*), gold, ivory, palm oil and precious woods; they took with them to those countries smoked fish cotton goods and other manufactured items. The same structure of trade accompanied the establishment and expansion of the empires or kingdoms of Songhay, Kānem-Borno, Mossi and Dagomba etc.

The black states developed diplomatic relations, by means of embassies, with the countries of North Africa (Morocco, Tunisia, Libya, Egypt) and occasionally by means of flamboyant progresses by rulers for the pilgrimage.

Four Arab writers have left us particularly valuable accounts of these regions during this period.

The first, Ibn K͟haldūn (1332–1406), was a brilliant historian and thinker who was involved in the vicissitudes of life in the princely courts of Fez, Tunis and Andalusia. His monumental *Universal History*, including the section translated as 'History of the Berbers', contains some celebrated passages on the empire of Mali; he set out the list of rulers until 1390. His *al-Mukaddima* (*Prolegomena*) laid the foundation of sociology and scientific history.

Ibn Baṭṭūṭa, an indefatigable traveller in the fourteenth century, travelled all over western, northern and eastern Africa and the Indian Ocean as far as India and China. He was interested in everything – in foods as much as in political institutions, in marriage customs and medicines as much as in trade routes. He had the advantage of having personally visited the court of Mansa Mūsā I, the emperor of Mali. He tells us, for example, that he saw the same cowries in his capital and in Gao as he had already observed in the Maldive Islands and which served as currency 'at 1150 to one gold dinar'.

As for Al-'Umarī, he gives us vital information acquired in his position as secretary to the Mamlūk court between 1340 and 1348. He thus had access to the royal archives, and also sought information from the Sudanese consuls in Cairo, and from people who had met the Sudanese kings on their pilgrimages to the Holy Places. His 'Description of Africa excepting Egypt' has a remarkable accuracy and ring of authenticity.

Finally, at the beginning of the sixteenth century, Leo Africanus twice visited the Sudan and brought back a wealth of information on those regions, just at the beginning of the time of the caravels which coincided with the decline of the western Sudan.

In addition to the traditions and written sources, this region has also been revealed to us by archaeology. Following the excavation of Koumbi Saleh, the capital of Ghana, in 1914, it was the turn of Awdāghust to be excavated by professors J. Devisse and D. and S. Robert in 1965. Several levels of occupation were detected and treasures discovered which confirm that Awkār was indeed at this time, in al-Bakrī's words, the 'Land of Gold'. Further south, at Niani, the capital of Mali, a Guinean–Polish mission was working in 1968 on the tumuli of the site which has yielded remains that are full of information.

Beyond West Africa, at the other end of black Africa, the numerous Cyclopaean ruins of stone monuments called *zimbabwe* and *mapungubwe* (in Shona) are evidence of technical skill, population growth and political organization on a considerable scale.

After the extravagant hypotheses of colonial historians, light has now been thrown on the true origins of these impressive constructions initially attributed, among others, to the Phoenicians. In 1905 the Egyptologist David Randall MacIver declared unequivocally that the monuments are of African origin:

> There is no trace of any oriental or European style of any period whatever . . . the character of the dwellings enclosed in the stone ruins and forming an integral part of them is unmistakably African . . . The arts and techniques . . . are typically African.

After him other scholars said the same thing, such as Dr Gertrude Caton-Thompson and Basil Davidson. Professor B. M. Fagan sets out the same argument in this volume.

In reality, when the Portuguese moved up the east coast of Africa in the fifteenth century, they heard in Sofala of a powerful African empire inland, and even met some inhabitants of this state who had come to trade with the Arabs. They called this kingdom Benametapa. De Goes writes of it:

> In the middle of this country is a fortress built of large and heavy stones both within and without a very curious construction and well built, for it is said no mortar can be seen holding the stones together . . . The King of Benametapa lives in great style, and is served with great deference, on bended knee.

De Barros adds: 'the natives of this country call all these edifices 'Symbaoe', which in their tongue means (royal) "court" '. The joint efforts of linguists, archaeologists and anthropologists have already thrown much light on these buildings and the strict social and political organization of their creators. Like the *kaya maghan*, the *Mwenemutapa* (the royal title meaning the 'lord of metals') had a monopoly of gold. The whole of this region in the Zambezi basin (modern Zambia, Zimbabwe and Malawi) was very rich in copper, gold and iron. According to Basil Davidson, 'thousands of ancient mines have been discovered, perhaps as many as 60,000 or 70,000'. Although the chronology is not absolutely settled, what is certain is that when the Portuguese arrived, while the *Mwenemutapa* and Zimbabwe still appeared to be great powers, their decadence had already set in and it was to be accelerated by the depredations of the Portuguese and other Europeans. The peoples of these lands practised intensive terraced farming. They were Bantu who had superimposed themselves on earlier populations and driven the pygmies and other minority groups towards the forests and deserts.

Between West Africa and the empires of central and southern Africa, the presence of many other kingdoms and polities is recorded by various sources.

From the time they reached the estuary of the Senegal, in the twelfth century, the Portuguese expressed their admiration for the African kingdoms they encountered. In Senegambia, they heard talk of the Emperor or *mansa* of Mali and established relations with the kings of Wolof.

From Senegambia to the Niger delta stretches a region for which documentary sources are very patchy. But we know enough to assert that the forests were not an environment that was totally hostile to socio-political development. The cities of Benin and the lovely Yoruba sculptures developed in this forest environment. Here again, the imagination of numerous European authors was given free rein to invent imaginary non-African creators for these masterpieces, until their African origin was demonstrated and the natural connection established between the earthenware of Nok (500 years before the Christian era) and the Benin bronzes (tenth to fourteenth centuries).

This brief survey has shown that there were several types of socio-political structures in Africa during this period. In many human groups the clan and lineage claiming descent from a common ancestor were the norm, and they lived under the authority of a patriarch or a chief whose essential function was to ensure a fair distribution of the group's income. When this income grew so much that it generated a considerable surplus, the chief's power, formerly very limited, grew stronger and stronger. The clan was above all a biological grouping; it claimed to belong to a more or less clearly defined territory, but with the evolution of the clan, territory became the principal reference point.

The *kingdom* grouped together several clans; the chief of one of the clans had imposed himself on his peers, as was the case with the Keita clan that founded Mali. The king governed with the assistance of a council whose members he maintained. Although each clan had retained its particular customs and religious rites, it was integrated into the kingdom through allegiance to the king which was expressed by the payment of a tax (often in kind). The king retained his prerogatives as a religious chief which were now extended to the larger unit of the kingdom. His person was sacred as was the case in Mali, the Congo, Mwenemutapa, etc.

The *empire* implied an even larger territory, grouping several kingdoms above a certain stage. Such was the Almohad empire whose supreme sultan, although he came from a particular clan. (*ḳabīla*), reigned over other sultans scattered over a large part of the Maghrib. This was the case too with the emperor *mansa* of Mali who had 12 provinces, including two kingdoms, under his authority. The emperor's council, like the king's, functioned according to an unwritten constitution or custom and thus helped to moderate tendencies to autocracy. There were also small kingdoms that were no more than city-states plus their immediately surrounding territory. Such were the Hausa cities and the Yoruba cities of Benin, governed by sophisticated codes and ritually subject to a mother city: Daura for the Hausa cities and Ife for the Yoruba ones. Despite sporadic internecine wars, these cities remained linked by belonging to a common culture.

As can be seen, we have rejected such terms as 'segmented society' and 'stateless society': state functions can be fulfilled in various ways that differ from one civilization to another. We have also banished such words as 'tribe' and 'fetishism' which have pejorative connotations. We shall speak of 'people' or 'ethnic group', although this latter term has its problems too. The original African religion was neither 'fetishism' nor 'animism'; because of its complexity, despite appearances, it is better to describe it as 'traditional religion'. As for the word 'Hamitic', which was dealt with extensively in Volume I, it is rejected because, being derived from Ham (the biblical ancestor of the Blacks), its meaning was totally twisted to make it describe allegedly non-black peoples, who were supposed to have arrived in Africa as superior herdsmen bringing with them all the innovations of social progress. This was nothing but a mere mystifying ideology aimed at justifying the fact of colonialism. The way to decolonize history is to knock down these false theories and the prejudices they engender.

2 The Unification of the Maghrib under the Almohads

From the middle of the twelfth century to the middle of the thirteenth, the hegemony of the Almohads marks the high point of attempts to unify the Maghrib and even the whole Muslim West. The unification forged by the Almohads completely transcended that attempted by the Almoravids. It stemmed from a religious 'reform' led by the famous Mahdī Ibn Tūmart and rested on a highly organized community of *Muwahhidūn* ('unitarians'). It finally developed into a total political enterprise, whose leaders were the sultans of the dynasty founded by one of the Mahdī's earliest companions. The Muʿminids based their power on two key economic factors to build the unity of the Muslim West: on the one hand, the traffic along the trans-Saharan trade routes and the northern outlets for the gold of the Sudan; and on the other, the integration of the main economic growth points.

The religious situation in the Maghrib and the Almohad quest

Orthodoxy and Islam

In the middle of the eleventh century, Shīʿite proselytism was still very active, despite the decline of the Fāṭimids in Egypt; and the movement towards unification of the Islamic community remained fragmented. There were three approaches, each one claiming to lead to unification. The first was that of ascetic purification in the Sunni tradition sometimes with the risk of falling into the excesses of Sufism. Second, there was the codification of the law with its formalism and ritualism. Finally, there was the deepening of theological research towards a synthesis following on from al-Ashʿarī. The two adversaries fought by every tendency was Shīʿism and *falsafa* (philosophy). But in the Maghrib Islam encountered further difficulties. The anarchistic and egalitarian Khāridjite heresy was attractive to nomadic and rural societies. In particular, the Berbers had found in it the long-sought expression of their inborn resistance to the Arabization implied in Islamization. For Khāridjism rejected the principle of heredity in the succession to the caliphate, and also the principle that any given *ḳabīla* had primacy. The long survival of Berber customary law aggravated this latent mentality of spiritual dissent that only the Almoravids and Almohads succeeded in reducing.

The other problem of Islam in the Maghrib arose from Mālikism itself. This latter imposed itself at a very early date through the preaching of the disciples of Mālik b. ʿAnas, such as the doctor of the law Ibn al-Ḳasim and Imām Sahnun (776–854) who made Kayrawan the principal centre of Mālikism. But Mālikism was liable to regrettable deviations. The doctors of the law, who had often become big landowners, turned away from the spiritualist deepening of the foundations of the religion (the Koran and the *ḥadīths*), an exercise that was highly valued in the Muslim East, and rather devoted themselves simply to *furūʿ* (textbooks of applied jurisprudence). By refusing to make any attempt to interpret the basic texts, by making salvation dependent on external observance and scorning inner spirituality endeavouring to raise themselves to God, and by becoming sectarians and persecutors, the Mālikite jurists caused themselves to be called narrow-minded, mechanical 'anthropomorphists'. Faced with the intellectual and spiritual quest of the Muʿtazilites, the Mālikite way, concerned solely with laws and rituals, and with calculations to capitalize on merit to earn a reward, seemed very impoverished and sterile. It is easy to understand why such great thinkers as al-G͟hazālī and Ibn Ḥazm should have lambasted such an approach to the faith, and the practice of many jurists handsomely paid to administer pious foundations; while their contorted and over-clever casuistry made them the servile acolytes of rulers. In his work 'The revival of religious learning' al-G͟hazālī, whose tendencies to mysticism were violently rejected by the Mālikites, pleaded for a return to the use of the 'life-giving waters', the springs of the Koran and the *sunna*.

Ibn Tūmart's education

Little is known of Ibn Tūmart whose reputation has come down to us surrounded with legends. He was born in about 1075 in the Anti-Atlas mountains of Morocco, descended through his parents from two Maṣmuda *ḳabila*s known today as S͟hlūḥ, and later fabricated a Sharifian ancestry for the needs of the cause. His father was well off and this enabled him to pursue his studies in the East and, according to Ibn K͟haldūn, to earn the appellation *asafū* ('torch' in S͟hlūḥ) for his fervour.

He never met al-G͟hazālī, although al-G͟hazālī's prestige was subsequently mobilized to support his preaching. Ibn Tūmart was successively: the censor of morals; the theologian asserting himself in Marrakesh; the head of a new school at Ag͟hmāt; and the leader of a communal party entrenched at Tinmallal. He gradually but inflexibly asserted his aims. On his return from the east towards Morocco, he made a long stop at Bidjaya (Bougie) in Ifrīḳiya in a retreat devoted to prayer, study and meditation. It was there that he met his future successor ʿAbd-al-Muʿmin, then on an educational journey to the east. He persuaded him to abandon it and join him. After this meeting, his movement westward was more organized with stops, contacts with men of religion, and improvised or planned discussion sessions, and the number of his disciples grew steadily. Between Sale and Marrakesh he symbolically refused to pay the toll; then in the Almoravid capital the famous debate took place with the court

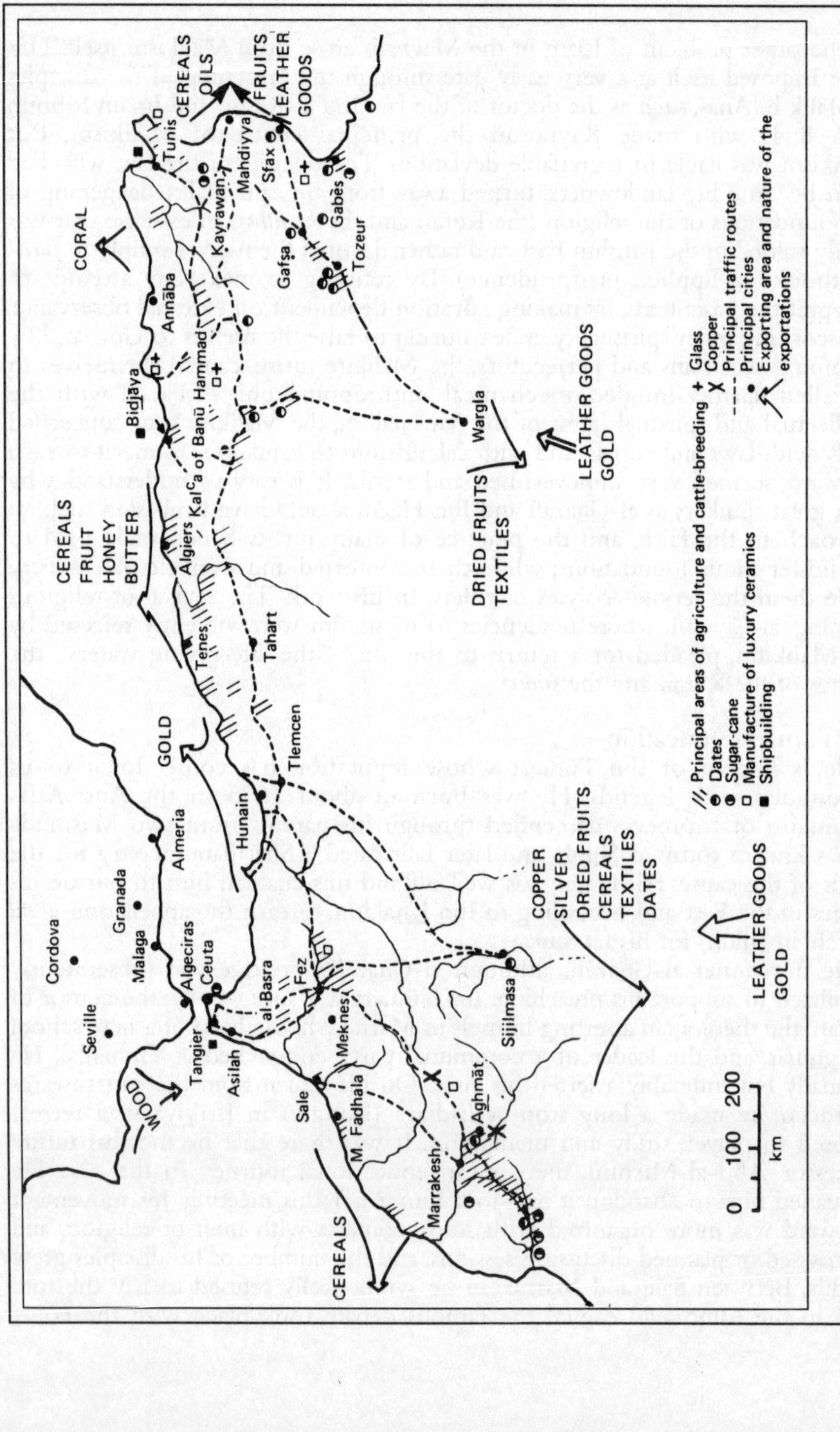

2.1 *The Maghrib during the twelfth century – economic activities. (J. Devisse, based on originals by O. Saïdi and C. Vanacker)*

jurists in the presence of the Almoravid amīr ʿAlī Ibn Yūsuf, in the course of which Ibn Tūmart's adversaries, who dominated the ruler, were reduced to silence by his performance. The threat to him became political, and the vizier advised that he be physically eliminated; but another notable persuaded him to leave and helped him to flee.

A new phase began. He withdraw to Aghmāt and went into open rebellion against the Almoravids, refusing for example to go to Marrakesh when ordered to by the amīr. From then on he was the head of larger and larger forces, that were motivated far more by clanic anti-Almoravid feeling than by the desire for religious reform. A clash was inevitable.

Ibn Tūmart's Almohad reforms

Eventually Ibn Tūmart settled with his companions in a cave in his native village of Igilliz. His theses on dogma, mortality and the law, which had taken shape gradually, were crystallized into a few basic principles.

The first point of course was the affirmation of the oneness of God (the *tawhīd*) which was erected into a mystical profession of faith marked by the influence of al-Ghazālī. The very name Almohads derives from that: the members of the movement were believers in oneness, *al-Muwaḥḥid*, whence the name Almohads. They stood out by their moral sobriety which was approved by the Berbers in the countryside, especially as the Mahdī preached in the Berber language and used it even in some of his writings. Furthermore, in accordance with the rules of the Shlūḥ *ḳabīla*, he relied on the advice of a council of notables. Following the ideas of the Muʿtazilites and reacting against the comparative interpretation of the Almoravids speaking of the attributes of God from human realities, Ibn Tūmart strongly asserted that the divine being was pure spirit, so that certain verses of the Koran could only be given an allegorical interpretation. Conversely, the Almoravids were declared guilty of anthropomorphism (*tadjsim*) an error attributable to the Almoravids alone since they were responsible for their subjects and, in his view, merited excommunication.

The second principle was the eternity of God: God as creator is the first and will remain the last, having no end.

The third principle was the omnipotence of God.

On a fourth point, the justification of the prophetic mission by extraordinary signs, proofs (*āyāt*), Ibn Tūmart's position was the same as that of the Sunnites.

Conversely, as regards belief in the Mahdī (the impeccable guide), who is guided by God, he differed sharply from the Sunnites, for whom the Mahdī was to appear only just before the end of the world. But Ibn Tūmart placed his own mission immediately after the death of ʿAlī in 661. In making this choice, he mobilized behind him powerful popular aspirations towards the era of justice that the Madhī would inaugurate and which Ibn Khaldūn testifies to for this period. By the same token it became obligatory to obey him blindly and to subordinate deeper theological inquiry into the faith to the achievement of the Mahdī's main priority programme, the elimination of the existing unjust government.

2.2 *The* Kibla, *or eastern wall, of the mosque at Tinmallal (Morocco). As the first major oratory of the Almohad community, the mosque is an example of the architectural and decorative austerity that the Almohads wanted to impose. (J. L. Arbey)*

2.3 *The inner courtyard of the mosque at Tinmallal. (J. L. Arbey)*

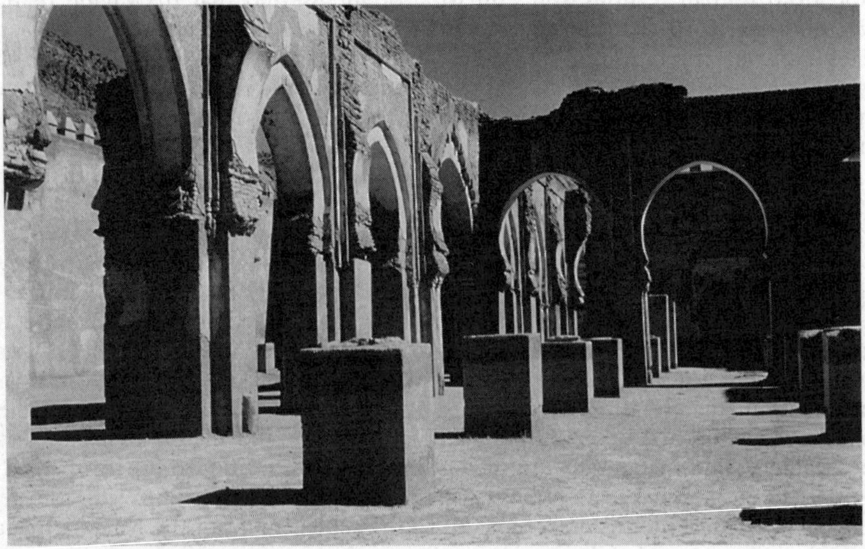

While recognizing the Koran and the *sunna* as fundamental sources of the laws of religion, Ibn Tūmart nevertheless, in certain conditions, accepted consensus, (*idjmā*ʾ), limited to the companions of the Prophet and reasoning by non-speculative analogy. Conversely, he absolutely rejected the exclusive resort to legal treatises and casuistry instead of direct recourse to the sources.

The organization of the Almohad movement: a party of propaganda, indoctrination and battle

After he withdraw to Aghmāt, Ibn Tūmart gave his movement political goals in addition to its religious ones. Just as he had intended to imitate the Prophet by settling himself in a cave, he continued on this path by having himself proclaimed the Mahdī by ten of his companions including ʿAbd al-Muʾmin, under a tree. Similarly, his withdrawal to Tīnmallal came to be called a *hidjra* (hegira) and his campaigns to be described, like the Prophet's, as *maghāzī*.

There were soon skirmishes between his followers and the Almoravid forces. With the support of all the *ḳabīlas* of the Masmūda, he secured control over the greater part of the Anti-Atlas. But the Almoravids' sharp response led him to 'emigrate' to Tīnmallal in 1123. There, despite the internal tensions that divided his Masmūda followers, and taking advantage of the reverses that the Almoravids were suffering in Spain, he succeeded in setting up an institutional structure whose main organs were the 'ten', the 'fifty' and the *ṭalaba* group.

The ten

The ten, also called the 'people of the community' (Ahl al-Djamaʿa), the number of whom must have fluctuated, were so called by analogy with the companions of the Prophet. It was the privy council, the 'people of the house' (Ahl al-Dār), headed by ʿAbd al-Muʾmin, the successor to al-Bashīr. The members of the council of ten were in a way the Mahdī's ministers, helping in the preparation and execution of major decision, in the civilian, administrative and military areas.

The council of fifty

Here again, the figure fluctuated. It was a consultative council representing the *ḳabīlas* which had joined, the seven leading ones coming from the three most important *ḳabīlas*: the Hargha, the Mahdī's *ḳabīla*, the Ahl Tīnmallal and the Djanfisa.

The ṭalaba

These were disciples collected by the Mahdī through his teaching during his wanderings.

Al-ḳāffa

This expression described the mass of the followers organized into *ḳabīlas* (socio-political and religious entities) subdivided into sections made up of ten people (*naḳib*) ranked in a hierarchy (*ruṭba*). This tight organization made possible intensive indoctrination, a deep feeling of identity and an attitude of violent hostility towards others, particularly the Almoravids. The Almohads had to be distinguished from others even by their dress, and they had to avoid those who did not believe in the divine unity and join their co-religionists. The doctrine of the *tawhid* was systematically inculcated through treatises in both Berber and Arabic, taking care to link knowledge and action (*ʿilm* and *ʿamal*). This rigorous training developed such blind obedience in the followers that they could even execute their own relatives if necessary. This gave rise to massive bloody purges. After Ibn Tūmart's death, the ten and the council of fifty are mentioned only on the occasion of the *bayʿa*, the oath of allegiance, to ʿAbd al-Muʿmin. In fact, ʿAbd al-Muʿmin had deemed it wise to work with the members of the council on a personal basis, rather than through the councils to which they belonged. From now on it was the council of Almohad shaykhs which seems to have replaced the two councils established at the beginning of the movement. This led to tension that was sometimes very serious. The shaykhs tended to constitute a power parallel to that of the caliphs. Caliph al-Nāṣir in particular dealt a heavy blow to their power on the eve of the battle of Las Navas de Tolosa, which may have contributed to the crushing defeat then suffered by the Almohads. On the other hand, the decline of the authority of the caliphs led to an increase in the power of the shaykhs who formed themselves into a sort of clan or caste whose control became intolerable to Caliph al-Maʿmun. The most numerous and influential of the shaykhs were descendants of the members of the group of ten and the council of fifty, except that the representatives of the Mahdī's own *ḳabīla* did not occupy a prominent place among them – a situation which led to the later revolt by the Mahdī's brothers. In fact the council of shaykhs marked a broadening of the original leadership bodies to organize the newly recruited sectors; thus there appeared a council of Arab shaykhs and a council of Andalusian shaykhs of Djund. As for the corps of the *ṭalaba*, it was the object of particular attention by ʿAbd al-Muʿmin, because of their role as propagandists.

However, they acquired other responsibilities in various spheres: education, administration, the army (political commissariat). It was their duty 'to enjoin the good and to forbid the evil'.

The movement's sectarianism was maintained for a long time; but to the extent that it constituted a political factor, al-Maʿmun reduced it by abandoning the dogma of Madhīsm.

Unification of the Maghrib by the Almohad Muʿminid caliphs

The first phase of hostilities against the Almoravids was marked by three very different events: the Almoravids failed against Aghmāt; while the Almohads were victorious at Kik in 1122 and then went on to lay siege to Marrakesh. But the Almoravid cavalry inflicted the disaster of al-Buḥayrā on them where the Mahdī's principal companion, al-Bashīr, perished; while ʿAbd al-Muʿmin, who was wounded, brought the remnants of the troops back to Tīnmallal. It was at this point that Ibn Tūmart, the founder of the movement, died in 1130.

Period of ʿAbd al-Muʿmin and the foundation of the empire (1133–63)

The rather long period of crisis following Ibn Tūmart's death which ended in ʿAbd al-Muʿmin's accession and consolidation cannot be explained solely by tribalist considerations. What was happening was the transcending of a local messianism in a much larger-scale project: the reunification of the Maghrib in the interests of a strict observance of Islam and in the interests of ʿAbd al-Muʿmin's family. During his 30-year-long reign, ʿAbd al-Muʿmin was to display remarkable qualities as a military strategist and a statesman. The chief stages of this great enterprise were as follows; the conquest of Morocco, the conquest of the central Maghrib, the consolidation of power, the conquest of Ifriḳiya and the beginning of the intervention in Andalusia.

The conquest of Morocco

Drawing a lesson from the disaster at al-Buḥayra (defeat being attributed to the fact that the plains favoured the Almoravid cavalry), ʿAbd al-Muʿmin set out to conquer the Berber mountains beginning with the south which secured him control of both their mineral wealth and the trade routes to the Sudan; which, together with the subjugation of the Sūs and the Draʿa ensured him considerable income. Then, the Almoravid army followed the route along the ridges, moving north-east in order to isolate the Almoravid heartland. They took the Middle Atlas and the Tafilālet oases during 1040–41; finally, they debouched in northern Morocco and seized the fortresses in the Tāzā region and won over the sub-Mediterranean *kabila*s. The Almoravid dispositions were thus surrounded. Equipped with ample means in men and resources, ʿAbd al-Muʿmin decided to move down into the plains where favourable conditions helped his offensive: the discord between the Lemtūna and Masūfa chiefs after the death of Amīr ʿAli ibn Yūsuf Ibn Tas͟hfin in 1143; the death in 1145 of the Catalan, Reverter (al-Ruburṭayr), leader of the Almoravids' Christian militia; and the rallying to the cause (*tawḥid*) of the Zenāta Berbers. When, after the Almoravids had taken Tlemcen, the Almoravid amīr Tas͟hfin Ibn ʿAli withdrew to Oran where he met an accidental death, Morocco was virtually conquered by the Almohads who controlled the vital trade route linking the Sudan to the Mediterranean. In that situation, internal revolts, such as one by the al-Harg͟hi of Ibn Tūmart's own *ḳabīla*, or external ones, inspired by supporters of the Almoravids in the Sūs and between Ceuta and Agadir could no longer seriously threaten the new power, which bloodily put down every sign of rebellion. For the Almoravids, with a society whose structure was relatively flexible, and following a Mālikism that they had adopted easily, did not appear as ungodly. That is why, except in the Maṣmūda mountains, the Almohads were not welcomed as liberators. Hence the numerous acts of rejection by a society radically challenged by an 'exclusivist' and implacable Almohad community.

The conquest of the central Maghrib

ʿAbd al-Muʾmin could now move on to conquer the rest of the Maghrib. Before embarking on that, he responded to the appeal from the people of Andalusia who could no longer tolerate the Almoravid yoke and feared the growing danger from Castile. Some towns such as Seville and Cordova came over and were received by the Almohad expeditionary force, but the eastern provinces remained cautious; and when, in 1150, an Andalusian delegation came to take an oath of allegiance to ʿAbd al-Muʾmin, the Almohad leader did not think of pushing further into Spain and preferred first to look eastward with the idea of unifying the Maghrib.

In Ifrīḳiya itself, there was also a Christian threat: the Normans under Roger II of Sicily were gaining a foothold on the coasts, while the Ṣanhādjan dynasties of Ḳayrawān and Bidjāya (Bougie) were being threatened by the Ṣanhādjan and Arab principalities in the hinterland.

In 1152, ʿAbd al-Muʾmin, using forced marches, reached the central Maghrib with the advantage of surprise. He seized Algiers and Bidjaya and, thanks to the Ḥammādid ruler's vizier's coming over, he entered Constantine. Using harsh measures, he dispersed the Ṣanhādja, Luwāta and Kutāma. Their Arab allies or clients, who had so far been cautious, threw themselves into battle and were cut to pieces in the plain of Setif in 1153 after putting up a heroic resistance. The Almohad caliph showed them unusual clemency. Perhaps after showing his strength he was already thinking of broadening the bases of the empire and making with Arabs allies in the name of the *djihād*, in order to attack Andalusia. That is why, leaving behind governors and garrisons in the central Maghrib, he returned to Morocco.

Consolidation of Muʾminid power

Fearing that the recent victories might reinforce the power of the caliph, Mahdī Ibn Tūmart's own relatives among the Hargha and the people of Tīnmallal revolted; they were crushed and deported; while, to calm the people, the caliph went on a pilgrimage to the Mahdī's sanctuary, distributed gifts there and had the mosque enlarged.

But, in 1156–7, encamped at Sale, he had his eldest son Muḥammad recognized as heir presumptive, and his other sons as governors of the chief cities of the empire with the title of *sayyid*; each of them however was to be seconded by an Almohad shaykh as vizier and adviser. The establishment of the dynasty had been made possible by the support of new imperial forces: the Hilāl Arabs and the Ṣanhādjan *ḳabīlas* in the east.

But the new order once again provoked rebellions in the south-east among the Lamṭa and Lamtūna, while in Marrakesh, a serious plot mounted by the Mahdī Ibn Tūmart's two brothers shook the regime to its very foundations. The repression was pitiless.

The result of these testing times was that ʿAbd al-Muʾmin was now the head not of a great community of believers that had been seriously shaken but of a patrimonial empire. He stopped relying exclusively on the ruling 'clan', the

Maṣmūda, and began to think of enlarging the bases of the empire with the support of the *ḳabīla*s of the central Maghrib and the Hilāl Arabs. From being based on a clan and a religion, power now became above all political and inter-ethnic.

The conquest of Ifrīḳiya

In 1159, after putting down various challenges, ʿAbd al-Muʾmin embarked on his second campaign in the east, at the end of which the Maghrib would for the first time be unified under one single authority. The people of Ifrīḳiya made repeated appeals for help against intrusions by the Christians.

At the head of very large land forces and a powerful fleet steering a parallel course towards the east, ʿAbd al-Muʾmin laid siege to Tunis which soon fell. But it took a seven-month blockade to secure the surrender of Mahdīyya which had been in the hands of the Christian Normans for 12 years. Gabes, Gafsa, Sfax and Tripoli fell in turn, and the hinterland of Ifrīḳiya, caught in a pincer movement between the attacks of the fleet and the breaches made by the cavalry in the south, was eventually subdued. The principalities that had succeeded the Zīrīd kingdom were dismantled, the Normans were removed from the coast and the Maghrib was united.

Preparations for the intervention in Andalusia, and the end of ʿAbd al-Muʾmin's reign

Andalusian lords, representatives of the Almoravid dynasty and Christian groups were challenging the caliph's authority and making more and more incursions against northern Andalusia. ʿAbd al-Muʾmin first sent detachments that won some victories, for example at Badajoz. But then the caliph died in Sale just when he was about to start out for Spain. He was buried in Tīnmallal near the tomb of Ibn Tūmart. He had been an outstanding military leader and organizer who never lost sight of economic objectives, for example when he shifted the terminus of the trans-Saharan routes from the Atlantic coast of Morocco to Oran from Draʿa, thus replacing the Almoravid axis with an Almohad axis for the route taken by gold from the Sudan. The caliph was forced to look both northwards in order to contain the Christian offensive in the Iberian peninsula and eastwards towards Ifrīḳiya to ensure the dearly won unity of the Maghrib. But it was very difficult to attain both these objectives at the same time.

The Almohads had added political and administrative unity to the existing economic and cultural unity. Breaking with Almoravid tradition, which had been inspired by Hispano-ʿUmayyad organization, ʿAbd al-Muʾmin set up an administrative system which took account both of the requirements of an enormous empire and of the susceptibilities of his Berber entourage. On the technical level, to ensure a degree of efficiency, he made use of Andalusians. On the political level, the duality between the Muʾminid *sayyid* and the Almohad shaykh guaranteed the necessary balance. Finally, on the ideological level, the *ṭalaba* as 'political commissars' ensured loyalty to the regime. Some aspects of the modern Moroccan Makhzen are still based on this system.

This new administration was financed by an updated tax system. In 1160, on his return from Ifrīḳiya, it seems that the caliph caused a survey to be made of the whole of the Maghrib, from Tripoli to southern Morocco. Except for one-third of the land (mountains or unproductive land), all the rest was made liable to the *kharādj* (land tax). There had been no land register since Roman times. But it is possible too that he was influenced by the Hilālian tax. Considerable resources were thus generated, for only the Almohad 'unitarians' (*muwaḥḥidūn*) were exempted from paying the tax.

The central Maghrib and Ifrīḳiya were thus treated as non-Muslim lands, which gave the inhabitants of those areas a rather bitter idea of the unity that had been achieved, especially as Almohad sectarianism did not promote 'a calming of minds'.

Furthermore, even though the revised tax system made it possible to establish an army and navy that were famous throughout the Mediterranean, these armed forces were never really homogeneous, which was a real danger in the long run. As for the transfer of the Hilālians to the Maghrib, it never had the catastrophic character that R. Le Tourneau attributes to it.

The period of balance

Abū Yūsuf Yaʿḳūb (1163–84)

A time of serious unrest followed the death of caliph ʿAbd al-Muʾmin. There were various reasons for it: first, the hostility between the heir presumptive Muḥammad and his brothers, one of whom (Abū Yūsuf) emerged victorious. Next, the uprising of the Ghumāra in northern Morocco, caused probably by the disbanding of the army mustered for the Andalusian expedition. Finally, the Mālikite resistance in the Ceuta region was perhaps partly behind it too. This rebellion was drowned in blood by the new caliph who only then took the title *Amīr al-Muʾminin* (1168) and appointed his brother governor of Ceuta with the responsibility of watching over the Rīf.

The Andalusian Campaign

The caliph and his brothers defeated the Andalusian prince Ibn Mardanīsh and his Christian mercenaries in 1165 but failed to take his capital, Murcia. But the caliph's forces could only escape the counter-offensive by the famous captain Giraldo Sempavor at Badajoz, by the intervention of their Spanish ally Ferdinand II of Leon. Ibn Mardanīsh's forces soon broke up and many of his men joined the caliphal army, but the approach of the Castilians forced the Almohads to withdraw to Murcia where the troops were disbanded. The caliph returned to Marrakesh in 1181–2.

Abū Yūsuf Yaʿḳūb al-Manṣūr (1184–99)

When he was designated by the Almohads as successor to his father, there were a number of challenges; but the fact that he had been his father's vizier and close associate, not to mention his qualities of dynamism and gallantry, meant that the grand electors had to choose him. Nevertheless, the beginning of his reign was marked by fierce opposition from new actors in the history of the Maghrib: the Banū Ghāniya.

The Banū Ghāniya in the central Maghrib

They derived their name from an Almoravid princess, Ghāniya, who was given in marriage by the Almoravid Yūsuf Ibn Tāshfin to ʿAlī Ibn Yūsuf al-Masufi, who had two sons by her, Yaḥyā and Muḥammad. This latter was governor of the Balearics at the time of the collapse of Almoravid power. His son, Isḥāḳ, turned this haven into a prosperous kingdom through piracy; and his grandson swore to bring down the Almohads, keep the islands out of their hands and even carry the war into the Maghrib, also for reasons of trade. Taking advantage of the fact that the Ḥammādid Ṣanhādja of Bidjāya were still hoping to regain power, the Majorcan Almoravids backed them up with a detachment of 20 units and 4,200 armed men, landed at Bidjaya and seized the town; they then replaced them. ʿAli Ibn Ghāniya, helped by the Riyāh Arabs, occupied Algiers and then Constantine and only withdrew when the Almohad army approached.

Despite its failure, this Almoravid venture caused a considerable stir. The anti-Almohad forces had now found their leader. Among these forces, Ibn Khaldūn notes in particular the zeal with which the Arabs supported rule by the Banū Ghāniya. Setting out from Ceuta, the new caliph launched a combined expedition by land and sea to retake Algiers, while Ibn Ghāniya fled south towards the Mzāb.

The Banū Ghāniya in Ifrīḳiya

With their fleet lost and their base at Bidjaya retaken by the Almohads, the Banū Ghāniya shifted to guerilla war, using the desert, which was in a state of perpetual rebellion, as a base for withdrawal and regrouping. ʿAli Ibn Ghāniya allied with the Lemtūna and Masūfa Berbers, the Banū Sulaym Arabs and the Armenian Ḳarākūsh, a freedman of a nephew of Ṣalāḥ al-Dīn (Saladin). ʿAlī even sent an oath of allegiance to the Abbasid Caliph al-Nāṣir who promised his support while the Armenian, master of Tripolitania, occupied the town of Gabès. ʿAlī Ibn Ghāniya set up his main base in the Djarīd, in the south-west of Tunisia.

ʿAbū Yūsue Yaʿḳūb's intervention in Ifrīḳiya

In 1186, the caliph decided to march on Tunis with an army of 20,000 horsemen. Ibn Ghāniya disengaged his troops and withdrew to the Djarīd, where he enticed a force of 6,000 horsemen whom he cut to pieces near Gafsa in 1187. The caliph then decided to take part in the operations himself. Ibn Ghāniya was defeated and wounded at al-Ḥāmma, and then 'vanished' in the desert. The caliph defeated and captured Ḳaraḳush at Gabès, mopped up throughout the rich Djarīd basin, retook Gafsa, punished the Almoravid officials severely and deported their Arab allies en masse to the Tāmasnā in Morocco.

The reappearance of the Banū Ghāniya

Succeeding his brother ʿAlī, Yaḥyā Ibn Ghāniya was in turn to pursue the struggle against the Almohad empire implacably, undermining its eastern province of Ifrīḳiya and weakening its power. Yaḥyā renewed the alliance with Ḳaraḳush who had not been executed. Going round Ifrīḳiya, where his deported Arab allies were no longer very numerous, he attacked the central Maghrib. Soon, with the Armenian, they controlled the whole of the interior of Tunisia. When they quarrelled and Ḳaraḳush was defeated and driven back into the Djabāl Nafūsa, Yaḥyā controlled a vast territory stretching from Tripolitania to the Djarīd. This position was further strengthened by the Almohads' internal dissensions and the support of the Khāridjites in the Djabal Nafūsa; so that in the end Ibn Ghāniya was master of the eastern half of the Maghrib.

The al-ʿArak (Alarcos) campaign and the end of Yaʿḳūb's reign

Simultaneously, serious difficulties arose in Spain, bringing out into the open the great contradiction in Almohad policy: intervention on two fronts, in the Iberian peninsula and in the Maghrib. From 1194, the caliph sacrificed Ifrīḳiya to Spain. In July 1195, he crushed the Castilians at Alarcos (al-ʿArak), which earned him the title of *al-manṣūr billāh* ('the victor through God's will'). Disagreements among the Spaniards enabled him to wage a campaign of devastation as far as Madrid where he accepted an offer of a truce from Castile which was allied to Aragon against Leon. He was ill, and returned to Morocco to die.

Abū ʿAbdallāh Muḥammdad Al-Nāṣir (1199–1214)

Muḥammad inherited a difficult situation; both Ifrīḳiya and Spain continued to be threatened. The new caliph gave priority to Ifrīḳiya where Ibn Ghāniya was extending his possessions westward and having prayers said in the name of the 'Abbasid' caliph of Baghdad. But in Morocco itself, he had to put down an uprising in the Sūs, led by Abū Ḳaṣāba who claimed to be the expected *ḳaḥtani*; thus Mahdīsm was being turned against the Almohads, who had used it to establish their power. It was a subject of great bitterness. Moreover, among the caliph's advisers, only one advised him against making peace with Ibn Ghāniya the Almoravid.

Al-Nāṣir's offensive against the Banū Ghāniya and the reorganization of Almohad power in Ifrīḳiya

Using a new strategy, the caliph first took Majorca, in 1203, thus depriving the Banū Ghāniya of their refuge in the Balearics which they had used as a military and commercial base that enabled them to maintain links with Aragon, Genoa and Pisa against the Almohads. But the Banū Ghāniya responded by seizing Tunis. The caliph succeeded in winning it back, along with Mahdīyya. Ibn Ghāniya, whose nephew surrendered then, was himself vainly pursued as far as the Barḳa area. Appointed governor and virtual viceroy of Ifrīḳiya, Abū Muḥammad ʿAbd al-Wāḥid, the very one who had advised the campaign, remained in Tunis, while the caliph set off back to Morocco in 1207. Ibn Ghāniya rallied a number of Arab groups, including the Riyāḥ, the Sulaym and the Dawawida, with whom he first attempted, but failed, to cut the caliph's return route. Then he laid waste the Tlemcen region and the whole of the central Maghrib which, in the fourteenth century, according to Ibn Khaldūn, still bore the mark of it. There followed the fierce and implacable confrontation between ʿAbd al-Wāḥid, the new governor, and Ibn Ghāniya supported by his Arab allies. The clash took place at the foot of the Djabāl Nafūsa in 1210. There, with his Arab and Zenata contingents, the Almoravid was overwhelmingly defeated. He then moved southward into the Waddān and was only captured in 1233 by the governor ʿAbd al-Wāḥid's successor.

The stormy epic of the Banū Ghāniya cannot be analysed simply as an extension of the Hilālian Arab 'catastrophe' carried by the Majorcans into the central Maghrib as Georges Marçais argues. For half a century it assumed a major strategic dimension, by endeavouring, as at the beginning of the Almoravid epic, to combine the nomadic Saharan dimension and the maritime dimension. It demonstrated a remarkable constancy and consistency, and it cannot be perceived as a mere rebellion devoid of profound political aims.

In reality it was a power struggle in which the Banū Ghāniya attempted to present themselves as an alternative to the Almohad power. In this struggle, the ideological and political dimension was the most important, for it united all those opposing the caliph: fallen former dynasties, Mālikites, nomad Arab *ḳabilas* and Berbers in Tripolitania. Geopolitical and economic aspects may also help us understand the relative success of this enterprise: first, the trading and diplomatic base constituted by the island of Majorca, but also the fact that the movement's sphere of influence extended from the Waddān and southern Tripolitania to the former Khāridjite settlements in the central Maghrib. This strip included the Maghrib from Tripoli to the borders of Morocco, and embraced a series of dissident mountain 'tribes' and rich oases situated at the outlet of the great trans-Saharan routes. The struggle of the Banū Ghāniya was thus designed to recover the heritage of the Fāṭimids, Zīrīds and Almoravids in the control of trade between the Mediterranean and the Sudan; whereas the Almohad project, despite the attraction of Spain, remained on an east-west axis, across the Maghrib, without that Saharan and Sudanese dimension that carried the African gold that was vital to the Mediterranean economy.

The defeat of al-ʿIḳāb (Las Navas de Tolosa) and the end of al-Nāṣir's reign

Put on their guard by their defeat at Alarcos in 1195, the Christians had reorganized, and, despite the truce, had resumed hostilities in 1200, under the impetus of Alfonso VIII of Castile and Pedro II of Leon, encouraged by the offensive spirit of the famous bishop of Toledo, Rodrigo Jimenez de Rada, who convince Pope Innocent III to declare a crusade. The Almohads lacked unity. When Caliph al-Nāṣir decided to counter-attack in Spain, he purged his army by executing senior officers. This was followed, on 16 July 1212, by the crushing defeat at Las Navas de Tolosa, which the Christians exaggerated, but which was nevertheless the first major victory by the united Christians over the Muslims of Spain and the Maghrib, led by their caliph in person. It caused a considerable sensation, for more than just a military reverse, it was a political setback due to a loss of morale among the troops. It is a remarkable fact that this sign of the disintegration of the Almohad regime did not lead to any comeback on the part of the Muslim West. There was rather indifference. It is easy then to understand the depression into which the caliph sank when he hurriedly returned to Marrakesh, and which was to afflict him until his death in 1213.

Disintegration of the Almohad system

Caliph al-Mustanṣir, who succeeded al-Nāṣir, was only a young boy whose power was limited by the Almohad leaders: he could not keep the army in enemy territory for as long as he wanted. Furthermore, the calm that marked his reign was disturbed by Christian attacks, the revival of the Banū Ghāniya and the incursions of the Banū Marīn hitherto held back beyond the Saharan borders. The viziers were also seizing more and more power. After al-Mustanṣir's death and despite the energetic attempts at recovery by al-Maʿmūn (1227–32) and al-Ṣʿaīd (1242–8), the forces of disintegration grew stronger; the heterogeneous army was on the defensive against the Christian crusade. There was a muted hostility between the Muʾminids and the Almohad shaykhs. The latter, unable to take the lead doctrinally, began more and more to present themselves as defenders of the people against the demands of the tax collector. In the internecine strife that now pitted pretenders to the caliphal title against one another, the role of the Christians and the Arab *ḳabīla*s grew. Thanks to his agreement with Ferdinand III of Castile, al-Maʿmūn was able to recruit a Christian militia and overcome his rival proclaimed in Marrakesh. Master of the empire, he took two key decisions: tolerance for Christians and a solemn renunciation of Almohad doctrine, including the principle of the Mahdī and his infallibility. The Almohad aristocracy was confused by this initiative: it was an opportunistic gesture of conciliation towards the Mālikites, but it still in fact destroyed the regime's ideological legitimacy.

From 1230 onwards, al-Mamʿūn, now wholly dependent on Christian mercenaries, had to grant more and more privileges to Christian trade and the Hilālian Arabs in order to hold his rival, who had not given up, in check. His son, al-Rashīd (1232–42), only reigned thanks to the action of his mother, Habbada, a slave of Christian origin, and the Christian leader of the militia.

The European factions and the Banū Marīn took great advantage of the situation. When in 1242, al-Ṣaʿīd, son of al-Mamʿūn and a black slave, came to power, the centrifugal forces grew stronger. After him, the Banū Marīn took Marrakesh. Ifrīḳiya broke away in two stages: the first was the rebellion and secession of Yaḥyā Ibn Ghāniya, who was captured by Abū Zakariyyā, son of the Ḥafṣid, ʿAbd al-Wāḥid. Abu Zakariyyā took power in 1228, and in 1233, proclaimed his independence; he even laid claim to the office of caliph.

Meanwhile, Almohad Spain was disintegrating, the governors giving way to Andalusians who ended up submitting to the Christian kings. The former pre-Almohad local dynasties, such as the Beni Mardanīsh, sometimes resurfaced, but only at once to become vassals of the Christian rulers. By 1230, Almohad power had vanished from Spain and been replaced by the remote suzerainty of the 'Abbasids' or the nearer suzerainty of the Ḥafṣids of Ifrīḳiya. This new situation simply gave a new impulse to the expansion of the kings of Castile and Aragon.

3 The Spread of Civilization in the Maghrib and its Impact on Western Civilization

The Almohad century

The apogee

Was the apogee of the civilization of the Maghrib reached under the Aghlabids in the ninth century, when the forces of Ifrīḳiya ruled the Mediterranean and threatened the city of Rome? Or in the tenth century, when the Fāṭimids made Mahdiyyā the seat of a rival caliphate to that of Baghdad? Or again in the twelfth and thirteenth centuries, when the Almohads led by a Berber dynasty built a Eurafrican empire stretching from Tripoli to Seville? This last period was in any event one of the most brilliant ones. As for Spain, it was to the Maghrib as Rome was to Greece: twice Spain conquered its uncouth Berber conquerors, captivating the Almoravids and Almohads to make them builders of a Hispano-Maghribi civilization which reached far beyond the Mediterranean Sudanese blacks, then present in large numbers throughout the Maghrib, also contributed to this cultural mix, as did those of mixed ancestry who were the fruit of this presence, just as in Spain, especially in Seville and Granada, where they introduced black African customs, and sometimes made their presence felt in intellectual life, like Jean Latin, a university professor.

Art

It was chiefly in the western half of the Maghrib that Almohad art was visible, since Ifrīḳiya had declined greatly. Furthermore, the time of the Almoravids and the Almohads forms a whole, since Almohad art was the culmination of the preceding period. The Almoravids were great builders. Both their civil and their military architecture (palaces and fortresses, irrigation works etc.) were magnificent, but much has been destroyed. On the other hand, the religious monuments are much better preserved, especially in Algeria. Thus, the Great Mosque of Marrakesh has disappeared. The Great Mosque at Algiers, built in 1096, has not suffered unduly from later alterations. But it is undeniably the Great Mosque of Tlemcen which remains the most remarkable evidence of Almoravid art and architecture. It was completed in 1136, and is an imposing building combining the solid and sober majesty of Saharan buildings with the refined delicacy of Andalusian art. The ribbed dome, typical of Andalusian art, is associated with Iranian-inspired features.

In the balance of its volume and the richness of its ornament, Almohad art simply enhanced the nobility and grace of the previous style. Its most complete expression is *D̲jāmiʾ al-Kutubiyyīn*[1] (the Mosque of the Booksellers) in Marrakesh, one of the jewels of Islamic art, built by ʿAbd al-Muʾmin himself. Its six-storey minaret is 67 m high. Five stalactite domes, which may be considered masterpieces of the style, adorn the transverse nave. Lobate or scalloped arches span the 17 naves and seven bays, magnificently enlarging the space. The Great Mosque of Seville, another pearl of Almohad art, was built by ʿAbd al-Muʾmin's successor, Abū Yūsuf Yaʿḳūb (1163–84). It was converted into a cathedral and today only the minaret, the famous Giralda, remains. The most grandiose monument, the Mosque of Ḥasān, begun in Rabat by al-Mansūr, remained unfinished; but its monumental minaret (the Ḥasān tower) still survives to impress us today. Little survives either of the civil architecture of the Almohads; among others, there survive the two great gates of al-Mansūr in Rabat, the *ḳaṣaba* of Badajoz, the famous Tower of Gold which overlooked the ships on the Guadalquivir. Almohad art, further enriched by the profusion of colours due in particular to the use of polychrome faience, was an art of maturity, strength and grandeur.

Literature

The literary flowering after the short period of reservation at the beginning of Almoravid rule, was due to the fact that Arab rulers were traditionally patrons. In this area and for the period we are concerned with, Ifrīḳiya did not shine. We should nevertheless mention the great poet Ibn Ḥāmdis, born in Sicily who spent most of his life in Ifrīḳiya.

The regions most fertile in great talents were undoubtedly the far Maghrib and above all Andalusia. Ibn Baḳi (d. 1150), who spent his life journeying back and forth between these two regions; Ibn Diḥya, who left Spain, travelled all through the Maghrib and died in Cairo; finally, Ibn Ṣāḥl (d. 1251), a native of Seville, of Jewish origin, were outstanding men of letters. But two names shine with particular brilliance: Ibn K̲h̲afad̲ja (1058–1139) and Ibn Ḳuzmān (d. 1160). The former was an inspired and unequalled poet of nature who merited the nickname al-D̲jannān (the gardener) because of the freshness, sensuality and romantic nature of his poems which tell of the beauty of nature and the joys of existence. He has remained one of the classic Arab poets down to the present day.

Ibn Ḳuzmān was truly the 'prince of popular poetry' (*imām al-zad̲jd̲jalīn*). He abandoned literary language and manipulated colloquial Hispano-Arabic like a master. He was ugly and dissipated, and led an openly dissolute and licentious life. He was always short of money, suffered imprisonment and barely escaped the death penalty. In very short ballads in which he created new metres and rhyme schemes, he praises love and wine, refined pleasures full of pretty

1. From *Kitab*, 'book' in Arabic.

women, sometimes giving way to a popular coarseness which always stops short of obscenity. His compatriot Madg͟hālis and many others, even in the East, endeavoured long afterwards to equal the inspired verve of Ibn Ḳuzmān.

In the field of literary criticism mention may be made of Ibn Bassām (d. 1148) who compiled a vast and intelligent anthology in his *Dhāk͟hira*, in order to fight the alleged superiority of the East; this task was later taken up by Ibn Bas͟hkuwāl (d. 1183) who collected together the biographies of 1,400 celebrities of Islamic Spain.

Mention must also be made of Ibn Madaʾ al-Ḳurṭubi (d. 1195), a specialist in philology, who advocated simplifying Arabic grammar even at that early date; and above all the distinguished historian and geographer al-Idrīsī (1099–c.1166) who lived at the court of Roger II of Sicily.

Philosophy, medicine and science

Philosophy flourished to a rare degree under the Almohads, who were the protectors of a galaxy of great minds, such as Ibn Bad͟jd͟ja (Avempace, d. 1139), Ibn Rus͟hd (Averroes, 1126–98), Ibn Maymūn (Moses Maimonides, 1135–1204) among others. These scholars devoted themselves to the practical sciences too – medicine, mathematics and astronomy. The Latin deformation of their names is clear evidence that they were adopted by Europe in the Middle Ages. This was particularly the case with the greatest of them, Ibn Rus͟hd. After having been a *ḳādī*, he wrote a medical book and worked on astronomy, before being invited by Caliph Abū Yaʿḳūb Yūsuf to elucidate obscurities in the works of the great Greek philosopher Aristotle. Ibn Rus͟hd then showed his full genius. But the theologians disapproved, and he was condemned, disgraced and exiled, while his works were consigned to the flames. They have come down to us mostly only in their Latin or Hebrew translation. Besides the *Commentaries* on Aristotle, there is the *Faṣl al-Maḳal* ('The Positive Treatise') in which he tackles the difficult problem of the conflict between reason and faith, and the *Taḥafūt al-Taḥafūt*, in which he refutes in detail the theses of the greatest theologian of orthodox Islam, al-G͟hazālī.

Ibn Rus͟hd's ideas are controversial, and in particular, some have criticized the ambiguity of a thought that swings between a sort of materialist rationalism reserved for the elite of readers and a cover of orthodox discourse intended for ordinary people. The fact is that Ibn Rus͟hd's thought reflects the contexts within which he lived his life. This gives it a richness and depth that has not yet been totally elucidated. He certainly owes a great deal to Aristotle on whom he was the greatest commentator, but he was also linked to a whole current of Arab philosophy which he accepted only with a powerful critical mind marked by a remarkably original genius equally at ease in theology and in law or pure philosophy (*Taḥafūt*). The Almohad century also saw, especially in the twelfth century, great specialists in the practical sciences too such as the botanist Ibn al-Bayṭar, and above all the astronomers and mathematicians D͟jabir Aflaḥ and al-Zarḳali.

The splendour of a setting sun

After the disaster at Las Navas de Tolosa (1212), the Almohad empire disintegrated leaving four successor kingdoms: one in Spain and three in the Maghrib.

Granada, or a last and splendid flowering

The little kingdom of Granada was the beautiful pinnacle of the great and eventful history of the caliphate of Cordova. The dynasty of Granada, the Nāṣrids, left many civil and military monuments. There is nothing new architecturally, except that there is, above all, a perfect marriage between the skilful balance of volumes and forms which is so striking from outside, and the exuberant and refined sumptuousness of the decoration: twin pairs of doors and windows, rows of stone-laced arches surmounting slender marble columns, bays of light and patches of shade. With its walls covered with tracery of floral, epigraphic or geometric motifs coming together from all directions in a sort of subtle and never-ending music with its symphony of discreet or dazzling colours, the art of Granada is the last marvellous and enchanting but exhausted song of Spanish-Maghribi art. Its most beautiful flower remains the Alhambra.

Culture evolved in the same pattern: whereas philosophy declined and the practical sciences marked time or lost ground (although mention should be made of the physician Ibn Khaṭima and the mathematician Al-Kalasadi (1412–86) poets, philologists and stylists producing highly wrought, refined prose remained as good as ever, in particular with two magicians of the word in both prose and verse. The first, Lisān al-Dīn Ibn al-Khāṭib (1313–75), an unrivalled humanist equally at home in history, medicine and mystical theology, was already highly regarded by his friend Ibn Khaldūn and still remains one of the great classical Arabic writers. But he was falsely accused of being a heretic by powerful personages, including his own protégé, Ibn Zāmrak, who succeeded him as vizier, and was strangled in his dungeon; his body was burnt. But Ibn Zāmrak, whose virtuosity in writing rivalled his, was himself murdered on the sultan's order. In short, Granada swung between the refinements of an exquisite art and the barbarous practices of a decadent power.

The heirs of the Almohads in the Maghrib

The same loss of vitality affected the heirs of the empire in the Maghrib: the Marinids in Morocco, the Abd al-Wādīds in the central Maghrib and the Ḥafṣids in Ifrīḳiya, a situation that lasted up to the late sixteenth century.

While the European West was undergoing a real demographic explosion, the Muslim West was becoming depopulated, the critical point being reached in the mid-fourteenth century. Ibn Khaldūn, who saw population decline as one of the factors in the decline of a civilization, observed this phenomenon and all that ensued: the shrinking of agriculture, arboriculture and towns, and the spread of nomadism. Ḳayrawān changed from having hundreds of thousands of inhabitants in the ninth century to being no more than a small town in the

3.1 *The Alhambra of Granada: a room adjoining the Court of the Lions, fourteenth-century decorative sculpture.* (*J. Devisse*)

fourteenth. According to Leo Africanus, Bidjayā was reduced to one-third of its previous population. The total population seems to have fallen by two-thirds. Epidemics were both cause and consequence of this tragic shift, which, as Ibn Khaldūn observed, plunged the southern shores of the Mediterranean into dusk just when the northern shores were seeing the dawning of the Renaissance.

In architecture, the influence of Granada was felt above all in Morocco and western Algeria. The Marinids were the only great builders. During the thirteenth century two new types of monument appeared. First, there was the *madrasa*, a college of higher education borrowed from the East, with its inner courtyard surrounded by balconies with student rooms leading off them, and on one side a large room furnished with a *miḥrāb* serving as both classroom and oratory. The largest one is the Abū ʿInāniyya in Fez. The other was the *zāwiya*, which was both the hall of a confraternity and the burial sanctuary of its founding saint.

The style of these monuments shows both perfect technique and the absence of any new creativity. It was, so to speak, the same with culture. As Ibn Khaldūn notes: 'the progress of learning had totally stagnated'. The rational sciences in particular were kept under close, obscurantist surveillance by conservative theologians. The Moroccan Ibn al-Banna (1256–1321) was the last mathematician, the Ifrīḳiyan Ibn al-Ḳammād, the last astronomer. The Moroccan Ibn Baṭṭūta

(1304–c.1377), a great traveller who visited Africa, the Middle East, India and China, was a master of descriptive geography in the form of the travel narrative (*riḥla*). Finally, among the historians the great figure of Ibn Khaldūn (1332–1406), trained by al-ʿAbīlī of Tlemcen, stands out. But on the whole, the world of letters was decadent. The panegyrics and funeral orations exuded artifice and hypocrisy. Cold stereotypes and even the equivocations of erotic poetry had replaced the spirit of earlier times. And yet, the external form of the literary morsels was finely crafted.

They nevertheless bore witness to the presence among this educated bourgeoisie, including women, of a culture that was inherited and learned rather than an instrument of intellectual and artistic creativity. They adored music, in which Andalusian influence (the *maʿlūf*) was predominant, and appreciated dancing; as Leo Africanus notes, about the people of high society in Bidjayā: 'The civilization of rentiers was following the more vigorous era of pioneers and inventors.'

The impact of the Maghrib on western civilization

Although they took different and contrasting paths, the Muslim West and the Christian West had never stopped being engaged in many-sided exchanges.

Material exchanges

Trade with Spain and other European countries was governed by treaties that also regulated the settlement of individuals. Thus the Europeans controlled the *funduk* in the main towns of the Maghrib (Tlemcen, Marrakesh etc.) that were at once inns, places of worship and business offices, managed by consuls accredited by the authorities.

But the reverse did not happen; traders of the Maghrib did not succeed in structuring their own maritime transport or in stimulating home production for export. The taxes paid by foreigners were used essentially to fill the state treasuries.

The structure of trade moreover was typical of the disparity in commercial exchanges. In theory, there was no limitation on imports on either side; whereas, for exports, some strategic goods were prohibited or subject to quotas, such as arms, iron, wood etc. Notwithstanding these official rules, the Iberians exported to the Maghrib metals, wood, ironmongery, spices, wine, paper and especially textiles. They imported wool, skins, wax (the town of Bidjayā (Bougie, in French) gave its name to the French language as a word for wax candle), dates and carpets and other craft products. The kingdom of Aragon endeavoured to control the Barcelona–Majorca–Tlemcen–Sidjilmāsa route, which was the route by which the gold of the Sudan reached the Mediterranean basin.

The Maghrib ran a deficit on the plane of material exchanges, but it was a major exporter of the achievements of its cultural heritage which it was no longer able to build on.

Cultural exchanges

During this period, the Maghrib transferred its own cultural legacy while also acting as the channel for the transmission of Muslim values emerging from Egypt and the East.

Atmosphere and motivation

In the twelfth and thirteenth centuries the Christian West was very tolerant of contributions from the Maghrib and continued to be so up the fall of Granada in 1492, when the Inquisition radically transformed attitudes.

There were two main reasons for the original openness: disinterested curiosity or sympathy, and spiritual strategy. Roger II of Sicily (1105–54) and Frederick II (1194–1250) surrounded themselves with Arab scholars. Peter I of Aragon (1094–1104) signed his letters in Arabic and struck Muslim-type coins.

But the Dominicans and Franciscans dreamed of spiritual conquest. Ramón Llull (1235–1315) devoted his life to 'dialogue' with the Muslims, writing treatises in Arabic, preaching in the Maghrib, and seeking to use philosophy as well as crusades to put an end to Islam. He urged the popes and European kings to adopt the same approach. At the Council of Vienna in 1311, he proposed the foundation of colleges for Arabic studies, and the creation of a military order to crush Islam. And yet Ramón Llull was deeply influenced by Ibn al-ʿArabī (1165–1240), the greatest mystic of Spanish Islam, so much so that he was later to be known as the 'Christian *ṣūfi*'.

The Studia Arabica

Muslim and Arab influences moved along two main routes: the Italian one through Sicily and the Iberian one into southern France. Compared to them, the crusades seem to have been superficial phenomena, acting in the opposite direction.

The Italian school's influence spread out from Salerno where Constantine the African (Constantinus Africanus), a physician and businessman from Tunis converted to Christianity, ended up as abbot of the Monastery of Monte Cassino. But it was above all at Palermo, in Sicily, thanks to the encouragement given by Frederick II (1194–1250) and the early Angevin rulers, that the great period of translations from Arabic into Latin developed, with the astrologer Theodore and above all the Scotsman Michael Scot and the Jew Faradj b. Salim of Agrigento.

In Spain, the movement began in the tenth century in Catalonia, at the famous monastery of Ripoll. But it was in the twelfth century that Barcelona became the leading centre for translations, with Plato Tiburtinus and the Andalusian Jew Savasorda (Ṣāḥib al-Shurṭa) who made available several works of astrology and astronomy, including the important tables drawn up by al-Baṭṭani (Albatenius). Toledo was the next to attract scholars from all over Europe, playing the same role in the foundation of the culture of the Christian West that Baghdad had played in the ninth century gathering the Hellenic heritage for the Arab world; Alfonso X the Wise (1252–84) was the counterpart of al-Maʾmūn (813–33), who dreamed of Aristotle. Two archbishops, Raymond and then Rodrigo Jimenez de Rada (1170–1247), followed one another as heads of this school of Toledo whose original initiators were Jews and Mozarabs. Indeed, the first translations were made into Hebrew before Castilian and Latin.

Among distinguished translators were the great philosopher Dominicus Gondisalvius of Segovia, and the Englishman Robert of Ketton who made for Peter the Venerable, the reformer of Cluny, the first Latin translation of the Koran; but above all Gerard of Cremona (1114–87) whose tireless zeal enabled him to translate no fewer than 70 works. The second period of the Toledo school was dominated by Michael Scot.

This example had wide-reaching effects. *Studia Arabica* multiplied. In 1250, Ibn Rashīq of Murcia met, in the monastery of that city, Dominicans totally familiar with Arabic and the Koran. Moreover, Alfonso X entrusted the direction of the school in Murcia to a Muslim philosopher of the region. In 1250 too, the *Studium Arabicum* of Tunis founded by the Dominicans benefited from the contribution of Ramón Marti, to whom is attributed an Arabic-Latin dictionary. In 1276, the Franciscan Ramón Llull founded, in Majorca, the famous Miramar College where monks were initiated into the study of Arabic before going to evangelize the lands of Islam. Finally, following a proposal by the Council of Vienna, *Studia Arabica* were opened at Oxford, Paris, Rome and Bologna, where Leo Africanus was still teaching in the sixteenth century. At Marseilles, a Jewish family from Granada, the Ibn Tibbon family, made their mark as translators of Arabic works into Hebrew.

Translations of works from Andalusia and the Maghrib and their impact

Philosophy

The Christian Middle Ages discovered, understood and appreciated ancient thought through the philosophers of the Maghrib and Muslim Andalusia. Ibn Badjdja (Avempace) and Abubacer were known in the Latin Middle Ages, although only Hebrew translations of their works date from this period. The first Latin translation of Abubacer, entitled *Philosophus Autodidactus*, dates from as late as 1671. But the grand master was indisputably Ibn Rūshd (Averroes), most of whose works have come down to us in Latin or Hebrew translations. He was passionately discussed. Among his numerous translators and propagators mention should be made of the Scotsman Michael Scot (d. 1235) and the Tibbonids of Provence. Ibn Rūshd, al-Ghāzali's adversary and author of the *Tahafūt*, translated under the title of *Destructio destructionis*, easily appeared as the champion of rationalism and anti-dogmatism. Thus, two irreconcilable camps came into being. Among the Averroists was Siger of Brabant of the University of Paris. But when Averroes asserted the eternity of the world and denied the immortality of the individual soul, he was vigorously challenged by Albertus Magnus (1206–80) and Ramón Llull among others. Averroism divided the great minds that passionately took sides. Siger was excommunicated and imprisoned, and met a tragic end in 1281.

Painters portrayed Averroes in their pictures: for example, at Pisa, Andrea Orcagna places him beside Muḥammad and the Antichrist in his hell. Francesco Traini pictures him, about 1340, upside down beneath the feet of St Thomas Aquinas. It has been said that St Thomas 'was at once the most serious adversary and the chief discipline of Averroes' (Ernest Renan). Five hundred and three quotations from Ibn Rūshd have been counted in St Thomas Aquinas. Expurgated or better understood, Ibn Rūshd triumphed yet again in the fourteenth century. And in the fifteenth, when Louis XI of France reorganized the teaching of philosophy, he recommended the doctrine of 'Aristotle and his commentator Averroes, long recognized as wholesome and sure'. At the University of Padua, Averroism had its most brilliant effects which lasted into the eighteenth century.

Science

Ibn Rūshd's medical works were translated in Padua by the Jew Bonacossa; similarly, the best works of the famous medical school of Ḳayrawān (Isḥāḳ ben ʿImrān), translated by Constantinus Africanus in the eleventh century, were used in teaching at Salerno. Isḥāḳ al-Isrāʾili's medical works continued in high favour until the sixteenth century. The *Kitāb al-Taʿrif* of the Andalusian Abū Al-Ḳāsim (Abulcasis 936–1013) enjoyed immense renown throughout the Middle Ages; though less than Avicenna's work the *Canon of Medicine* regarded as the Bible of their profession by all medieval doctors. Similarly, medieval pharmacology owes much to the Andalusian Ibn Wāfid (Abenguefit, 988–1074) thanks to his work translated under the title *De medicamentis sipplicibus*. The contribution of Andalusia and the Maghrib to the mathematical and astronomical sciences was also vital. Adelard of Bath translated the *Astronomical Tables* of Maslama al-Madjriṭi, which had been drawn up around the year 1600, following Al-Khuwārizmī.

The thirteenth century also saw the translation of the vast astrological encyclopedia of the Ifrīḳiyān Ibn Abī al-Ridjal by Yehuda ben Moshe; while Gerard of Cremona translated the *Tables* of Al-Zarḳālī (Azarquiel), which become well known throughout medieval Europe as the *Tablas Toledanas*. Between the thirteenth and sixteenth century, the *Treatise on Astronomy* of al-Bitrūdjī (Alpetragius) was translated several times, which shows its continuing success. As for the mathematical genius Leonardo of Pisa (b. c.1175), who lived for a long while in Bidjayā, (Bougie) he owed much to the Arabs both in algebra and for the numerical system that he introduced into Europe.

Language, letters and art

The subject of the influence of literature in Arabic on medieval Europe has been passionately debated.

Was the poetry of the troubadours, with its themes of courtly love in the twelfth and thirteenth centuries using new forms of prosody, Arab in origin? No, says Jean Anglade. Yes, say other writers including Ramon Menendez Pidal, who shows the striking resemblances between the poetry of Ibn Kusmān and the poetry of Languedoc represented by Guillaume IX of Poitiers. This type of influence appears to be the normal result of the symbiosis which, before the twelfth century, marked the economic and socio-cultural relations of which Andalusia was the main crucible.

On the other hand, the undeniable Muslim Arab influence on Dante's *Divine Comedy* are today universally recognized; especially since the discovery of the translation of the *Mi'rādj,* a popular tale of Muḥammad's ascension into heaven which had a great vogue in Muslim Spain. It has been established that Dante knew it; which, of course, in no way detracts from his own genius.

The long intimacy between the Muslim West and the Christian West left many traces in Europe languages. Words like algebra, logarithm, zenith, azimuth, alembic, alcohol, cipher, tariff, syrup, sugar and hundreds of others to do with mathematics, astronomy, medicine, chemistry, botany etc. are of Arabic origin. In Spanish, such words number about 4,000. The artistic influences went beyond Andalusian architecture and affected Romanesque art, as Mâle pointed out, and even the culinary art of medieval Europe.

Conclusion

Across the two bridges of Sicily and Spain, African culture in its Andalusian-Maghribi form penetrated the culture of western Europe up to the fourteenth century. Until the time when, because of political decline and demographic collapse, this culture ceased to be a living force in its country of origin, and was taken over by a Europe in full demographic expansion which, perceiving the priceless strategic value of what it had acquired, was to turn it into one of the tools of its irresistible historical rise.

4 The Disintegration of Political Unity in the Maghrib

The downfall of the Almohads

After the defeat at the battle of Las Navas de Tolosa, the disintegration of Almohad power proceeded slowly but surely; the first territories to secede were in Africa and al-Andalus and then in the central Maghrib (Tlemcen) and finally Morocco, ending with the original southern core of Almohad power which was conquered by the Marinids in 1269.

The causes of this decline were, first, the sheer size of the empire which dissipated the caliph's energies between the eastern Maghrib and Spain, and made any central administration very difficult, while the geographical eccentricity of the capital, Marrakesh, compounded the existing difficulties.

This explains the numerous rebellions of nomad Arabs, the Banū Ghāniya, and townspeople. Increasingly, the dynasty had to turn to Arab, Berber and even Christian mercenaries, thus destroying the original feeling of unity. Furthermore, the Almohad aristocracy was intent on retaining its privileges, treating all other non-Almohad Muslims as infidels. But this aristocracy was itself split into two clans: on the one hand, the descendants of ʿAbd al-Muʾmin, known as *sayyids*, and on the other, the Masmūda Almohads and the religious shaykhs. These latter clashed with the Andalusian bureaucracy, which recognized only the power of the caliph.

The conflict between the dynasty and the shaykhs was brought out into the open in 1230, when one of the princes, Yaʿḳūb al-Maʾmūn, landed from Spain at the head of a force of Christian horsemen, defeated the army of the reigning caliph and proclaimed himself *Amīr al-Muʾminin* and persecuted the shaykhs, going so far as to repudiate the Almohad confession. When his successor, al-Rashīd (1232–42), attempted, in agreement with the shaykhs, to restore the doctrine of the Mahdī, it was too late. Anarchy had become incurable. The last Almohad caliph al-Wathiḳ was deposed by the Marinids in 1269.

The threefold partition of the Maghrib

This brought about a return to the situation before the rule of the Fāṭimids: three independent states weakened by chronic upheavals from within and from

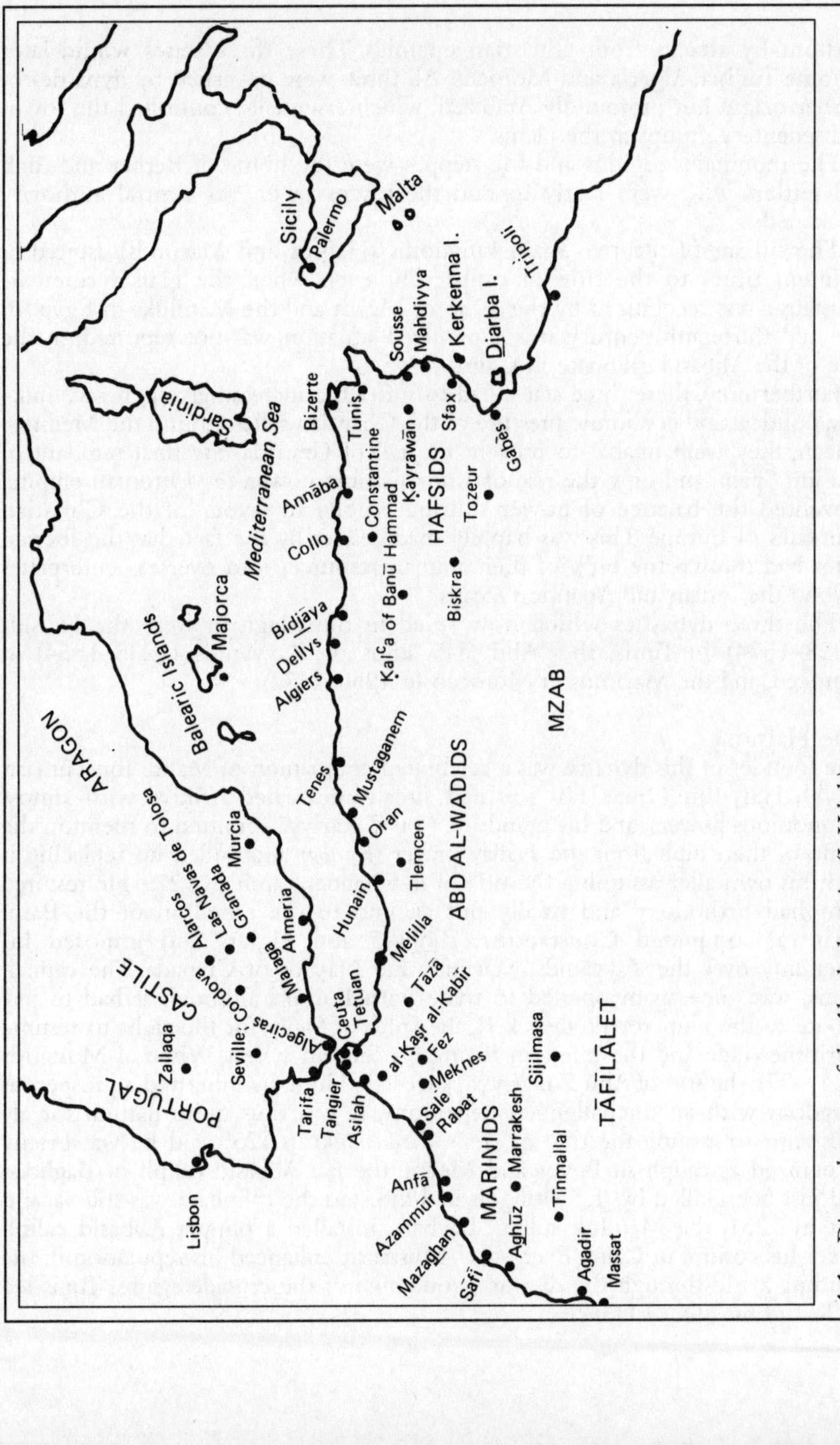

4.1 *Dismemberment of the Almohad empire (I. Hrbek).*

without by attacks from Christian enemies. These three states would later become Tunisia, Algeria and Morocco. All three were governed by dynasties of Berber origin but profoundly Arabized, which essentially controlled the towns and sedentary groups in the plains.

The mountains regions and the steppes were the home of Berber and Arab hill-settlers who were ready to raid the towns whenever central authority weakened.

The sultans of the two main kingdoms (Ḥafṣids and Marinids) aspired at different times to the title of caliph; but even when the Ḥafṣid ruler al-Mustanṣir was recognized by the *s̲h̲ārīfs* of Mecca and the Mamluks in Egypt in the mid-thirteenth century, this short-lived situation was not repeated, in the face of the Abbasid caliphate in Cairo.

Furthermore, these three states had to suffer the increasingly aggressive military, political and economic pressure of the Christian states around the Mediterranean; they were unable to prevent the fall of Granada, the final remnant of Muslim Spain; and only the rise of a new Islamic power, the Ottoman empire, prevented the balance of power shifting wholly in favour of the Christian countries of Europe. This was happily made easier by the fact that the Iberian states had thrown the bulk of their human resources into overseas enterprises beyond the Indian and Atlantic Oceans.

The three dynasties which now ruled in the Maghrib were the Ḥafṣids (1228–1574) in Tunis, the ʿAbd al-Wādīds or Zayyānids (1235–1554) at Tlemcen, and the Marinids in Morocco (c. 1230–1472).

The Ḥafṣids

The founder of this dynasty was a celebrated companion of Mahdī Ibn Tūmart, s̲h̲ayk̲h̲ Ḥafṣ Ibn ʿUmar. His son had already governed Ifrīḳiya with almost autonomous powers, and his grandson, Abū Zakariyyāʾ, omitted to mention the name of the caliph from the Friday prayer (*k̲h̲uṭba*) and ended up replacing it with his own after assuming the title of independent amīr in 1229. He restored Almohad orthodoxy and finally put an end to the rebellion of the Banū G̲h̲āniya, conquered Constantine, Bid̲j̲jayā and Algiers and imposed his suzerainty over the Zayyānids, Marinids and Nāṣrids of Granada. The capital, Tunis, was once again opened to trade with Europe, although it had to pay tribute to the emperor Frederick II, the ruler of Sicily, for the right to resume maritime trade and the freedom to import Sicilian wheat. When al-Mustanṣir (1249–77), the son of Abū Zakariyyāʾ, succeeded him, he inherited a prosperous kingdom with an unchallenged hegemony. It was thus quite natural for al-Mustanṣir to assume the title of *Amīr al-Muʾminin* in 1259 and he was briefly recognized as caliph in Egypt and Mecca; the last Abbasid caliph of Baghdad had just been killed by the Mongols in 1258, and the caliphate was still vacant. But in 1261, the Mamluk sultan, Baybars, installed a puppet Abbasid caliph under his control in Cairo. Even so, al-Mustanṣir enhanced his reputation in the Muslim world through the disastrous outcome of the crusade against Tunis led by King Louis IX of France.

Whether King Louis was misled into believing that the Ḥafṣid ruler intended to convert to Christianity, or was encouraged by some Provencal merchants anxious to recover their debts, it was lamentably misguided. His brother Charles of Anjou, king of Sicily, quickly concluded peace with Tunis, which agreed to continue to pay tribute; and commercial relations resumed on a larger scale. Thus, under these two regions of Abū Zakariyyā' and al-Mustanṣir, the authority of the Ḥafṣids was recognized from the Ḥidjāz to Andalusia.

After al-Mustanṣir, for almost a century, there was chaos, marked by internecine struggles, Arab revolts and recurrent outbreaks of dissidence, for example in the towns of Constantine and Bidjayā. It was during these periods when centrifugal processes were at work that the Marinids of Morocco twice (in 1348 and 1357) occupied large areas of Ḥafṣid territory, including Tunis.

It was Abū-al-ʿAbbas (1370–94) who restored the prestige of the dynasty by reunifying and reorganizing the country. The open hostility between Tlemcen and the Marinids of Morocco relieved him of any worry in the west. His son, Abū Fāris (1394–1434), during his long reign, consolidated this work, choosing governors from among freedmen. His authority was accepted as far away as Tlemcen, in Morocco and even in Andalusia. Abū Fāris achieved his success through his concern for justice, for example among the various communities of the kingdom (Almohads, Arabs and Andalusians), through his spirit of tolerance towards the Jews, his generosity towards the religious authorities (ʿulamā) or sharīfs) and also through the building of numerous monuments, the suppression of illegal taxes and the grandiose celebration of Muslim festivals.

His grandson and successor, ʿUthmān (1434–88) enjoyed a long reign disturbed only by the agitation of some of the princes and by outbreaks of famine and plague.

After him, this second period of Ḥafṣid hegemony collapsed as suddenly as the first, giving way after the end of the fifteenth century to anarchy, so that the dynasty was unable to exploit the great clash between Spain and the Ottoman empire for hegemony in the Mediterranean.

The Marinids

The Marinids were originally from the Mzāb where they belonged to the noblest among the Zenāta. They knew neither money nor agriculture nor trade, they valued only camels, horses and slaves. Their fate is a marvellous illustration of Ibn Khaldūn's theory about the importance of 'clan spirit' (ʿ*aṣabiyya*) for conquering territory and establishing states. After the defeat at Las Navas de Tolosa (1212), the Banū Marin who were settled in the pre-Saharan steppes embarked on an invasion of north-eastern Morocco, establishing their rule and exacting tribute from agriculturalists or towns such as Fez and Taza. Political ambitions followed. The long time it took for them to complete their conquest of power, from 1240, when they were defeated by the Almohad army before Meknès, and 1269, when they captured Marrakesh, can doubtless be explained by their total lack of any religious motivation. All this took place in the reign of Abū Yūsuf Yaʿḳūb (1258–86) who made Fas al-Djadīd (New Fez) his capital.

Before long, the Marinids, men of the desert, were gripped by the mirage of the north and the green plains of al-Andalus, like the Almoravids and Almohads before them. Here again, as with the Ḥafṣids, there were two high periods. The first, from 1258 to 1307, under Abū Yūsuf Ya'ḳub and his son, Abū Ya'ḳūb Yūsuf; the second under Abū al-Ḥasan (1331–48) and his son, Abū 'Inān Fāris (1349–58). It was only during the latter period that the Marinids could briefly lay claim to hegemony over the Maghrib.

One of the most important developments under the Marinids was the growing importance of the Arabs. The Marinids made a political calculation and observed that their Zenāta supporters were only a small minority; they therefore allied with the Arabs to whom they were already highly assimilated. Arab nomads were encouraged to immigrate. Numerous Berber groups were Arabized, and Berber, which was the language of the Almoravid and Almohad armies, gave way to Arabic, which became the official language. This process, which favoured the Arab nomads, led them to encroach on the area of the agriculturalists: fields, gardens and forests were taken over as pastures. The more fixed structuring into three social groups – nomads, townspeople and mountain dwellers – came into being in this period. The towns and their surrounding areas alone were under the direct administration of the sultan, while the *makhzan ḳabīla*, the Arabs and the Zenāta, enjoyed a wide degree of autonomy. As for the Berbers of the Atlas, the Rif and the Djabal, they remained outside any authority, even of an indirect sort, and, whenever the central government weakened, would make incursions into the *bilād al-makhzan* and incorporate it, if only briefly, into the 'land of dissidence' (*bilād al-sibā*). Against all these risks, the sultans turned increasingly to the system of mercenary slave armies garrisoned in the towns.

The counterpart of this influx of nomads was the contribution of Andalusian immigrants which involved a more refined style in the arts and crafts and customs of the large towns. Fez succeeded Marrakesh which was in decline, and became a major cultural centre. It was organized around its university, al-Ḳarāwiyyīn, and numerous *madrasas*, where, under the patronage of the sultan, the orthodox Mālikite rite was preponderant; the rural populations, on the other hand, were rather attracted by the mystic brotherhoods (*tariḳas*), the *zawiyas* and local holy men or marabouts. The Almohads had incorporated the mystical doctrine of al-Ghazālī (d. 1111) into their teaching, and the reign of the Marinids saw the appearance of several *Ṣufi* (mystic) orders, which were for the most part offshoots of the Ḳādirīyya. It was in this popular form that Islam reached the remotest parts of Morocco.

As for the challenge of Christian expansionism, Abū Yūsuf Ya'ḳūb took it up four times, landing in Spain and defeating the Castilians on land and sea; this succeeded in containing the Christian threat for a while. The fourth campaign ended in 1285 with a treaty under which the king of Castile undertook not to intervene in the affairs of the Muslim territories in Spain, and to hand back Arabic manuscripts previously captured.

Sultan Abū Ya'ḳāb divided his time between campaigns against internal revolts, against Tlemcen and against the king of Castile, who had broken the

1285 agreement. After the sultan's murder, there was a period of disorder marked by the revolt of a dissident prince, who succeeded in taking control of the trans-Saharan trade, paralysing the expansionism of the dynasty in Spain and the Maghrib. Only Abū al-Ḥasan put an end to this revolt. Faced with attacks by Castile on Granada, he allied with the Nāṣrid amīr of Granada, retook Algeciras and threatened Castile which then made an alliance with Aragon. Despite a decisive naval victory by the Marinid navy reinforced by some Ḥafṣid vessels, the fiercely fought battle of Rio Salada (1340) ended in a severe defeat. The sultan of Morocco then abandoned his dreams of Spain and the emirate of Granada was abandoned to its fate.

The Marinids, like the Zayyānids, took advantage of the weakness of the Ḥafṣids in the first half of the fourteenth century to expand their respective territories. Abū al-Ḥasan seized this opportunity to conquer Tlemcen, the Zayyānid capital, after a lengthy siege, and then Tunis (1347), establishing Marinid control over the whole of the Maghrib. But intervention in the affairs of the Arab *ḳabīla*s of Ifrīḳiya soon set off a general uprising which crushed Abū al-Ḥasan's army at Kayrawan and went on to besiege him in his capital from where he managed to escape only to find himself confronted with the rebellion of his own son Abū ʿInān who laid claim to the throne. The greatness and the tragic end of Abū al-Ḥasan in the mountains, is like the rerun of the model of the recurrent history of the dynasties of the Maghrib: the slow accumulation of forces, the breakthrough into a period of successes and the sudden disaster. And it was always for the same reasons: geographical dispersion of resources, inability to do justice to local particularisms, and a precarious fiscal situation.

When the ambitious Abū ʿInān succeeded his father, he assumed the caliphal title and again conquered Tlemcen and Tunis; but the Arabs' response obliged him to evacuate them, and he was murdered by one of his viziers.

From then on, anarchy and decadence ruled. The viziers and in particular, after 1420, the Zenāta clan of the Banū Waṭṭas held effective power, making and unmaking rulers until 1472, when Muḥammad al-S͟hayk͟h was proclaimed sultan, after a bitter struggle against the *s͟hārīf*s associated with the cult of saints and the blessing (*baraka*) of the marabouts. the first Waṭṭasid sultans succeeded in containing the s͟hārīfian movement, but not Portuguese expansion along the Atlantic coast. They were soon confined to the region of Fez, with the south of the country beyond their control. It was from there that popular forces assembled by a s͟hārīfian family embarked on a holy war against the Portuguese, sounding the death knell of the Waṭṭasid dynasty.

The Zayyānids (ʿAbd al-Wādids)

Yaghmuraṣān Ibn Zayyān, the Almohad governor of Tlemcen (Tilimsān), who came from a junior branch of the Zenāta clan, broke away from the sultan's control and founded his own dynasty, which survived for three centuries, despite the pressures from western or eastern neighbours and the incursions by Arabs from the south. That it did so was due to the skilful policies of a number of rulers who were usually on the defensive, but were often able to go over to

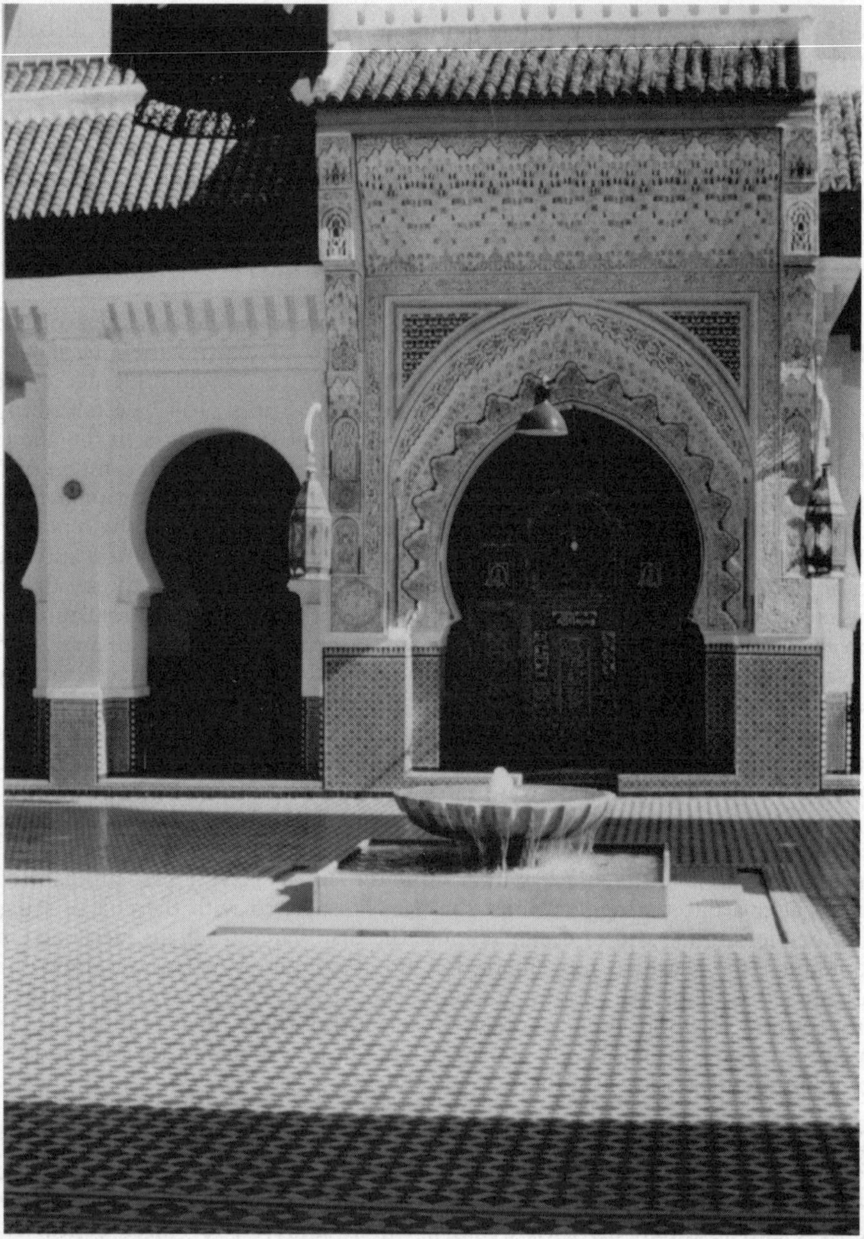

4.2 *The Ḳarawiyyīn Mosque at Fez: restoration was carried out during the Almoravid era; in the courtyard, the main entrance of the prayer room.* (*J. L. Arbey*)

the offensive against Fez in the west and the Chelif valley in the east. Under their rule, the Arabization of the Zenāta Berbers went on with increasing intensity, so much so that western Algeria lost its former predominantly Berber character.

The kingdom's fragile economic base on the least fertile part of the Tell with very few sedentary inhabitants and many nomads harassed by the Arabs, explains its chronic instability and internecine strife. And yet this state survived until the Ottoman conquest, in the mid-sixteenth century. Its main asset was its capital, Tlemcen, which had replaced Tāhart as the main commercial entrepôt of the central Maghrib, located where the east–west route linking Fez to the Ifrīḳiya crossed the north–south route which went from Europe to the Sudan through Oran and the Saharan oases. The town was also directly linked to Sidjilmāsa which was conquered in 1264, thereby, for ten years, bringing the two main outlets of trans-Saharan trade under a single authority for the first time.

The two rival dynasties of the Marinids and the Zayyānids, as well as the Ḥafṣids, fought repeatedly for control of this trade. Between 1299 and 1307, Abū Yūsuf Yaʿḳūb laid siege to Tlemcen and built a new town opposite, called Tilimsān al-Djadid (New Tlemcen) which soon captured most of the trade until its destruction after the relief of Tlemcen. An old and famous proverb current in Tlemcen says: 'The best remedy against poverty is the Sudan.' Thus the kingdom skilfully exploited the periods of weakness of its two powerful neighbours. On the other hand, when the Marinid Abū al-Hasān conquered Tlemcen in 1337, he seized the outlets of trans-Saharan trade. During the latter half of the fifteenth century, prosperity returned with the reign of Abū Ḥāmmū Mūṣā II, an able ruler (1359–89), although there were problems arising from two periods of occupation by the Marinids and uprisings of Arab nomads. It was among these latter that the great historian Ibn Khaldūn intervened on behalf of Abū Ḥāmmū, which gave him an insight into the wellsprings of the turbulent politics of the Maghrib. He testifies to Zayyānid culture: 'Here [in Tlemcen] science and arts developed with success; here were born scholars and outstanding men, whose glory penetrated into other countries.' And many monuments are still there to bear witness to this flowering. But when Abū Tashfin dethroned his father, Abū Ḥāmmū, in 1389, it marked the beginning of a long period of decline. Tlemcen was intermittently the vassal either of Tunis or of Fez, and after the fifteenth century, of Aragon, until the arrival of the Ottoman empire which put an end to the Zayyānid dynasty in 1554.

The challenge of Christian Europe

If the Maghrib was divided, its Christian adversaries to the north of the Mediterranean were even more so: the kingdoms of Castile and Aragon, the Italian towns of Pisa, Genoa and Venice, Sicily and Portugal pursued competing policies. After the adventure of St Louis, France withdrew into itself. Every possible diplomatic and commercial permutation were tried, which shows that it was not at all simply a religious confrontation between two monolithic blocs. In reality, it was above all economic interests that account for the tangle of alliances between Muslims and Christians against other coalitions of Christians and Muslims.

But the mid-thirteenth century marked a decisive turning-point when most towns in the Iberian peninsula and the Balearic Islands came under Christian control, leaving the tiny emirate of Granada to enjoy a respite until 1492. The balance of power had shifted in the western Mediterranean. This was when the Maghrib was quite clearly driven on to the defensive.

Internal factors played a major role in this process, in particular the ever-present thrust of centrifugal forces represented in the Muslim states by dissident princes, heads of nomad *ḳabilās*, Christian mercenaries and religious leaders (*shaykhs* or *shārīfs*) all attached to their own particular interests. Added to those there was the antagonism between the countryside, on the one hand, and the towns geared to business and money-making without regard for nation or religion, on the other; between nomads and sedentary populations etc. In addition to that there was the falling rate of population growth, aggravated by the Black Death in the mid-fourteenth century and scarcely made up for by the influx of Andalusian Muslim refugees, as well as the rural exodus due to the constraint of the feudal regime and the deterioration of the soil associated with use by nomadic groups. The list shows that there were many negative internal factors.

Externally, it is important to observe that trans-Saharan trade, which for centuries had fuelled economic prosperity, began from the 1350s onwards to be increasingly directed towards Egypt, thus diverting the many economic and financial side benefits (such as customs duties) of this trade.

But at the same time, the Christian states were consolidating their power. Even the power of the Ḥafṣids, which was farthest away from their reach, did not escape the incursions, raids and annexations of maritime bases by Aragon, Sicily, Genoa and Venice. Djarba remained in Christian hands until 1335, and throughout the fifteenth century, several ports between Tripoli and Algiers were the targets of attacks, worsening relations between the Ḥafṣids and the Christian states.

The situation in the central and western Maghrib was more complicated. Whereas, until the mid-fifteenth century, Aragon maintained friendly relations with Morocco in the framework of a hegemonic strategy, Castile, as well as Portugal, kept alive the crusading spirit and the desire to eliminate the activities of corsairs.

Piracy in the Mediterranean had existed from time immemorial, but the Christian reconquest of Spain gave it a religious colouring; the Muslim corsairs, especially those expelled from al-Andalus, considered their reprisals a kind of holy war (*djihād*). From naval bases christened republics they launched operations that were outside the control of the authorities. Moreover, the Marinids, like the Waṭṭaṣids and the Ḥafṣids, adopted an ambiguous attitude towards the corsairs, congratulating them on their aggressiveness towards the Christian challenge, which they themselves were too weakened to take up, but anxious not to provoke too many counter-attacks from the corsairs or the Christian states.

The Muslim corsairs, like the Moroccan *s̲h̲ārifs* and marabouts in the fifteenth and sixteenth centuries who stirred up popular anger against the Portuguese, denounced compromises with the Christians. But before the union of Castile and Aragon (1479), no concerted European action was possible against the Maghrib. Only the liquidation of Granada (1492) made this a real prospect. Portugal, on the other hand, motivated by religious, political or basely material feelings, was to prove much more offensive.

In 1415, the conquest of Ceuta, undertaken by two princes, one of whom was the future Henry the Navigator, marked the beginning of Portuguese and even European colonial expansion. It was the preface to a new chapter in world history, despite the precedents of the crusades; but these were in the last analysis no more than sporadic thrusts confined to the Mediterranean. Henceforth, the Atlantic Ocean entered the stage, with all the continents.

The Portuguese failed once again before Tangiers in 1437, and King Duarte of Portugal preferred to let his brother Fernando, who had been taken hostage, die in captivity in Fez than hand back Ceuta to Morocco. Portugal concluded that it could not defeat Morocco and get to the gold of the Sudan along the trans-Saharan routes by a frontal attack. This explains the project to get round Morocco by the Atlantic. From the mid-fifteenth century onwards, numerous coastal towns were occupied by the Portuguese: ʿAnfā, Arsīla, Massat, Agadir, and Tangiers finally fell into their hands in 1471.

The coasts of West Africa had already been reconnoitred and in addition to the booty that the operations against the Moroccan coasts and cities brought them, the Portuguese initiated a circular trade which consisted in purchasing woollen textiles, cereals and horses in Morocco which they bartered in Black Africa for slaves and gold.

While Portugal, seeking the legendary 'Prester John', was attempting to take the Muslim world from behind, the marriage of Ferdinand of Aragon and Isabella of Castile in 1469 was followed by the fall of Granada in 1492 and Christopher Columbus' first voyage across the Atlantic in the same year.

In 1494, the Pope sanctioned the agreement between the two Iberian kingdoms to divide the Maghrib between them: the Spanish got numerous ports in the central and eastern Maghrib (Melilla, Oran, Bid̲j̲ayā, Tripoli) without being able to move into the hinterland.

The end of the fifteenth century thus saw the decay of Islamic power in the Maghrib. It was divided, undermined by internecine quarrels and drained of manpower, demographically and economically just when the positive factors making for political integration and economic expansion were helping Europe.

The sixteenth century saw a revival of the Maghrib, with, in the west, the popular movements, and, in the east, the counter-offensive by the Turkish corsairs, and later the Ottoman empire. But the era of Muslim hegemony marked by the Almoravids, Almohads and the early Ḥafṣid and Marinid rulers was well and truly over.

5 Society in the Maghrib after the disappearance of the Almohads

The predominance of nomadism: life in towns

The nomads

After the eleventh century, the balance between nomads and sedentary populations was upset in favour of the former with the arrival of the Banū Hilāl, followed in the twelfth century by the Banū Sulaym. For strategic reasons, the Almohads gave over the Atlantic plains to them, while the Banū Maʿḳil settled in the south and east of the Moroccan Atlas range. The western Maghrib was thus cut off from the east and forced back towards the Mediterranean coast.

The rural population

Peasants made up the vast majority of the population living in symbiosis with the towns. Serfdom did not exist; small family farms predominated in the context of joint and collective ownership, although there were some large estates. Numerous plots were *habous* (religious endowments) which the assigns had cultivated by tenant-farmers. Various forms of contract bound the owners to the farmers, in particular share-cropping for a fifth of the crops. But the share-croppers (*k͟hammas*) were often wretched. Rural markets often grew into market towns, centres for contact between sedentary people and nomads.

The isolated Berber-speaking areas were the ones where the most archaic forms of organization persisted longest.

The townspeople

In general, Muslim Arab society in the Maghrib was characterized by the patriarchal family, the separation of the sexes, the separation between free men and slaves, and between Muslims and tributaries.

The traditional layout of the town included the great mosque amid the *souk*s (side streets) and *ḥammām* (hot steam baths), with ramparts pierced by gates leading to the suburbs and cemeteries. The *funduḳ*s (caravanserai) in the ports were inhabited by European merchants and corsairs returning with slaves.

The Jews played an important role thanks to their capital, their skills and their European connections. Their numbers increased with the influx of refugees fleeing persecutions. They were in general well received, and in Morocco often attained high office, but they did not escape outbreaks of xenophobia (pogroms), as at the beginning and end of the Marinid dynasty, as well as in the Tuāt oasis in the late fifteenth century.

But from the beginning of the thirteenth century to the end of the fifteenth, the most important contribution was that of the Muslim Spaniards. They settled in coherent groups, and these Andalusians were to be found from top to bottom of the social hierarchy, from the sultans' favourites to gardeners and masons, including writers, musicians, secretaries, merchants and soldiers.

Concubinage with black women, of whom there were many among the slaves, led to a considerable amount of racial mixing. The high degree of symbiosis between Arabs and Berbers in the towns did not destroy 'tribalism'.

The triumph of Mālikism: mystical tendencies

Under the Marinids and ʿAbd al-Wadids, Almohadism, the religious ideology of the former power, was replaced by orthodox Mālikism which had not disappeared and which was to revive with the support of the Andalusians in numerous *madrasas*. As for the Ḥafṣids, who were long-standing Almohads, they tried vainly to maintain the dynastic doctrine among the Ifrīḳiyans who had remained faithful to Mālikism which eminent doctors were to revive during the second half of the twelfth century through the *madrasas*, the magistracy and religious institutions. The Ḥafṣids agreed to collaborate and, thanks to the renowned Ibn ʿArafa, Mālikism triumphed in the second half of the fourteenth century.

But alongside orthodox Mālikism, whose narrow-minded legalism had led under the Almoravids to the *auto-da-fé* of the works of al-G͟hāzali, the Moroccan people seeking a more fervent faith turned to Andalusian Ṣūfism which rekindled a local asceticism. Many mystic leaders became popular holy men. Abū Madȳan al-Andalusi, an Iberian, crossed Morocco to go and immerse himself in the eastern source of mysticism. He later lived in Bid͟jayā and died at Tlemcen in 1198, leaving disciples, including al-Dahmānī and al-Mahdāwi. Al-S͟hadili born near Tetuan, began his preaching in a Tunisian retreat in the D͟jabel Zag͟houān. He claimed to be a *s͟hārīf* and died in the East, leaving a multitude of followers imbued with his fervent but simple Ṣūfism. Shādilism was much given to the cult of saints (maraboutism, *baraka*, fervent appeals for miracles) and was linked to the brotherhoods and the *zāwiya*. Among them, a woman, Lāllā Mānnūbiyya (thirteenth century), became famous by her demented behaviour and the fear and veneration that she aroused in Ifrīḳiya. With al-Murd͟jani these popular tendencies were accepted even by theologians at the court.

Then came the Ifrīḳiyan Sīdī Ben ʿArūs (d. 1463), a wandering and outrageous Ṣūfi marabout who in the end won over everyone and died with the reputation of a saint. In the sixteenth century, his numerous followers formed the brotherhood of the ʿArusiyya.

But it was Morocco, from where its founder set out, that produced most Shadilist experiences; particularly in Aghmat and Marrakesh with the *zāwiya* of the Ragraga. Finally, in the fifteenth century, al-Djazūlī, a Berber from the south, who according to legend was descended from the Prophet, brought Ṣūfism, the cult of marabouts and the cult of *shārīfs* together. At that time the Idrīsid *shārīfs* formed powerful groups which the Marinids permitted. Al-Djazūlī, a follower of Shadilism, trained a multitude of marabouts who swarmed north and east as far as Tripolitania.

After his death, there were violent incidents around his coffin which for years was carried around before it was transferred in 1524 by the Sa'dian *shārīf* al-A'radj to the same mausoleum as his own father, thus sealing the alliance between the new dynasty and djazūlīsm and ensuring its triumph.

It was also in Morocco that the *mawlid* – the feast of the birth of the Prophet, which had already been celebrated in the east at the beginning of the thirteenth century – spread among the Berbers and the feast was made official by Abū Ya'ḳūb in 1292. After a period of resistance from Tunisian jurists, it was under Abū Fāris (1394–1434) that Ifrīḳiya adopted the *mawlid* with much reciting of poems, illuminations and songs. Everywhere the *shārīfs* and brotherhoods took over organizing it and derived great prestige from doing so.

Dynastic power and social structure

Theoretically, Maghribi society was organized around two poles: the Berber conquerors (Marinids, 'Abd al-Wādīds, Ḥafṣids) identified with the state (*makhzan*) and the rest; or again the *khāṣṣa* (aristocracy, elite, literates etc.) and the *āmma* (commoners, masses, illiterates). But this second distinction was not identical with the first – not to mention the fact that a middle class upset this bipolarization: the petty bourgeoisie trying to rise up the social hierarchy through good fortune, knowledge or piety, relying on a great man.

The Marinids

The Marinid horsemen and the Zenāta aristocracy, the source of viziers and war leaders, were joined by a variety of Turkoman, Frankish, Andalusian or renegade mercenaries. The great Banū Waṭṭas family emerged at the end of the Marinid dynasty. The chancellor's office was entrusted to secretaries (*katib*). The *hadjib* were chamberlains, freedmen, who had no power, except for one Jew who became head of the government under Abū Ya'ḳūb Yūsuf. Various bodyguards and chiefs of protocol controlled etiquette in the audience chamber (*dār al-'umma*) of the house of the people.

The heir presumptive was closely associated with the exercise of power. The great provincial governors were chosen from the royal family and the Zonāta or the Arabs. The Atlas was virtually autonomous; the Arab *ḳabīlas* were permitted to levy a tax (*iḳṭā*) from which the brotherhoods were exempt, while the *shārīfs* and holy men received a share of it. The Marinids left Marrakesh, the Almoravid capital, for Fez which reached its apogee in the fourteenth century with a royal quarter, another one known as the Christians' quarter and a third one reserved for Jews, the *mallah*. But many of them did not live in it and preferred to go into trade. In the fourteenth century, Abū Yūsuf Yaʿḳūb founded in the old city the famous Marinid *madrasas* endowed by *habous* foundations.

There was a brisk trade with Portugal, Spain, Genoa and Venice. The Christian and Jewish merchants had their own autonomous structures and were controlled by the *muḥtasib*, similar to a *ḳāḍī* for commercial transactions. With the fall of the dynasty, Fez declined, and Marrakesh, chosen as capital by the Saʿdians, was revitalized.

The ʿAbd al-Wādids

The founder, Yag͟hmurasān (1235–83), a Zenāta nomad who settled at Tlemcen, was still living under canvas when he was thirty, and spoke only Berber. The office of vizier was first entrusted to relatives of the kings, but then passed into the hands of an Iberian family of money-changers. A Jew became minister of finance. The chancellor-accountant was selected from among the jurists, while Abū Tas͟hfin (1318–37) appointed an Andalusian freedman as great chamberlain. Kurdish and Christian mercenaries were used, but the Banū Hilāl, who were granted important fiscal concessions, made up the bulk of the army. Yag͟hmurasān built minarets on the great mosques of Tlemcen and Agadir, and palace fortress. His successors created *madrasas*. Tlemcen was then at the peak of its prosperity. Thus, under Abū Hāmmū II (1359–89), who built religious foundations, a family mausoleum and a *madrasa*, and *mawlid* nights were particularly splendid; and an enormous clock with moving figures was much admired.

When in the fourteenth century, the Marinids twice took Tlemcen, they added their buildings too, for example by adding a mosque and a *madrasa* to the mausoleum of Abū Madyan, which they embellished. In short, despite the political vicissitudes, Tlemcen enjoyed unbroken success. The goods derived from flourishing foreign trade were displayed around the Great Mosque. Craftsmen produced woollen fabrics, rugs, earthenware, harnesses etc. feeding the sea-borne traffic which went mostly through Oran. The gold and slaves of the Sudan came through Sid͟jlmāsa to Tlemcen which seems to have taken most of the trans-Saharan trade from Marrakesh. Bid͟jayā with its trading port, its corsair base, and its shipyards was an essentially Kabyle and Andalusian intellectual and religious centre rivalling Tlemcen; Constantine was very busy too and had an old and wealthy bourgeoisie which included many Jews.

The Ḥafṣids

The Ḥafṣids perpetuated the Almohad order with its amīrs. Amīrs were provincial governors, whose children, together with those of the sultan, acted as *sibyān* (pages) at court. Mercenaries who had previously been slaves and renegades played an increasing role in the army and upper echelons of the administration. The *s͟hayk͟hs* controlled the various original Almohad *ḳabīla*. Out of a concern for equality, they were paid the same salary as the sultan. But their influence declined to the advantage of the Andalusians and freedmen in the council (*shurā*) and with the caliph who personally saw to the repression of abuses.

Under Abū Zakariyyā' (1228–49) there were three viziers: one for the army, who functioned as prime minister; one for finance; and one for the chancellor's office. At the end of the thirteenth century there emerged the office of chamberlain (*ḥadjib*), who, in the fourteenth century, became prime minister. The comptroller of the royal household finally gained control over public finance, while the *mazwār* (majordomo and chief of the palace guards), came to rank second controlling the administration of the army. The scribes, initially Andalusians, were gradually supplanted by Ifrīḳiyans.

The Almohad *shaykhs* who were provincial governors gave way to freedmen and close kinsmen of the sultan. The 'tribal' *shaykhs* commanded the contingent of their *ḳabīla* and enjoyed fiscal concessions.

The army was heterogeneous, and was made up of Almohads, Nomadic Arabs, Ifrīḳiyan Berbers, Orientals, Andalusians, Franks etc., and its generals were often freedmen or renegades. At sea, the corsairs were commissioned by the rulers or by businessmen; and in the towns an Andalusian militia lived side by side with a militia of Christian cavalry who acted as the sultan's guard, and Turkoman mercenaries.

The Ḥafṣids abandoned the old capital, Kayrawan, which had been reduced to insignificance by the Banū Ḥilāl, and turned towards the sea.

Tunis was a thriving metropolis. Abū Zakariyya' transformed the Almohad *ḳaṣaba* there into a government centre and in 1240, near the Great Mosque of the Zāytūna, he built the oldest *madrasa* in North Africa. There were numerous *zāwiya, funduk*s, gardens and orchards maintained by Andalusians, and parks and princely residences, including the Bardo palace (1420)

It was in Tunis that the most representative figure of this time, Ibn Khaldūn (1332–1406), was born. The Khaldūn were of Yemeni origin, and had settled in Spain. They left Spain after the Christian *reconquista*. Ibn Khaldūn's ancestors were statesmen in the service of the Ḥafṣids. He too joined their service, but soon fled before the invasion of Ifrīḳiya by the amīr of Constantine. He entered the service of the Marinid Abū 'Inān in Fez. He joined a conspiracy and spent two years in prison. Intrigues and volte-faces followed one after the other in Granada, Seville, Bidjayā, Constantine, Tunis and Tlemcen. At one time Ibn Khaldūn was recruiting Arab mercenaries for the Marinids of Fez, and then he went into retreat near Tiaret for four years to compose his famous *Muḳaddima*.

It was in Tunis, in 1378, that he completed his *Universal History*. Then, the target of a cabal, he left on the pilgrimage to Mecca in 1382 and returned and settled in Cairo where he was a teacher and the Mālikite Grand *ḳāḍī*. In Damascus, besieged by Tamerlane, he had the opportunity before his death to meet the great Mongol conqueror.

From his experience in the Maghrib, Ibn Khaldūn drew conclusions of astonishing originality. He founded a scientific philosophy of history based on

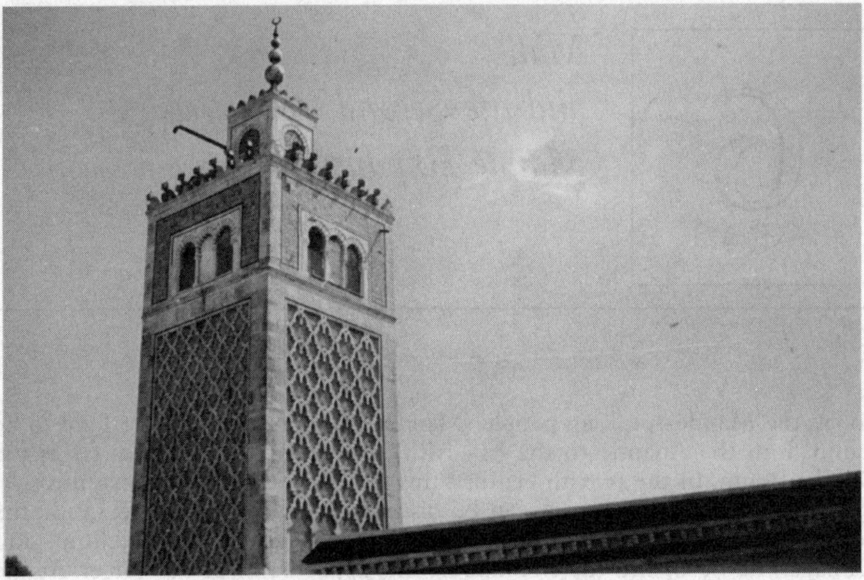

5.1 *The Ḳaṣaba Mosque at Tunis.* (B. Nantet)

the laws of a process made up of open cycles; nomadic groups endowed with a virtue of group consciousness (*ʿaṣabiyya*) conquered the plains, the cities and power; but, once they had become sedentary, they lost that living force to other nomad groups who established themselves in turn. In his view, the Banū Hilāl and the Black Death sapped the vitality of the Maghrib faced with a West with a growing population. According to his theory, sovereignty lasts for only four generations. In his *Universal History*, he studied in detail the Arab and Berber *ḳabīla*s and dynasties.

Ibn Khaldūn is valuable for two reasons: he provides information of exceptional quality derived from his position as a privileged witness of his time. But above all, his profound theories based on a realism that was at once empirical and rationalist, even determinist, enabled him to elaborate laws of historical evolution which have caused him to be seen, rather boldly, as a precursor of historical materialism.

6 Mali and the Second Mande Expansion

Today, the Mande-speaking people (Mandingo, Mandenka, Mander) are to be found from the Atlantic to the Air, with pockets of settlement as far as the Gulf of Benin. In the twelfth century, this habitat was much less extensive. At that time, three major groups can be distinguished, from north to south: the Soninke (or Sarakolle), the founders of Ghana, in Wagadu, Bakhunu and Kaniaga; the Soso; and the Malinke in the upper basin of the Niger. At the time when the Almoravids were putting an end to the empire of Ghana, some Soninke, in particular the Marka or Wakore (Wangara), perhaps in quest of gold, were founding new settlements further south, one of the models for which was the city-state of Jenne. The excavations at the site of Jenne-Jeno have uncovered a settlement dating back to the third century before the Christian era. The development of the city was thus not due to the trans-Saharan trade but was created by interactions between local herdsmen, fishermen, farmers and smiths.

By the beginning of the Christian era, African rice (*Oryza glaberrima*) was being cultivated on the rich silt at the confluence of the Niger and the Banī where Jenne-Jeno was situated, in the midst of a string of large villages.

At the beginning of the sixth century of the Christian era, the presence of copper objects, the raw materials which could only have come from the Saharan mines at Takedda, are evidence of the flourishing state of trans-Saharan trade. The transfer of Jenne-Jeno to its present site at Jenne was probably connected with the desire of the Muslims and traders to separate themselves from the majority of the inhabitants who still followed the traditional religion. Copper was exchanged southwards for gold, kola nuts and ivory.

The discovery of copper at Jenne and Igbo-Ukwu in the Niger delta shows that trans-Saharan trade did not begin with the Arabs; long before them, it was initiated by the Wangara (or Diola) who extended it southwards, sometimes by force of arms. There are few written documents about the period between the fall of Koumbi Saleh, the capital of Ghana, in about 1076, and the birth of Mali with the victory of Sundiata over the Soso in 1235. This marked the beginning of the second Mande expansion which took Malinke clans from the upper Niger to the Atlantic coast in Senegambia. Moreover, Mandenka traders and marabouts moved eastwards into Hausa country, and southwards where trading centres such as Begho were founded towards areas rich in gold, such as the Akan countries.

First we shall describe the peoples and kingdoms of the western Sudan at the beginning of the twelfth century; then the initial development of this expansion of the Mande people; and finally the principal features of the civilization that they created.

Kingdoms and provinces of the western Sudan in the twelfth century

Before the conquest of Koumbi Saleh in about 1076 by the Almoravids, al-Bakrī gives valuable information on the western Sudan; this is filled out by al-Idrīsī in the mid-twelfth century. The written sources accumulated since then and based, like the *Ta'rikh*s of the seventeenth century, on oral traditions, and archaeological work at Koumbi Saleh, Awdāghust and Niani, also confirming what oral traditions have to say, provide the pieces of evidence that make it possible to give a broad outline picture of the western Sudan at that time.

Takrūr

In the mid-eleventh century, Wardjabi, king of Takrūr, who had converted to Islam, and his son, Labī, had thrown off their dependence on Ghana. They had even contributed to its downfall by allying with the Almoravids.

They controlled the river Senegal, which was navigable as far as Gondiouru (region of Kayes) where salt was transported from the Awlīl mines which were under their control, as were the gold mines of Galam. While civil war ravaged the Soninke provinces of Wagadu, Bakhunu and Kaniaga, Takrūr was conquering Barissa on the river, thus becoming, as al-Idrīsī testifies, a powerful kingdom whose name replaced that of Ghana in the twelfth century and was used by the Arabs to describe the whole of the western Sudan. As at Koumbi Saleh, the town of Takrūr included a Berber Arab quarter; but its area of authority and influence was limited to the Senegal basin.

Songhay

This very ancient kingdom, which lay outside the orbit of Ghana, had Muslim kings by the beginning of the eleventh century, and welcomed Berber Arab traders and scholars. The capital was transferred from Kukya to Gao; and Timbuktu, where river and land routes met, was founded in about 1100. Before long Songhay's influence was felt all along the Niger Bend.

The Soninke provinces

By the eighth century, there were trade relations between Koumbi Saleh and the northern edge of the Sahara: Berber Arab Muslims occupied senior positions there; and although the majority of the inhabitants remained true to their traditional religion, conversion to Islam had even reached the family of king Beci, for example in the person of his son, Canmer, who nevertheless 'hid his religion'. Those who rejected the new religion fled to the province of Mema. The same troubles also affected Kaniaga (Diafunu), where the old capital, called Sain Demba, was situated; Maḥmud Kāʿti says that it was ruined after the fall of Ghana, and replaced by the town of Zara. Some of the inhabitants of the empire, the Kussa, emigrated to Kussata. The rest went to Zara which was in turn conquered by the *Kaniaga faren* who extended his kingdom towards the desert where he came into conflict with the Soso.

Soso supremacy

Soso supremacy lasted for about half a century after 1180. The capital of the Soso was probably near Kulikoro (north of Bamako), in the mountains occupied by a Maninka clan of smiths who were hostile to Islam. We are told that the Soninke clan of the Diarisso (Jariso) had freed itself from Ghana even before the fall of Koumbi Saleh. Towards the end of the twelfth century, the Soso king Kemoko united Kaniaga and Soso, which he ruled until c. 1200, when his son Sumaoro Kante (or Sumanguru) took up the reins of power. After conquering the Soninke provinces, Sumaoro attacked Mande which put up a fierce resistance through nine successive attacks.

Mansa Dankaran Tuman succeeded his father, Nare Fa Maghan, but preferred to make peace with Sumaoro, to whom he gave his sister, Nana Triban, in marriage.

Sumaoro was then at the height of his power which extended over the Soninke provinces and involved the virtual allegiance of the Maninka. He inspired such terror that, we are told, 'men did not dare to meet in parley for fear that the wind might carry their words to the king'. He is supposed to have been a powerful magician and sorcerer. But he is also credited with the invention of the balafone (xylophone) and the dan, a four-stringed guitar used by the hunters' *griot*, or praise singer. Inquiries among the Kante smiths suggest another reason for his opposition to the Mande and Soninke: he was fiercely opposed to the slave trade as well as Islam. The people of Mande revolted against his exactions and called on their king, Dankaran Tuman, to resume the struggle; but he preferred to take refuge in the south, where he founded Kisidugu (the 'city of salvation'). The insurgents then appealed to his brother, Sundiata Keita, who was living in exile in Mema.

Mande before Sundiata

Written sources

First al-Bakrī, then al-Idrīsī, mention the two kingdoms of Malel (Mali) and Do; they refer to 'Nungharmata' (Wangara) traders who procured slaves in the country of the Lem-Lem, a local population who scarified their faces and 'carried gold dust from Irseni (Barīssā) to other countries'. According to al-Bakrī, the king of Malel had the title of al-Muslimani.

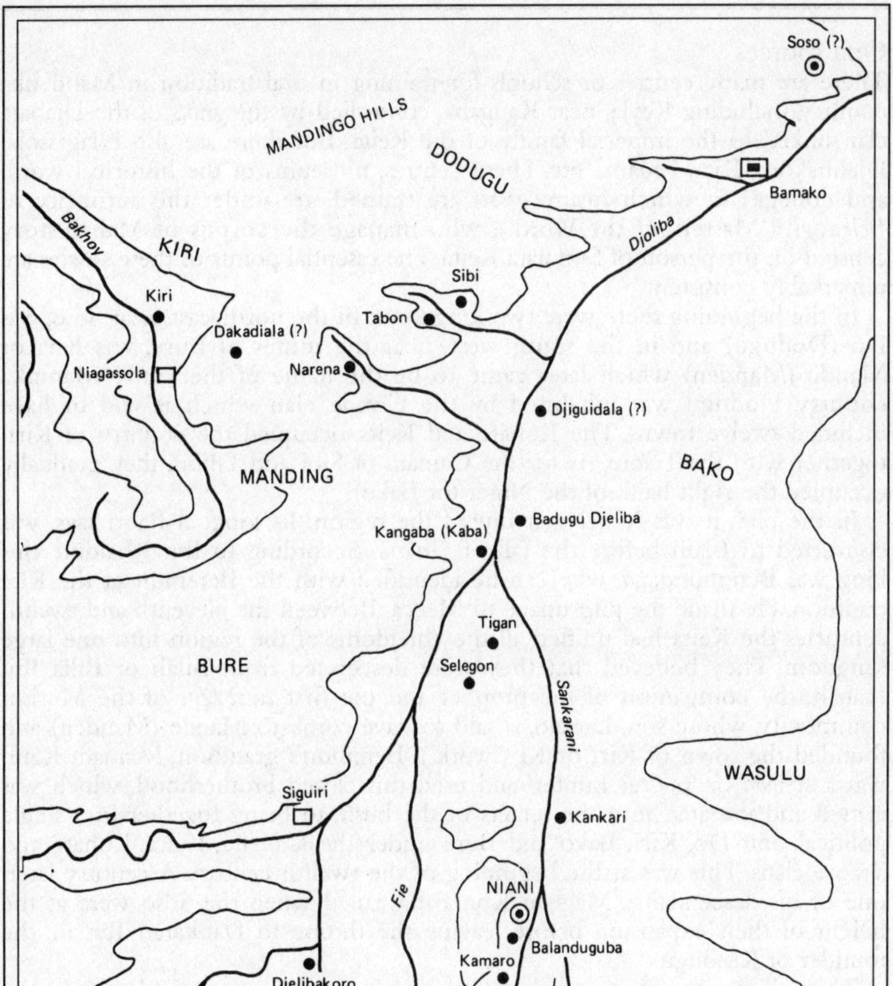

6.1 *Old Mande. (D. T. Niane)*

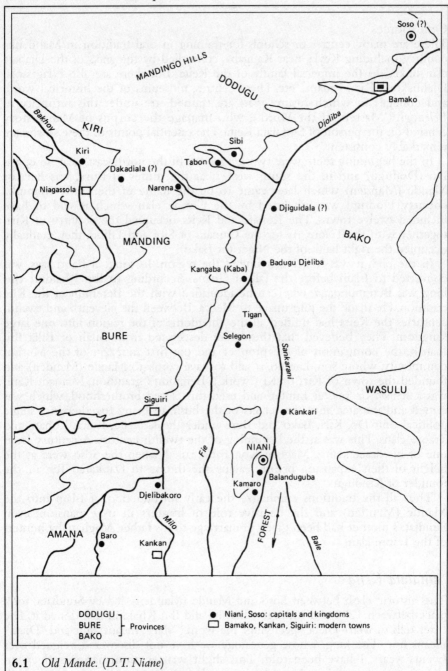

Oral sources

There are many centres or schools for training in oral tradition in Mandenka country, including Keyla, near Kangaba, controlled by the *griots* of the Diabate clan linked to the imperial family of the Keita. But there are also Niagassola, Djelibakoro, Kita, Fadama etc. These centres, museums of the historical word, and colleges in which future *griots* are trained, are under the authority of *Belentigi*. ('Masters of the Word'), who manage the corpus of Mali history centred on the person of Sundiata Keita. The essential points of these stories are remarkably consistent.

In the beginning there were two kingdoms. In the north-east, near Soso, was Do (Dodugu) and in the south-west, near the mines of Bure, was Kiri or Mande (Manden) which later came to be the name of the entire Maninka country. Dodugu was inhabited by the Conde clan which is said to have included twelve towns. The Konate and Keita occupied the country of Kiri, together with the Traore. As for the Camara of Sibi and Tabön, they gradually occupied the right bank of the Niger (or Bako).

In the end, it was Malel that united the region. Its king, al-Bakrī says, was converted to Islam before the fall of Ghana. According to Ibn Khaldūn, this king was Beremundana, who can be identified with the Beremun of the Kita tradition. He made the pilgrimage to Mecca. Between the eleventh and twelfth centuries the Keita had unified all the chiefdoms of the region into one large kingdom. They believed that they were descended from Bilāli or Bilāl Ibn Rabāḥ, the companion of the prophet and the first muezzin of the Muslim community, whose son, Lawalo, is said to have come to Mande (Manden) and founded the town of Kiri or Ki ('work'). Beremun's grandson, Mamadi Kani, was a *simbon* or 'master hunter' and used this closed brotherhood, which was armed and initiated into the secrets of the bush, to bring together in a single political unit Do, Kiri, Bako and Bure under the Camara, Keita, Konate and Traore clans. This was at the beginning of the twelfth century. A century later, one of his descendants, Maghan Kön Fatta, ruled when the Soso were at the height of their expansion before leaving the throne to Dankaran Tuman, the founder of Kisidugu.

Thus all the traditions emphasize the early introduction of Islam into the Mande (Manden) and the decisive role of hunters in its expansion; even Sundiata's mother had been given in marriage to his father, Maghan, by hunters of the Traore clan.

Sundiata Keita

The historic clash between Soso and Mande (Manden), led by Sundiata, took place between 1200 and 1235. Ibn Baṭṭūṭa and Ibn Khaldūn mentioned it. The latter tells of Mari-Diata, specifying: 'the word "Mari" means amir and "Diata" means lion. The king, whose genealogy we have not discovered, reigned over twenty years, I have been told.' This slight written information reflects an abundant oral tradition. According to oral tradition, Sundiata had a difficult childhood and was crippled for a long time. Because of that, his other was the laughing stock of her co-wives. He eventually began to walk under strange circumstances, then became the leader of his age group and was persecuted by his brother, Dankaran Tuman. He decided to go into exile and this flight (*bori*) lasted many years, taking him to Ghana and Mema whose king appreciated his courage and gave him a senior post. It was there that Mande messengers found him, and he agreed to accompany them with a force of soldiers given by the king of Mema.

His return aroused great enthusiasm among the Maninka. The war chiefs, who had been of the same age-group as Sundiata were ready to unite: Tabön-Wana (Ghana), Kamadian Camara of Sibi, Faony Conde, Siara Kuman Konate and Tiramaghan Traore. They sealed the alliance with Sundiata on the plain of Sibi. On the right bank, the rebellion against Sumaoro. Kante was led by Mansa Kara Noro whose soldiers wore iron armour. Only the skill and cunning of Fakoli, Sumaoro's military leader, overcame it. But during the festivities celebrating this victory, Sumaoro took the liberty of seducing Keleya, Fakoli's wife. This latter was furious and crossed the Niger with his army to join the allies gathered at Sibi. Despite this setback, Sumaoro went on the offensive. After two indecisive battles, the decisive encounter took place at Kirina. Sumaoro arrived with his famous cavalry backed up by two major allies: Jolofing, king of Jolof, a famed magician, and the chief of the Tunkara of Kita. Sundiata was all the more confident because his sister, Nana Triban, who had formerly been forced to marry Sumaoro had fled with the help of the latter's *griot* Balla Fasseke Kuyate, carrying with her the secret of her ex-husband's totem (*tana*): a white cockspur. Thus, Sumaoro went into battle with a serious psychological handicap. He was completely routed. Sundiata pursued him to Kulikoro, although he did not succeed in capturing him. Kulikoro was taken and shortly afterwards Soso was razed to the ground. The victory at Kirina was not just a fortunate victory: it sealed the alliance between the clans gathered at Sibi; it ensured that Mali inherited the legacy of the empire of Ghana in the western Sudan; it finally opened the way for the southward expansion of Islam.

It is the last point that Arab authors such as Ibn Baṭṭūṭa mention; but they do not mention the victory at Kirina which made possible the massive Islamization of the Bilād al-Sudān. Here as elsewhere, the oral sources thus fill out the written ones.

Achievements of Sundiata Keita

Military conquests

Aided by brilliant generals, Sundiata conquered the lands of Ghana. Tiramaghan Traore was sent to the west against the Wolof king, Jolofing, who had intercepted a caravan of traders sent by Sundiata to buy horses. After defeating Jolofing, Tiramaghan waged war in the Senegal and Gambia basins, conquering the Casamance and the highlands of present-day Guinea-Bissau, and founded the vast Senegambian kingdom of Kaabu or Gabu.

Fakoli Koroma was sent to the south and conquered the area of the upper Senegal river and the areas bordering the forest. Sundiata himself took Diafunu and Kita. After him, the conquest of Gao and Takrūr for the first time completed the unity of the western Sudan.

The constitution of Mali

Tradition attributes to Sundiata the codification of the social and political norms that still in part govern the Mande peoples. He was given many names: *Simbon Salaba* (master hunter, whose head commands reverence), *Mari Diata* (Lord lion) and, in Soninke, *Maghan Sundiata* (King Sundiata). According to tradition, it was on a large plain near Kangaba, at Kurukanfuga, that the *Gbara* or great assembly took place, which was in fact that constituent assembly of the Mandenka clans.

(a) Sundiata Keita was proclaimed supreme king there (*mansa* or *maghan*); the other leaders became *farin* in their provinces except for the chiefs of Mema and Wagadu who were given the title of king.
(b) The assembly decreed that the emperor would in future be chosen from the line of Sundiata fratrilineally; he was recognized as the supreme judge and father of all, whence the title Nfa Mansa (my father, the king).
(c) Sixteen clans of 'quiver-bearing' freedmen were formed.
(d) Five marabout clans, the first of Sundiata's allies, including the Sise Cisse of Wagadu, the Toure and the Berete, were proclaimed the five guardians of the faith.
(e) Men practising special trades – *griots*, shoemakers, smiths and weavers – were divided into four clans.
(f) The names of clans were recognized as corresponding to the clan names of other ethnic groups, thus creating *sanankuya*: kinship involving solidarity, and also joking relationships. This was a structure that helped reduce tension.
(g) The Somono and Bozo boatmen were proclaimed 'masters of the water'.

In short, Sundiata 'divided up the world', with each knowing his rights and duties. Trades were made hereditary, which does not seem to have been the case in the time of Ghana.

Sundiata's government

Sundiata's companions made up the government. In addition to them there were black scholars of the marabout clans and perhaps a few Arab traders. According to Ibn Baṭṭūṭa, Mari Diata was converted by a certain Mudrik whose descendant was living at Mansa Sulaymān's court in the fourteenth century.

In addition to the kingdoms of Ghana and Mema, the conquered chiefdoms were incorporated flexibly, adding a governor (*farin*) alongside the traditional chief. Thus the empire was rather a federation of kingdoms and chiefdoms, with Mandenka garrisons in the principal provinces guaranteeing both security and a degree of integration. The empire was divided into two large military regions:

one for the north under the *sura farin* (chief of the northern area) and one for the south.

Niani, capital of Mali

The town of Niani, on the Sankarani, was in Camara territory. Sundiata preferred this area that was rich in iron and gold to Narena or Dakadiala where the Keita had originally lived.

The fact is that the clan of the direct kin rarely constituted a reliable environment, as witness the disputes between Dankaran Tuman and his elder brother. Moreover, the site of Dakadiala in the mountains was difficult of access; whereas the site of Niani on a plain alongside the Sankarani, navigable all the year round, but surrounded by a ring of hills dominated by a rocky peak, combined the advantages of both communication and security.

In addition, Niani was on the edge of the forest, a source of gold, kola nuts, palm oil and ivory, which Maninka traders purchased in exchange for cotton and copper goods and salt. This site, far removed from the Sahelian areas in the north exposed to incursions by nomads, was even more secure. It thus developed rapidly as an outlet for two main routes, one northward, called the 'Mande route', the other southward, known as the 'Sarakolle route'. Ibn Baṭṭūṭa, who passed through there in the fourteenth century, called it Mali. But al-ʿUmarī, had already given it the name Nyeni (Niani), going on to specify that it is 'the official name of Mali . . . because it is the capital of the regions of this kingdom'.

It is this text of al-ʿUmarī that enabled Maurice Delafosse, after numerous earlier controversies, to identify the location of Niani on the Sankarani, on the present border between Mali and Guinea.

The site of Niani was identified in the 1920s, but serious excavations were undertaken only after 1968, with a Guinean-Polish mission. The Arab quarter and the royal town have been identified: foundations of stone houses, the *mihrab* of a mosque and the walls around the royal town. The buildings were of bricks of beaten earth, as al-ʿUmari wrote, adding: 'The ceilings are made of beams and reeds. They are mostly in the shape of a cupola [i.e. conical] or a camel's hump, like vaulted arches. The floors of the houses are of earth mixed with sand . . . The king has a group of palaces surrounded by a circular wall.' Archaeologists have compared these written texts with the oral traditions and reality on the ground. The ruins stretch today from Niani up to Sidikila, 25 km away, with a host of villages for various trade clans.

Sundiata declared Niani imperial territory, a common homeland for all his peoples. The population was cosmopolitan. As in the time of the kings of Ghana, the sons of *farin*s and vassal kings were brought up there.

The death of Sundiata

Here we can only theorize because there are various traditions and because it is forbidden in Mande country to disclose the burial place of great kings. According to Maurice Delafosse, Sundiata was accidentally killed by an arrow during a ceremony; it is more likely that he was drowned in the waters of the Sankarani, for 10 km upstream from Niani is a place called *Sundiata-dun* (Sundiata's deep water). This part of the river has many eddies. On the banks at this point, ritual sacrifices are periodically made by the nearest descendants of the conqueror. At Kirina, the 'traditionalists', the Mamissoko, offer sacrifices in a sacred forest. At Tigan, among the Camara, there is a pile of ashes called *bundalin* under which there are believed to be shoes, a knife and a suit of armour belonging to Sundiata. Finally, there is a ceremony every seven years around the sanctuary called *Kamablon* at Kangaba: there too there are said to be objects belonging to Sundiata.

Classical Mande music began in Sundiata's time (*Sundiata tele*). The sage of the conqueror, called *Sundiata fassa*, composed by his *griot*, Balla Fasseke, was accompanied by particular music. Sundiata made the song called *Boloba* (the great music), composed by the *griots* of Sumaoro Kante, the music of every Maninka warrior, who could ask for it. *Duga* ('vulture') was reserved for the most renowned warriors. As for *Janjon* ('glory to the warrior'), it was dedicated to Fakoli Koroma and *Tiramaghan faso*, the conqueror of the western provinces.

Sundiata Keita's successors

In his remarkable *History of the Berbers* and his *Prolegomena*, Ibn Khaldūn acknowledges the political and economic importance of Mali in the Muslim world of the fourteenth century. He got his information from Arab traders and Mali's embassies in Cairo. His presentation corresponds at many points to the information given in the traditions.

The old principle of fratrilineal succession was not observed after Sundiata's death. His eldest son, Mansa Oulin, reigned from 1250 to 1270. The Mande consolidated their positions in Takrūr and Senegambia and established settlements there. After his death, palace intrigues threatened the integrity of the empire. Sakura, an energetic general, put an end to these disturbances by conquests in the north against the Tuareg and in the Niger valley as far as Gao; he was murdered on the way home from the pilgrimage and was buried with royal honours in Mali. After a period of mediocre rulers, Sundiata's nephew, Kanku Mūsā I, reigned from 1307 to c.1332. This marked the apogee of Mali, and his pilgrimage was 'covered' admiringly by many authors.

After his son, Maghan I, it was his brother, Mansa Sulaymān, who maintained the greatness of the empire. Subsequently, the political 'clans' renewed their infighting. Mansa Sulaymān's son, Fomba, reigned only one year. He was dethroned by Sundiata II, who was a despot who ruined the empire and exhausted the treasury, even, according to Ibn Khaldūn, selling for less than it was worth the enormous gold ingot weighing 25 kg to Egyptian merchants. He was struck down by sleeping sickness, and was replaced by his son, Mansa Mūsā II (1374–87), under whom power really lay in the hands of a general who put down a rising at Takedda, the copper town. Then, intrigues fomented by the princesses shook the empire but that did not prevent it enjoying lasting prestige.

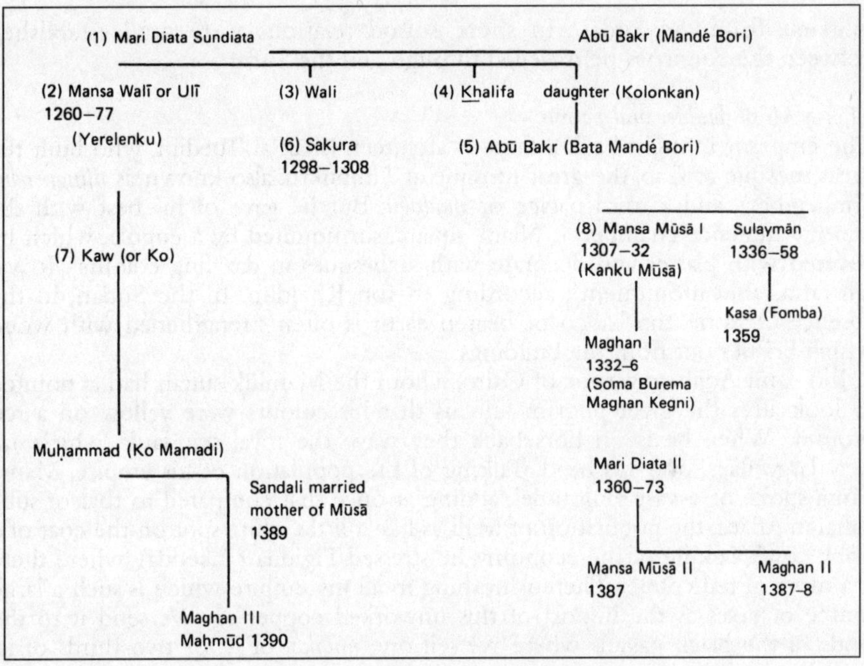

6.2 *Genealogy of the* mansas *of Mali according to Ibn Khaldūn.*
Note: the names given by oral tradition are in parentheses. (*D. T. Niane*)

Triumph of Islam under Mansa Mūsā

Mansa Mūsā I (1307–32)

It was Mansa Mūsā who projected the image of Mali to North Africa and the Near East, giving away so much gold that it made the gold price fall. From that time on, the Sudan haunted men's minds, as, later, Eldorado did. In order to consolidate central authority, he had the help of a remarkably able general, Saran Mandian, who brought the Saharan nomad, who were inclined to pillage, under control and pushed the expansion in the Niger valley beyond Gao.

To prepare for his pilgrimage, he levied special contributions from every trading town and every province. His retinue was enormous: 60,000 porters, 500 servants decked in gold, each carrying a golden staff. These exaggerations nevertheless give some idea of the scale. In Cairo, Mansa Mūsā I seemed like one of the kings of the Arabian Nights.

Al-Maḳrīzī left a laudatory portrait of him: 'He was a young man with a brown skin, a pleasant face and good figure, instructed in the Malikite rite . . . His gifts amazed the eye with their beauty and splendour.' According to tradition, he bought land and houses in Cairo and Mecca to accommodate pilgrims from the Sudan. In short, sound relations were now established between the countries he travelled through and the Sudan.

Mansa Mūsā, builder and patron

The emperor brought back a famous architect, Isḥāḳ al-Tuedjin, who built the great mosque at Gao, the great mosque at Timbuktu, also known as *djinguereber* (Jingereber), and a royal palace or *madugu*. But he gave of his best with the famous audience chamber at Niani 'square, surmounted by a cupola, which he covered with plaster and decorate with arabesques in dazzling colours'. It was 'an admirable monument', according to Ibn Khaldūn. In the Sudan, in the absence of stone, the banco or beaten earth is often strengthened with wood which bristles out from the buildings.

Ibn Amīr Adjib, governor of Cairo, whom the Mamlūk sultan had appointed to look after the great pilgrim tells us that his colours were yellow on a red ground: 'When he is on horseback they wave the royal standards, which are very large flags, over his head.' Talking of the population of his empire, Mansa Mūsā spoke of 'a vast multitude', adding at once that compared to that of sub-Saharan Africa, the population of Mali 'is like a little white spot on the coat of a black cow'. Talking of the economy, he stressed Tigidda (Takedda) 'where there is a mine of red copper. There is nothing in all my empire which is such a large source of taxes as the import of this unworked copper . . . We send it to the lands of the black pagans where we sell one *mithḳal* of it for two-thirds of its weight in gold.'

On the political and technical level, Mansa Mūsā I revealed that his predecessor had died at sea: 'for this king would not listen to those who told him that it was impossible to get to the other side of the sea, and obstinately persisted in his purpose.' So much so that he fitted out 200 ships that were engulfed in the sea; then 2,000, of which he took charge . . . never to return.

On this point, numerous authors, such as Wiener and Jeffreys, have discussed the problem of the arrival of blacks in the Americas before Christopher Columbus, and indeed a number of resemblances have been detected between elements in Mexican civilization and elements in black Africa.

At least the episode mentioned by the emperor of Mali shows that, at the beginning of the fourteenth century, the Sudanese leaders were concerned about the problems of sea navigation.

On his return to Mali, Mansa Mūsā I, who was skilled in Arabic, but always used interpreters with his Arab interlocutors, brought back with him an Arabic library and Arab secretaries, *ḳāḍīs* and teachers; but these trained men failed to transform the administrative and political apparatus. Intellectual and trading groups associated with the schools opened and the contacts made Walāta, Jenne and Timbuktu into trading and university cities worthy of their counterparts in North Africa, since in the fifteenth and sixteenth centuries they produced a whole Arabic-language black literature.

Diplomatic relations were established and there were, for example, exchanges of ambassadors and gifts between Mali and the Marinids of Fez.

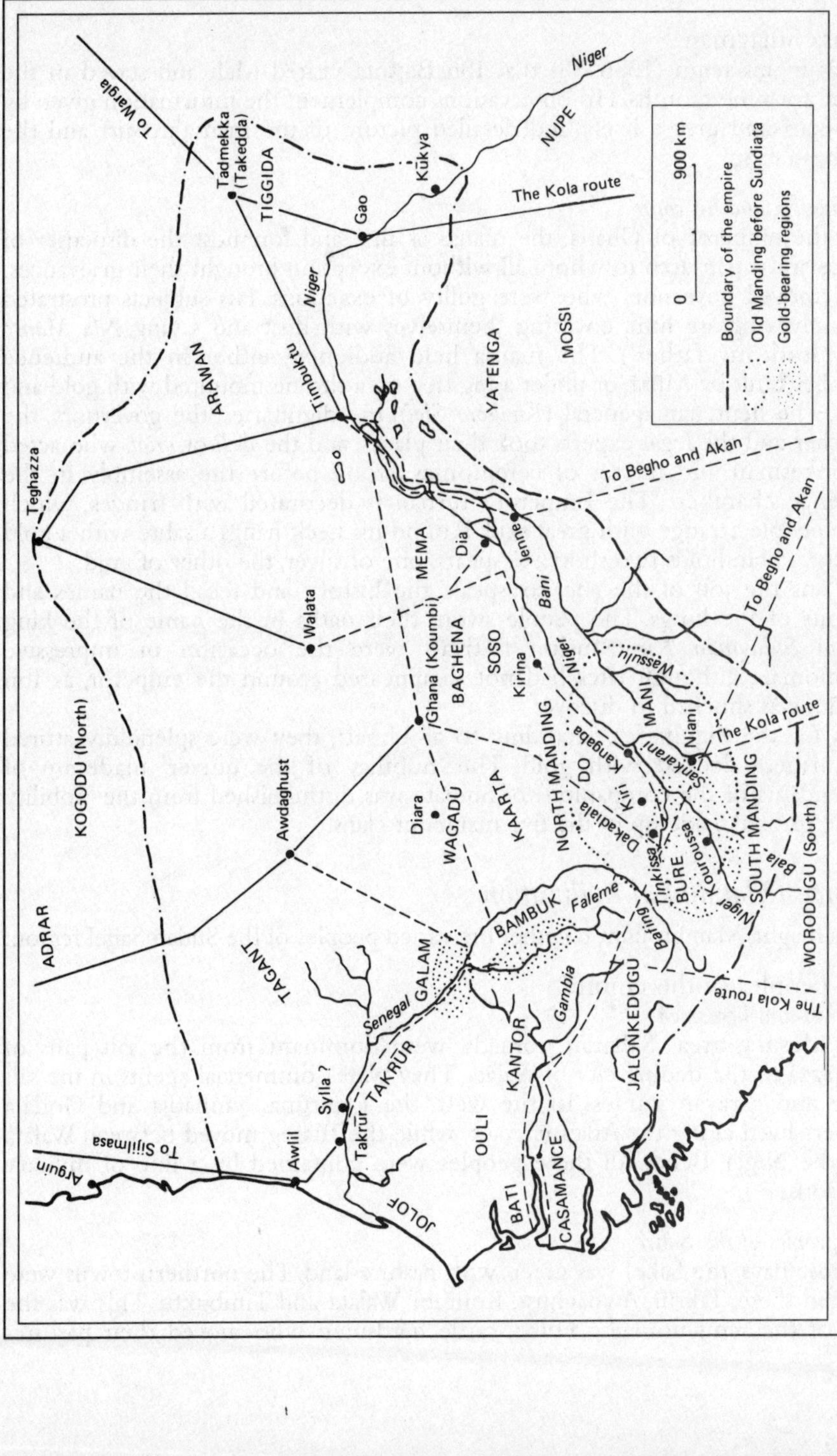

6.3 *The Mali empire, 1325.* (D. T. Niane)

Mansa Sulaymān

It was in his reign (1336–58) that Ibn Baṭṭūta visited Mali and stayed in the capital for nine months. His observations complement the information given by al-ʿUmarī and give a lively and detailed picture of the mansa's court and the administration.

The mansa and his court

Like the emperor of Ghana, the mansa as first and foremost the dispenser of justice and a patriarch to whom all without exception brought their grievances. He removed governors who were guilty of exactions. His subjects prostrated themselves before him, covering themselves with dust and saying *Nfa Mansa* ('My lord, my father'). The mansa held audiences either in the audience chamber built by Mūsā, or under a big tree on a throne mounted with gold and ivory. The lieutenant-general (*Kankoro Sigi*), the dignitaries, the governors, the preacher and the legal experts took their places, and the *d̲jeli* or *griot*, who acted as spokesman and master of ceremonies, stood before the assembly in the audience chamber: 'The Emperor's turban is decorated with fringes, which these people arrange with great skill. Round his neck hangs a sabre with a gold sheath . . . He holds two short . . . spears, one of silver, the other of gold.'

It was the job of the *griot* to 'speak' the history and recall the names and exploits of the kings. The people swore their oaths in the name of the king *Mansa Sulaymān Kib* Muslim festivals were the occasion of impressive ceremonials, although rites had not disappeared around the emperor, as Ibn Baṭṭūta was shocked to discover.

As for the dignitaries, according to al-ʿUmarī, they were splendidly attired and armed, decked with gold. The 'nobility of the quiver' made up of descendants of the companions of Sudiata was distinguished from the 'nobility of the turban' made up of the five marabout clans.

Mande (Mandinka) civilization

At its height, Mali brought together the varied peoples of the Sudan Sahel region:

The peoples of the empire

Nomads and herdsmen

The Mesufa, great Saharan nomads, were dominant from the salt-pans of Teghāzza to the trading city of Walāta. They were commercial agents in the salt trade and caravan guides. In the west, the Lamtūna, Ṣanhād̲ja and Godala Berbers lived along the Atlantic coast, while the Tuareg moved between Walāta and the Niger Bend. All these peoples were contained by a line of military garrisons.

The peoples of the Sahel

In those days, the Sahel was green with pasture land. The northern towns were situated there: Takrūr, Awdāg̲hust, Koumbi, Walāta and Timbuktu. This was the area of the semi-nomadic Fulbe, cattle herdsmen who moved their pastures

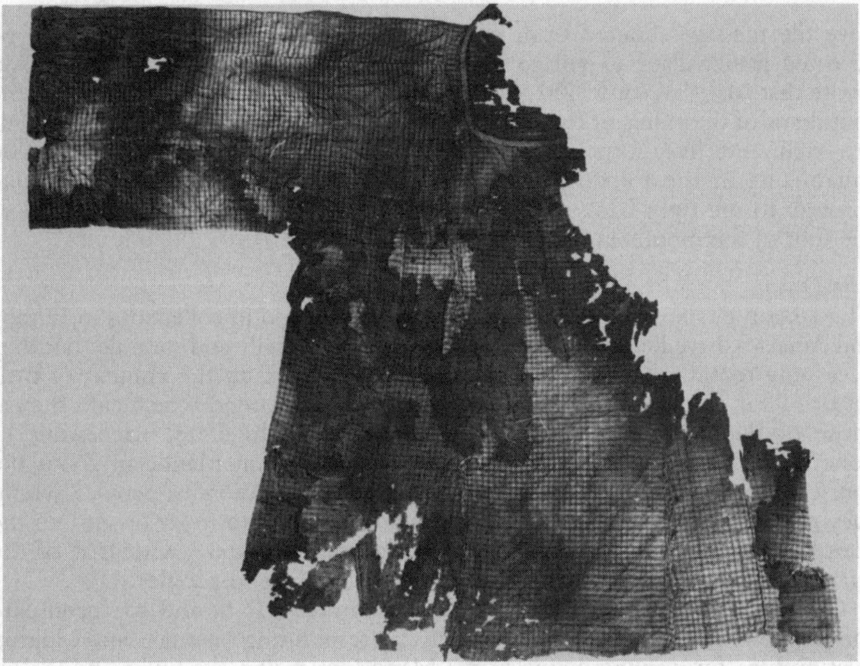

6.4 *Pégué: a Tellem cotton tunic found in cave C (phase 2 Tellem, eleventh to twelfth century).* (*R. M. A. Bedaux, 1977*)

according to the seasons; there were also more or less sedentarized pioneer groups further south. The farmer cultivators – the Tukuloor (Toucouleur), Soninke and Songhay peoples – had been converted to Islam at an early date (the eleventh and twelfth centuries). They lived in large towns which were later to become cities.

The peoples of the savannah

From west to east these were the Wolof, the Sereer, the Mande and the Soninke; but even before the thirteenth century, Soninke and Mande traders and marabouts were to be found in Senegambia. On the coast between the Gambia and the Rio Grande lived communities of Beafada, Balante, Diola, Felupe and Bainunke peasants and fishermen, noted for rice cultivation. The Portuguese arrived in this region in the fifteenth century and it is from them that we learn that it had been strongly influenced by the Mande.

Mali was very densely populated, especially along the rivers and around the big agricultural and trading centres. For example, according to the *Ta'rikh al-Sudan*, the territory of Jenne contained 7,077 villages that were so close to each other than when the king wished to summon a subject, all he had to do was to have the message shouted from one of the gates of the ramparts for it to be repeated from village to village until it reached its destination. Maḥmūd Kāti wrote that Mali 'has some 400 towns' and that 'its soil is most fertile. Among the kingdoms of the rulers of the world, only Syria is more beautiful. Its inhabitants are rich and live comfortably.' The capital, Niani, had at least 100,000 inhabitants in the fourteenth century. Moreover, the rulers of Gao broke through to the right bank of the Niger and placed a governor at Hombori, at the foot of the mountains of Dogon country.

The Dogon

The Dogon people, whose works of art are to be found in collections in Europe and America, have been extensively studied ethnologically and statically, but they have only recently been studied (by R. M. A. Bedaux) in the context of their historical relations with the other peoples of the Niger Bend, where cliffs such as those of Bandiagara, shelter their villages perched high up, inaccessible to conquerors. The Dogon are said to have migrated from Mande in about the fourteenth century to the mountains where the autochthonous peoples, whom they called *Tellem* (meaning 'we found them there'), had to move down into the plains of Yatenga. Comparison of Dogon stemmed pottery with that of the Maninka of Niani suggests close contacts between the two peoples.

Overall, the framework created by the empire was bound to accentuate differences, through the system of corresponding names and joking relationships, for example between the Mande and Fulbe, the Fulbe and Wolof, between the Mande and coastal peoples etc.

Political and administrative organization

The central power

The Mali confederation was placed under the authority of the mansa assisted by a council of dignitaries descended from Sundiata's companions. At the base, in Mande, there were villages grouped into provinces or *kafu* (*jamana*).

Alongside the ruler there was the influential presence of the *griot*, the spokesman of the emperor (who had to speak softly) but also of the people, and of delegations received at the court; and he was also the tutor of princes, the master of ceremonies and the leader of the royal orchestra.

In the fourteenth century, the mansa had a staff of secretaries who were only used when messages were sent to the ruler's counterparts abroad. The rest of the time, messages were transmitted or received orally.

As the 'father of his people' and dispenser of justice, the emperor, whether in his palace or travelling, sat as of right in his palace. In the provinces he was represented by *ḳāḍīs*.

Officials

Apart from the *griot*, there is mention of the lieutenant-general, the chief of the armed forces, and the *santigi* (initially master of the granaries, later of the treasury). Originally this job was done by a crown slave.

All the trade clans were represented before the mansa by delegated 'chiefs'.

Provincial government

In the twelfth century, the empire had twelve provinces each headed by a governor (or *farin*). The most important ones were Takrūr, along the middle and lower Senegal; Bambugu, with its famous gold-mines; Dia or Diafunu on the middle Niger; Gao or Songhay, which freed itself at the end of the fourteenth century; Sanagana, mentioned by al-ʿUmarī, the country of the Ṣanhādja and Godala. Each province had subdivisions, which were occasionally clan units, and included a court around the *farin* which was the local replica of the mansa's court.

Ghana and Mema were two vassal allied kingdoms.

This flexible organization, in which the security of goods and of persons was guaranteed by an army that long remained undefeated, gave Mali considerable stability.

The army

Arab documents mention 100,000 men under arms. The strength of this military force lay in its core of warlike and disciplined Mande. Normally, it was garrisoned in numerous towns, and its writ ran as far away as Teghazza. Even deposed princes of the Maghrib sought the help of Mansa Mūsā to recover their thrones.

The cavalry, an elite corps, was reserved for the aristocracy of the *ton-tigi* (quiver- and bow-bearers), but they also knew how to use spears and sabres. They were directly under the orders of the mansa.

The horses initially came from Takrūr and Jolof; but horse-breeding soon prospered in the Niger valley. The infantry marched under the orders of the minor nobility. Those from the Sahara fought with the famous skin shields. Slave battalions only appeared much later.

Economic life

Agriculture

Although it was known abroad for the 'gold of the Sudan', Mali was essentially an agricultural and pastoral country. Written documents all mention the abundance of foodstuffs; rice was cultivated in the river valleys and above all in Kaabu. Millet, the main crop, was grown in the driest terrain. There were also beans, yams and many other vegetables. Ibn Baṭṭūṭa assures us that the traveller did not need to carry provisions because each village was well supplied.

Such resources provided the wherewithal to maintain the army and the court. The mansa collected the first fruits of the harvests. To refuse this contribution was tantamount to rebellion.

In the fifteenth century, Portuguese sailors observed that cotton was one of the chief resources of the Casamance.

Animal-rearing and fishing

Animal-rearing was principally the speciality of the Fulbe; but the valley peasants also engaged in it, especially in smaller livestock.

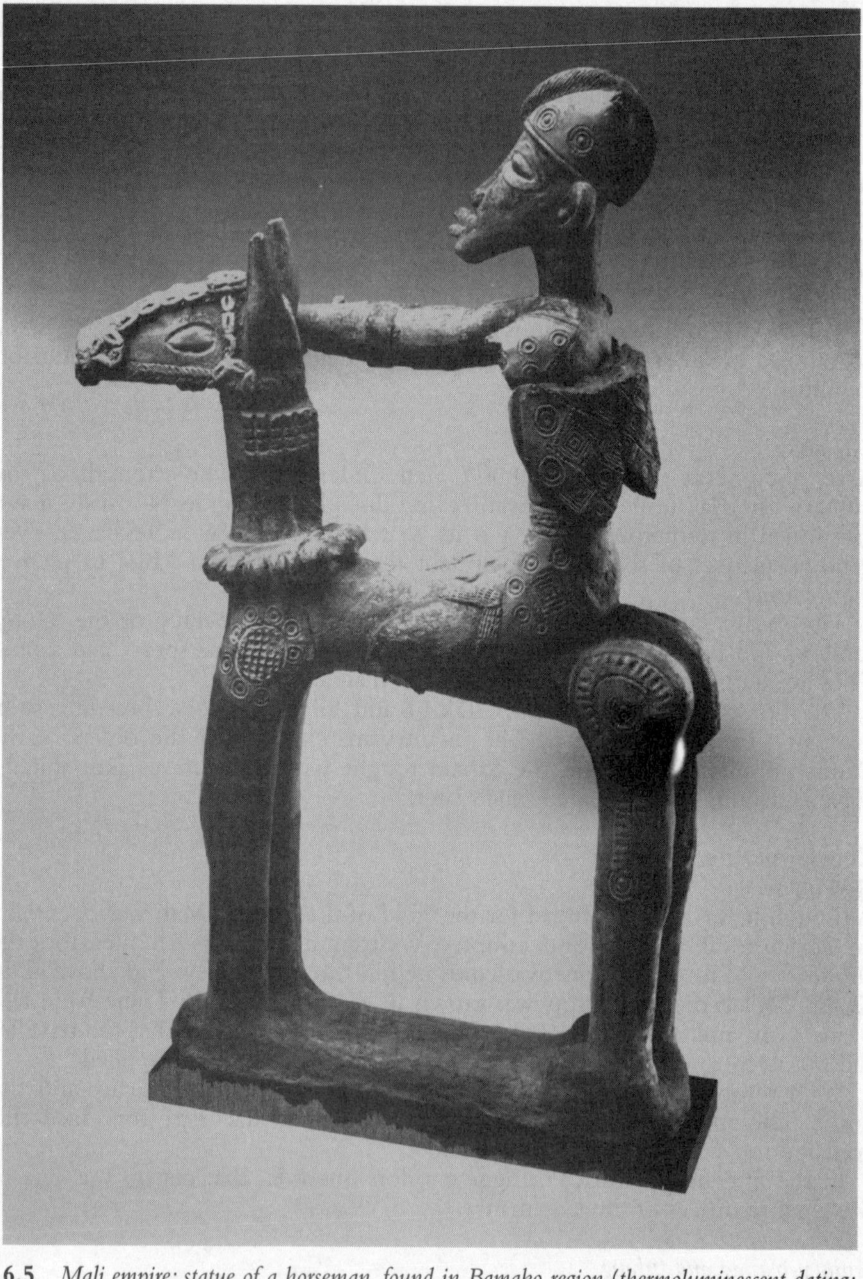

6.5 *Mali empire: statue of a horseman, found in Bamako region (thermoluminescent dating: 680 ± 105 years before 1979; 1194–1404).* (B. de Grunne, 1980)

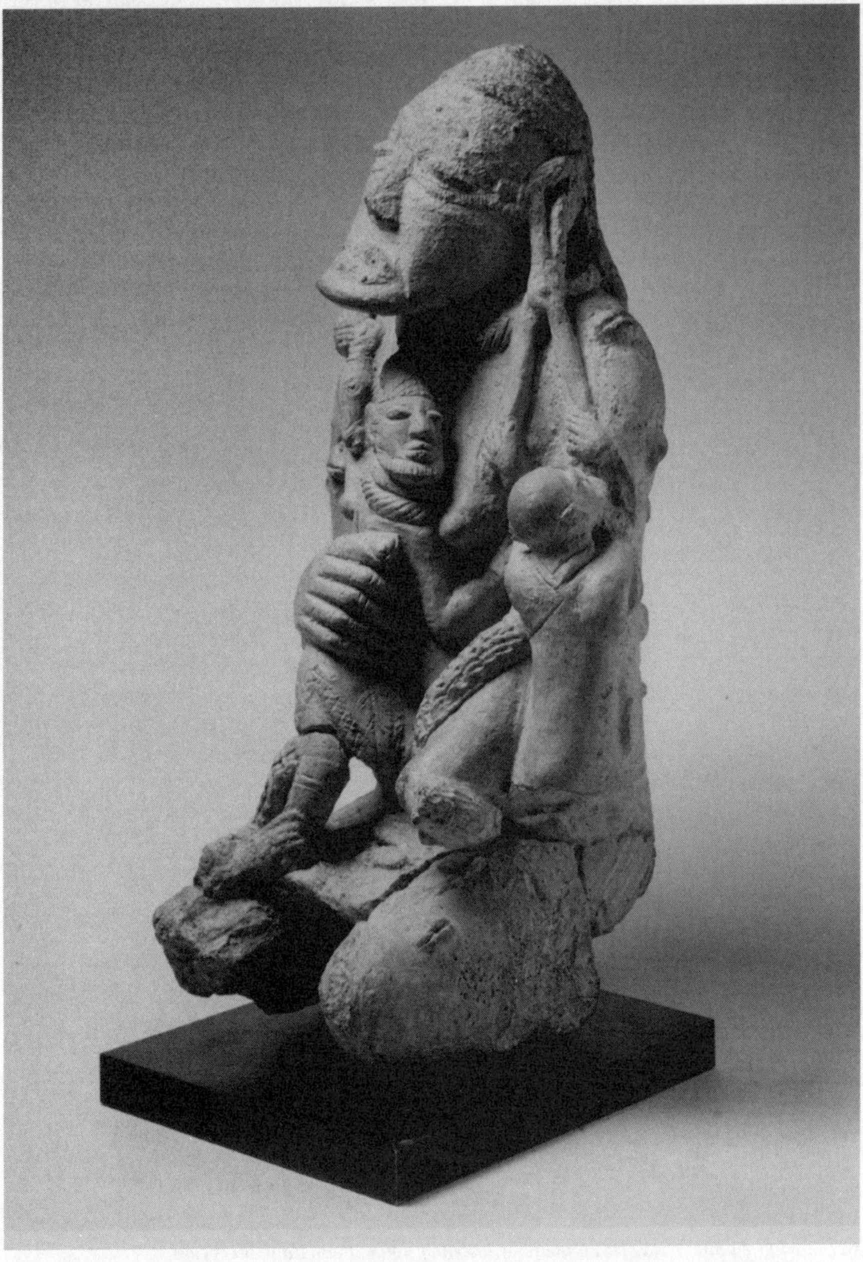

6.6 *Mali empire: terracotta statuette of mother and child (thermoluminescent dating: 690 ± 105 years before 1979: 1184–1394). (B. de Grunne, 1980)*

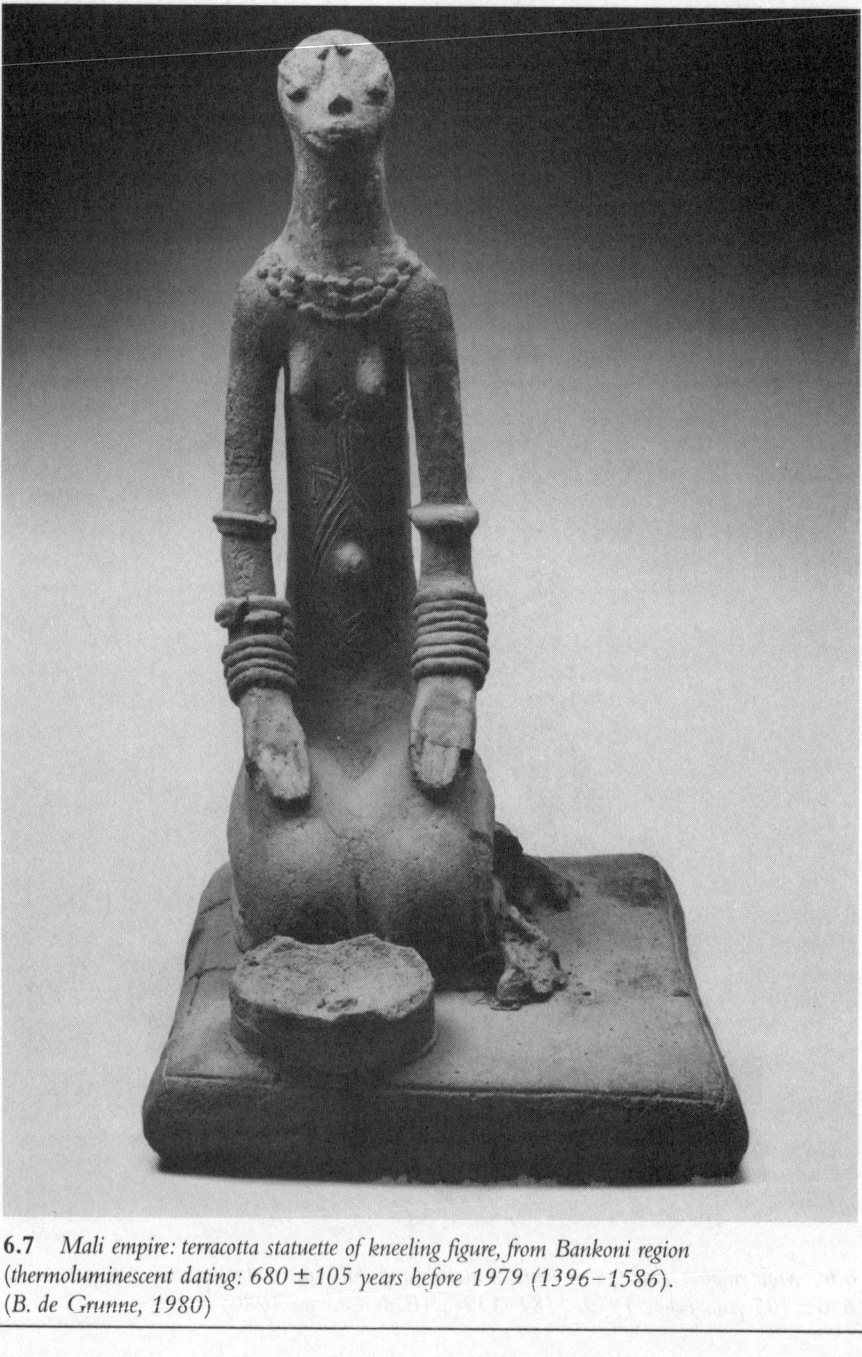

6.7 *Mali empire: terracotta statuette of kneeling figure, from Bankoni region (thermoluminescent dating: 680 ± 105 years before 1979 (1396–1586).* (*B. de Grunne, 1980*)

Fishing was the specialized activity of certain ethnic groups such as the Somono of the upper Niger, the Bozo of the middle Niger and the Sorko between Timbuktu and Gao. Smoked or dried fish was packed in large baskets and marketed as far away as the forest.

Craftsmen

The working of iron and leather and weaving was restricted to certain clans. Iron was abundant in the Mande mountains and the smiths who had large workshops at Niani made implements and weapons.

Weavers marketed rolls of cotton; cloth dyed with indigo became the speciality of the Tukuloor and Soninke peoples, thanks to the Mabo clan.

Endogamy was the rule among the craftsmen whose duties as well as rights were precisely laid down.

Trade

Gold, salt, copper, kola nuts, cloth and fish were some of the numerous products moving along the roads of Mali.

Gold, of which Mali was the principal producer before the discovery of the new world, came from the mines of Bure on the upper Niger, Bambuk and Galam on the upper Senegal. Niani was situated on the edge of the gold-bearing areas of Bure. The mansa, like the ruler of Ghana, had an exclusive right to gold nuggets. But some regions situated further south (Volta, Akan country) also supplied Mali with gold.

Sea-salt from Senegambia and rock salt mainly from Teg͟hāzzā and Id͟jīl circulated throughout West Africa. The same is true of copper which was retailed from the north to the Akan country and the kingdom of Benin.

The marketing of kola nuts brought the *Dioula* and *Wangara* traders into contract with the Akan and the Guro peoples of the forest.

Along these trade routes, the Mande built staging posts, some of which later became major trading cities, such as Kong and Begho. They propagated Islam as far as Hausaland. They sent caravans of donkeys and slave porters laden with salt, cotton goods, fish and copper objects as they moved down towards the forest, and returned with gold, ivory and kola nuts.

7 The Decline of the Empire of Mali: the Fifteenth to Sixteenth Centuries

Introduction: the sources

After the fourteenth century, dominated by the great figure of Mansa Kanku Mūsā, Mali went through a long period of gradual decline, marked by a shift of its centre of interest towards the west. The Muslim monopoly on trans-Saharan trade remained intact in Songhay and Kānem, whereas Malian trade, which had lost the markets of Timbuktu and Jenne to Songhay, turned towards Sutuco and the Senegambian coast where the European were now arriving.

There are few sources for this period. After Ibn Khaldūn, more than a century passed before Leo Africanus' *Africae Descriptio*, the last Arab evidence on the empire. On the other hand, the number of Portuguese accounts was increasing. Ca da Mosto and Diego Gomes were the first to sail up the river Gambia, between 1455 and 1456. At the beginning of the sixteenth century, there are Duarte Pacheco Pereira and Valentim Fernandes and above all, at the end of the century there is the *Tratado Breve dos Rios de Guiné* By Alvares d'Almada, a Portuguese born on the island of Santiago do Cabo-Verde, who traded in the region he describes.

The Sudanese chronicle dating from the seventeenth century, although biased in some respects, are useful for knowledge of Mali during this period.

Finally, the oral traditions of the western Malians, particularly those of the kingdom of Kaabu or Gabu, throw light on the economic role of these regions while the traditions of Futa Toro and Futa Jallon give information on the relations between the Mande empire and the Fulani state of Futa Toro.

The Mali empire loses control of trans-Saharan trade

It was the nomads, before Songhay, who shook Mali.

The Tuareg and the Berbers

Mali had various Berber groups such as the Kel Antasar and the Lamtūna under its rule. They had begun to live a sedentary life and paid tribute to the *mansa*. But the nomads in the Air and the Adrār des Ifogha continued to resist and were only effectively subdued in the reigns of strong rulers such as Kankū Mūsā

7.1 *View of Kamalia (south-west of Kangaba, Mali), from Mungo Park's Travels in the Interior Districts of Africa (1799). (Bibliothèque Nationale, Paris)*

and Sulaymān. On the death of Mūsā II, a succession crisis pitted the descendants of Sundiata against those of his younger brother, Mande Bory. Rulers were assassinated and royal power was weakened. In the fifteenth century, the Tuareg finally conquered Timbuktu, Walāta and Nema. This affected Mali's trans-Saharan relations. The emergence of Songhay under Sonnī ʿAlī was a decisive setback both for the expansion of the Tuareg and for Malian hegemony, which was only given a second breath by trade with the Portuguese.

The western Malian provinces

With the arrival of the Portuguese, the western provinces, which had hitherto been of marginal importance, now took on a key role. After commercial ties had been opened up, Mali and Portugal established diplomatic relations.

Trade

Mali retained control of the Bure gold-mines and also acquired gold through trade from as far south as Asante. Caravans took this gold to the Gambian coast and exchanged it for copper, cotton goods from India and luxury cloths. The Wangara came with their weights and measures; and although they were sometimes forced to take some of their gold back with them, they almost always made a handsome profit from it.

The Europeans introduced more flexibility into the trade by for example buying horses in Futa and selling them in the Gambia to the Malian governors and in Jolof. Slaves were soon introduced into this circuit at eight and later fifteen slaves for one horse. The Malian army supplied more and more, many of whom had settled in Portugal.

Alvares d'Almada was right to write: 'It is in the Gambia that there is the largest volume of trade in all Guinea.'

Agriculture and animal-rearing

The vast majority of the population was occupied in this sector. The Gambia is an abundant river whose floods were then such that boats sometimes left the bed and ended up among the trees. The alluvial soils of numerous rivers produced fine fields of rice and cotton. In the forest galleries, hunting based on some knowledge of nature and magical secrets was fruitful, especially given the great herds of elephants which supplied the ivory trade. In addition to the pastoral Fulbe the peasants raised mainly small livestock. The trade in skins developed mainly at the end of the period.

Social life

Succession was matrilineal as in Ghana, according to al-Bakrī. The certainty of blood links on the mother's side led to the nephew being preferred. Thus *farin* Sangoli, supreme chief of the Gambia, was represented at Niumi by one of his nephews. The prince nominated to succeed was sometimes required to go on a retreat for a year in order to purify himself. The regency was then assured by a general of the previous king. This gave rise to a great deal of intriguing.

Adherence to the traditional religion did not rule out deviations. Thus the numerous lawsuits for 'sorcery' were settled by 'the red water ordeal', the red water being a drink obtained from *cailcedra* roots. The loser was reduced to captivity. This gave rise to abuses by certain chiefs who used this method to increase the number of their slaves.

Moreover, Islam was often simply a veneer. Thus, before embarking on a war, a Muslim king of Casamance would make the imām himself consult the soothsayers, and poured libations to the dead. In the fields, stakes daubed with rice or maize flour mixed with goat's blood were supposed to ensure good harvests. Agrarian cults remained very much alive.

Nevertheless, Islam was making progress, even if the chiefs had no hesitation in moving from the Koran to Christianity. The marabouts obstinately pursued their task. The traditional equilibrium was subverted by all the influences that came in the wake of trade and new religions.

Furthermore, the political authority of Niani was remote. It was supplemented and then gradually supplanted by the king of Kaabu who took the title

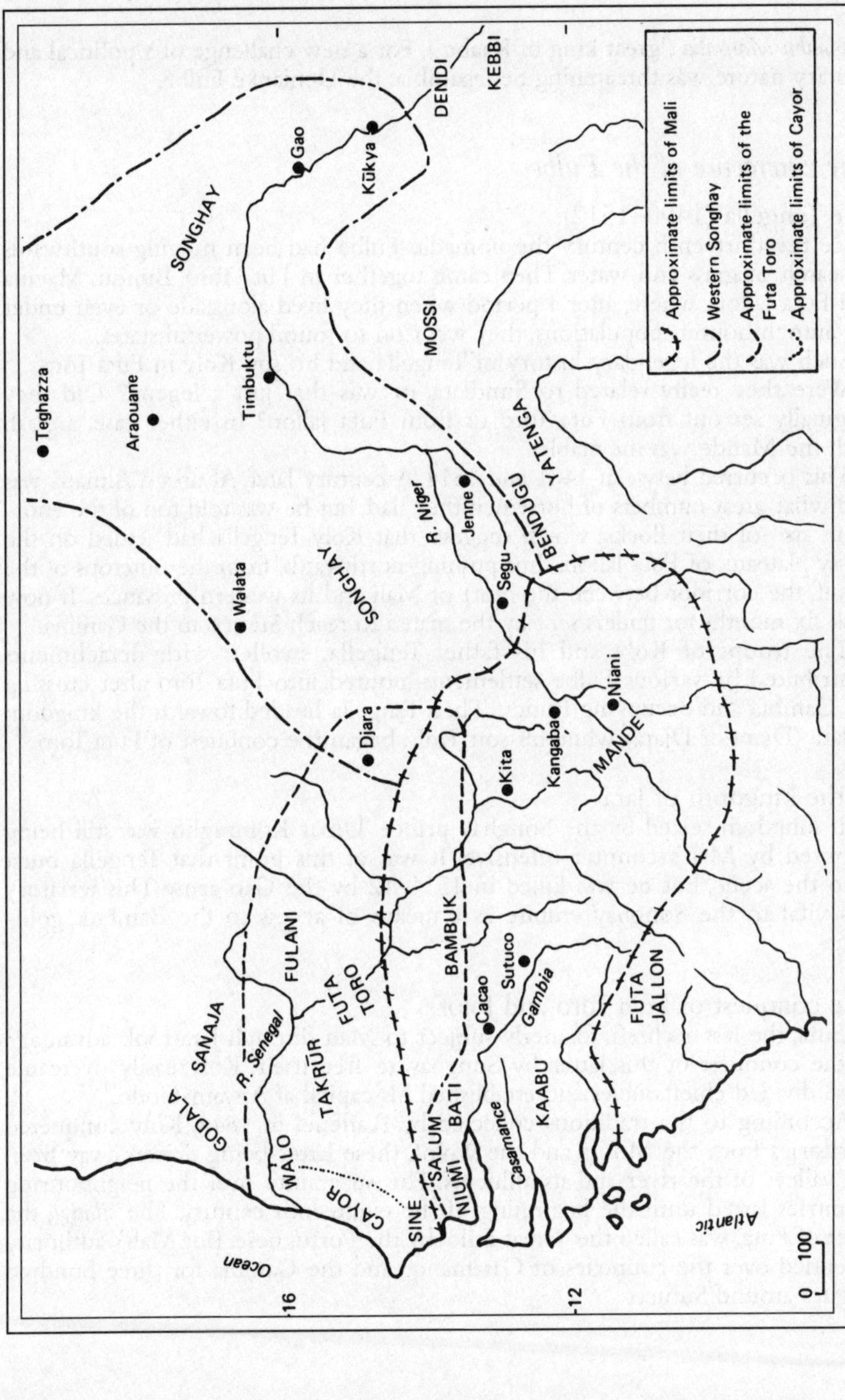

7.2 *The states of the Sudan in the sixteenth century (after Madina Ly-Tall)*

of *Kaabu Mansaba* ('great king of Kaabu'). For a new challenge of a political and military nature was threatening Senegambia: the Denianke Fulbe.

The emergence of the Fulbe

The Tengella (1490–1512)

Since the thirteenth century the nomadic Fulbe had been moving southwards in search of grass and water. They came together in Futa Toro, Bundu, Macina and Futa Jallon, where, after a period when they lived alongside or even under the autochthonous populations, they went on to found powerful states.

Such was the legendary history of Tengella and his son Koly in Futa Toro.

Were they really related to Sundiata, or was that just a legend? Did they originally set out from Futa Toro or from Futa Jallon? In either case, a clash with the Mande was inevitable.

This occurred between 1481 and 1514. A century later, Alvares d'Almada was told what great numbers of horsemen they had; but he was told too of the enormous size of their flocks; which suggests that Koly Tengella had settled on the grassy plateaux of Futa Jallon, thus pushing northwards, from the outcrops of the massif, the corridor between the heart of Mali and its western provinces. It now took six months for traders sent by the mansa to reach Sutuco in the Gambia.

The troops of Koly and his father Tengella, swollen with detachments contributed by various Fulbe settlements, poured into Futa Toro after crossing the Gambia and occupying Bundu. Then Tengella headed towards the kingdom of Jara (Diara or Djara) while his son, Koly, began the conquest of Futa Toro.

In the kingdom of Jara

This kingdom seized by the Songhay prince 'Umar Komzagho was still being disputed by Mali's counter-offensive. It was at this point that Tengella burst onto the scene, but he was killed in 1511–12 by the Gao army. This territory was vital to the Songhay empire as a means of access to the Bambuk gold-mines.

The conquest of Futa Toro and Jolof

In Futa, the lesser chiefs, formerly subject to Mali through Jara took advantage of the conquest of this latter by Songhay to free itself. Koly easily overcame these divided chieftaincies and established his capital at Anyam-Godo.

According to the traditions collected by Raffenel in 1846, Koly conquered territories from the Moors and the Wolof, these latter being driven away from the valleys of the river and its affluents. This suzerainty over the neighbouring countries lasted until the beginning of the eighteenth century. The *silatigi*, the ruler of Futa, was called the 'Great Fulo' by the Portuguese. But Mali's authority extended over the countries of Casamance and the Gambia for three hundred leagues around Sutuco.

The end of the Mali empire

In addition to the Songhay threat in the east and Denianke power in the west, Mali had to face interference by the Portuguese. After vainly attempting to use force against the coastal populations, they tried the diplomatic path at the end of the fifteenth century, with embassies sent by king John II of Portugal to the king of Futa, the *koi* of Timbuktu and the *mansa* of Mali. Given its importance Mali was even sent two delegations, one going up the Gambia and the other leaving from the fort at El Mina. In a letter to the king of Portugal, Mansa Maḥmūd III compared his empire to that of Cairo and Baghdad. The Portuguese mission sent in 1534 from El Mina went to negotiate on various questions concerning trade on the river Gambia.

But the Portuguese were already meddling in the domestic conflicts of the coastal countries. Thus, in about 1482, they attempted to put the regent, Bemoy, onto the throne. Furthermore, through friendship missions, they were accumulating information, and they were using trade to attempt to detach the coastal chiefs from Mali's control.

A particular case where this happened is in the kingdom of Salum, founded in the late fifteenth century by M'Began N'Dur, king of Sine, which in about 1556 occupied the north of the river Gambia. The trader Alvares d'Almada tells of its efficient military structure with two captain-generals who, in the event of conflict, were charged by the king with assembling the troops. The Mande village chiefs provided contingents of horsemen whose mounts were purchased from the Fulbe and the Moors. Gradually, this kingdom freed itself from the Gambia and grew at its expense, until by the early seventeenth century the Gambia, a remote province of Mali, was no longer spoken of; in its place, there were three kingdoms: Salum, Wuli and Cantor. But this had been Mali's sole window on the outside world.

Mali's last bid

Maḥmūd IV tried to take advantage of the disastrous situation created in the inner Niger delta by the Moroccan occupation. With the support of most of the Fulbe and Bambara chiefs, he marched on Jenne. Then, one of the allies abandoned him at the last moment, and went over to the Moroccans who, thanks to his advice and despite their amazement at the size of the forces of Mali, got the better of them after a violent bombardment.

But even in defeat, the *mansa* received the honours due to him. The Moroccans' allies, says the *Ta'rīkh al-Sūdān*, 'having met him in a safe place, saluted him as sultan and bared their heads to do him honour, as was their custom'. The provinces of Mali freed themselves one by one giving rise to five small kingdoms. The most promising of them later brought together the centres and groups of Bambara migrants around the inner Niger delta. This was to be the basis of the Bambara kingdoms of Segu and Kaarta. Mali itself was reduced to a small kingdom around Kaabu and Kita.

Conclusion

Shorn of its northern provinces in the first half of the sixteenth century, to the advantage of the Tuareg and the Songhay, Mali survived another century and a half, thanks to the economic strength of its western provinces where the evidence of the Portuguese reveals political and social structures that were still firm.

The *farin* representing the *mansa* effectively controlled many village chiefs: *njoni-mansa, bati-mansa, casa-mansa* and so on. In the markets scattered along the river Gambia, such as Sutuco, Jamnam Sura etc., the Portuguese exchanged horses, wine, cloth, glass trinkets, nails and bracelets for foodstuffs, gold, slaves, ivory and craft products.

From the sixteenth century, Kaabu became a more powerful independent kingdom, and the great upheaval of the Denianke movement, at the same time as the presence of the Portuguese, considerably reduced the bases of the empire. Mali turned towards Worodugu (the land of kola nuts, the forest).

After the last clash with Songhay, it was reduced to a tiny rump by the beginning of the seventeenth century.

8 The Songhay from the Twelfth to the Sixteenth Century

After a long period of gestation lasting several centuries, the Songhay who had settled on both banks of the middle Niger, established a state in the fifteenth century which unified a large portion of the western Sudan and acted as the setting for a brilliant civilization.

The kingdom of Gao from the twelfth century to the advent of Sonnī ʿalī Ber in 1464

This first period is rather obscure, and, despite the existence of a few chronicles or traditions, can do no more than provide hypotheses for research.

The kingdom of Gao in the twelfth century

By its geographical position on the Niger Bend, facing the immensity of the central Sudan, Gao became in the twelfth century the capital of the newly established Songhay state and ended up by eclipsing the old city of Kūkya as Arab authors call it.

Salt from the desert, merchandise from Egypt, Libya and Ifrīḳiya via Tadmekka and Tūwāt made Gao a great cosmopolitan market. Al-Bakrī and al-Idrīsī testify to the existence of Gao and Kūkya, a town surrounded with a wall, in the twelfth century.

The kingdom which stretched along both banks of the river from Dendi to Gao, was governed by the Jaa or Zaa, probably a Songhay clan who had intermarried with Berbers. Islam was introduced to the court in the time of the king, the *Jaa Kosoy* in 1019. But the mass of the people remained faithful to their traditional religion. The funerary stelae of Gao-Sane, which are evidence of a profound Islamic faith, seem to have been imported.

Mande domination and the Sonnī dynasty

At the end of the thirteenth century, Mali conquered the kingdom of Gao, and Kankū Mūsā, on his return from the pilgrimage, built a mosque at Gao where he put a governor. But the Jaa did not hesitate to shake off control from Niani on occasion.

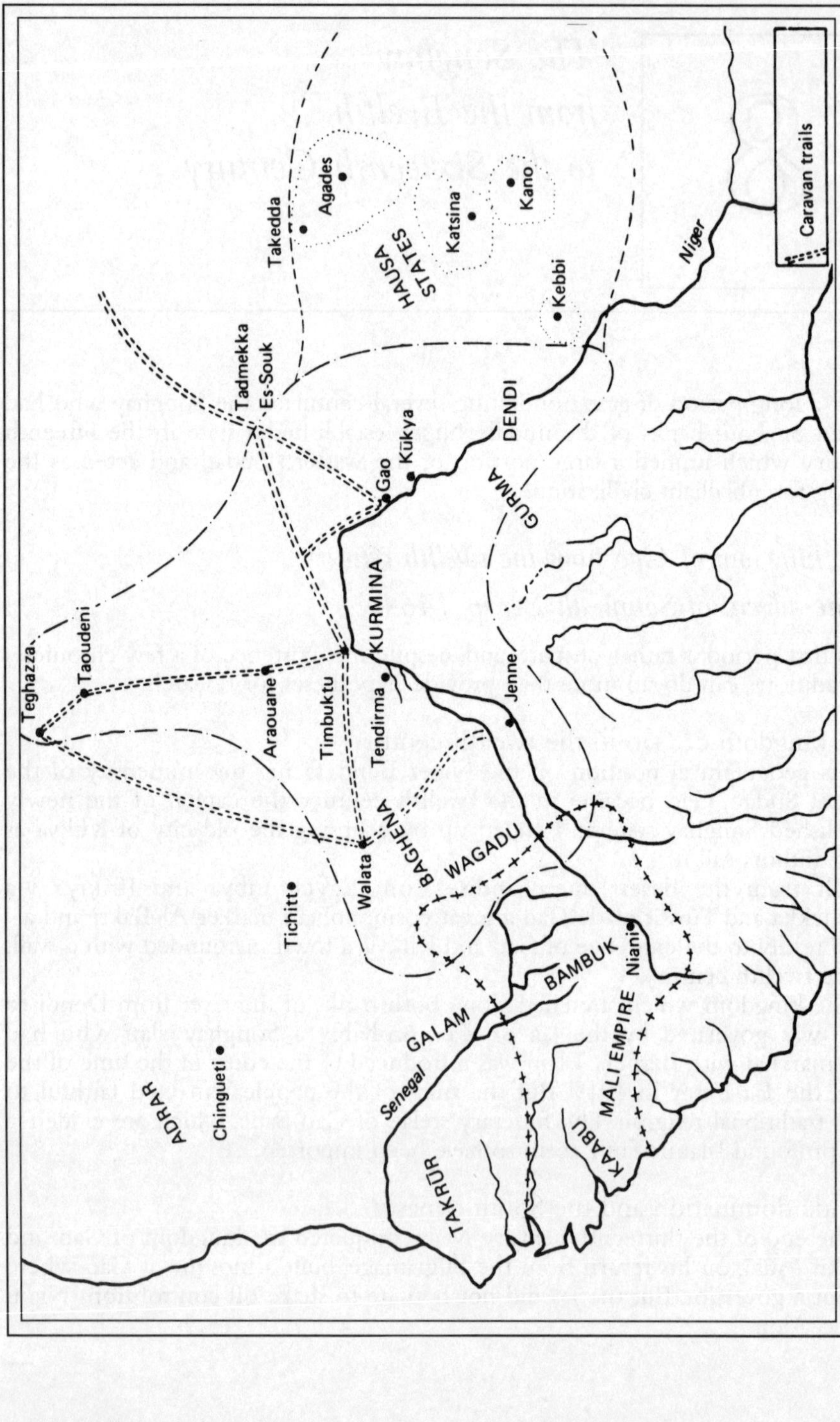

8.1 *Songhay empire towards the end of the sixteenth century. (D. T. Niane)*

In the thirteenth century, a new dynasty, that of the Sonnī, founded by ʿAlī Kolon, freed itself.

According to Boubou Hama, the Sonnī, or Sii or Shi, were warriors from Kūkya who conquered Macina, the Soninke province of Mema, and even the capital, Niani, from where Sonnī Madawu is said to have brought back 24 slave clans which went to increase the monarchy's scope for action.

The Songhay empire in the fifteenth and sixteenth centuries

Sonnī ʿAlī abandoned sporadic raiding and opted instead for territorial occupation. He reorganized the army which was equipped with a fleet on the Niger commanded by the *hi-koy*, a body of foot soldiers which took in the best of the defeated, and above all an elite cavalry which, by the speed and toughness of its actions all over the Niger region, imposed itself as the principal military force in the Sudan.

Reputed to be a magician and called *daali* ('the Most High'), Sonnī ʿAlī inspired terror. He took Jenne, and part of Macina where many Fulbe were executed; then it was the turn of Timbuktu (1468).

The Tuareg in the north, the Dogon and the Bariba in the south suffered his attacks. In 1483, near Jenne, he surprised and defeated the Mossi king, Nasere I, who was returning from Walāta laden with a valuable booty. He thus put an end to Yatenga's incursions into the Niger valley. The Songhay empire stretched from Dendi to Macina; it was better organized and placed under governors who bore the title *fari, farma* in Mande and *Koy, mondzo* in Songhay. Sonnī ʿAlī appointed a *ḳāḍī* in Timbuktu, but failed in his plan to build a canal between the Niger and Walāta. At least he built dykes which encouraged agriculture.

In religion, he was presented in later writings by the Muslim scholars of Timbuktu as tyrannical, cruel and impious. In reality, Sonnī ʿAlī, brought up in Sokoto, his mother's country, remained attached to pre-Islamic rites and opposed the *ʿulamā* for their alliance with the Tuareg whom he was trying hard to defeat. It was thus an ideological and political conflict that pitted him against the jurists of the great cities of the Niger region.

The askiyas (1492–1592)

The last Sonnī, rejecting Islam, was driven from power by the *Hombori-Koy* Toure or Sylla, a convinced Muslim, who created the dynastic title of *askiya*.

This scholar, of Soninke and Takrūr origin, a balanced and moderate man, mobilized the Islamic force to consolidate and strengthen the achievements of the Sunni.

Taking with him 300,000 dinars, he went to Mecca with a retinue of 800 horsemen and *ʿulamā*. He met the grand master of al-Azhār University in Cairo. In Mecca he acquired a concession for pilgrims from the Sudan and obtained from the *sharīf* of Mecca the title of caliph of the Sudan. With his power thus legitimized, he returned to work with his brother ʿUmar Komdiagho to extend the conquests to Macina and Jara where Tengella was killed, the mines at

Teghāzza, Agades and the Hausa towns of Katsina and Kano. But the southern frontier of the empire scarcely moved despite attacks on the Dogon, the Mossi and the Bariba.

ʿUmar Komdiagho, appointed *kurmina fari*, created the town of Tendirma. The *askiya* appointed governors loyal to himself for the new provinces and *ḳāḍīs* in all the Muslim cities. He reorganized the court and the imperial council, giving pride of place to the religious authorities.

In order to encourage trade, he strengthened the market police and the control of weights and measures. In order to stimulate agricultural production, he set up farming settlements for slaves taken in war and reduced the taxes levied on the harvests. The advancement of learning was ensured by deference towards the *ʿulamāʾ*, who were moreover showered with gifts. Askiya Muḥammad became old and blind and he was overthrown by a conspiracy led by his eldest son Mūsā.

The successors of Askiya Muḥammad

The sons of Askiya Muḥammad no longer had any conquests to make; rather they made raids which alternated with intrigues and palace revolutions, while the prickly problem of the Teghāzza salt-mines coveted by Morocco precipitated the end of the regime.

We shall see how these problems appeared through the reigns of the three most representative askiyas.

Isḥāḳ I (1539–49)

It was under this authoritarian prince that the Saʿdian sultan Muḥammad al-Shaykh claimed ownership of the Teghāzza salt-mines. Isḥāk I replied by sending a troop of Tuareg horsemen to sack the Moroccan Draʿa.

Dāwūd (1549–83)

This long and prosperous reign of an open-minded prince, who head learned to be wily in the intrigues of the previous reigns and the high office he assumed, coincided with the apogee of the empire. There was a remarkable economic and intellectual flowering. The trans-Saharan caravans still got the better of the Atlantic caraval. Careful management of the resources derived from economic activities enabled the *askiya* to build up a treasury of coins and vast storehouses of cereals. These enormous resources served partly for the upkeep of men of letters, the poor and mosques. In addition to raids on the Mossi and against Macina, the Askiya Dāwūd succeeded in reaching a compromise with the Sultan Aḥmad al-Manṣūr that safeguarded Songhay ownership of Teghāzza. But under his successor, Askiya Muḥammad III (1583–86), the occupation of the mines by the Moroccans led the Tuareg to move southwards to exploit the salt-pans of Taoudeni. And Teghāzza fell into ruins.

The election of *Muḥammad IV Bāno* as *askiya* in 1586 sparked off a civil war. Several of his brothers, including the *balama* al-Ṣaḍḍiḳ, marched on Gao in

1588 at the head of troops from the west. The revolt was cruelly put down and the empire was virtually divided. The west was disillusioned and lost interest in Gao; it had no qualms about welcoming the Moroccan invaders in 1591. The empire had worked to bring about its own destruction.

The civilization of the Songhay

Political and organizational structures

The hierarchy of centralized absolute power gave the Gao monarchy a 'modern' flavour which broke with the more flexible federal system that existed in the time of Ghana and Mali.

The monarchy

The king as father and wielder of a sacred power that guaranteed the prosperity of all was venerated. It was possible to approach him only in a prostrate position. In addition to Sudanese tradition there was the Islamic tradition brought to the fore by Askiya Muḥammad and Askiya Dāwūd.

In Gao the court included the members of his family, the dignitaries and the *griots* (*gesere* and *mabo*). The king sat on a raised platform surrounded by 700 eunuchs. The Wandu (chief *griot*) acted as a herald. In principle, on the death of an askiya, his eldest brother succeeded. The successor was proclaimed by the court and enthroned at Kūkya. In practice, the decisive factor was the balance of power between the claimants.

Royal government

(1) The central government was formed by the top office holders sitting in the imperial council.

A chancellor-secretary dealt with correspondence and minutes, charters or conventions for internal and external use. In the absence of a strict specialization of functions, the *Taʿrikh*s give a list of areas with those heading them.

The *hi koy* or 'master of the water' was the commander of the fleet. He was a sort of minister of home affairs with authority over the governors, if only because of the role played by the river in the life of the empire.

The *fari mondzo* was the minister of agriculture. This key office which involved control over vast imperial estates was generally held by princes of the blood or even crown princes. The *saw farma*, the commissioner of forests, performed similar but lower-level functions.

The *kalisa farma* or 'finance minister' was doubtless in charge of the imperial treasury. He was backed up by the *werney farma*, in charge of property, the *bana farma*, responsible for wages, and the *doy farma*, in charge of purchases. The *balama* was the commander of the army whose responsibility was later limited to the command of the army corps stationed in the Kabara–Timbuktu region. At that time, he was then, most likely, dependent on the *kurmina fari*. The *korey farma* was the minister in charge of white foreigners. In addition there was a large number of imperial commissioners appointed periodically for particular tasks.

(2) The government of the provinces had two sides:

(a) The first group of provinces included the conquered territories administered directly by the askiya who appointed governors (*fari, farba, farma*) to head them. The *koy* or *mandzo* were chiefs of lesser importance. Justice was reserved for the *ḳāḍī* alone.

The empire included two major provinces: Kurmina in the west and Dendi in the south-east. The *kurmina fari* or *kanfari* ranked second in the state; it was often the crown prince who held this office. He resided at Tendirma and seems to have exercised his authority throughout the territory west of Timbuktu, especially at the end of the sixteenth century. At that time he had a powerful army able to counter-balance the power of Gao, something which was attempted on several occasions.

The *dendi fari* supervised the south-east. He ranked third in the state and was responsible for the southern marches.

Some particular provinces were governed autonomously by local chiefs appointed by the *askiya* (such as the *Hombori-Koy* and the *arabinda farma*). Similar arrangements applied to the main trading towns (Timbuktu, Jenne, Walāta and Teghāzza) which enjoyed administrative autonomy under their *koy* or *mondzo* assisted by numerous specialized agents; the *asara mondzo*, the commissioner responsible for policing markets and for carrying out the sentences passed by the *ḳāḍī*, weights and measures inspectors, tax inspectors in the markets, customs officials from Kabara, masters of the guilds, chiefs of ethnic groups and so on.

(b) The vassal or tributary countries were governed by local law: their appointed chief was simply recognized by the *askiya*, who would however intervene and impose his own candidate in the event of disputes among claimants or rebellions. These countries included Macina, the Hausa states (Kano and Katsina), the kingdom of Agades and the Tuareg Kel Antassar federation. Their allegiance was expressed in tribute, the provision of armed contingents at the request of the emperor, visits, gifts and marriages.

With this framework of norms and institutions of both endogenous and Islamic origin, Songhay ensured the security of goods and persons as well as the survival of an impersonal power over and beyond any incidental crises. This original experience of the development of the African state was brutally interrupted by the Moroccan conquest.

The state apparatus

The state had a standing army to ensure internal and external security. Its abundant and regular resources enabled it to ensure its independence. The independence of justice entrusted to the *ḳāḍī*s and customary chiefs protected people's freedom and rights.

The army

The nobility constituted the backbone of the cavalry which wore iron breastplates beneath their battle tunics. Horses were expensive (each equal to ten captives), so the cavalry were a privileged élite. The infantry were made up mostly of freemen and captives and were armed with spears, arrows and leather or copper shields. Military music was produced by a group of long trumpeters, *kakaki*, and big standards preceded the troops. According to the *Ta'ri͟kh al-Fatta͟sh*: 'The great men of the Songhay were versed in the art of war. They were very brave, very bold and most expert in the deployment of military stratagems.' The total army assembled at the battle of Tondibi in 1591 comprised 30,000 infantry and 10,000 horsemen including the sovereign's personal bodyguard. It was the largest organized force in the western Sudan; it was a political instrument, but also an economic weapon by virtue of the booty it brought in.

Financial resources

These were many: revenues from imperial estates; the *zakāt* or tithe, for the poor; taxes in kind levied on harvests, herds and fishing; taxes and customs duties on commercial transactions; special levies on the merchants in the towns; the spoils of almost annual war etc. This income paid for the upkeep of the court, the administration and the army, and for giving presents and alms.

Justice

Two kinds of jurisdiction co-existed in the empire. One was based on Mālikite Muslim law; the *ḳāḍī* was the supreme and independent judge appointed by the emperor for life. The post was not greatly sought after, and sometimes people had to be forced to fill it. In Timbuktu, the post was occupied for the whole of the sixteenth century by the distinguished family of the Ḳāḍī Maḥmūd ben ʿUmar al-ʿAḳit. The *ḳāḍī* was assisted by secretaries, clerks of the court and notaries. He acted as a kind of registrar, recording the freeing of slaves, successions, the validation of private documents etc. He protected certain basic freedoms. He was the real master of Timbuktu.

Customary justice, the most widespread in the empire, was exercised amicably through the traditional agencies. The imperial council sat as a political tribunal to pronounce judgement in affairs of state.

Economic development

The rural sector

Techniques have not greatly changed since those times: the hoe (light or heavy), animal manure and horticulture in the valleys, shifting cultivation in the savannah. The Niger valley was then more densely populated. Large estates worked by servile labour belonged to notables. The *askiya* was the largest landowner, and his estates were put under overseers called *fanfa*.

Fish were plentiful and fishing was practised by the Sorko, the Do and the Bozo. Animal-raising, widely practised in some provinces such as Macina and

Bakhunu, provided milk, meat and skins especially for the urban populations, the country dwellers receiving manufactured products and salt in exchange.

The commercial sector

The principal trans-Saharan routes were the following: from Timbuktu to Tlemcen via Teghāzza; from Timbuktu to Fez via Walāta, Tishīt, Wadān and the Dra'a; from Gao to Tunis, Tripoli and Cairo, either via Tuwāt or via the Fezzān or via the eastern route through Hausaland or Kānem to end up on the lower Nile.

Trans-Saharan trade was in the hands of Berber Arabs. The Sudanese (Wangara), Wakore (Soninke), Mossi, Hausa and Songhay took over in the towns bordering the desert where brokers did good business, following the fluctuations in prices and organizing themselves to use the available transport: fleet on the river, camels, pack oxen and donkeys. On his arrival in Kabara, Leo Africanus observed that the port of Timbuktu was congested with all sorts of merchandise.

Exchanges were effected by barter or through the intermediary of a commodity currency – cowries, gold, salt, copper. The Sudan imported salt from the desert in the form of rock salt, cloth, arms, horses, copper, glassware, sugar and North African craft products. The empire exported gold, ivory, spices, kola nuts slaves, cotton goods, all coming from the same sources as in the time of Mali. Internal trade interfered with long-distance trade, for example for cereals, dried or smoked fish and craft products. In this whole system, the town of Jenne acted as the major centre for redistributing goods and providing the impetus for trade.

Nevertheless, this trade, which considerably enriched some sections of the urban populations, affected local production relatively little. The bulk of the trade involved the products of mining and gathering. Trans-Saharan trade was thus more a matter of trading local produce for imported goods than a real market economy based on local production. This explains why there was little transformation in the social structures and techniques despite the innovations in housing, food and dress for the notables in the cities.

Organization of Niger society

The whole of Songhay society was marked by the importance of ties of kinship. The clans were of varying antiquity: the Soninke (Ture, Sylla, Tunkara, Cisse, Jakhite, Drame and Jaware), Songhay (Maiga), Mande (Traore, Keita and Jamara) etc. In addition there were those of mixed blood resulting from the mixed character of the towns associated with the presence of the Berbers.

Ethnic specialization also meant occupational specialization for the Fulbe or for the war captives conscripted into the army or agricultural work. This functional specialization marked by hierarchical ranking can also be seen in the social stratification into orders or classes of nobles, free men, members of guilds and slaves. Free men were independent farmers; slaves were subordinate workers; guild members were specialized and endogamous craftsmen; while nobles reserved for themselves the tasks of administration, power and war.

Rural society

Most people lived in villages, as in contemporary African kingdoms and empires. Craftsmen, like fishermen, also engaged in agriculture. People were probably not as wretched as Leo Africanus claims. Security was general and famine rare. There is no mention of peasant revolts. The inventory of the goods of an imperial steward in Dendi shows that there were big rural landowners. The existence of rural markets testifies to the reality of peasant surpluses.

Towns and urban society

The great commercial expansion enabled a true urban civilization to develop in the Sudan-Sahel region. The towns included a centre, formed of houses built of masonry in the Sudanese style, with a space set aside for the market and another for the mosque; while the suburbs of tents and straw huts housed a floating population.

Three towns stand out: Timbuktu, Jenne and Gao. Timbuktu, conquered by Sonnī ʿAlī Ber in 1468, was the pearl of the Sudan in the sixteenth century, as a town of scholars and holy men, and as an economic capital. Jenne, spiritually and economically linked to Timbuktu, was dominated by its mosque, one of the jewels of the eastern Sudan, and was the principal entrepôt with the vast world of the savannah and the forest. Gao, the political capital, had even more inhabitants (100,000) and looked towards the central Sudan, Libya and Egypt.

In these towns Songhay was the dominant language for the cosmopolitan population and Arabic for the educated. The criterion of social differentiation tended here to be above all economic both among the 'politicos' and among the merchants, craftsmen or 'intellectuals' (both masters and students). The refinement consequent upon the mixing of populations and the abundance of goods showed itself in some moral laxity among the aristocracy and the growing number of courtesans; there was a growing contrast between this insular urban society and the global society.

Religious and intellectual development

Religious life

Islam made uneven progress depending on the region but did not take root deeply or widely during this period. In the urban areas a privileged minority fully assumed the Islamic message and became its leading thinkers, respected in the known world of the time and maintained by the generosity of rulers, such as Askiya Muḥammad, the founder of the dynasty. But the great mass of the population remained attached to its ancestral beliefs. The Songhay worshipped *hole* (spiritual doubles) and spirits inhabiting nature who had to be propitiated. Two spirits were particularly important: Harake Dikko, the spirit of the river, and Dongo, the spirit of thunder. The *sonianke*, healer priests, regarded as descendants of the Sunni dynasty, still enjoyed popular veneration and protected society from evil spirits and sorcerers or *tierkei*. The cult of the dead was perpetuated by each clan chief. Thus, black Islam had to adapt and become tolerant in order to spread.

Aristocratic and urban, Islam was supported by rulers such as Askiya Muḥammad. Obedient to the advice of the doctors, al-Maghhīlī of Tuwāt and al-Suyūṭī of Cairo, he destroyed 'fetishes' and persecuted the companions of Sonnī. He imposed the Mālikite rite and waged a holy war (*djihād*) against the followers of the traditional religion in the south, in particular the Mossi. The merchants, with their own methods, carried Islam down into the forest.

Islam was thus established in the urban spheres of power. From this point of view, Timbuktu was a model with its three great mosques: the Jingereber, the Sīdī Yaḥya and the Sankore, and the fame of its doctors and saints (Sharīf Sīdī Yaḥya, who died in 1464; *Ḳāḍī* Mahmud). Timbuktu became the holy city of the Sudan.

Intellectual life

The Sudanese elite, trained in the universities of Karawiyyin in Fez and al-Azhār in Cairo, became emancipated and by its own efforts reached the heights of Islamic learning. The economic surplus made possible the development of a class of scholars given over to worship and study. It also attracted scholars from the Sudan, North Africa and even the Near East. The two historical *Ta'rikh*s produced by intellectuals of the Songhay empire testify to the level reached by these universities which were less strictly organized than in North Africa. They were independent schools and open mosques.

In the sixteenth century, Timbuktu had some 180 Koranic schools and thousands of students from far and near. The masters, unpaid, but protected from need, worked day and night. Study was at two levels: the Koranic school for the memorization of texts; and the level of the *madrasa* and university learning for interpretation and creative work. Here as elsewhere, the Muslim 'humanities' included theology (*tawḥīh*), exegesis (*tafṣīr*), traditions (*ḥadīth*), jurisprudence (*fiḳh*), grammar, rhetoric, logic, astrology, astronomy, history and geography. The predominance of Mālikite law and simple commentary of the texts following scholastic methods among the Sudanese 'jurists' left very little room for the sciences.

Among these masters, mention should be made in the fifteenth century of *Shaykh* Sīdī Yāhyā and Muḥammad al-Kabarī (from Kabara). In the sixteenth century, two great Berber families supplied the majority of scholars: the 'Aḳits and the Anda Ag Muḥammads. Among them, was the famous 'Abbās Aḥmad Bābā, famed throughout the Muslim world, even in the East. But he quoted and venerated as his master the celebrated Baghayogho of Jenne.

This intellectual effort of learning and faith must not be underestimated. But because it was elitist and urban, because it was written down in a language that took no account of the autochthonous languages and cultures, it remained marginal to society, and collapsed with the cities where it had flourished.

9 The Peoples and Kingdoms of the Niger Bend and the Volta Basin from the Twelfth to the Sixteenth Century

The Mossi of the Niger Bend

In the Niger Bend we shall deal principally with the Mamprusi, Dagomba and Mossi kingdoms – for two reasons. First, they are far better known than other historical formations of the region such as the Gurma or *a fortiori* the societies without a centralized system of political power. The second reason is that the problem arises of identifying the Mossi referred to in the *Taʾrīkh al-Sūdān* and *Taʾrīkh al-fattāsh*, and the definition of a satisfactory chronological framework for the whole of the area depends upon a solution to this problem.

The *Taʾrīkh al-fattāsh* speaks of Mossi incursions into the Songhay kingdom around the middle of the thirteenth century in the time of *Za* Baray, who may be identified with *Za* Beirafoloko. It was during the reign of his successor, *Za* Asibay, that the kingdom of Gao passed under the control of Mali then ruled by Mansa Wālī (1260–77).

The *Taʾrīkh* uses the expression *Mossi Koy* for the chief or king of the Mossi.

These incursions were not by anarchic bands, but organized forces of a military society capable of confronting the principal hegemonies which shared the Niger Bend. The fact that Timbuktu was one of the objectives also shows the desire of the Mossi to control West African trade.

It was during the reign of one of the successors of Mansa Kanku Mūsā (1312–37) that, according to the *Taʾrikh al-Sūdān*, the Mossi erupted onto the scene: 'The sultan of the Mossi entered the town, pillaged it, set fire to it, reduced it to ruins and, after putting to death everyone he could lay hands on and seizing all the wealth he could find, he returned to his country.'

These events probably occurred in the years following the death of Kanku Mūsā. i.e. a century after the attack mentioned by the *Taʾrikh al-fattāsh*, which suggests a stable power, strong enough to launch such expeditions over such a great distance and such a long period. The *Taʾrikh al-Sūdān* records a third raid by the Mossi against Benka shortly before 1433.

For the reign of Sonnī ʿAlī we have the following points of reference. In 1464–5, the Mossi king Komdao was defeated by Sonnī ʿAlī who led an expedition into Mossi territory in 1471–2. In 1477–8, the Mossi penetrated into Songhay territory where they remained for four years after taking the towns of Sama and Walāta. At the end of this expedition, the Mossi were intercepted, defeated and pursued by the Songhay who seized the king's *smala* and booty.

What happened between the middle of the fourteenth century, marked in particular by the raid against Benka, and the middle of the following century, which seems to mark the height of Mossi expansionism as far as Walāta? What seems clear is that for Sonnī ʿAlī, the principal enemy was the Mossi against whom he waged an implacable war which was continued by his successors.

Askiya Muḥammad (1493–1529) transformed the Songhay offensive against the Mossi into a holy war, since the Mossi were followers of the traditional religion like the inhabitants of Gurma. The Songhay army was victorious against 'sultan' Naʾaṣira, and many mothers and their children were carried off into captivity.

At the time of the second expedition by Askiya Dāwūd (1549–83), 'the chief (of the Mossi) abandoned the country with all his troops'. Another expedition by Dāwūd seems to have run into a scorched earth policy since the Songhay army came back 'without having pillaged anything'.

Thus, for three centuries, a conquering military society fought against the Songhay with a view to gaining control of the river after establishing their ascendancy within the Bend. Finally, the Mossi were defeated; the political antagonism was reinforced by religious antagonism after the reign of Muḥammad.

Who were these Mossi of the *Taʾrikh*? In the absence of any help from oral tradition, we have to rely on what archaeological excavations can tell us.

According to Boubou Hama, citing an Arabic manuscript by a certain Ould ʿAoudar (doubtless the *Taʾrikh of Say*), the Mossi, who had come from the east, first founded on the left bank of the Niger a state by the name of Dyamare, the capital of which was Rozi. After five centuries (eighth to twelfth centuries) and under pressure from the Berbers, the Mossi migrated to Mindji, the capital of a second Dyamare, which they left soon afterwards, crossing the river and establishing a third Dyamare at the expense of the autochthonous Kurumba and Gurmankyeba peoples.

According to al-ʿUmarī, in one of his discussions with Cairo notables, the emperor of Mali, Mansa Mūsā, said: 'We have a relentless enemy who, among the blacks, is for us what the Tartars are for you . . . [They] are skilled in shooting arrows [and have] gelded horses, with split noses.' We may wonder whether these horsemen were northern Mossi.

The Genoese merchant Antonio Malfante, who visited Tuwāt in 1447, refers to the siege of Vallo (Walāta?) by 'a fetishistic king with five hundred thousand men'. According to Yves Person, this may well be the king of the northern Mossi. Finally, in his *Decadas da Asia* (1553), João de Barros speaks of the 'Mossi people' mentioned by the Wolof prince Bemoy in 1488 when he visited Portugal. According to him, the territory of the 'Moses' extended eastward from Timbuktu. The king of Portugal was impressed and identified the king of the Moses with the legendary Prester John, who, he thought, was fighting against the Muslim power of the Mande *Mansa*.

Claude Meillassoux, collecting oral traditions, found between Niamina and Nara (in the republic of Mali) a line of wells said to have been dug by the Mossi who are said to have defeated the Sumare, whereas the Jariso (Dyariso) clans held out victoriously. In the Hōdh, the Mossi are said to have set up a territorial command centred in Gara and invaded Daole-Gilbe, near Kumbi Ṣāleḥ.

The Mossi of the Niger Bend and the Volta basin: the classical thesis

The earliest authors based their analyses on the oral tradition which traces all the Mossi royal dynasties to a single ancestor, Naaba Wedraogo, and establishes an explicit relation between the origin of the Mossi kingdoms and that of the Mamprusi-Nanumba-Dagomba states.

In current Mossi traditions, there is nowhere any mention of expeditions against the Songhay. But Dalafosse, Frobenius and Tauxier, from the *Taʿrīkh*s, were very familiar with this ancient presence of the northern Mossi in the countries of the inner delta of the Niger and beyond. Basing themselves on the slightest of hints, for instance, the similarity between the Naʿasira of the *Taʿrīkh*s and the name of a ruler of Yatenga, the first historiographers of the Mossi identified the Mossi of the Niger Bend with those of the White Volta, thus giving the history of the present-day Mossi kingdoms a much greater chronological depth than the study of oral traditions and of the neighbouring historical formations warrants. This thesis implied the following hypothesis: the Mossi were only able to embark on their wide-ranging military campaigns after they had firmly established their power over the autochthonous populations of the Volta; thus the actions recorded in the *Tarʿīkh*s must, it was thought, have occurred late in a history pushed back into the remote past of the origins put by Delafosse in the tenth century. This hypothesis could only be defended if the lengths of the reigns of the monarchs mentioned by the traditions were considerably lengthened, or if it was believed that there are gaps in the regnal lists.

In 1907, Captain Lambert criticized the identification of the present-day Mossi with the Mossi of the *Taʿrīkh*s. But this study remained unpublished. That is why John Fage's radical criticism directed against Delafosse's thesis was perceived as an overall reinterpretation of the history of the Mossi. He drew a clear distinction between the Mossi of the Niger Bend and those of the Volta basin, although he did not rule out the possibility of relations between them. This basic choice led him to place the chronology of the beginnings of the present-day kingdoms much more recently; for example, he dates the founder of the Dagomba kingdom at about 1480. For John Fage, the northern Mossi must be considered to have been evolving in a pre-state framework. Nehemiah Levtzion, comparing the evolution of the states of the Volta basin, reaches a similar conclusion, that is, between 1380 and 1480. Michel Izard, analysing Mossi genealogical material in order to compare the present-day kingdoms, especially those of Wagadugu and Yatenga, began by defining the pivotal date of the foundation of Yatenga as being in 1540. From there, he extrapolated back to the first king of Wagadugu, Naaba Wubri, dated to 1495. Going back even further, he placed the first ruler of the genealogy (Na Bawa) between 1375 and 1420.

The origin of the states of the Volta basin: the present state of our knowledge

The proto-Mossi of Dyamare II (Minji) crossed the river in the region of Say in the first half of the thirteenth century and founded Dyamare III within the Bend on the Gurma bank. From then until 1575, there were repeated attempts to seize control of the rich outlets of trans-Saharan trade. But this area was already occupied by the two great empires of the Sudan, Mali and Gao.

Is there a relationship between these northern proto-Mossi and the Mamprusi kingdom from which came the Nanumba and Dagomba formations, the present-day Mossi and the present dynasty of Nungu (Fada Ngurma)? What was occurring in fact was the diffusion of a pattern of political organization from Bornu to King Bawa of Mamprusi by way of the Hausa country of Zamfara.

According to the tradition recorded by E. Tamakloe, Tohajiye, the 'red hunter', then his son, Kpogonumbo, had been the allies of the king of Mali. Then Kpogonumbo set off westward where in Gurma, he eventually married Soyini, one of the king's daughters, who bore the future Na Bawa (Gbewa) of the Mamprusi (known to the Dagomba and the Mossi as Na Nedega) who settled at Pusuga where he consolidated his power by waging war against the Kusasi and the Bisa. Zirili, the eldest son of Na Bawa, was initially kept off the throne by his father but ended up succeeding to it after killing his brother and ousting his sister, who had been invested before him, from power. He organized Mamprusi. On his death, his three younger brothers took possession of the three present-day kingdoms: Mamprusi, Nanumba and Dagomba.

There are numerous variants of this general tradition. If there is a relationship between the Mossi of the Niger Bend and the ancestors of the Mamprusi it must date back to the time of Dyamare II (on the Hausa bank of the Niger) and Dyamare III (on the Gurma bank). Perhaps it was then that detachments of mercenary warriors left to settle in the region of Pusuga.

The alliance with Mali that is mentioned in one of the stories mentioned above referred, not to the (western) Mali of the *Taʿrikh*s, but to an eastern Mali of which the Mossi of Yatenga speak and which was the country of origin of the Kurumba of Lurum.

According to the dominant tradition in the Mossi country, notably at Wagadugu, the eponymous ancestor was Na Nedega (and not Na Bawa), king of the Dagomba (and not of the Mamprusi). He reigned at Gambaga, and his eldest daughter, Yenenga (and not Kachiogo), whom he refused to give in marriage in order to be able to make use of her skills as a warrior, ended up fleeing and/or getting lost on a stallion, in a forest near Bitu. There she met a prince of Bisa-Mande origin (Ryale or Ryare), an elephant hunter.

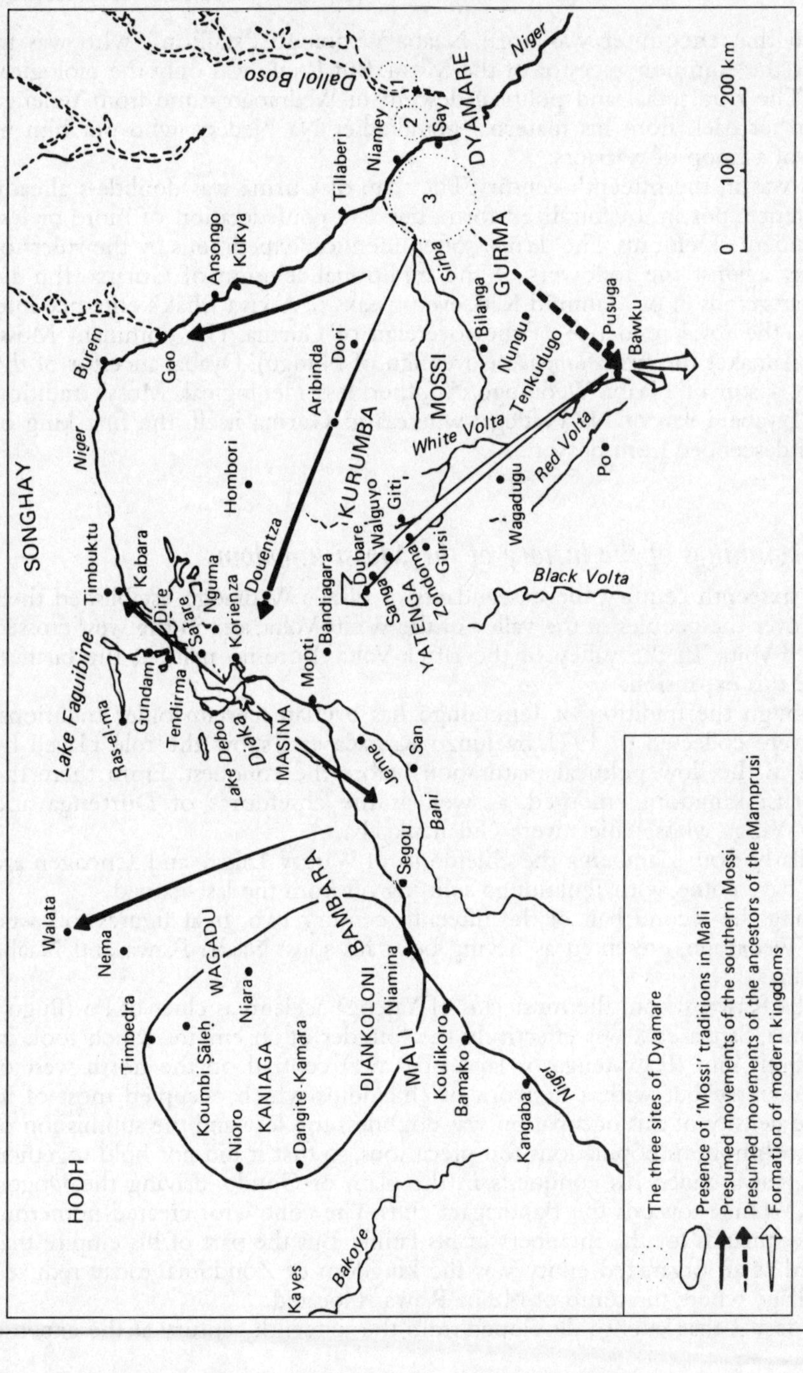

9.1 *The Niger Bend and the Volta basin, 1100–1600.*
Source: M. Izard in 'Introduction à l'Historie des Royaumes Mossi' (doctoral dissertation, Paris University, 1970)

From that encounter was born Naaba Wedraogo ('stallion') who was to become the common ancestor of the Mossi. But Ryale was only the biological father. The true social and political descent of Wedraogo came from Yenenga and further back from his maternal grandfather Na Nedega who put him in charge of a troop of warriors.

This was in the fifteenth century. The state of Gurma was doubtless already in existence; not in a centralized form, but as a confederation of more or less independent chiefdoms. The *Ta'rikhs* often mention expeditions by the rulers of Songhay against the followers of the traditional religion of Gurma. Ibn al-Mukhtar grandson of Maḥmūd Kātī, even speaks of Askiya Isḥāḳ's entrance into Bilanga, the royal residence of the sovereign of Gurma. The dominant Mossi tradition makes the first *Nunbado* (sovereign of Nungu), Dyaba, ancestor of the Lompo, a son of Naaba Wedraogo. Another, less ideological, Mossi tradition makes Dyaba a son of Na Nedega; whereas in Gurma itself, the first king of Nungu descended from heaven.

The beginnings of the history of the Mossi kingdoms

In the sixteenth century, the descendants of Naaba Wedraogo established their power over the peoples of the valley of the White Volta, and in the west crossed the Red Volta. In the valley of the Black Volta, Boromo marked the farthest limit of this expansion.

Although the tradition of Tenkudugo has overlain certain older traditions, these were collected in 1971 by Junzo Kawada and show the role played by Pusuga in the slow political maturation before the conquest. From there the Mamprusi kingdom emerged, as well as the chiefdoms of Durtenga and Komin-Yanga whose chiefs were Gurmankyeba.

Similarly, from Zambarga the chiefdoms of Wargay, Lalgay and Tenoagen are said to have come, with Tenkudugo splitting off from the last-named.

During the second half of the fifteenth century, two great figures followed Naaba Wedraogo, presented as having been his sons: Naaba Rawa and Naaba Zungrana.

Naaba Rawa, whom the musicians of Yatenga acclaim as chief of Po (Pugo), Zôndoma, Sanga etc., was effectively the founder of an empire which took its name from him (Rawatenga or land of Rawa) centred on the north-west of Mossi country, but with a network of chiefdoms which occupied most of it. But the density of this occupation was doubtless too low and the submission of the autochthonous populations too precarious, so that it did not hold together. Naaba Rawa ended his conquests in the plain of Gondo, driving the Dogon out of Yatenga towards the Bandiagara cliffs. The conqueror created numerous local commands for the members of his family. But the part of his empire that survived as an organized entity was the kingdom of Zôndoma, today reduced to a village where the tomb of Naaba Rawa is located.

The fact is that Yatenga developed from the sixteenth century at the expense of the kingdom of Zôndoma. The name of Naaba Zûngrana, who is much less known, is linked to the small kingdoms of Ratenga and Zitenga, in south-eastern Yatenga.

At that time, there were five major streams of Mossi penetration into the central area of the White Volta basin, setting up chiefdoms in all directions: in the west, in the regions of Kombisiri and Manga; in the region of Kugupela (Koupela); on the shores of the lake of Bam (Ratenga and Zitenga); the region of Bulsa, with Naaba Gigma; and the principal centre where Wubritenga was to be founded by Naaba Wubri, the son of Naaba Zûngrana. Two figures stand out in this period: Naaba Gigma and Naaba Wubri. Naaba Gigma led the expansion eastward and northward to the present borders of Liptako. At the time a large section of this frontier ran along the edge of the territory of Gurma, which was organized enough to stand up to the Mossi. Naaba Wubri, founder of the kingdom of Wagadugu, whose ruler bears the title of *Moogo Naaba*, 'chief of the Mossi' (the country being conceived of as the world); he lived during the early years of the sixteenth century.

From the region of Zinyare (the original name of Wubritenga) Naaba Wubri extended his authority eastward and north-eastward, setting up chiefdoms at Lay, Yako and finally Kudugo where he died. His remains were placed in Gilongu and Lumbila. His successors continued his work by extending Mossi influence westward.

Some of his descendants set off towards Yatenga, such as Naaba Wûmtane, the founder of the kingdom of Giti which pursued the struggle against the Dogon and enslaved the smiths. The accession of Naaba Kûmdumye, grandson of Naaba Wûbri, coincided with the departure of Naaba Yadega, another grandson of Naaba Wûbri, for Gursi. The two princes were pretenders to the throne of Wagadugu. Having been defeated by his rival, Naaba Yadega went off, accompanied by his eldest sister, Pabre, who had stolen for him the regalia placed in her custody. This, in our view happened in about 1540. Naaba Kûmdumye played a considerable role in the establishment of the present-day kingdoms of Konkistenga, Yako, Tema, Mane and Busuma; he also made a real, though short-lived, push into Gurunsi territory. With Naaba Kuda, the son of Naaba Kûmdumye, the central Mossi territory assumed the historical shape it was to retain for centuries.

In Gursi, Naaba Yadega had found a network of Mossi commands, the principal one being the kingdom of Zôndoma. From Gursi to the borders of San (Samo) territory, Naaba Yadega consolidated his position at the expense of his adoptive father, Naaba Swida. He finally settled at Lago. During the reign of his second son, Naaba Geda (late sixteenth century), the newly founded kingdom of Yatenga broke all its links with the kingdom of Wagadugu. They now constituted the two territorial poles of Mossi hegemony.

Three main phases stand out in the history of the Mossi: a phase of preparation (second half of the fifteenth century); a phase of conquest (first half of the sixteenth century); finally, a phase of stabilization (second half of the sixteenth century).

The Mossi political system

The basic fact here is the distinction between those who held the mastery of the land (*tengsobondo*) and those who held power (*naam*). The former are the representatives of the autochthonous people ('sons of the land'). The latter are in principle the Mossi; but this term ended up describing all those who were assimilated, such as,, for example, the crown captives. Thus, in contrast to the *naaba* holding political power, there was the *tengsoba* ('master of the land'). This duality is reflected in religious ideology, since the *tengsoba* was associated with the worship of the 'earth goddess'; whereas the chiefs recognized the celestial and solar 'god' (*Naaba Wende*). The union of the two seals the unity of society.

The autochthonous peoples can be divided into three broad groups: (1) the so-called Gurunsi groups, speaking Voltaic or Gur languages, in which may also be included the Kurumba (Fulse); (2) the Dogon, who were particularly victimized; and (3) the San (Samo) and Bisa peoples who are today separated territorially.

The autochthonous peoples were responsible for the annual fertility rites. It was only after certain sacrifices on land altars that a newly designated king (called only *naaba*) could be enthroned and receive the title of *rima*, which entitled him to be buried in the royal cemetery, and his son to aspire to the throne.

In Yatenga, the holders of royal power may be divided into three categories: the people of the king's household (*nayirdemba*); the masters of war (*tasobanamba*); and the members of the royal lineage (*nakombse*). The first two categories were made up either of Mossi or of captives of the crown and dignitaries descended from the great pre-Yatenga families. They were closest to the king, whereas he tended to be suspicious of the *nakombse* who were closest biologically.

Each of the four royal residences had four groups of servants each headed by a dignitary. These were, respectively: the *togo naaba*, the *balum naaba*, the *weranga naaba* and the *rasam naaba*. These dignitaries were called *nesomba*; on the one hand, they shared the tasks of central government, under the orders of the king, and on the other, on his death, they became an electoral college. Over time, the system of inheritance from brother to brother was overlain with a system in which the eldest of a group of brothers, all sons of the same king, could claim power. In the absence of a fixed rule, clashes between opposing factions often led to civil wars, despite the increasing centralization of power in the hands of the king, to the detriment of potential candidates to the throne.

But unity was achieved through language and cultural, social and political acceptance of the system of government.

The peoples without centralized political systems

The governance of such societies generally implies less attachment to a chronological framework of traditions articulated around rulers and their reigns and deeds. That is why these peoples seem to have less historical depth, although they have in fact been longer settled. Thus very little is known of history of such peoples between 1200 and 1600.

The Gur languages have been studied by many experts, such as Gabriel Manessy, De Lavergne de Tressan, Westermann and Bryan, Greenberg and Köhler among others. Their classifications and the criteria on which they are based often diverge, not to mention the problems of genetic affiliation between languages, which pose even more complex problems. Briefly, we can distinguish: (1) a large Mossi group comprising three subgroups: Mossi (Moore), Dagomba and Birifor-Dagari-Wile; (2) a Gurunsi group (eastern, western and northern); and (3) a Gurma group.

These cultural relationships do not necessarily imply any homogeneity in the socio-political system of highly centralized peoples living side by side with others speaking related languages, but living in a more dispersed and 'self-managing' social system. This is the case of the Mossi and Dagari. But it can be observed that the number of dialects of a given language varies with the degree of centralization of power.

A question arises as to the direction in which acculturation worked. Did the conquerors impose their language? Or were they assimilated culturally as happened elsewhere?

But at this level, it must be remembered that cultural and linguistic spaces do not coincide exactly. For example, the Bwa speak a Gur language, but are of Mande culture, like their Bobo neighbours, who speak a Mande language.

In an anthropological approach to the societies of the Volta basin, Guy Le Moal distinguishes the following groupings: Mossi, Gurunsi, Bobo, Mande and Senufo. He puts together under a common heading the peoples of the south-western part of present-day Burkina Faso.

With the Mossi must be associated pre-Mossi peoples such as the Kurumba who, in the kingdom of Lurum, had a political formation comprising some elements of centralized power initially based on the concept of 'divine kingship'. In Yatenga, the Kurumba (Fulse) belonged to the groups of 'people of the land', in the same way as the 'Maranse', who were of Songhay origin, or the Yarse or the Kambosi who were of Mande origin.

The Gurunsi are divided into the following six segmented peoples: Lela, Nuna, Kasena, Sisola, Ko and Puguli. They are associated with the Talensi, the Kunsasi and the Nakansi. Culturally, and often territorially autonomous these peoples were considered by neighbouring states to be tributary societies. The Bobo comprise essentially the Bwa (Bobo-Wule) and the Bobo proper (Bobo-Fing). In these societies, initiation linked to *do* worship played an important role, and political organization was based on autonomous village communities.

The Dafing (Marka) were scattered from the Suru valley, in the north, to the region of Bobo-Dyulaso, in the south. The Dafing were traders and warriors, Muslims with large minorities that had retained their traditional religion. They created numerous small centralized states.

The Karaboro, the Tusya, the Turka, the Gwê and the Wara were related to the Senufo. Thus the Tusya had a secret society, the *lo*, which had features similar to the *poro* of the Senufo. In the south-west, the Wile, the Dagari, the Birifo, the Lobi and the Dya came from present-day Ghana in successive waves from the sixteenth century. The Wile, who were the first to arrive, drove back the Puguli; they were followed by the Dagari, who had affinities with the Wile but whose descent system was bilateral, comparable to that of the Birifo.

The Wile, the Dagari and the Birifo had a language belonging to the Mossi group; one common characteristic they had was the importance assumed in their social life by secret initiation into the *bagre*. The Birifo and the Dya were culturally close to the Lobi among whom matrilineal elements were largely predominant, while initiation into the *poro* played an essential role in social control. All these peoples, unlike the Gurunsi, had no forms of centralized power.

The Fulbe of the Black Volta valley, the Suru valley, the Gondo plain, Jelgoji and Liptako, set up numerous chiefdoms, such as Barani, Jibo, Barabulle, Tongomayel and, later, the kingdom of Liptako.

The economic approach

In the savannah zone, agriculture was dominated by millet, which was replaced in the north by varieties of *fonio* and, in the south, by tubers. Cotton had been cultivated for a very long time; at the time of the establishment of the first Mossi kingdoms, weaving was widespread, with long loose garments being reserved for chiefs. A weaver is said to have made such clothes for Naaba Wubri. The Yarse, who had come from Mande, were associated with weaving. Dyeing, a Songhay speciality, was well-organized, thanks to indigo and *Anogeissus leicarpus*, giving a khaki-coloured dye. Cattle-rearing was the business of the Fulbe.

Yatenga exported donkeys to central and southern Mossi country, while the eastern zones were noted for the quality of their Dongolawi horses, introduced long before from Upper Egypt. Five races of horses have been identified: Yatenga, Jelgoji, and Kurumba country, the Gondo plane and Barani. Metal-working, favoured by the abundance of ores, and pottery industries, were practised in association. As for trade, it seems that when the Mossi arrived, it was already being conducted by the Yarse. The establishment of kingdoms simply developed it. Weaving was directly linked to the development of trade, as Yarse weavers and traders used cotton strips as local freight merchandise and also as currency in the north–south trade in which the north supplied block salt from the Sahara, but also dried fish and mats; the south mainly kola nuts and gold. Apart from barter, the currency was the cowrie and various other standards such as the cubit of cotton fabric, and horses being paid for in captives.

The smiths themselves conducted the trade in finished products (tools and weapons) or balls of iron. The history of settlement reveals the age of some of the trading centres. But in the absence of archaeological data, oral traditions, narrative accounts of the African *Ta'rikh* and extrapolation of information based on the texts of European travellers remain the principal sources of reconstituting the past of the Volta basin.

10 The Kingdoms and Peoples of Chad

In the twelfth century, the major part of the region of Lake Chad lay under the sway of a powerful kingdom, Kānem. Other kingdoms developed but most of the inhabitants lived in separate clans and ethnic groups. Kānem, known in very early times to Arab travellers and geographers, held sway between the Nuba of the Nile valley and the Kaw-Kaw of the Niger Bend. There are numerous sources for this empire, and it will be the main subject of this survey, but we must not forget all the other peoples who escaped the attention of the chroniclers.

The main internal source is the *Dīwān* of the sultans of Kānem-Borno, the origins of which go back to the first half of the thirteen century and which was constantly updated until the end of the Sēfuwa dynasty in the nineteenth century. In this modest manuscript containing half a dozen pages is to be found the dynastic history of Kānem-Borno. In addition, there are the records of al-Idrisi (1154), Ibn Saʿīd (d. 1286) and al-Maḳrīzī (d. 1442). These two series of records complement one another, the Africans being concerned mainly with the temporal framework, and the Arab geographers with the spatial dimension.

The Sēfuwa dynasty

The Zaghawa ruled Kānem until about the end of the eleventh century. The Sēfuwa were so named because they claimed descent from the Yemenite hero Ṣayf ben Dhi Yazan. The founder of the dynasty, Ḥummay (1078–80), seems to have come from a Berber family. In the time of al-Idrīsī, the inhabitants of Kawār wore the *litham* (*mulaththamūn*). The claim to a Yemeni ancestry is understandable among people who claimed to be North African Berbers to distinguish themselves from the Arabs of the region who claimed to be of Himyarite descent. But at the beginning of the thirteenth century, the trend shifted, and Ḥummay's genealogy was emptied of its Berber content and replaced with the Ḳurayshi ancestors of the tribe of the prophet; the aim then was to demonstrate their long fidelity to Islam.

Conversely, the need to appear rooted in Kānem meant that the thirteenth-century chroniclers' record of Salmama b. ʿAbd Allāh (c. 1182–1210), said that he was 'very dark', while Ibn Saʿīd writes: 'The sultan of Kanem . . . is Muhammadi ben Djabl, of the lineage of Sayf . . . The capital of his infidel ancestors, prior to their conversion to Islam, was Manan.' But Muḥammad was simply the name by which the great king Dūnama Dībalāmi (c. 1210–48) was known to the outside world. At that time, the Sēfuwa were considered to be the direct descendants of the Duguwa (Zag̲h̲āwa kings) despite the conversion and the change of capital. The fact is that this highly structured state, to which the *Dīwān* bears witness, probably dated back to the sixth century and had its political centre in Manan under the Duguwa for at least a century and in Djimi under the Sēfuwa for three centuries.

This change of capital doubtless also reflected a reversal in the balance of power in favour of the sedentary peoples at the expense of the semi-nomads of the Sahel. This 'de-Berberization' of the new dynasty can be seen in the evolution of the ethnic origins of the queen-mothers.

It can be observed that the Tomag̲h̲ra, who provided two queen-mothers in the Duguwa period, are not mentioned under the Sēfuwa. Yet these Tubu clans still survive today in Tibesti and Kawār.

In contrast, the Ḳay are mentioned in connection with both dynasties, which implies that their political status remained unchanged. Today, the Ḳay (Koyam) live on the edge of Borno, near the Komadugu Yoo. The Tubu appear in the *Dīwān* solely in connection with the Sēfuwa. Ḥummay's principal wife was Tubu, and it is likely that the Tubu contributed to the fall of the Duguwa. What was their relationship to the Zag̲h̲āwa whom the Arab authors located between Kānem and Nubia? Some Tubu (the Daza or Gorhan) still live in this area. But the true Tubu are in the mountains of Tibesti. (The word *tu-bu* is taken to mean 'inhabitant of the mountain'.)

The Dabīr (Dibbīri) and the Kunkuna mentioned in the *Dīwān* no longer exist today. They were mentioned in the nineteenth century by Nachtigal and Barth as old sedentary Kanembu people.

Lastly, the Magomi were the nucleus of a people (the Kanuri) which was gradually formed from the Sēfuwa dynasty; but this implies that the origin of the state of Kānem-Borno ante-dated that of the people who today form its main substratum.

Before the emergence of the Kanuri people, the Kānem kings derived their power from different nomadic and sedentary ethnic groups speaking sub-Saharan languages (Tubu, Zag̲h̲āwa and Kanuri) or Chad languages. Berber speaking groups, who were at times integrated into this group, as in the thirteenth century, seem always to have been in the minority. According to the *Dīwān*, there were three successive phases in the development and reinforcement of the ethnic base of the Sēfuwa kings.

The first phase extended from the advent of Ḥummay to the middle of the thirteenth century and saw the domination of two nomadic groups – the Tubu and the Ḳay. In the second phase, the sedentary Dabir and Kunkuna peoples became the main allies of the Sēfuwa. In the third phase, from the time of the Magomi mother of Dūnama Dībalāmi (c. 1210–48), the political power of the royal lineage of the Magomi became more firmly established. A century later, the *Dīwāh* ceased to indicate the ethnic origins of the queen-mothers, which suggests that by the beginning of the fourteenth century, the Magomi had eclipsed the other sedentary groups of Kānem. This might explain why Dūnama Dībalāmi, in whose reign the Magomi group rose to prominence, began a long war against the Tubu. It might also explain why the relatively peaceful period of succession from father to son came to an end when the Sēfuwa kings ceased to take foreign wives as their (principal) wives and married women from their own lineage.

Kānem at its zenith

Between the Lake Chad region and the Mediterranean there had existed, at least since Roman times, a direct route through the Fezzān and the oases of Kawār. To the east, there was also the very difficult trail through the Kufra oases and to the west the trail through Takedda or Agades. These trans-Saharan trade routes certainly influenced the growth of Kānem.

Political structure

Until the reign of Dūnama Dībalāmi, the royal clan occupied the premier position. From the thirteenth century, when there were open conflicts between the sultans and their sons, the latter were excluded in favour of foreigners or local chiefs. The titles of *yerima* (governor of the north) and *kayghamma* (governor of the south) probably date from the period of Borno.

The queen-mother and her clan played a major role even in the selection of a new sultan. Later, the king's first wife (the *gumsu*) became the most important wife, since the king designated his successor (the *shiroma*) from among her sons.

At the end of the fifteenth century, the Sēfuwa ruled over 12 vassal kingdoms. Direct administration, often entrusted to crown slaves, extended over a more limited area. The texts distinguish between a *djūnūd*, a soldier called up for a campaign, and an *ʿaṣākir*, or professional soldier.

Despite attempts to introduce the Muslim *sharīʿa*, as in the time of Idris Alawoma, justice seems to have been a royal prerogative, as it was with the *mansa* of Mali.

This political structure influenced people in neighbouring countries such as the Hausa, the Baghirmi and others.

Trade and commerce

The region to the west of Lake Chad was important for Kānem, situated as it was to the east of the lake. The principal objective was to control the trade out of Kawar. This trade had two dimensions: the massive export of salt from Bilma and Agram to the countries of the Sahel, on the one hand; and, on the other, according to al-Idrīsī, the lucrative export of alum (used in dyeing and tanning) to Egypt and the Maghrib.

But for trans-Saharan trade, the Fezzān had an importance far beyond that of Kawār. The Fezzān was strategically situated at the crossroads of the north–south route between Kānem and North Africa, on the one hand, and, on the other, the trails linking the empires of the southern fringes of the Sahara with Egypt and the Middle East. Security on the caravan routes and control of the staging posts were thus among the primary objectives of Kānem-Borno.

The structure of this trade varied hardly at all between the advent of Islam and the nineteenth century. Al-Yaʿḳūbī records that Berber traders brought numerous black slaves from Kawār to Zawīla, the capital of the Fezzān.

At the beginning of the sixteenth century, Leo Africanus tells us that North African traders travelled to Borno to exchange horses for slaves. The raids by the sultan of Borno against the non-Muslim peoples of the south did not suffice to meet the demand. And the inhabitants of Kānem-Borno themselves sometimes paid the price of this when the empire was weakened. At the end of the fourteenth century, in a letter to Sultan Baybars of Egypt, Bīr ben Idris complained that the Arabs were reducing his Muslim subjects to slavery.

Other products exported from Kānem were elephant tusks, ostrich feathers and live animals, such as the giraffe that Ibn Khaldūn records was sent by the 'sovereign of Kanem and lord of Bornu' to the Ḥafṣid sultan, al-Mustanṣir. Tin from the Nigerian plateau was also being exported through Borno to Tripoli at the least in the seventeenth century and probably earlier.

In reality, Kānem-Borno owed its prosperity far more to its agricultural and pastoral activities and mining than it did to the income derived from the slave trade; in addition there were craft products such as the embroidered garments mentioned by Ibn Baṭṭūṭa.

Imports consisted of war horses which were added to the horses of Kānem which al-Maḳrīzī describes as smaller. The chroniclers state that the cavalry of Dūnama Dībalāmi comprised 41,000 horses.

Manufactured goods such as garments and iron weapons were also imported. Al-Muhallabī tells us that the king of the Zaghāwa wore woollen and silk garments from Sūs (Sousse) although local weaving of cotton strips used as a standard of value was well-developed.

Finally, here as in Mali, copper from the Takedda was traded southwards.

The volume of trade depended on security on the routes. It was only guaranteed by three powers: in the north, the kingdom of the Fezzān, dominated by the Banū Khaṭṭāb Berbers; in the centre, the Berber chiefdoms of Kawār; in the south, Kānem. But in 1172, Sharīf al-Dīn Karakūsh, the Mamluk war leader, devastated the Fezzān. In order to restore order, Dūnama Dībalāmi (in the thirteenth century) seized Kawār and the Fezzān. This is confirmed by al-ʿUmarī in the fourteenth century: 'The empire of Kānem commences on the Egyptian side at a town called Zella [north-east of the Fezzān] and ends on the other side at a town called Kaka; a three-month journey separates these two towns.' Ibn Saʿīd specifies that the king of Kānem held the town of Takedda in the west and ruled over the Tādjuwa (Dadjo) and the Zaghāwa in the east. It would be rash, however, to see in this authority of the rulers of Kānem over remote marches a highly structured organization. For example, the Tubu of the Baḥr al-Ghazāl were probably independent. The peoples settled around Lake

Chad and on the lacustrine islands, some of whom are mentioned by al-Maḳrīzī (the Bāḍī, the Ankazār, the Kūrī), continued to defend their independence successfully.

The peoples of traditional religion such as the Afnū (a Kanuri name for the Hausa) and the Kotoko paid a heavy tribute in captives in raids by the kings of Kānem. In short, it was not in the interests of these latter to facilitate the expansion of Islam beyond certain limits, since slaves constituted the central Sudan's main input into trans-Saharan trade.

Even in Kānem, Islam did not take deep root before the thirteenth century. Contrary to what al-Maḳrīzī says, Dūnama Dībalāmi was not the first Muslim king of Kānem, since, according to the *Dīwān*, all the Sēfuwa were Muslims: and the second ruler of the dynasty, Dūnama b. Ḥummay (c. 1086–1140), is said to have performed the pilgrimage twice. It is likely rather than orthodox Islam only took deep root among the mass of the population in the time of Dūnama Dībalāmi. He was a great Muslim reformer. He destroyed the *mune*, a ritual object of a pre-Islamic royal cult. Imām Furṭū, following the authors of the *Dīwān*, criticized him for this action which is said to have caused a series of disturbances including a long war against the Tubu. Dūnama Dībalāmi surrounded himself with Muslim jurists, founded a *madrasa* in Cairo for the people of Kānem, and also waged relentless holy war on both the Berbers and the Blacks of traditional religion.

In the reign of Bir ben Dūnama (1277–96), there is mention of a visit to Kānem by two Fulbe (fellata) shaykhs from Mali. Al-ʿUmari mentions the minimal resources possessed by this empire, but praises on the contrary 'the ardent faith' and justice that reigned there.

The Fezzān was also probably still part of its territory, but Takedda had freed itself.

In fact, by the second half of the fourteenth century, chronic troubles had begun. And when, at the end of the century, the Bulala succeeded in conquering Kānem and breaking the empire's monopoly over trans-Saharan trade, it was the beginning of a dark period of decline for the Sēfuwa.

From Kānem to Borno

By the twelfth century, at the latest, a major movement of peoples was underway from the east to west of Lake Chad, i.e. to Borno. These included the Tomaghra, the Tūra, the Ḳay (Koyām), the oldest Magomi groups. This movement continued until the sixteenth century, in particular after the victorious campaigns of Idrīs Alawōma, with the departure from Kānem of numerous Tubu and Arabs, attracted by the more fertile and safer lands to the west.

There, autochthonous sedentary peoples lived, speaking Chad languages, who were given the collective name of Sao. The chroniclers record that in the middle of the fourteenth century four Sēfuwa kings fell in battle against the Sao. In the sixteenth century, Leo Africanus mentions their presence west of

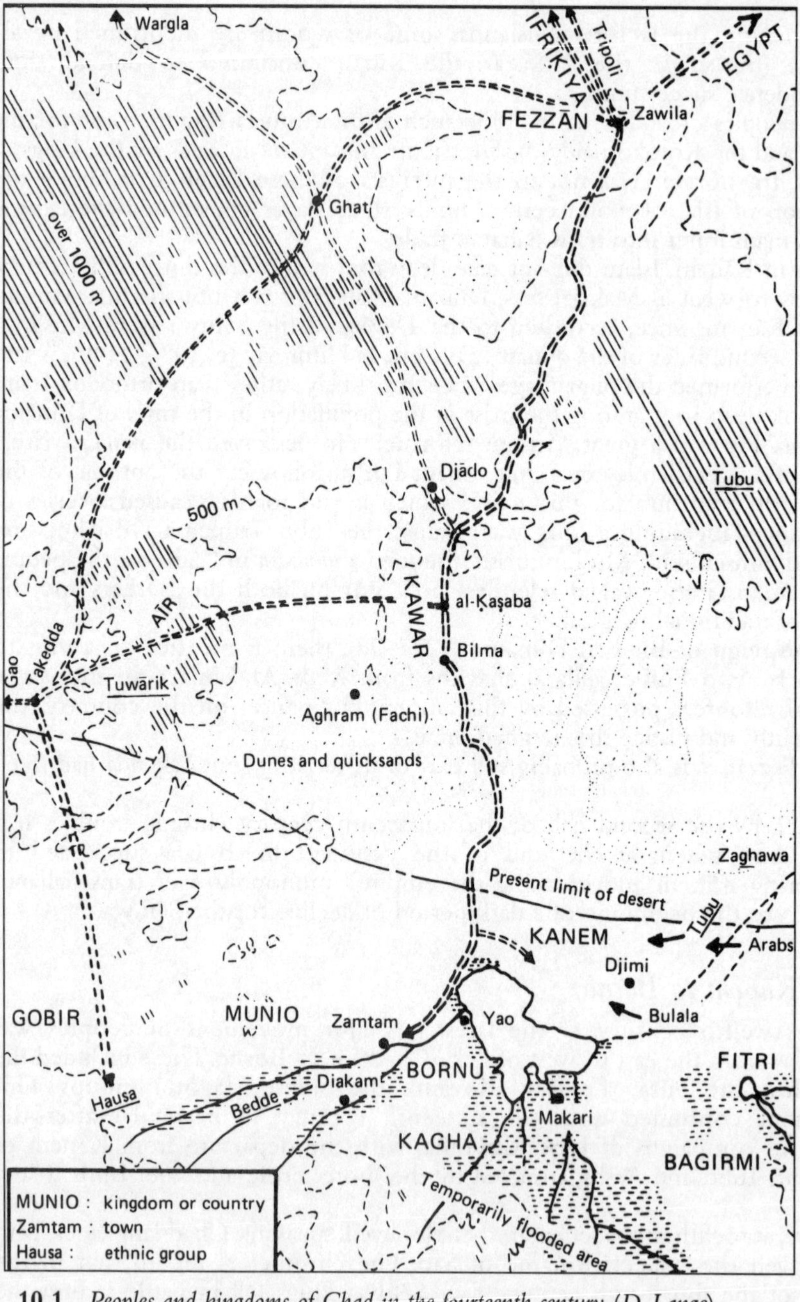

10.1 *Peoples and kingdoms of Chad in the fourteenth century.* (*D. Lange*)

Lake Chad and south of Borno. Idrīs Alawōma (1564–96) launched a series of murderous attacks on them which forced them from their ancestral homes; some took refuge on the islands in the lake.

From the end of the thirteenth century, Borno began to gain in importance. It is very likely that it had existed as an independent kingdom before then with a capital mentioned by al-Maghribī Ibn Saʿīd named Djadja. The Arab authors moreover always distinguish the two powers. Al-Makrīzī writes that Ibrāhīm ben Bir (1296–1315) held the thrones of Kānem and Borno. Ibn Khaldū speaks of the 'sovereign of Kanem and lord of Bornu'.

In the middle of the fourteenth century, Al-ʿUmarī mentions that the Mamluk sultans of Egypt exchanged letters with both the king of Kānem and the king of Borno. All these pieces of evidence suggest that Kānem and Borno were initially two separate kingdoms, but from the thirteenth century on were brought under the rule of the Sēfuwa, whose suzerainty over Borno did not prevent this latter enjoying a degree of autonomy.

This situation was radically altered when the attacks by the Bulala and the Arabs forced the Sēfuwa to abandon Kānem and settle finally in Borno. The Bulala, who were a pastoral people settled initially in the region of Lake Fitri, and ruled over the Kuba there, seem to have been driven westward by the Arab migration following the dislocation of the Christian kingdom of Nubia at the beginning of the fourteenth century. But they were also attracted westward by the weakening of the power of the Sēfuwa consequent upon dynastic conflicts, particularly between Dāwūd ben Ibrāhīm Nikale (fourteenth century) and the sons of his brother and predecessor, Idrīs. Dāwūd and his three successors fell in battle against the Bulala. ʿUmār ben Idrīs (1382–87) had to evacuate Djimī and it was only at the beginning of the fifteenth century that the threat from these redoubtable foes was finally averted by the Sēfuwa.

Al-Makrīzī echoes these events when he says that in about 800 (1400) the people of Kānem revolted against these kings and renounced the faith. Borno remained true to the faith and waged holy war against the people of Kānem. But the *Dīwān* does not confirm that the Bulala were 'pagans'; on the contrary, the new Bornoan empire of the Sēfuwa with Kaka as the new capital was the new big political reality of the central Sudan.

The Bulala established a powerful empire in Kānem, known to Leo Africanus by the name of Gaoga. It was allied with the Tubu and the Arabs, and maintained excellent relations with the caliph of Egypt. It was only at the beginning of the sixteenth century that Borno recaptured Djimi from the Bulala, who were later finally crushed by Idrīs Alawōma.

Dynastic and political crises

The *Dīwān* informs us about the successive reigns in Kānem-Borno and the genealogical relationships between the various kings. It follows that the election of a ruler probably depended partly on a favourable balance of power, but above all on the legitimacy conferred on him by unwritten rules, precedents and customs which imposed a decision in his favour more certainly than a written code. These rules varied only over long periods or as a result of serious upheavals.

But the first six kings succeeded one another from father to son. This mode of succession seems to have originated from the chiefs of Kawār, the probable ancestors of Ḥummay, who founded the new Sēfuwa dynasty.

It was under the son of Dūnama Dībalāmi that the first collateral succession (from brother to brother) occurred. Kaday and Bir, both sons of Dūnama, but by different mothers, for the first time created factions, so the *Dīwān* tells us; behind these clashes probably lay the rivalry between the royal lineage of the Magomi and the sedentary lineages of Kānem. Moreover, it should be noted that Kaday died in battle against one of the great vassals of the empire. After the reign of his brother Bir, the son of this latter, Ibrāhīm Nikale (c. 1296–1315), succeeded according to the old rule, but died fighting another great vassal.

He was followed by a son of Kaday, ʿAbd Allāh, who was succeeded by his own son. Thus, until the beginning of the fourteenth century, the old rule of succession in the direct line was broken only by resorting to violence.

Subsequently, collateral succession increasingly prevailed. Four sons of ʿAbd Allāh followed one another on the throne before relinquishing power to a grandson of Bir, Idris ben Ibrāhīm Nikāle, who succeeded in conciliating the indigenous Sao. On his death, it was one of his brothers, Dāwūd, who was chosen; but his sons fought bitterly against their uncle. There was a civil war, which facilitated the expansion of the Bulala. The two rival factions, the Dāwūdids and the Idrīsids, succeeded one another in power chiefly on the collateral principle, but also depending on the political imperatives of the moment. It was in this context that a non-Sēfuwa, Saʿīd (c. 1387–88), succeeded ʿUmār after the latter had moved from Kānem to Borno.

The Idrīsids and Dāwūdids were increasingly supplanted by individuals from outside the royal clan, in particular the great officials: the *kayghamma* (chief of the army) and the *yerima* (governor) who had no hesitation in removing one another, manipulating the oscillation of power as they pleased. Moreover, it was during the reign of Bir ʿUthmān (c. 1389–1421), after the Bulala had been driven back by the army, that the *kayghamma* turned this service to account to make his political weight felt. The upheavals thus engineered continued, some kings not lasting more than year on the throne.

It was only in the middle of the fifteenth century, after a century of storms that the Dāwūdids were finally eliminated. But the principle of collateral succession that was now established led to tensions within the Idrīsid clan itself. Thus ʿAlī Ghadjideni (c. 1465–97), who had won the victory over the Dāwūdids, had to leave the throne to his brothers before finally acceding to it himself. He built the new Sēfuwa capital, which remained so for three centuries, at Gazargamo, situated between Kano and Lake Chad. But after him, there was a return to succession in the direct line from father to son, which took Borno full circle back to the earliest days of the Sēfuwa dynasty.

11 *The Hausa and their Neighbours in the Central Sudan*

Hausaland extends from the Air mountains in the north to the Jos plateau in the south and from Borno in the east to the Niger valley in the west. *Kasar hausa* ('the country of the Hausa language') was the name given to the region, although non-Hausa peoples such as the Tuareg, the Zabarma (Djerma) and the Fulbe were also settled there. The brilliant civilization that was to develop here owed a great deal to this cultural assimilation through language which inevitably facilitated the homogenization of customs and political institutions to make it one of the most important ethnic groups in Africa.

Hausa origins

There are four main theories abut the origins of the Hausa:

The first theory, now abandoned, based on an erroneous interpretation of the Bayajida (or Daura) legend, claims that the ancestors of the Hausa were Arabs from Baghdad. According to Abdullahi Smith, if the Bayajida legend means anything, it is the influence of Borno on the political institutions of the Hausa, as is shown by the Kanuri words in the Hausa vocabulary.

The second theory maintains that the Hausa peoples were originally settled in the southern Sahara and moved southwards as it became a desert, pushing back the autochthonous peoples to the Bauchi plateau where the linguistic picture is different from Hausa. This second thesis is plausible but it is not backed by any factual data. It is only a hypothesis.

The third thesis asserts that the ancestors of the Hausa were the inhabitants of the western shore of Lake Chad, and when the lake began to shrink, they settled as sedentary cultivators on the land thus freed, spreading northward and westward from a nucleus constituted by the kingdoms of Daura, Kano, Rano and Garun Gobas, to include Katsina, Zazzau, Gobir, Zamfara and Kebbi. But there is no decisive proof to confirm this thesis.

The fourth thesis, proposed by Mahdi Adamu, stresses the autochthonous character of the Hausa people, based on the fact that no section of it has any tradition of migration. It is said that 'the ancestors came out of holes in the ground'. The original groups later benefited greatly, of course, from the immigration of Wangarawa (Wangara, Dyula) and Fulbe peoples. Naturally the process of ethnogenesis is difficult to reconstruct, but there is nothing to disprove it; and it is likely that, in very ancient times, this original home of the Hausa included parts of the Sahara, in particular Air (Azbin) conquered in the fourteenth and fifteenth centuries by the Tuareg who pushed the Hausa back towards Gobir. The term Hausa moreover only appeared in about the sixteenth century. Until then, the inhabitants were described by the names of kingdoms: Katsinawa, Kanawa, Gobirawa and so on. The Egyptian al-Suyūtī (1445–1505) used the term 'Hausa' in his *Epistles to the Kings of the Sudan, Hausa and al-Takrur*. The authors of the Timbuktu *Ta'rikh* regularly employed the term to refer to the left bank of the Niger in contrast to Gurma.

Originally, the term Hausa referred to the language, the inhabitants describing themselves as 'Hausawa' (meaning speakers of the Hausa language). Later and by a process of restriction, the term served to describe those living near the Songhay empire who directly represented the Hausa collectivity, that is the former kingdoms of Zamfara, Kebbi and Gobir. The non-Muslims, who were yet Hausa-speakers were called Maguzawa, or Azna, that is 'pagans' (from the Arabic *mādjūs*). That shows the relatively recent character of the ethnonym Hausa. We shall use the term Hausa to describe all the Hausa-speaking peoples without exception.

The birth and evolution of the Hausa states

According to the common legend, Prince Bayajida came from Baghdad and received an ambiguous reception from the *mai* (king of Kanem-Borno) which led him to flee westward. He came to a town which was ruled by a queen, Daura, but terrorized by a snake. After killing the snake, he married the queen who gave him a son, Bawogari, while a concubine gave him another son, Karbogari.

Bawogari had six sons who became the chiefs of Kano, Daura, Gobir, Zazzau (Zaria), Katsina and Rano respectively. Together with Biram, which was ruled by the son of the Borno princess, these seven states were called the *hausa bakwai*. The sons of Karbogari founded another seven states: Kebbi, Zamfara, Gwari, Jukun (Kwararafa), Yoruba, Nupe and Yawuri, the so-called *banza bakwai* (the 'seven bastards').

This legend surely reflects a real situation – the situation in the sixteenth century, when the seven states that had survived the surrounding conflicts legitimized themselves by a legend claiming a prestigious eastern ancestry. But the proof that it was not a civilizing hero who brought centralized government to the area is that when Bayajida arrived in Daura, he found a queen there already. Furthermore, the late origin of the story also emerges from the fact that mention is made in it of the division of functions among the Hausa cities.

Kano and Rano were *sarakunan babba* (kings of indigo), Katsina and Daura *sarakunan kasuwa* (kings of the market), Gobir *sarkin yaki* (the king of war) and, finally, Zaria was *sarkin bayi* (the king of slaves), according to the roles played by these cities in dyeing, trade, defence or the supply of servile labour. This nomenclature described the general situation.

The appearance of centralized states seems to have been linked with the foundation of fortified cities called *birane* (sing. *birni*).

Kano

The history of Kano is the best known because of its chronicles and wealth of oral tradition. Initially, there were small ritual chiefdoms, for example at Dala. It is estimated that the entry of Bagauda into the Kano area occurred in 999. It was his grandson, Gijimasu (1095–1134), who founded Kano at the foot of Dala hill. He started to build the city walls which were completed by his son, Tsaraki (1136–94).

Under Yaji (1349–85) the process of subjugating and integrating the surrounding population was completed, although not without difficulties. Even Rano was conquered the never regained its full independence. Even the resistance of Santolo was put down thanks to the support of Muslim Wangarawa who had recently arrived. This traditional religious centre was razed. The opposition to the regime of Kano, which is depicted as an anti-Islamic resistance, is better seen as the reaction of notables or popular groups against the process of despotic concentration of powers. The expansion of Kano was directed southwards and this led to a first clash with the forces of Kwararafa/Jukun. The outcome of the battle was indecisive; the Jukun refused to pay tribute, but delivered a single consignment of slaves.

Kananeji (1390–1410) continued the policy of expansion and subdued Zaria. External contacts were stepped up, as shown by the introduction of *lifidi* (the quilted protection for war-horses), iron helmets and coats of mail. Under Dauda (1421–38), the arrival of a refugee Borno prince brought more sophisticated concepts of administration, as well as trumpets and flags. Borno titles such as *galadima, chiroma* and *kaigama* came into use in Kano.

From this period, the commercial activities of the Kanawa became increasingly more important than acts of war. A trans-African route was opened between Borno and Gonja. There were more and more caravans of camels laden with Saharan salt, more and more convoys of kola nuts and eunuchs. The prosperity and progress of Islam attracted religious figures. In about 1450, Fulbe from Mali brought 'books of divinity', whereas formerly only books on law and the traditions had existed. The end of the century witnessed the arrival of a number of *s͟hārīfs*, followed by the uncompromising reformer, al-Mag͟hīlī.

The *Kano Chronicle* (translated by H. R. Palmer, 1909) ascribes to Muḥammad Rumfa (1463–99) a number of important innovations: the extension of the city walls, the appointment of eunuchs to political offices, the establishment of the great market and the setting up of a council of nine leading state office-holders (*tara-ta-Kano* 'the Nine of Kano') who formed a kind of cabinet. Some of these innovations suggest copying of what was happening in neighbouring Borno: the construction of a new palace (*gidan Rumfa*), the use of long trumpets and ostrich-feather fans, the establishment of a harem with 1,000 wives and the splendour of the festivities marking the end of Ramāḍān (*ʿId al-fiṭr*). Yet Kano still had to pay a humiliating tribute to Borno and to wage a hundred years' war against Katsina.

Katsina

Katsina's development seems to have closely parallelled that of Kano, but with a time-lag. There too, small chiefdoms, including that at Durbi, came together to form the city-state. From the time of *Sarki* (king) Muḥammad Korau (1445–95) we are on firmer historical ground. Korau built the walled city (*birni*) of Katsina at the meeting point of several trade routes, near an iron-mine and a shrine, known as Bawada.

The neighbouring chiefs came to pay tributes in the form of iron bars, and this was the beginning of *haraji* or poll-tax.

From this base, Korau, the first Muslim ruler, launched expeditions to enlarge his territory southwards, built the Gobarau mosque, modelled on the mosques of Gao and Jenne, and received al-Maghīlī.

The *Katsina Chronicle* records mainly the war against Nupe.

Among Korau's successors, Ibrāhīm Sura (1453–99) fought against those who refused to accept Islam and corresponded with al-Suyūṭī. After him ʿAlī, whose long reign covered the first quarter of the sixteenth century, was called *murābiṭ*, perhaps to commemorate his fortification of the city.

Zaria

Here, the historical materials are even more limited. Over a period lasting perhaps a millennium, and starting from Turunku, the chiefs brought together or annexed neighbouring territories before settling on the site of Zaria, probably at the end of the fifteenth century. Such is Abdullahi Smith's view. Murray Last presents a different scenario. He suggests that as early as the end of the thirteenth century a Kangoma federation of non-Hausa groups existed, the heir to the Nok culture and based on trade in metals. When this federation broke up, a kingdom of Kangoma took over the Turunku. And it was only in the seventeenth century that the Hausa came to rule Zaria. This is a very bold hypothesis.

Abdullahi Smith puts his position by saying that about the end of the fourteenth century, several towns including Turunku and Kufena appeared in this area. They remained independent until the time when Bakwa of Turunku seized power at Kufena near which was built the new capital, called Zaria after a daughter of Bakwa. It was her sister, Amīna, a true amazon, who led the armies of Zaria as far as Nupe country and Kwararafa. In the *Kano Chronicle* it is stated that 'the *Sarkin Nupe* sent her [the princess] forty eunuchs and 10,000 kola nuts. She was the first in Hausaland to own eunuchs and kola nuts'. Amīna is also said to have fortified Zaria and Kufena. She was a leading *gimbiya* (princess), but she was never a queen.

Gobir

Gobir was the northernmost state whose original territory included the Air massif. The Gobirawa were pushed back by the Tuareg into the plains of Adar and towards present-day Gobir, taking with them salt as an ordinary commodity and maize, after having halted before the fifteenth century in a kingdom situated in present-day Niger with its capital at Marandet. This commercial and industrial centre based on trans-Saharan trade is known from the ninth century. Gobir was naturally the defender of Hausaland's northern borders.

Rano

This kingdom is presented as having existed since the eleventh century, before it was annexed by Kano. In fact the *Kano Chronicle* does not record this state before the fifteenth century. There was a Hausa chiefdom of Zamnagaba, which was perhaps connected to Santolo and was conquered at the end of the reign of *Sarkin* Yaji (1349–85). Perhaps Zamnagaba should replace Rano in the list of *hausa bakwai*.

Zamfara

It was only in the sixteenth century that this political entity clearly emerged. In the beginning, there were a few chiefdoms, including Dutsi, Togno and Jata, in which an administration developed near iron ore and hills with traditional altars. Dutsi took the lead in the process of centralization. The establishment of Birnin Zamfara dates from the middle of the sixteenth century when this state sent out numerous expeditions, for example as far as Yawuri in the Niger basin.

Kebbi

The people of Kebbi, says Muḥammad Bello, are descended from a Katsina mother and a Songhay father. In the time of Sunni ʿAlī (1464–92) there were, in this area that had fallen under Songhay control, clan chiefs (*magaji*) who were soon eclipsed by an immigrant from Katsina, Muḥammadu Kanta. He was a great military leader who became the master of this province of the Songhay empire whose army he joined. On his return from the campaign against the Sultan of Agades, discontented with his share of the spoils, he broke away, and encouraged resistance to Songhay by building a series of fortifications culminating in the fortress of Birnin Kebbi, he founded the nation-state of Kebbi.

He seized Air (Agades) from Songhay control. According to Muḥammad Bello, he conquered the whole of Hausaland and parts of Borno, and also invaded southwards as far as Nupe. All these exploits did not result in a centralized empire but in a network of tributary territories. In the sixteenth century, Kebbi was a great power counterbalancing Songhay in the west and Borno in the east. Borno was crushed when it attempted to subdue Kebbi, but Kanta died on his return from a victorious campaign, in 1556. The Hausa states then shook off the yoke and helped Agades to free itself. Kebbi reverted to its previous status of a local kingdom.

In short, between 1200 and 1600 the Hausa people organized themselves into powerful city-states playing an important and sometimes primary role in the central Sudan economically, politically and militarily.

Relations of the Hausa with neighbouring peoples

Among the non-Hausa peoples who were the partners and adversaries of the Hausa people should be mentioned the Jukun, the Kwararafa, the Yoruba, the Nupe and the Yawuri, and of course the two great neighbours, Borno and Songhay.

The Hausa called the inhabitants of Kānem-Borno (Kānembu, Kanuri) *Beriberi*. Through their leaders, merchants and clerics, the cultural influence of Kānem-Borno transmitted numerous elements that are today inseparable from Hausa civilization. These inflows were above all decisive with the transfer of Sēfuwa power from Kānem to Borno and from the second half of the fifteenth century with the return of stability in Borno and the establishment of Ngazargumu. ʿUthmān Kalnama, a Borno refugee in Kano, played an important role there in the first half of the fifteenth century. Borno reacted by reducing numerous Hausa towns to vassal status, although this relationship needs further research.

But the principal channel for the influences of Borno was Kano, while Kebbi under Kanta took the lead in the Hausa counter-attack, even liberating some Hausa city-states from Borno's tutelage.

In the west there was essentially Songhay, since Mali now exercised only religious and commercial influence. Historians long believed that Askiya Muḥammad (1492–1528) had invaded and subjugated the whole of Hausaland. But the only source for this episode was the account of Leo Africanus. Yet the *Kano Chronicle* is absolutely silent on this point, whereas it willingly acknowledges invasions by smaller states. Furthermore, the Timbuktu *Taʾrīkhs*, which tell the tale from the Songhay point of view, do not say a word about this alleged invasion. There are good grounds therefore for rejecting Leo Africanus' account.

The Jukun were established in the south-east of Hausaland, along the middle Benue. In their time they played a much more important role than their present numbers would lead one to believe. Some say they came from the Nile valley and Kordofan at the same time as the Kanuri, but it is much more likely that they came from nearer, passing between Lake Chad and the Mandara highlands. But linguistically they belong to the Benue-Congo sub-family like Ibibio and Efik, which would rather suggest a southern origin. In short, they may have been the last wave of a series of migratory movements from the north-east.

Some argue that the first main power base of the Jukun was in the south, on the middle Benue. The ruins of Kwararafa survive there to this day; as do those of Wukari which succeeded it at the end of the eighteenth century. It was there that the Jukun moved north, especially to Kasar Chiki whose traditions confirm this southern origin.

But another theory claims rather that Jukun political power was first organized in the Gongola valley and the upper Benue basin before moving southwards.

These two theories are not incompatible if it is accepted that the Jukun had two political bases. Some of the attacks on the Hausa states from the Gongola valley may have been ordered by the *aku* (the Jukun king) established in the south where the largest concentration of power lay.

It may even be that there were two Jukun states, one called Kwana by the Kanuri and based in the north, and the other mentioned in the fourteenth century by the *Kano Chronicle* and which was situated further south. What is certain is that between 1200 and 1600, the Jukun were settled on the middle Benue and in the Gongola valley. They had a powerful state which reached its peak at the end of the sixteenth century; but its cultural influence also marked many ethnic groups of the region, such as the Igala, the Idoma and a number of others.

Nupe was on the edge of the forest, like a bridge towards it at the Niger–Benue confluence. It was a country that was naturally a meeting-point. Its mythical founding hero was Tsoede, but before him there was the Beni confederacy made up of five clans, including the Ebe, the Bini etc. There must have been kings before Tsoede who stands out rather as the figure who symbolizes the process of monarchical centralization, which must probably be dated to the sixteenth century, although references to Nupe in the Hausa sources go back to the fifteenth century. A supra-ethnic culture assimilating external elements that had come from Yoruba territory, Borno and Igala proved to be extremely dynamic. The kings of Nupe established diplomatic and commercial contacts with many neighbouring states, and especially the Hausa cities.

The inhabitants of Bauchi, a country situated south of Hausaland, were important partners for the Hausa. Apart from the Kambari, they were small ethnic groups. Relations seem to have consisted mainly in Hausa migrations into these territories either to take refuge there or for trading or military purposes. Numerous Hausa ended up being culturally absorbed into these peoples. The area also served as a favoured territory for slave raiding. Only the Kambari and Kamuku among the Bauchi peoples seem to have established centralized government. The Kambari did so at Maginga in the thirteenth century, while Hausa rule only came at the end of the fourteenth century. As for the Kamuku, it may be possible to identify them with the kingdom of Kankuma mentioned by al-Maḳrīzī.

Major developments in Hausaland

Immigration

Migrants came into Hausaland mainly from the north, from Borno in the east and from Mali and Songhay in the west. They were herdsmen, fishermen, agriculturalists, traders, scholars (*mallams*), clerics and princes.

The herdsmen were mainly Fulbe, followed by Tuareg. The Fulbe came from the west. They first reached Katsina in the fifteenth century. Shortly afterwards, the *Kano Chronicle* records their arrival in the following terms:

> In Yak'ubu's time (1452–63) the Fulani [Fulbe] came to Hausaland from Melle, bringing with them books on divinity and etymology . . . The Fulani [Fulbe] passed by and went to Bornu, leaving a few men in Hausaland, together with some slaves and people who were tired of journeying.

In fact the vast majority of these Fulbe were shepherds in search of new grazing lands who remained faithful to their traditional religion. They were very numerous especially in the central region of Kano, northern Katsina and the Rima valley (Kebbi). The Muslim clerics were concentrated in the towns.

The Tuareg arrived from Air in the late fourteenth century, pushing the autochthonous Hausa southwards and establishing the sultanate of Agades. The Tuareg, being essentially nomads, did not settle; they exchanged cattle or craft products for agricultural commodities and engaged in raids on sedentary peoples.

Migrations from Borno began at a very early date; but it is only in the fifteenth century that they are mentioned in written documents. Immigration developed above all before 1600 and was made up of refugee aristocrats, scholars and merchants who settled chiefly in Kano, Katsina and Zaria.

The Wangarawa (Dyula) also arrived from the west in the fourteenth and fifteenth centuries. They were predominantly merchants and settled in Kano, Yandoto and Kuyambana and were ultimately absorbed into the Hausa social system.

Groups of Songhay fishermen also came from the west and settled in the lower Rima valley. They had superior equipment. But they eventually merged completely into the Hausa people, thus creating the western marches of Hausaland.

Finally, there was the arrival of Arab and Berber merchants and scholars who had come from Timbuktu or North Africa from the second half of the fifteenth century and who settled chiefly in Kano, attracted by the prosperity and the adoption of Islam.

Emigration

But people were also leaving Hausaland, moving southwards and westwards, and had been doing so since time immemorial. The southward movement was, for example, associated with military campaigns launched by Kano and Katsina against the non-Hausa peoples of Bauchi, Gongola, Jukun and Yawuri. The sieges and 'pacification' operations took time. Numerous non-military Hausa followed the troops for trade or for various religious or social services. Many never returned home. Thus the Kuyambana area of southern Katsina established Hausa rule in Yawuri in the second half of the fourteenth century. Kanawa also reached Borno in the fifteenth century. But the great expansion of the Hausa diaspora in West Africa came only after the sixteenth century.

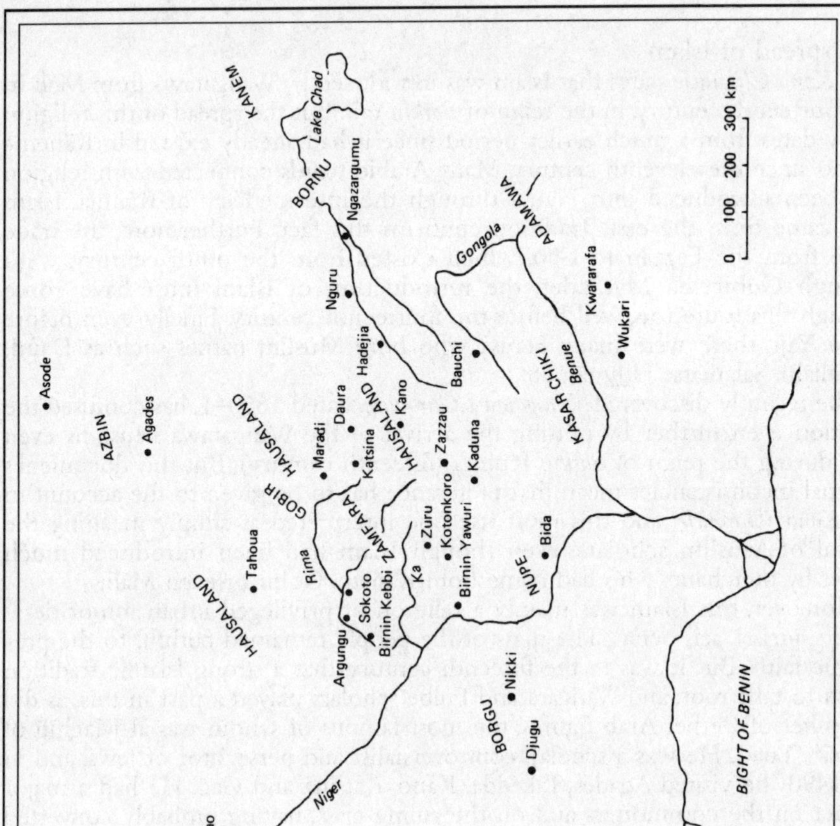

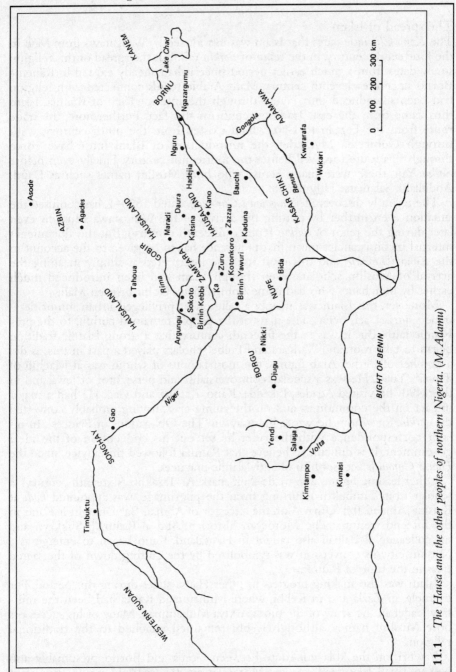

11.1 *The Hausa and the other peoples of northern Nigeria. (M. Adamu)*

The spread of Islam

The *Kano Chronicle* states that Islam was introduced by Wangarawa from Mali in the fourteenth century, in the reign of *Sarkin* Yaji. But the spread of this religion surely dates from a much earlier period since it had already existed in Kānem-Borno since the eleventh century. Many Arabic words connected with religion had been introduced into Hausa through the intermediary of Kanuri. Islam thus came from the east. Tradition confirms this fact. Furthermore, the trade route from the Fezzān to Gao, which existed from the ninth century, went through Gobir via Marandet; the introduction of Islam must have come through this route too, well before the fourteenth century. Finally, even before *Sarkin* Yaji, there were many Hausa who bore Muslim names such as Daud, Abdūllaḥi, Salamata, ʿUt͟hmān etc.

The recently discovered *Wangarawa Chronicle*, dated 1650–1, has confused the situation even further by putting the arrival of the Wangarawa Muslims even later during the reign of *Sarkin* Rumfa (fifteenth century). But this document's internal inconsistencies mean that preference has to be given to the account in the *Kano Chronicle*; and this must itself be interpreted as simply meaning the arrival of Muslim scholars, even though Islam had been introduced much earlier by merchants who had come from Kānem, Gobir or even Mali.

Moreover, this Islam was mainly a religion of privileged urban minorities – traders, jurists, aristocrats. The mass of the people remained faithful to the pre-Islamic faith. But it was in the fifteenth century that a strong Islamic tradition began to take root, and Wangara and Fulbe scholars played a part in this, as did a number of Berber Arab figures, the most famous of whom was al-Mag͟hīlī of Tūwāt (Tūāt). He was a scholar, controversialist and persecutor of Jews, and in the 1490s he visited Agades, Takedda, Kano, Katsina and Gao. He had a major impact on the commoners and on the ruling class, having probably converted the *sarkin*, for whom he wrote his essay on 'The Obligations of Princes'. In his later correspondence with the ruler he set out his conception of the ideal government. It is difficult to believe that Rumfa followed this advice, since the *Hausa Chronicle* accuses him of anti-Islamic practices.

Other leading figures also made their mark. Al-Tazak͟hti (sixteenth century), a scholar from Timbuktu returning from the pilgrimage, was appointed *kādī* at Katsina. Ahmad Ibn ʿUmar Aḳit, the ancestor of Aḥmad Baba, taught it Kano in the fifteenth century. The Moroccan historian ʿAbd al-Raḥmān Suḳḳayn and his colleague al-Balbalī also taught in Hausaland. Kano began to emerge as a Muslim city; its conversion was symbolized by the cutting down of the sacred trees in the time of Rumfa.

Islam was also making progress in other Hausa states during this period. For example, in Zaria and in Kebbi, where Muḥammad Kanta had been the military leader in the army of the pious Askiya Muḥammad. Many of his successors bore Muslim names, although Kebbi remained attached to the traditional religion.

Yawuri, on the kola-nut route between Gonja and Borno, presumably also had its small Islamized groups. Moreover, up to a certain point, this Islam adapted itself to the religious views and earlier socio-cultural practices of the Hausa; this was the price it paid to get accepted and make progress. That is why, even though the elite of scholars and their pupils observed Islam in its purity, many syncretic forms prevailed among the masses.

In the political sphere, Islam contributed to the process of centralizing power, by dismantling the traditional structure based on the control of traditional places of worship. The *Kano Chronicle*, which presents the official viewpoint of the Muslim rulers, is full of stories recording the resistance of local chiefs depicted as 'unbelievers'. These notables, opposed to centralization in the hands of the Muslim rulers of Kano, had to watch the massive and systematic destruction of their places and objects of worship. Santolo was the last of these sanctuaries to be destroyed.

Finally, the influx of Muslim scholars meant the arrival of new ideas, the spread of literacy in Arabic (the *ajami* system). Commercial and administrative management benefited from these developments.

Political and administrative organization

The two basic features of the organizational form common to the Hausa states were, first, the identical socio-cultural base marked by a common language and, second, the influence of Kānem-Borno which long constituted the model of civilization. Despite the raids by Borno and the tribute it exacted, it was never looked upon as an enemy in the same way that Songhay or Kwararafa were.

The Hausa also created a symbiosis established from their own original circumstances. At the base of the pyramid was the family clan (*gida*). At the next level came the village and its chief (*sarkin gari*). At the apex was the fortified city ruled by a *sarkin kasa* (chief of the 'country'). These fortified cities typical of the country had a growing role as socio-political catalysts thanks to the abundance of farming and craft resources, to long-distance trade and finally, to the guaranteed protection in the event of conflict.

Their cosmopolitan population was a factor of innovation. The *sarkin* (king), whose person was sacred, was responsible for the general welfare and had absolute power shared with a few officials of his lineage or closely related lineages. A council of state was responsible for advising the ruler and choosing his successor. In Gobir it was called *tara ta Gobir*, 'the nine of Gobir' and in Kano (*tara ta Kano*), 'the Kano nine'. Crown slaves played an increasing role in household and state offices.

The office of *galadima*, a sort of vizier, was sometimes entrusted to the heir apparent. A powerful *galadima* could make the *sarkin* a puppet; he controlled a host of dignitaries and officials ranked in a hierarchy.

It was above all from about 1530 that the centralization of power accelerated with Islam, the growth of the slave trade and the influence of crown slaves in the state machinery, which tended to weaken the previous power of the lineages. Rumfa's innovations (the seizure of property and women, the right to mobilize subjects for forced labour) illustrate these far-reaching changes in the social structure.

Economic development

Hausaland had considerable economic resources.

Deposits of iron ore were exploited that were close to wooded areas so that the necessary firewood was readily available. Archaeological research confirms the *Kano Chronicle* on this point. The rich soils made agriculture far and away the most important activity throughout the Hausa states. Despite the absence of historical statistics, the number of villages and towns suggests that Hausaland was densely populated and that the population was evenly distributed. Furthermore, the geographical position of Hausaland in the Sudan between the east and west of this vast area and also between the desert and the forest, gave it an advantage for all types of trade in every direction. That is why trade and crafts developed early in this area.

But although he was particularly well-equipped in these areas, each Hausa was first and foremost a farmer. Land belonged to the community and was never sold. Each individual enjoyed only the usufruct of it under the supervision of the chief of the community. With the growing centalization and personalization of power, the *sarkin* began to assign land to individuals. The farmers were placed under a 'chief of crops' (*Sarkin noma*) who was responsible for watching the rhythms of the seasons and performing the rituals necessary to ensure a good harvest.

Eventually, three kinds of farm came to prevail: the *gandum sarkin* the king's field, characterized by its large size; the *gandum gide*, the family field; and lastly, *gayauna*, the individual field. Slave labour played a major role on the *gandum sarkin* as well as on the large estates of the state dignitaries. In the reign of the *Sarkin* of Kano ʿAbdullāh Burja (1438–52), thousands of slaves lived in Kano and its environs, and most of them were certainly employed in agriculture. The main crops were millet, sorghum, fonio and rice (particularly in Kebbi and the western districts). Cotton and indigo were grown as commercial crops.

Handicrafts were the second key sector in the Hausa economy which had reached an advanced degree of specialization. The leading place was occupied by the textile and dyeing industry, followed by leather working which produced a vast range of articles sold as far away as North Africa.

Smiths renowned for their skill produced all the weapons and implements and utensils that the community needed from iron ores (*marmara*) Pottery developed similarly.

Most of the craft occupations were governed by guilds, each of which had a leader appointed by the king, occasionally on the nomination of members. They exercised control over production methods, standards of workmanship, prices and admission to the guild. The preferred venue for commerce was the market fair (*kasuwa*) and the person in charge of the market (the *sarkin kasuwa*) with his assistants, kept order, settled disputes and collected taxes, both in money and in kind. The market was also a focus of social life and a place for social meetings.

The Hausa drew a clear distinction between local trade, regional trade and

From Casamance to Mount Kakulima

Immediately to the south of Senegambia in the network of inlets and estuaries of Casamance and the Rio Cacheu live the Balante, the Dyola (Diola, Joola) and the Felupe. The Bainuk are considered to be autochthonous; the Biafada and the Landuma were under the rule of the Mande *mansa* until the middle of the sixteenth century, when they became autonomous chiefdoms. The Biafada clashed with the Bijago who lived on fortified islands and raided the mainland right up to the nineteenth century. Their large boats could carry up to 120 people.

Inland, from the upper Gambia to the foothills of the Futa Jallon, the Tenda peoples (the Bassari, Koniagi and Badiaranke) lived in autonomous rural communities and stubbornly resisted domination by Mande and Fulbe warriors.

The lands of the Landuma, Baga and Nalu extended from the Rio Grande to the Rio Pongo. They were rice-growers and fishermen who lived in villages built in the middle of mudflats or occasionally on dikes.

The Portuguese navigators report that these coasts were densely populated; but the 'kings' that they mention were doubtless rather patriarchs or clan chiefs. Valentim Fernandes wrote of the free help given to the 'kings' by their subjects for field work or building. But when it was a matter of going to war, the council of elders could insist on peace if they found 'that the war is not justified or that the enemy is too strong'. They were thus village democracies.

The traditional religion ruled here unchallenged. People paid honour to 'spirits' represented by statues made of wood, the chief one being called Kru. Animals were sacrificed to the dead of whom statuettes of soapstone or wood were made. These are known as *nomoli* or *pomta*.

From Mount Kakulima to Kru country

The Temne ruled the area south of Mount Kakulima; their neighbours were the Bulom and also, in the interior, the Kissi. These two groups spoke the Sherbro language. These peoples lived in autonomous villages (with up to 3,000 inhabitants among the Bulom) under the authority of esoteric 'mask' societies which were responsible for initiation, like the *Simo* society. Rice-growing produced a surplus which the Portuguese purchased. The Bulom, who were great fishermen using enormous boats, were also excellent artists, producing wood and ivory carvings; they sold their work to the Portuguese.

Temne culture, which dates from the thirteenth or fourteenth century, was spread in the hinterland when the Portuguese arrived. But the Soso, the vanguard of the Mande were already beginning to push them southwards. The 'empire of Sapes' that the Portuguese mention in connection with the Temne was never anything more than a series of chiefdoms or lineages united by a common culture moving forward by slow diffusion rather than by sudden massive population movements.

Further south, there were the Kru peoples, as far as the Bandama, in the forest zone. They were chiefly fishermen, as rice, which had come from Mande country, was not very widely grown. Their territory then extended as far as Seguela from where the Maninka drove them back in the sixteenth century.

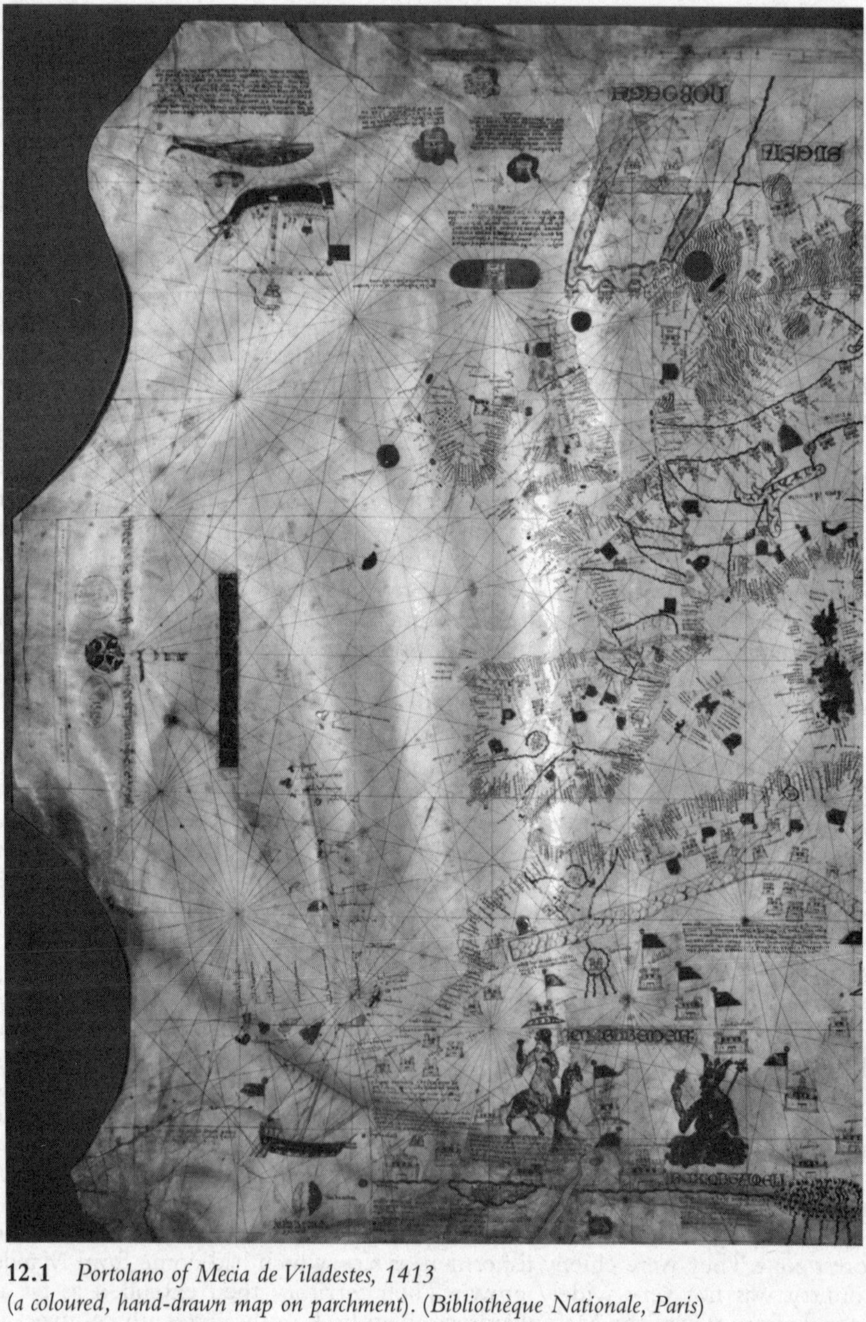

12.1 *Portolano of Mecia de Viladestes, 1413*
(*a coloured, hand-drawn map on parchment*). (*Bibliothèque Nationale, Paris*)

12.1 (*Continued*)

12.2 *African ivory of Portuguese ship and warriors, in detail.*
(*W. Fagg, Afro-Portuguese ivories, 1970, London. Photo © Werner Forman Archive*)

The influence of the savannah

The main peoples involved in contacts with this region were the Mande and the Fulbe. The Mande were organized into villages grouped together to form *kafu*, small-scale territorial units, then into kingdoms and finally into an empire which does not seem to have established unbroken political sway beyond a line running from Kurusa through Kankan to Odienne. But the rulers seem always to have encouraged good relations with the forest chiefs.

To the east of Futa Jallon where the authority of Mali seems to have been non-existent, the lead in very gradual expansion was taken by the peasantry backed by warriors. Then, great noble lineages imposed their rule, such as the Konde over the upper Niger, the Kuruma and Konate from Kankan to Odienne in the fourteenth and fifteenth centuries.

Further south, the firstcomers seem to have been the Dyula who reached the Gulf of Guinea. Their disputes with autochthonous peoples led them to call on Maninka warriors, who brought in peasants and politically organized the autochthonous peoples (the Kuranko, the Konianke etc). Some of them, such as the Vai and the Kono, reached the sea as early as the fifteenth century. It was almost certainly the Camara of Konianke who were responsible for the Somba invasion which reached the coast in about 1550.

But this pioneer front of the Maninka was oriented not towards the sea, but towards the commercial and political life of the Sahel and the north. It was only late in the seventeenth century that the slave trade made the coast the predominant influence and set off the eruption of the Upper Niger peoples disrupting the coastal peoples and also, as a consequence, the other Mande peoples of the interior.

The Mande states or provinces of the coast

In the thirteenth century, Sundiata's companion, Tiramaghan Traore, imposed the hegemony of the Mali empire, which controlled the gold-bearing regions of the upper Senegal and upper Niger, over Senegambia. This control was particularly enduring from the Gambia to the foothills of Futa Jallon. This large state of Kaabu survived until the nineteenth century. It provided Mali with an outlet to the sea. It brought together under its sway a series of kingdoms often inhabited by non-Mande peoples (Kokoli, Biafada, Niumi, Badibu, Wuli etc.). The Balante continued to be recalcitrant. Mande culture was dominant here but the autonomy of this kingdom was very real and the aristocracy adopted a system of matrilineal succession. The Gelowa of the Sereer kingdoms emerged from this aristocracy before the arrival of the Portuguese.

On the lower Casamance, the Bainuk-Kassanga, whose royal title (*Kasa-Mansa*) gave its name to the river, preserved their identity until their destruction by the Balante in the nineteenth century.

The event which had most impact here was the arrival of the Portuguese in 1446 on the Gambia and 1456 on the Rio Grande. This marked the opening to a new world for Mali, especially as the Gambia was a waterway on which navigation was remarkably easy and it became one of the main access routes into the heart of the continent. This was the route through which gold and slaves from Mali were exported, and through which the Portuguese embassies to Mali passed in the fifteenth century. As the Sereer kingdom of Salum gained in strength in the seventeenth century, this enabled it to bring under its sway the Maninka kingdoms to the north of the Gambia (Niumi, Nyaani). By then the slave trade dominated everything.

As for Kaabu, still loyal to the Mali empire, it was confined to the southern bank of the Gambia (Kantora) and made contact with the Portuguese on the Rio Cacheu and the Rio Grande. Bambugu remained under the control of Mali until the final defeat before Jenne in 1599. The mines were then conquered on behalf of the Denianke of Futa Toro (known as the 'empire of the great Ful') by Portuguese mercenaries under the command of the Jew Ganagoga. From that time, Kaabu was cut off from Mali as it declined (c. 1600).

Further south, in the plateaux of the Futa Jallon, lived the Jallonke and the Soso speaking Mande dialects. The former were organized into small chiefdoms within Mali's sphere of influence. The Soso were much less structured, with the Simo initiation society, which was Temne or Baga in origin. The Baga and the Nalu were still numerous in the valleys of the Futa Jallon; they were later driven out of it in the eighteenth century by the Fulbe *djihād*.

The Fulbe and the peoples of the Futa Jallon

It was in about 1450 that Dulo Demba, belonging to the Fulbe group that had set out from Futa Toro, attacked the Biafada who were still vassals of Mali. It was in Jallonke country where he had settled that Tengella set out to fight Kaabu and later Songhay troops, before his son Koly founded the Denianke dynasty in the Futa Toro.

The Futa Jallon was only symbolically linked to the empire of the 'great Ful', but the Denianke did not take all the Fulbe with them when they left. Many settled among the Soso and the Jallonke. They joined with the Soso to halt the Mane invasion which had overrun the regions to the south. These Fulbe retained their marginal role until the influx of Muslims enabled them to subjugate the Jallonke in the seventeenth century after a *djihād*.

But the situation of the Soso was totally transformed first by the new traffic in gold carried by the Diakhanke caravans of Bure to the Portuguese caravels. The Soso, following this movement, pushed back the Baga and Temne towards the Rio Pongo. Islam did not have a profound effect culturally until the end of the seventeenth century.

The forest front from the upper Niger to the Sassandra as occupied by southern Mande such as the Kuranko, (the Konianke and the Mau). The Dyula acting as brokers, organized the trade in kola nuts, whose producers they regarded as 'barbarians', whether they spoke Mande – like the Guro, Dan or Toma – or a Mel language like the Kissi. These autochthonous peoples were either assimilated or driven out, as settlements of warriors, peasants and traders established the present-day configuration of peoples from the fifteenth century, that is at the time when the retreat of Mali to the north turned men's energies towards the south instead.

The Mande in contact with the Kissi and Toma settled in Sankaran and Toron, east of the upper Niger, as early as the fourteenth century. At the end of the eleventh century, the Konianke and the Touba area, a high plateau strategically placed to dominate the coast, came under the hegemony of Camara and Dyomande clans. The Fulbe clans that arrived in the seventeenth century adopted the Maninka language.

On two occasions, the Mande attempted to break through the forest front.

The Kono and the Vai

Perhaps in quest of salt and fish, these Mande settled in the forest zone before the arrival of the Portuguese, led by the Camara, moved down towards the sea, towards the present-day border between Liberia and Sierra Leone. Some of them remained in the highlands after waiting in vain for a messenger from the vanguard group, for which reason they were called Kono (from *kono*, 'wait'). The others, led by Kamala the younger, organized the Vai people on the coast. They had so much poultry that the Portuguese christened them *Galinhas*. They seem to have retained a rather centralized political structure.

The Mane or Mande invasion

The Mane-Sumba and Kwoja-Karu invasions constitute one of those movements of peoples that have shaken whole regions of the continent, like those of the Jaga in Angola or the Zulu in the nineteenth century. But they did not transform the ethno-linguistic map.

The Mane invasion was of course responsible for the spread of the Mande language and even for the formation of the Loko group, but, above all, it contributed to the dissemination of centralized political institutions and to the extension of the long-distance trading network of the Sudan.

It seems that the Mane expansion was the work of Mande who were already familiar with the gold trade. Since the Portuguese had already been present for eighty years, the desire to open up a direct trade route to the coast seems obvious. This minority equipped with a superior political and military organization succeeded by mobilizing the autochthonous peoples one after the other, thus producing a snowball effect all the way to the coast.

The Cape Verde Islands

The arid, desert islands of Cape Verde were first settled in 1462 on the model of Madeira and then reverted to the Portuguese crown in 1484. The capital was established on Santiago, the island closest to the mainland, which became the residence of the governor and the bishop whose jurisdiction extended to the coast of the mainland.

The archipelago was quickly populated by slaves brought from the mainland. In 1582, the two main islands, Fogo and Santiago, had 1,600 white inhabitants, 400 free blacks and 13,7000 slaves. The economy was based on stock-raising, cotton-growing and weaving, using African techniques.

12.3 *An African village.* (*British Museum, London*)

12.4 *The king of Sestro* (*in the seventeenth century*). (*British Museum, London*)

Subsequently, slaves were imported for re-export to Spanish America in the sixteenth century, at the rate of about 3,000 a year, in exchange for cotton cloth from Cape Verde.

Portuguese colonization was based on the principle of a royal monopoly of trade, granted to concessionaires for clearly defined periods and regions. The Charter of 1466 granted the inhabitants of the islands the right to trade with the Senegambian coast, but the code of 1514 prohibited all contact with the mainland. The concern was to put a halt to the activities of the *lançados* (from *lançar*: to launch out on an adventure), who reached agreements with the African rulers to settle on the mainland, adopt local customs and set up as independent traders. And it was true that many of the lançados came from the fringes of society, especially the 'new Christians', the Jews who had been converted by force.

Conclusion

With the recent opening of the Lisbon archives and the beginning of archaeological studies, the history of this region will certainly be enriched. Already it is quite clear that it was not isolated and closed in on itself: the incursions and invasions of the Mande and Fulbe, the trade in kola nuts and other forest products, the powerful coastal kingdoms such as those of Kaabu and the Konianke, the activities of the Portuguese from the fifteenth century all linked it to the neighbouring African world and to Europe. Some of these peoples, such as the Nalu, the Baga and the Bulom, were noted for their sculpture. The rice-growing skill of many others made the region a granary for the savannah whose kings usually maintained good relations with the local chiefs.

13 From the Côte d'Ivoire Lagoons to the Volta

The country

From Cape Palmas the coast curves from south-west to north-east in an arc that forms the Gulf of Guinea. Another feature is the appearance of lagoons along the coast. The climate is equatorial, with heavy rainfall except towards the mouth of the Volta where the forest gives way to savannah.

The problem of sources

Written sources

From 1471, the land between Cape Palmas and the mouth of the Volta was explored by the Portuguese, who left accounts of their voyages. In 1481, they began to build the fort of El Mina, a strongpoint which controlled trade all along this stretch of coast. Duarte Pacheco Pereira's *Esmeraldo de situ orbis* (sixteenth century) and later Dapper's *Description of Africa*, a compilation of earlier accounts, are of the greatest value to the historian. For example, Pacheco Pereira's 'Eguorebo' are the Grebo of Cape Palmas. The rivers are carefully recorded. The Santo Andre or Sassandra has *harrari* or rice-fields. Rio Laguoa can be identified as great Lahu.

Beyond this point, Pacheco Pereira noted the Kru as bad men, hostile to the navigators. It was the discovery of gold in this region that precipitated the building of El Mina for which the king of Portugal sent nine ships laden with stone and lime; the fort was built despite the continuing threats of the local people who resented its construction. But it became a focus for Attie (Atty), Hacanys (Akan) Goroes (Abron) and Mandingo (Mande) merchants who bought and sold gold.

The land between the Bandama and Cape Three Points was called the Tooth (Ivory) Coast. The Gold Coast stretched from Cape Three Points to the Volta. Many villages are mentioned by the Portuguese who also give valuable information about the customs of the peoples.

Archaeological sources

Excavations at Begho, in Bron country, on the northern edge of the forest, show that many cultural objects came from Jenne. M. Posnansky thinks that

13.1 *Forearm sleeve bracelet found at the site of Séguié.* (*Institut d'Histoire, d'Art et d'Archaéologie Africains, Abidjan*)

intense trading relations of long standing existed between the forest and the savannah. The existence of a large colony of Dyula in this contact area is also evidence of such relations. From items recovered in the Nyarko area of Begho, this site began to be occupied around 1100. It was one of the leading markets for kola nuts and gold which were traded in increasing quantities as Mali developed. To the west, in Guro country, the even older Mande presence was associated with the kola-nut trade along the contact area marked by the 8° parallel of latitude between savannah and forest; there were many trading centres along that line, and in some sites such as Séguié (in the Côte d'Ivoire) there are oval-shaped ditches which resemble defensive areas. According to the Abe, they were there when they arrived before the great Akan migration of the eighteenth century. Research should be concentrated on the centres mentioned by the navigators. However, excavating in the lagoon area and mangrove swamps, where there are heavy accumulations of dead leaves, is very difficult. Three islands in the Aby lagoon have yielded piles of neolithic shells, burial places and bones, beads and bracelets.

Oral sources

These are abundant because each people has traditions or myths of origin. But enormous difficulties remain. First, the collective memory often does not go back beyond the eighteenth century. Furthermore, some ethnic groups claim that their ancestors came down from heaven, others out of a hole in the ground, with the obvious aim of muddying the tracks, or because they simply do not know. There is also contamination between one collective memory and another. The Avikam, for example, consider the Alladian to be their 'brothers'. Migrations are mentioned too. For example, the Adiukru believe they came from the west in eight successive waves. The Akan place their origin within the Republic of Ghana. The traditions of the Akwamu say their origins lie in the savannah, at Kong. Similarly, the Fanti of the coast say that their ancestors came from Tenkiyiman in north-west Ghana. Only systematic collection and comparison of data, based on interdisciplinary cooperation, can lead to explanatory hypotheses.

Collaboration between the University of Abidjan and the University of Ghana at Legon resulted in the Bonduku Seminar in 1974 on 'The Peoples common to the Côte d'Ivoire and Ghana'. The conclusion of this meeting looking at the data provided by oral tradition, archaeology and anthropology was that it is possible to reconstruct the historical process.

The fragmentation of peoples probably took place between the seventeenth and nineteenth centuries. Yet the Akan, the Kru and the Bron seem to have been settled where they are by the fifteenth century. According to the Ndenye, their ancestor called Ano Asena came from the east, from the country called Anyanya. He is said to have taught agriculture by introducing the yam and the banana. Cross-checking traditions dated this event to the seventeenth century. Claude Perrot's research is the archives have revealed that the origins of the Ndenye can be dated to around 1690.

But can agriculture really be of such recent date? What really happened is that at the end of the seventeenth century, following a dynastic dispute in the kingdom of Aowin in Ghana, Ano Asena left with his men and settled around Assini (Côte d'Ivoire). The Ndenye then reconstructed the myth of origin and attributed to Ano Asena developments that had happened much earlier, as if to eradicate everything that went before the migration that led to the formation of the presently existing people. It is by collating the various sources and by the disciplines working together that it will be possible to reconstruct the historical pattern from all the scattered or contradictory data.

The peoples of the coast and the interior

The theory that contrasts the peoples of the lagoons and the forest on the one hand to those of the savannah on the other, does not stand up to examination. Most belong to the Kwa language group. The Portuguese called part of the coast 'the coast of the Quaqua'.

According to A. Adu Boahen, the Akan, who constitute 45 per cent of the population in Ghana and 33 per cent in the Côte d'Ivoire have a remarkable linguistic unity. The involves the following groups: the Asante, Akyem, Wasa, Twifo, Akwamu, Sefwi, Nzima, Fanti and others in Ghana; the Abron, Agni, Sanwi, Baule, Attie, Abe, Abure, Alladian and others in the Côte d'Ivoire.

Before the seventeenth century, the current fragmentation into distinct dialects had probably not yet occurred. But the peoples of the lagoons belonged to the same Kwa language group as the Akan. They probably all came from the Chad-Benue region by stages, crossing the lower Niger and then present-day Benin and Togo while creating original institutions. Several migrant groups set

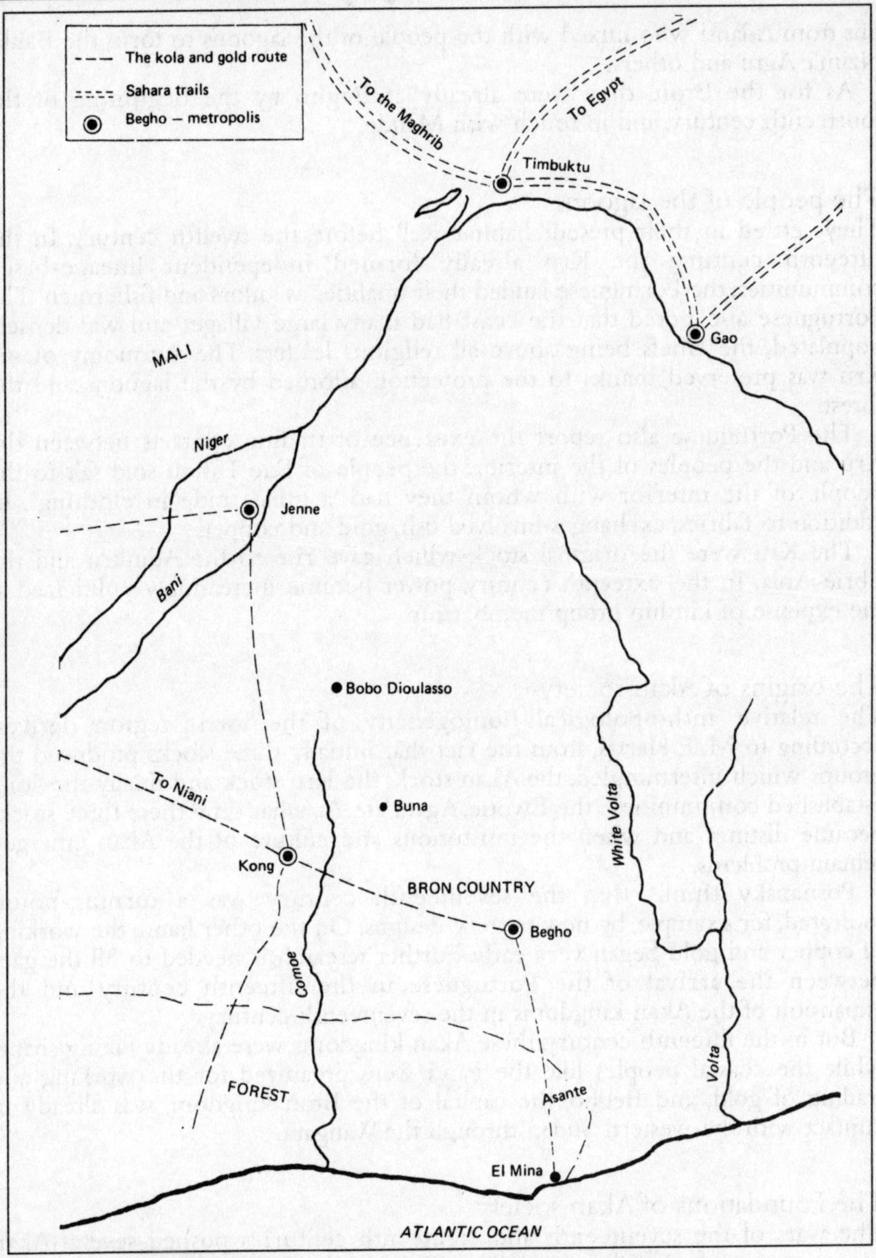

13.2 *Map of the area between the Niger valley and the Gulf of Guinea. (M. Posnansky, Bonduku Symposium, 1974)*

out from Adansi who mixed with the people of the lagoons to form the Baule, Nzima, Agni and others.

As for the Bron, they were already at Begho by the beginning of the fourteenth century, and in touch with Mande.

The people of the lagoons

They settled in their present habitat well before the twelfth century. In the fifteenth century, the Kru already formed independent lineage-based communities; the Portuguese lauded their qualities as sailors and fishermen. The Portuguese also noted that the coast had many large villages and was densely populated, the chiefs being above all religious leaders. The autonomy of the Kru was preserved thanks to the protection afforded by the lagoons and the forest.

The Portuguese also report the existence of trading contacts between the Kru and the peoples of the interior; the people of Rio Lahou sold salt to the people of the interior with whom they had 'a great trade in clothing'. In addition to fabrics, exchanges involved fish, gold and copper.

The Kru were the original stock which gave rise to the Adiukru and the Ebrié-Abia. In the sixteenth century, power became increasingly politicized at the expense of kinship group membership.

The origins of Akan society

The relative anthropological homogeneity of the forest region derives, according to M. F. Harris, from the fact that initially three stocks produced the groups which intermingled: the Akan stock, the Kru stock and finally the 'long established communities': the Ewotie, Agwa etc. At what time these three stocks became distinct and when the institutions and culture of the Akan emerged remain problems.

Posnansky thinks that the seventeenth century was a turning-point, indicated, for example, by new pottery designs. On the other hand, the working of copper and gold began very early. Further research is needed to fill the gaps between the arrival of the Portuguese in the fifteenth century and the expansion of the Akan kingdoms in the seventeenth century.

But in the fifteenth century, these Akan kingdoms were already taking shape, while the coastal peoples like the Fanti were organized for the working and trading of gold, and Begho, the capital of the Bron kingdom, was already in contact with the western Sudan through the Wangara.

The Foundations of Akan society

The wars of the seventeenth and eighteenth centuries pushed several Akan groups westwards. As Christophe Wondji observed, the word *Akan* is used in a political sense and the word *Twi* denotes the linguistic group to which all the Akan languages belong.

The principal socio-cultural and political traits as follows:

(1) The system of matrilineal inheritance of power.
(2) The system of giving children two names, one for the day of the week on which it is born and one selected from the father's clan.
(3) A 42-day calendar with religious significance, whose relationship to the Muslim calendar remains a matter of controversy.
(4) Festivals associated with the yam harvest.
(5) The complementary existence of eight matrilineal clans and 12 patrilineal clans, the matrilineage giving the blood and the patrilineage the character and spirit of a person.
(6) The highly centralized character of power incarnated in a queen or a king assisted by a priest who managed the 'national' or clan ceremonies and acts of worship.

According to Professor Diabaté, power was originally held by queens and this was the situation until the fifteenth century when the clans were isolated and autonomous. Subsequently, as the number of armed conflicts grew, they preferred a ruler who was always ready for war.

Conclusion

The lagoon zone from the twelfth to the fifteenth century saw the development of autonomous kinship societies, among whom some division of labour developed, especially in their relations with the peoples of the hinterland. These had sometimes come from the western Sudan to trade on the edge of the forest. Their main partners were the Akan peoples whose kingdoms began to be organized from the fifteenth century.

14 From the Volta to Cameroon

Ecology and language

The appearance of the coastal fringe of this region in the twelfth century was little different from what it is today, except that there had been less clearance. There were already swamps in the Niger delta, the rain-forest belts and the gap in the forest in the area of present-day Benin and Togo. The use of iron in the first centuries of the Christian era had made it possible to penetrate deeper into the forest zone and increase the density of settlement. Dialect analysis of the Yoruba language suggests that the migrations have been from the forest towards the savannah, which contradicts the historical traditions. The explanation may lie in the fact that, depending on the period considered, movements were sometimes from north to south and sometimes in the opposite direction.

Three main groups of Yoruba dialects have been identified. The two oldest groups are the central group (Ife and Ilesha) and the south-eastern group (Owo and Ijebu). In the twelfth century, these groups were in the forest zone. The north-western group (Ọyọ and Ibadan) is more recent. These conclusions of linguistic analysis bear out the tradition that places the creation of the earth at Ile-Ifẹ and the origin of the Yoruba east of Ọyọ.

An analysis of the Edo language distinguishes two clusters: a northern one and a southern one corresponding to the dialect of the kingdom of Benin, the focus of political and cultural development; but the historical significance of this linguistic finding is not yet clear.

Although dialect analysis of the Ibo language has not yet gone very far, it suggests a dispersal from a homeland around Owerri and Umuahia.

Furthermore, in the twelfth century the languages were certainly both closer to one another than they are today and also more numerous before the dynamism of some of them obliterated others that are today sometimes reduced to one or two villages. The period from the twelfth to the sixteenth century was precisely one that saw the imposition of the linguistic and political supremacy of some groups over wide areas in the framework of major states such as Ọyọ, Benin and Ifẹ, whereas other peoples did not develop in the same direction.

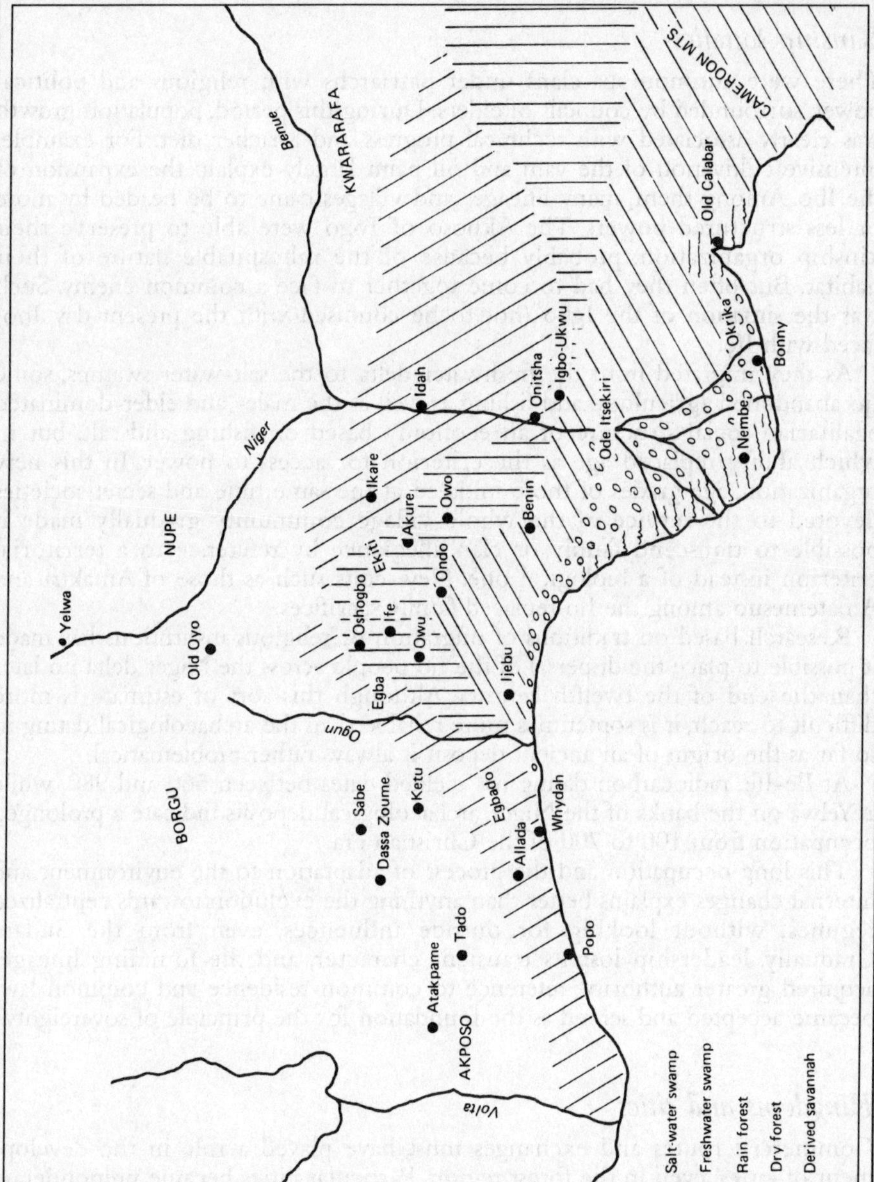

14.1 *Map of the area between the Volta and the Cameroon, 1100–1500 (A. F. C. Ryder)*

Kinship societies

These were autonomous clans under patriarchs with religious and political power, surrounded by councils of elders. During this period, population growth was clearly associated with technical progress and a richer diet. For example, intensive cultivation of the yam and oil palm largely explain the expansion of the Ibo. Among them, many lineages and villages came to be headed by more or less structured powers. The Akposo of Togo were able to preserve their kinship organization, probably because of the inhospitable nature of their habitat. But often they had to come together to face a common enemy. Such was the situation of the Igbo (not to be confused with the present-day Ibo) faced with Ifẹ.

As they migrated from the freshwater delta to the salt-water swamps, some Ijo abandoned agriculture and fishing as well as the male- and elder-dominated egalitarian social structure of an economy based on fishing and salt, but in which ability replaced age as the criterion for access to power. In this new organization, age grades of those initiated at the same time and secret societies devoted to the service of the whole village community gradually made it possible to transcend family or clan allegiance by reference to a territorial criterion instead of a biological one. New cults such as those of Amakiri and Amatemesuo among the Ijo replaced family sacrifices.

Research based on traditions of migration or religious institutions has made it possible to place the dispersal of the Ijo people across the Niger delta no later than the end of the twelfth century. Although this sort of estimate is more difficult to reach, it is sometimes more reliable than the archaeological dating in so far as the origin of an ancient deposit is always rather problematical.

At Ile-Ifẹ, radiocarbon dating has yielded dates between 560 and 980, while at Yelwa on the banks of the Niger, archaeological deposits indicate a prolonged occupation from 100 to 700 of the Christian era.

This long occupation and the process of adaptation to the environment and internal changes explains better than anything the evolution towards centralized regimes, without looking for outside influences, even from the Sudan. Gradually, leadership lost its transient character, and the founding lineages acquired greater authority; reference to common residence and common laws became accepted and served as the foundation for the principle of sovereignty.

Kingdoms and cities

Commercial routes and exchanges must have played a role in the development of cities, even in the forest region. Particular cities became preponderant through competition, even hostility. But the preponderant cities exercised direct power only over a rather limited area; beyond that, there was a system of vassal centres, and lineages remained powerful. Nevertheless, external influences on the development of the state system in the forest zone must not be altogether ruled out: a state might have borrowed aspects of its protocol from an external source, or ceremonial objects (ceremonial swords), or chieftaincy titles, or even leaders. The relations for which there is evidence since the existence of the empire of Ghana between the Sahel and the forest were not limited to the traffic in kola nuts, ivory and slaves; they also carried cultural and religious traits, and hence political and institutional ones. One can see, for example, how an Ijo village in the eastern Niger delta obliged to sell its fish and salt in exchange for foodstuffs that it could not produce, saw the trade assume growing importance and the earlier autonomous structure give way to a personalization and concentration of power, with the chief finally giving himself the significant title of *amanyamabo* ('owner of the town').

The Yoruba

The most important complex of states was that associated with the Yoruba-speaking peoples which extended from Atakpame in the west to Owo in the east. Two of these states – Ifẹ and Ọyọ – have coloured the traditions in the others to such an extent as to make it extremely difficult to discern the chronological sequence leading to the establishment of the system as a whole. Claims by peoples or dynasties to an Ifẹ origin can no more be taken at their face value than can the claims of numerous Ijo states to a Benin origin. When a group no longer remembers a prior place of origin, it is likely to align itself with the oldest and most prestigious contemporary state that is also distant enough not to threaten it in any way.

Linguistic references comparing the central Yoruba dialects with south-eastern ones suggest that the creators of the first Yoruba state whose eponymous and symbolic image is Oduduwa were in the region of Ifẹ. Moreover, no rival legend challenges this honour. Radiocarbon dates from the Ita-Yemoo site range from 960 to 1160, which confirms the tradition. Finally, the northern position of Ifẹ close to the savannah must have exposed it earlier than the others to the pressures that accelerated the processes of centralization.

Origins

According to Ifẹ tradition, a first generation of states arose under the grandchildren of Oduduwa, who had migrated from Ifẹ: Ketu, Benin, Popo, Ṣabẹ and Ọyọ. But it is unlikely that they all came into being at the same time, given the great variations in the number of rulers in the various king-lists, ranging from 27 in Ṣabẹ to 52 in Ijẹbu, which is not numbered among the earliest states.

The typical Yoruba city-state comprised one town and its surrounding villages, covering a very limited area. The towns were isolated or grouped into federations as among the Ẹgba and the Ijẹbu. There were also pockets of kinship groups.

The case of an 'imperial' state like Ọyọ arose only in the seventeenth century; and even then is probably to be explained more by its atypical savannah ecological environment which facilitated internal relations and relations with neighbouring states like Borgu and Nupe. Indeed, this latter invaded Ọyọ in the last quarter of the sixteenth century and it was not reoccupied until the end of the century.

Ifẹ

Paradoxically, despite the central position of Ifẹ in Yoruba history, after the wealth of details attached to Oduduwa, the legendary founder of the state, and his immediate successors, the tradition is full of gaps. Fortunately, the archaeological record has done something to fill them.

A first phase in the history of the state opened around the eleventh century. It was characterized by a scattered settlement pattern, a glass-bead industry, the use of floors made of potsherds set on edge, a very fine terracotta art and naturalistic figurines reminiscent of Nok culture, but above all related to the similar finds made all over Yorubaland, for example at Ire near Oṣogbo, at Idanre and at Ọwọ where these terracotta sculptures have been excavated in a fifteenth-century context. This widely distributed style which reached all the Yoruba towns from an unidentified source, seems to be associated with certain religious rites rather than political power. In this context, Ifẹ, far from having the monopoly was but one case among others of this artistic flowering. The potsherd floors, for example, are to be found as far away as Ketu in the Republic of Benin, as well as in northern Togo and at Daima near Lake Chad. At Ifẹ, they appeared between the twelfth and sixteenth century. Their sudden disappearance appears to be linked to some catastrophe that overwhelmed the town in the sixteenth century. But probably just before this event, the 25 Ifẹ 'bronze' heads (in fact brass and copper), which so perfectly reproduce the naturalistic style of the terracottas, had been cast. The break that occurred in Ifẹ in the sixteenth century can only really be explained by a change of dynasty. In this case the present ruler belongs to the new line which built the palace and the earliest of the walls around the central area of the town. It probably retained some of the political and social institutions of the old dynasty, which means that it is impossible to describe in detail the system that existed in the first period, nor to decide whether the relationship between the other Yoruba towns and Ifẹ dates from the later or the earlier period of Ifẹ history.

Thus, the installation rituals and royal insignia are very similar throughout Yorubaland, but they differ considerably from the insignia worn by notables who probably belong to the overthrown royal families of the first dynasty.

The influence of the states of the Sudan situated further north (the nearest ones being Borgu and Kwararafa) is also clear. Thus the Nupe drove the Yoruba out of Old Ọyọ early in the sixteenth century, and to recapture their capital the Ọyọ had reorganized their forces to give greater prominence to the cavalry, the striking force of the savannah states. From the Nupe the Ọyọ borrowed the *Egungun* cult of ancestors.

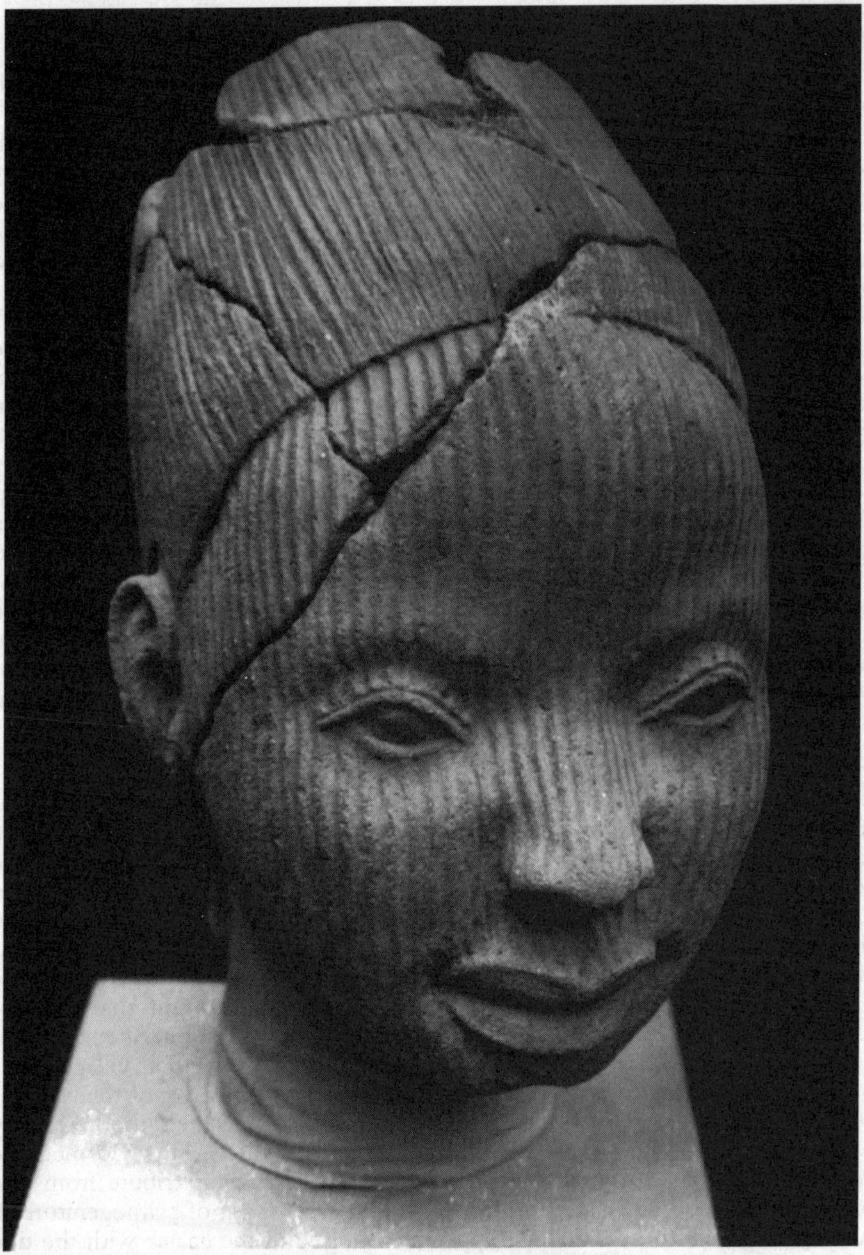

14.2 *Terracotta head (Owọ, Nigeria).*
(Nigeria, its archaeology and history, *London, Thames and Hudson, 1978*)

The kingdom of Benin

This was the first state on the coast to receive the Portuguese and establish trading and diplomatic relations with them.

Situated south-east of Ifẹ, Benin probably became a kingdom in the twelfth century. It seems to have undergone a transformation in the fifteenth century resembling that which befell Ifẹ in the sixteenth century. But the definitive establishment of the kingdom had meanwhile occurred at the beginning of the fourteenth century: the people of Benin, according to the tradition, had asked the king of Ifẹ, Oduduwa, for a prince and he sent them Oranyan. The powers of the first rulers were, we are told, limited by those of the indigenous chiefs known as the *ozama*; but it is possible that the powers of these latter were delegated by the dynasty itself. In fact here we have an example of the political role of the local chiefs, similar to that of the seven *oyomesi* of Ọyọ and, more generally, a pattern widespread in Africa of the division of powers between the king and the indigenous chiefs of descent groups.

After an armed struggle with *ozama*, the fourth ruler of the Benin dynasty is said to have succeeded in altering the balance in his favour. He thereupon built a more spacious palace, where the great title-holders owed their titles not to heredity but to a royal grant, but despite everything the power of the *ozama* was not destroyed and the ruler remained little more than *primus inter pares*. In the fifteenth century, however, a major upheaval resulted in the installation of an autocracy under Ewuare, who seized the throne after murdering his brother. But it is likely that this version conceals a change of dynasty, perhaps consequent upon outside intervention.

Ewuare's government

Ewuare rebuilt his capital to a new plan and gave it the name of Edo. It was surrounded by a huge ditch and ramparts. A broad avenue separated the palace from the quarters reserved for craftsmen and ritual dignitaries. The palace comprised a wardrobe, the ruler's personal attendants and a harem, each of these departments being graded into three age ranks analogous to the age grades of the Edo villages. Each 'town' guild had a similar grade structure and was affiliated to the appropriate palace department. Members of the senior palace grades bore individual titles conferred for life. It is thought that Ewuare associated all his free-born subjects with the palace organization. After they had completed their service, the majority of the men returned to their villages, after being given the facial scarification which marked them as 'slaves of the *oba*'.

Around the ruler, Ewuare placed three groups of titled chiefs: the hereditary *ozama*, the palace chiefs and a new order of 'town' chiefs. These formed the council of state each member of which was responsible for tribute from one part of the kingdom. Ewuare also introduced the principle of primogeniture in succession to the throne, the heir apparent sitting with the *ozama* with the title of *edaiken*. Ewuare is remembered as a great magician, and gave greater potency to his mystical powers by introducing the annual *Igwe* festival during which his vital forces were renewed.

14.3 *Benin: bronze flute-player. (W. Forman, B. Forman and P. Dark, 1960)*

Ewuare also embarked on vast conquests among the Edo, Ibo and Yoruba. The empire ultimately appeared as a series of concentric circles: in a radius of some 60 km around the capital there was direct rule where the king alone could impose the death penalty. Other territories were headed by princes of the blood royal and their structure was modelled on that of Edo. Further out, vassal and tributary kingdoms completed the political map of Benin.

The secret of such successes may well lie in Ewuare's success in mustering his subjects and instilling in them a 'national' spirit. His successors continued this warlike activity, the booty and tribute from which went precisely to sustain the military machine. In this way almost the whole of northern Edo country was integrated into Benin, as were areas of Yorubaland like Ọwọ and Ijẹbu. The Itsekiri were given a grandson of Ewuare as their ruler, which resulted in their acknowledging their allegiance to Benin for several centuries.

We have stressed the social and political structure of Benin because it is one of the few countries for which reasonably certain knowledge of institutions prior to the sixteenth century is available, and archaeological excavations have confirmed the traditions. Furthermore, this state was of crucial importance both for the Edo and for many neighbouring peoples. The excavations have also shed light on the evolution of the renowned Benin art. All brass objects earlier than the sixteenth century prove to have been made by a smithing and not a casting process. Although the *cire perdue* (lost-wax) technique may have been known at an earlier date, it only flourished when large quantities of European brass were imported.

Ifẹ art and the problem of the bronzes

The Ifẹ-Benin civilization enables us to situate African art in its historical and sociological context not simply its aesthetic one. The wood sculpture which prevails elsewhere in Africa provides only pieces of recent origin. The Ifẹ-Benin civilization with its terracottas and its bronzes is the brilliant exception.

We have already mentioned the historical and as it were genealogical link between the terracottas of Nok, dating from the iron age (fifth century before the Christian era), the terracotta figurines of Ifẹ, and finally the brass objects forged or cast by the *cire perdue* technique. This is an aspect and evidence of the age-old contacts between the countries of the savannah (in this case the Bauchi plateau) and those of the forest.

We shall leave aside the theories of European authors who refused to recognize the African provenance of these perfect masterpieces. The German Leo Frobenius had fortunately collected and objectively interpreted some of these pieces at Ifẹ in 1910. But we must not forget that Ifẹ was sacked at the end of the nineteenth century by a British military column which carried off many masterpieces.

An important group was again discovered in 1939 not far from the palace of the *Oni* of Ifẹ. Since then, other finds have followed.

Characteristics and development of Benin art

In a tomb at Abiri, Bernard Fagg discovered three terracotta heads, one of which is a model of the realistic and naturalistic style of Ifẹ, with that serenity that is calm with an interior equilibrium that confers upon it a striking density of expression, whereas the other two are of an extreme stylism, verging on abstract art: two holes represent the eyes, a horizontal slash the mouth. All are of the same origin and were made by the same firing technique.

It is a strange and almost unique phenomenon in the history of world culture to see the coexistence in the same culture of two contrasting arts. There is no need to look for outsiders to explain these two very different expressions: what is required is to understand the society that created these masterpieces, especially its religious life.

The fact is that these works, which usually represent the *Oni*, the political and religious chief, were executed after his death, to be placed in his tomb. It is therefore not surprising that this ritual character should inspire a variety of aesthetic approaches. The purpose was to perpetuate, in the hundred temples of Ifẹ, the memory of those who continue to watch over the living.

Tradition records that the *Oba* of Benin requested and received from the *Oni* of Ifẹ a skilled sculptor who taught the craftsmen of Benin. Thus, Ifẹ is truly the mother city whence came the religion and art by which one honours one's ancestors.

The problem of the bronzes

Outside the Ifẹ-Benin area, numerous bronzes have been discovered from the delta to the borders of Nupe. At Igbo-Ukwu, excavated in 1959, which represents an urban complex around the palace and temples, almost 800 bronze pieces in a style completely different from the Ifẹ-Benin bronzes have been brought to light.

The structures discovered are a great room where treasures were stored, a burial chamber of a great priest and a refuse hole.

The common feature that can be detected here is the background of ritual monarchy. The virtuosity of the Igbo-Ukwu artists is remarkable: for example, in the animal motifs of incredible mastery that decorate the bronze bowls and ceramic vases. The technology and aesthetics here were perfectly mastered. Igbo-Ukwu may have been the religious capital of a very vast kingdom, and it was there that the treasures were stored under the keeping of a priest–king. But radiocarbon dating indicates that this highly sophisticated culture already existed in the ninth century, two centuries before the prestigious culture of Ifẹ, and, furthermore, it was among the Ibo, a people with an allegedly 'segmentary' and stateless society, that such a culture flourished.

That is why the question of the chronological table and even the problem of the reliability of radiocarbon dating are being raised again by some authors. In short, Igbo-Ikwu is yet another enigma in African history.

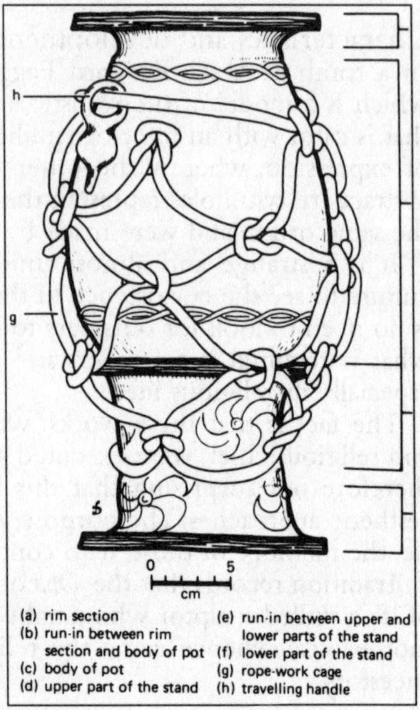

14.4 *Schematic drawing of the bronze roped pot.* (*after T. Shaw, 1970*)

14.5 *Bronze roped pot.* (*T. Shaw, 1970*)

14.6 *Large bronze bowl, viewed from above.* (*T. Shaw, 1970*)

14.7 *Large upturned bronze bowl, viewed from side.* (*T. Shaw, 1970*)

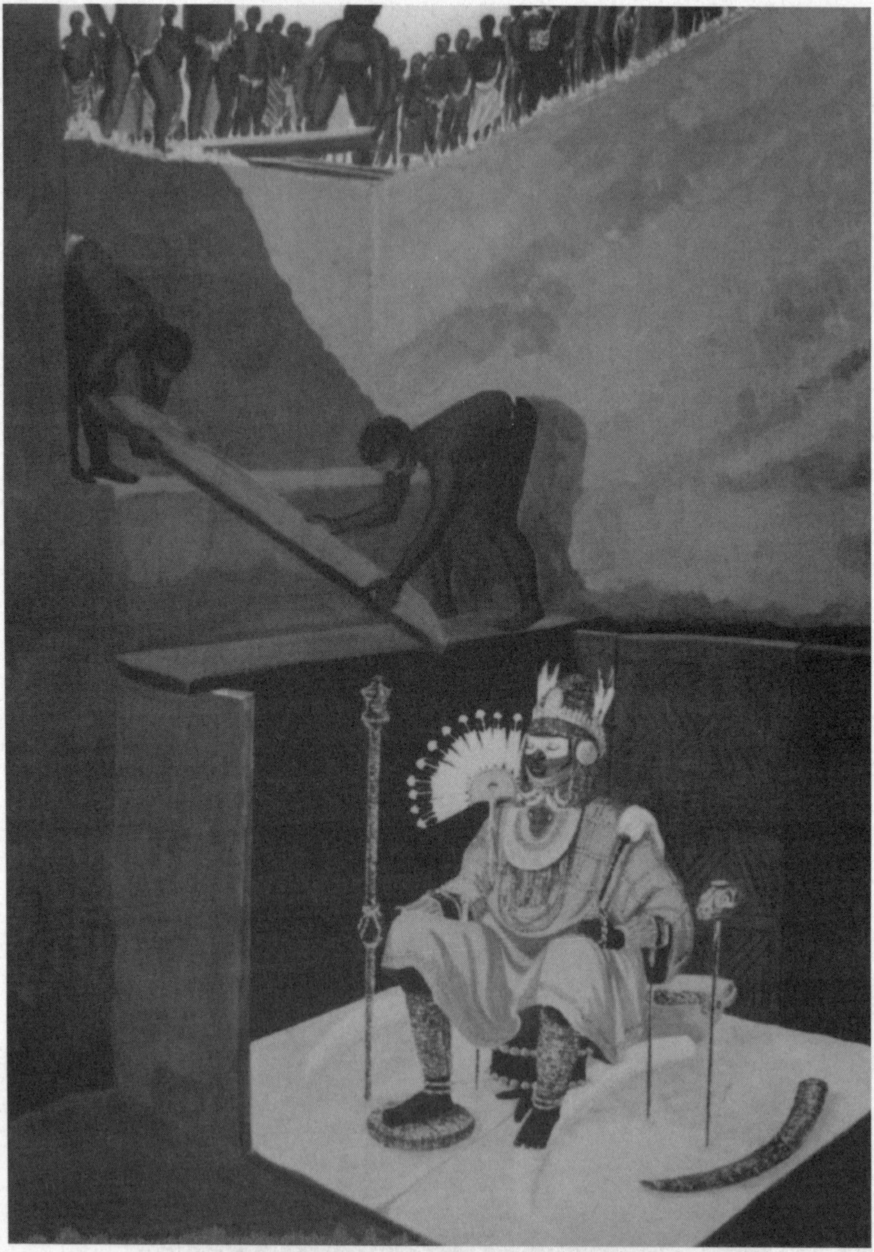

14.8 *Archaeologist's reconstruction of the burial of a ruler at Igbo-Ukwu.* (*T. Shaw, 1970*)

The Nupe bronzes
They were discovered between Busa and the confluence of the Benue. These are the famous 'Tsoede bronzes' said to have been brought in the sixteenth century by the founder of the kingdom of Nupe. He also brought from Igala a group of smiths to teach his subjects the *cire perdue* technique.

Many questions remain unanswered and particular attention will have to be paid to the study of north–south relations between the lower Niger area, a major consumer of copper and brass, and possible sources of these metals further north, in Africa (Takedda) or elsewhere.

In the Niger delta
Here kinship societies such as the semi–Bantu Ekoi (at least before their absorption by the Efik) or the Ibo, on the one hand, lived side by side with ethnic groups in which a process of political centralization was underway, like the Ijǫ, on the other. Okrika, Bonny and Nembe, established in about the middle of the fifteenth century, show this capacity to move in space, to absorb other groups like the Itsekiri and to adopt new cultural traits such as gods and state rituals. In their migration through the eastern part of the delta, the Ijǫ inspired the Ibibio and the Ndoki. The creation of the state of Calabar in the seventeenth century on the Cross River was the work of an Efik branch of the Ibibio.

Conclusion
At the end of the fifteenth century, when the Portuguese arrived on the coast, Ǫyǫ and Benin were the most important states. The process of state formation had quickened the tempo of cultural interaction between peoples, encouraging the diffusion of institutions, practices, religious cults and technology, including the technique of *cire perdue* casting previously associated with divine kingship.

By the considerable demand that they represented, the monarchies stimulated domestic production and trade through the collection and transport of produce, and the security that they guaranteed. The Ijǫ trading states were sending their large canoes laden with salt far into the interior. The *Oba* of Benin was organizing a large-scale trade in ivory, pepper and slaves. Ǫyǫ, owing to its frontier position between the forest and savannah states, controlled much of the trade passing between the two zones. Thus, when the Portuguese arrived, they found well-established states with an economy already adapted to the needs of international trade.

15 Egypt and the Muslim World from the Twelfth to the Beginning of the Sixteenth Century

Importance of Egypt in the political and economic life of the period

During this period, it might seem that Egypt turned its back on Africa. The Ayyūbid and, later, the Mamlūk empire which stretched as far as the Euphrates and Anatolia took the place of the Fāṭimid caliphate which had originated in the Maghrib.

And yet it was also the period of the great pilgrimages of the princes of Kānem, Mali and Songhay who passed through Cairo on their way to the Muslim Holy Places. It was, too, the period when the routes across the Sahara were at their busiest towards Egypt and carrying back into the centre of Africa, along with commodities, principles of conduct and frameworks of thought. Furthermore, the disappearance of the Shīʿite caliphate from the Nile valley brought closer together the Mālikite Maghrib, Egypt and the East, contributing to rebuilding the unitary aspect of Islam of which Cairo was the major school.

The resurgence of Egypt after the fall of the Fāṭimids (Ṣālaḥ al-Dīn and the rise of a new political territory)

Everything pointed out Ṣālaḥ al-Dīn Yūsuf ibn ʿAyyub (Saladīn) as the obvious person to lead Islam's struggle against the European crusaders. Neither the Abbasid caliph of Baghdad, dominated by the Turkish Seldjuk *amīrs*, recently arrived from the Asian steppes, nor the Fāṭimid caliphate of Cairo, under the sway of its military chiefs and threatened by the caliph of Baghdad, had been able to take up the challenge of the implantation of Europeans in Palestine and on the upper Euphrates.

The *amīr* who governed Mosul, Nūr al-Dīn, succeeded in putting a halt to this Christian advance eastward by reconquering the region of the upper Euphrates and inland Syria.

However, the caliph of Cairo was increasingly becoming the plaything of his military viziers who in their competition for this post even resorted to appealing to the Christians for support. It was then that the caliph accepted the help of the army corps sent from Damascus with the Kurd Shīrkūh, whose place was taken after his death by his nephew Ṣālaḥ al-Dīn. In 1171, this latter proclaimed the removal of the Shīʿite caliphate and allegiance to the Abbasid caliphate of Baghdad controlled by Nūr al-Dīn. A conflict might have arisen between the two strong men of eastern Islam. But the death of Nūr al-Dīn in 1174 left the way clear to Ṣālaḥ al-Dīn who reconquered the last territories on the Euphrates and then, in 1187, Jerusalem from the crusaders. With that, the unity of the eastern Muslim world was established around Egypt.

The ideology of the new power

The religious and political ideal was the reconstruction of Muslim Egypt. Shiʿism had not spread greatly among the masses except in Upper Egypt. It was held to be responsible for the weakness of Islam in the face of the West. What was needed was to re-establish firmly the Islam of tradition and of the community, Sunni Islam. The distant caliphs of Baghdad now regained some respect. The pilgrimage of Mecca which had been hindered by the Christian kingdom of Jerusalem, resumed on a larger scale, which greatly enhanced Ṣālaḥ al-Dīn's reputation as far away as Morocco.

In Egypt itself, the power created a class of men versed in religious and legal disciplines to sustain Sunnism. The *madrasas*, a system borrowed from Seldjuk Islam, were permanently developed on a large scale to produce the intellectual and religious manpower needed to act as social and cultural links between the rulers and the people. From the East and the Maghrib came mystics who settled in convents (*khanḳāhs*), or in solitude in the *ribāṭs* of Upper Egypt; they played a major role in teaching and sensitizing the masses. In about 1244, the Maghribi mystic Abū al-Ḥasan al-Shādhili settled in Alexandria.

The Ayyūbid peace

The construction of Sunni Egypt was favoured by the economic prosperity that resulted from the ending of hostilities. But the European counter-attack in the shape of the Third Crusade enabled the European rulers, not to retake Jerusalem, but to settle once again firmly on the Syrian and Palestinian coasts. This presence could be useful commercially to the Ayyūbid states. After the death of Ṣalaḥ al-Dīn in 1193, his successors took advantage of the goodwill in Christian circles to sign compromise agreements with the Christians. A period of remarkable economic prosperity ensued.

Sugar-cane was added to its traditional agricultural crops. Despite the embargo on strategic materials, the merchants of Venice and Genoa began once again to supply iron, structural timber and pitch, all essential for a war fleet. In return, Egypt offered alum for the textile industry and the valuable products of East Africa and Asia. The Ayyūbid state benefited from the efforts of the Fāṭimids to bring back to the Red Sea and Nile valley routes the historic Indian Ocean trade. For three centuries from the second half of the eleventh century, the merchandise unloaded at the port of ʿAydjāb on the Red Sea coast was transferred by caravan to the port of Ḳūs on the Nile and sent from there to Alexandria, where the European merchants had to wait for it, Cairo itself and the Red Sea being closed to them. An Ayyūbid prince governed the Yemen.

And the Kārimi, who specialized in this long-distance trade, worked this highly profitable circuit of which Egypt had secured a monopoly for itself and which contributed to the prosperity and unity of the Nile valley.

The state and its organization: the military class in power (the successors of Ṣālaḥ al-Dīn)

There was no break with Fāṭimid administration in which the Coptic Christians, heirs to a tried and tested bureaucratic technique, continued to play a major role. The ministerial functions (*dīwān*) continued their activities under the Ayyūbid sultans who had previously been viziers of the caliph and were always addressed by the title *mālik*.

But Ṣālaḥ al-Dīn, as a Kurdish *amīr* used to the ways of the Seldjuks whom his family had served, became concerned to please his army as the Fāṭimid army had been by the system of *iḳṭā*ʿ, that is to say the allocation to each amīr of the tax revenue of given areas.

But the Kurds and the Turks who benefited from this tax were perceived as foreigners by the Egyptians. Furthermore, Ṣālaḥ al-Dīn's familial view of power led him to grant provinces or towns, so that the empire resolved itself into a federation of principalities with Egypt in the centre reserved for the head of the family group. But rivalries soon arose between claimants who had no hesitation in seeking out allies even among the Christians. Right from the time of the death of Ṣālaḥ al-Dīn in 1193, there was a clash within the family and it was after dramatic events marked by the Christian counter-offensive of the Fifth Crusade that al-Mālik, Ṣālaḥ al-Dīn's great great nephew, finally established himself in Cairo in 1240. Experience had taught him that only a highly structured professional army devoted to the person and fate of the ruler could guarantee a minimum of stability. He decided to resort to Turkish slaves: the Mamlūks or Baḥri, so called because they were quartered on an island in the Nile (*Baḥr*).

The Turkish Mamlūks

The Mamlūks represented the establishment, at the head of society, of a powerful military caste which chose the sultans from among its own ranks, with no concern for dynastic continuity. The breach between the rulers and the ruled was consummated.

The origin of their power lay in the very serious dangers arising from the Mongol advance westward and the strong reaction on the part of the European crusaders. The installation of the first wave of Mongols in the lower Volga basin and Hungary had thrown on the market large numbers of Turkish slaves whom the Ayyūbids rushed to acquire; it was they who constituted the Baḥri regiment of Cairo. Then in 1249, the army of the Sixth Crusade, led by King Louis IX of France himself, landed at Damietta. This event coincided with the death of al-Mālik al-Ṣāliḥ while his successor, Turān Shāh, was for away on the Euphrates. It was the Baḥri regiment which saved Egypt by defeating Louis IX and taking him prisoner.

When, on his return, Turan Shāh sought to impose his authority over them, the Mamlūks assassinated him. He was the last Ayyūbid ruler, even though al-Mālik al-Ṣāliḥ's widow was raised to the sultanate as a matter of form by the Mamlūks. The Mamlūks were about to tear themselves apart when a second wave of Mongols took Baghdad in 1258, killed the Abbasid caliph and overran the Ayyūbid possessions as far as Gaza. By reason of the Mongols' internal dissensions, the Mamlūks succeeded in pushing them back beyond the Euphrates. They had saved Islam alone from the twin threat from the Christians and the Mongols, who fortunately did not combine in a joint offensive. They also benefited from the fact that the Mongols were divided into two blocs: the Ilkhāns, the descendants of Hūlāgū, the grandson of Ghenghis Khan, based in Persia, and the Khans of Kipčaḳ who had converted to Islam.

The Baḥri Mamlūks took advantage of these favourable circumstances to transform their de facto power usurped from the Ayyūbids into legitimate authority. To do that they gave themselves a sultan who was an undoubted military and political genius: Baybars (1260–77). He destroyed the main Christian strongholds in Syria and Palestine and led his troops as far as Anatolia against the Mongols. His successors continued the same task. The taking of the last crusader stronghold on the Palestinian coast, St John of Acre, in 1291, was a response to a new threat of an alliance between the Mongols and the European kings. When the Persian Ilkhāns also converted to Islam, that constituted a respite; but it was an Iranian-Mongol Shī'ite Islam which could itself constitute a threat to the Sunni Islam that was dominant in the Middle East and Egypt. Only the decline of the Ilkhān state in 1323 and the fact that the Ottoman Turks in the north were occupied fighting against what remained of Byzantium, and were not yet of great account, enabled the Mamlūk state to act as the great power of Islam.

Mamlūk power in Africa

Mamlūk prosperity owed much to Africa. The great trade with the Far East still went by way of the Red Sea and the Nile valley. Egypt consolidated its position on this route by hegemony over Yemen and an alliance with the *amīrs* of Dahlak. The Mongols attempted at one point to switch the Indian Ocean and eastern traffic back to the Persian Gulf and the land routes controlled by the Mongols. But, in about the middle of the fourteenth century, the great European ports acknowledged that the Red Sea and Nile route was unrivalled. The Kārimī merchants who controlled it developed their contacts as far away as Timbuktu.

Political and cultural relations between Egypt and Africa were flourishing. It was at this time that al-'Umarī wrote his geographical encyclopaedia. The people of Cairo witnessed the passage of the lords of the Sudan whose magnificent generosity became legendary. The ruler of Kānem founded a *madrasa* at Fusṭāṭ, while, in 1324, the Malian emperor Mansa Mūsā distributed

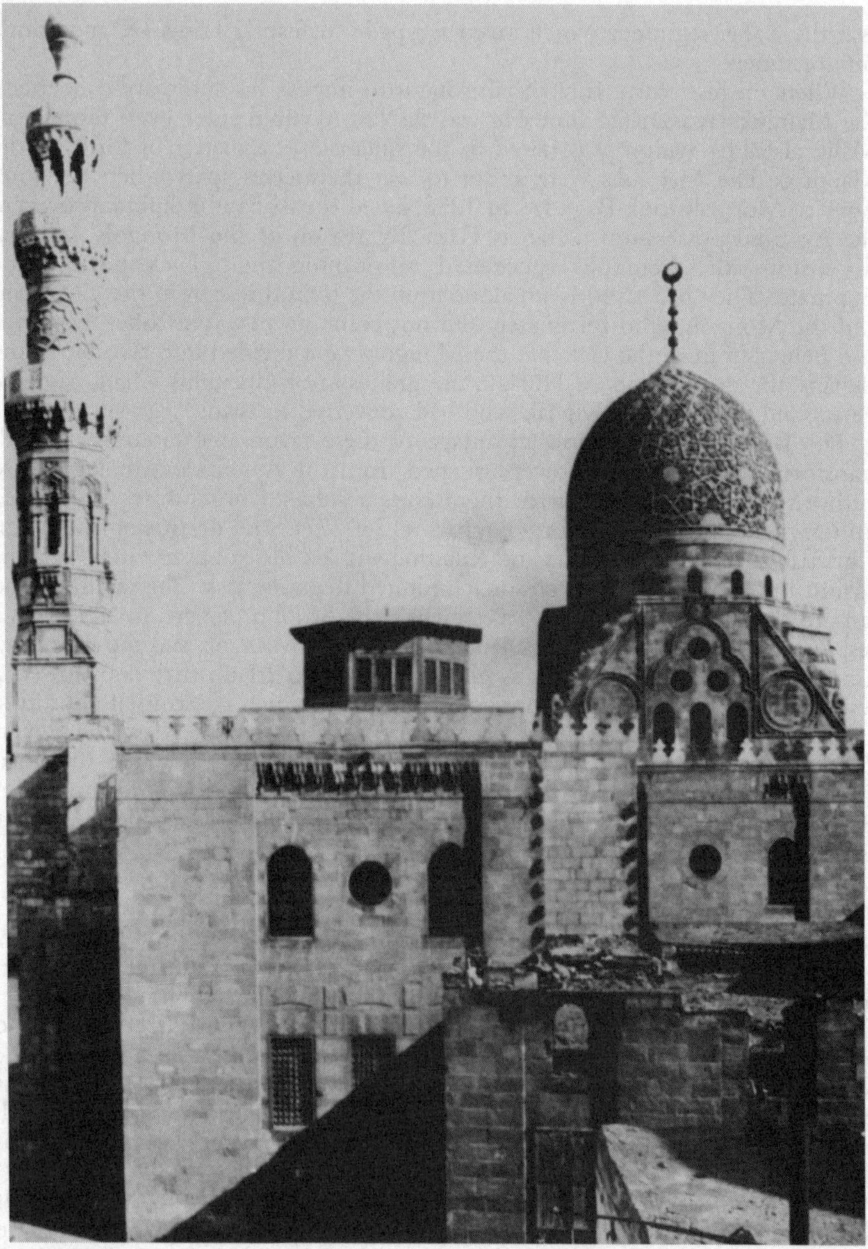

15.1 *Cairo: tomb of Kayt Bay* (*1472–4*) (*Mamlūk architecture*).
(*G. Wiet and L. Hautecoeur, 1932*)

enormous quantities of gold. The gold of the Sudan helped to supply the Egyptian mint. Valuable fabrics, books and the customs of the Mamlūk court and many other industrial and cultural products returned to the Sudan with the famous pilgrims.

But Egypt's attitude towards its immediate African neighbours was extremely brutal: in 1275, the northern part of the Christian kingdom of Nubia was annexed and vassal princes were installed there. In its destruction of Nubia, the Egyptian state found allies in the Beduins: the Banū Kanz and the Djuhayna 'tribes', the Bālī and others who were moving towards Darfūr and Central Africa. Egypt was only too happy to see these turbulent and anarchic groups, who helped to remove the Nubian obstacle, move on.

Islam in Egypt

It developed in the Ayyūbid tradition of Sunni teaching with its prestigious or modest *madrasa*s, increasing participation of the elite from the provinces in the life of the capital and a mystical current derived from the work of al-Ghazālī and his fraternal groups or *Shadili*s. The higher posts of the chancery recovered the glory of the Abbasid caliphate with Syrians like 'al-ʿUmarī' or, towards the end of the fourteenth century, the work of a man like al-Ḳalḳashandī.

The lawyers, however, remained decidedly critical of the Mamlūks despite their prestige as defenders of the faith against the Mongols: these battles had taken place far away, whereas the insolent luxury of *amīr*s who were more at home with Turkish than Arabic offended Egyptian popular feeling whose scholars gave voice to it. But the common people were also conscious of the resounding victories, the grandiose buildings of a Baybars or a Kalaʿūn, the pomp of the sultans and the strange rites of the fraternities from the Far East. In this the common people and the military caste were as one, especially as Baybars had received from the Abbasid caliph the official investiture legitimizing him as sultan. When the caliphs began to take refuge in Cairo, as in 1262, the prayers said in their name led to tension until the caliph was put under surveillance; but even his symbolic presence strengthened the glory of the sultan in the whole Muslim world of which Cairo had become the principal political and cultural centre. The 'Tales of a Thousand and One Nights' were nearing completion. Naturally this new more militant culture was less brilliant and less rich than had been the case in Baghdad; but it was reinterpreting the vast heritage of the caliphate in order to adapt it to the demands of the times. Such was the significance of the monumental historical work of Ibn Khaldūn who was several times the Mālikite grand *ḳāḍī* of Egypt where he arrived in 1382 and where, like many others, he taught in the *madrasa*s of Cairo.

The Mamlūk political system

The caste of Turkish Mamlūks came principally from the shores of the Black Sea, with a minority of other slaves including Mongols. They were sold by Genoese or Arab merchants. It was among these few tens of thousands of

15.2 *Egyptian lamp in enamelled glass (Mamlūk era).*
(G. Wiet and L. Hautecoeur, 1932)

armed men that the political game was played. The cohesion of this group depended on a common education, military and religious. The sultan and the *amīr*s shared the tax concessions which enabled them to keep the troops ready under the orders of their *amīr*s to respond to any instructions from the sultan. Selection was ruthless and unpredictable. And every *amīr* acceding to the sultanate was concerned only to strengthen the new group of Mamlūks who bore his name and shared his fate so long as he did not disappear by natural death or the brutal onslaught of another group laying claim to power.

In these circumstances, the dynastic continuity that can be seen in some of the names given to sultans of the Kalaʿūn family, for example, was more apparent than real. It is true that after Baybars (1260–77), Kalaʿūn succeeded in handing power to his son, but this latter was removed by Kalaʿūn's brother, Muḥammad, who returned to power three times. Great *amīr*s like Uūsun and Tār then took up the regency and contributed brilliantly to the urban architecture of Cairo, which boasted also the magnificent mosque of Sultan al-Nāṣir Ḥassān (1356–62). From the obscure period that followed, the *amīr* Barḳūḳ emerged and was sultan until 1399 thanks to the vigour of his ethnic group, the Circassians.

Egypt up to the end of the fifteenth century: African contacts (the Circassian Mamlūks)

This marks one of the turning-points in the long history of Egypt: the Circassian Mamlūk regime took Egypt out of the Middle Ages.

Far-reaching changes

The Mamlūks of the khanate of Ḳipčaḳ were no longer reaching Egypt in such large numbers as previously. Their place was taken by Circassians from the Caucasus who began to dominate by dint of their strict family, indeed almost racial solidarity which now monopolized access to the sultanate in favour of an even smaller group than before: a group of mercenaries who sold their support to the strongest.

But the resources extracted from tax concessions (*iḳṭāʿ*) were diminishing: Egypt was suffering from disastrous epidemics, including the Black Death in 1349. They decimated the population from the sultans downwards and reduced the yield of the *iḳṭāʿ*).

Last but not least, the Beduin 'tribes' which had been complacently allowed to ravage Nubia grew stronger in Upper Egypt too and became uncontrollable, going so far as to make the road between ʿAydhāb and Kūs impassable in the 1360s: so for a while the port of entry for the spice trade was transferred to the coast of the Sinai peninsula to escape exactions. The power of Barḳūḳ (1382–99) had for a while held up and reversed this decline; he had balanced the Berbers against the Arab *ḳabīla* in Upper Egypt and stiffened control of the provinces. The great days of the great sultans seemed to have returned.

The crisis at the beginning of the fifteenth century

But after the death of Barḳūḳ, the crisis erupted. It was both external and internal. Externally, the Mamlūk hegemony was threatened in Anatolia by a Turkoman principality, that of the Ottomans, who were on the offensive against the Europeans in the Balkans. But what was even more serious, in Central Asia, Tamerlane, an officer of the Mongol princes, was attempting to restore the great empire. He rapidly struck through as far as Damascus and then, by a miracle, instead of invading Egypt, turned towards Anatolia to crush the Ottomans. The two dangers threatening Egypt neutralized each other.

From now on, the Mamlūks, who had watched powerlessly the confrontation between the two new great powers, were to be caught up in their own inner rivalries.

After contesting the transfer of power to Barḳūḳ's son, Faradj, the military class proceeded to tear itself apart in bloody conflicts. For a while, the sultanate was even entrusted to the phantom Abbasid caliph. But meanwhile, the disasters were accumulating: the Nile floods failed; there was famine and plague in 1405; Berber and Arab nomads were ravaging Upper Egypt. Faced with this unprecedented crisis, the Mamlūk states had to change or perish.

Egypt facing the Christian danger: the struggle against the Portuguese – a new Egypt

It was Mamlūks from Barḳūḳ's group, namely Shaykh and al Barsbāy (1422–38), who restored order in Egyptian affairs, by pacifying Upper Egypt, thanks to the Hawwāra Berbers. In order to replenish the state's treasury depleted by losses caused by deaths due to the plague. Barsbāy decided to secure sole control of the spice trade which now came from Aden across Egypt by the shortest routes, from El Tūr in the Sinai peninsula to Alexandria or Damietta, or else to the Syrian ports. Barsbāy rationalized the circuit by requiring goods to come solely through the port of Jeddah (then an Egyptian port) where they were taxed and then sold through official channels. This was clearly detrimental to the interests of great private merchants, in particular the Kārimī, who disappeared, the Venetians, the main purchasers, and the Catalan and Genoese corsairs against whom he had to wage war. In this connexion, Cyprus was raided and its king taken prisoner. The monopoly provided Barsbāy and his successors with a more solid economic base whereas the *amīrs* had been reduced to living off the falling revenues yielded by the *iḳṭā'*. The central power was thus consolidated. The only problem was that the new recruits to the military class were nothing but mercenaries facing the privileged status of the Circassian group. Furthermore, it was no longer young *amīrs*, who, with the help of their men, attained power, but mature or older men, who behaved more as politicians than as soldiers. The sultanate, now legitimized, eclipsed the Abbasid caliphs while the ratio of Muslims to Christians was increasing, setting Muslim Egypt more sharply against the Christians, the corsairs and the merchants with their gold coins and costly fabrics. Thus, faced with European designs, Mamlūk society appeared stronger both economically and in terms of religion, but more fragile in the face of the commercial dynamism of the Christians and their now heightened ambition to bypass Egypt in order possibly to ally with the Negus of Ethiopia. A number of European travellers left precious accounts of their travels.

But the most numerous visitors were the African pilgrims from the Sudan, on their way to the Ḥidjāz for the Holy Places of Islam. The Sunnism propagated out of Egypt and Mecca to sub-Saharan Africa had borne fruit, as the *Taʾrīkh al-fattāsh* and the *Taʾrīkh al-Sūdān* show; and during the pilgrimage Sudanese rulers were sometimes invested by the Abbasid caliph during the pilgrimage, as happened to Askiya Muḥammad in 1496. The Egyptians saw the Sudan mainly as a plentiful source of gold. Upper Egypt contributed greatly to this trade now that the Beduin *amīrs* had become Muslims and merchants, and sold the horses they bred and the slaves they acquired from the Central Sudan.

But Upper Egypt, deprived of spices, began to appear poorer and life there moved at a slower pace than in Mediterranean Egypt with its teeming commerce and the appearance of grand buildings in a new style, especially during the long sultanate of Khāyt Bāy (1468–96), the summit of Mamlūk power, who gave Cairo the appearance it has preserved to this day.

Despite the signs of decline, the end of the fifteenth century still manifested the exceptional influence of Egypt in the majesty of the state and the blossoming of culture, as seen particularly in the Egyptian school of historians with names like al-Maḳrīī and the prolific al-Suyūṭī whose fame spread as far as Tākrūr.

A new international context

From the Timurids – the successors of Tamerlane – who had become peaceful Muslims and protectors of the arts, the strengthened Mamlūks no longer had anything to fear in the east; they could even, by their intervention in Anatolia, play a role as arbiter between the Turkomans; but this expansion eventually provoked the domination of one of the Turkish ethnic groups, the Ottomans.

The Ottomans, initially divided and defeated, reorganized, and under Meḥmed II (1451–81) took Constantinople in 1453, appearing as the new champions of Islam, especially as the position of the Mamlūks was becoming difficult with their Turkoman protegés in Anatolia forced to come to terms with the Christians in order to avoid their own absorption by the Ottomans. A clash between Ottomans and Mamlūks was becoming inevitable. It came several times, starting in the sultanate of Khāyt Bāy. Despite the mastery of firearms that the Ottomans had acquired from the West, the Mamlūks were able to hold out thanks to the intervention of the Iraqi Turkomans, the Ottomans' concentration on the holy war in the Mediterranean, and, finally the emergence at the beginning of the sixteenth century of Safavid power uniting Turkomans and Iranians in an Iran that was now officially Shīʿite for the first time – a danger that was assuredly greater for the Ottomans than for the Mamlūks.

But it was Portuguese expansion in the Indian Ocean that swung the balance, ruining the economic bases of Mamlūk power. From the voyage of Vasco da Gama, the Portuguese were buying spices there directly and organized a blockade of the Red Sea. After the defeat of the Egyptian squadron at Diu on the west coast of India in 1509, the Mamlūk empire was reduced to the defence of the Red Sea. When the Safavids, egged on by the West, attacked the Ottomans, the latter were abandoned by the Mamlūks, even though the Ottomans had helped the Egyptians in the Red Sea. As a result of using firearms, they nevertheless succeeded in 1514 in containing the expansion of Shī'ism to Iran. In 1516, at the battle of Mardj Dabīk, near Aleppo, with the use of modern weapons which decimated the old-fashioned Circassian cavalry, the Ottomans forced the Mamlūk to recognize them as the leading Sunni power in the Mediterranean and Africa.

Conclusion

Mamlūk power, reduced to the Circassians, was limited to a very small political group. When it lost its economic base situated in the Indian Ocean and its religious legitimacy as the defender of Islam, it had to yield to the Ottomans who installed a governor in Cairo. But for a very long time yet Egyptian society was to bear the mark of the political and cultural enterprise of the Mamlūks, so magnificent for Islam and for Africa.

16 Nubia from the late Twelfth Century to the Funj Conquest in the early Sixteenth Century

The Decline and disappearance of the Christian Nubian states

Despite a few minor clashes, the *baḳt*, an international agreement between Muslim Egypt and Christian Nubia, remained in force for six centuries. In addition to having a political, military and religious dimension, it set the seal on economic interdependence.

This formula of tolerance was especially effective under the Fāṭimids, who wanted peace and slaves for their army at a time when Nubia was reaching the zenith of its power. The period covered here, the period of the Ayyūbids (1171–1250) and the Mamlūks (1250–1517), saw the progressive deterioration of relations between Egypt and Nubia owing to the growing pressure of Cairo on a weakening Nubia and the increasing, and destructive, infiltration of Arab nomadic groups.

The documents that reveal this process to us are almost all of Egyptian provenance. Local records, which are scarce and not very relevant, have been enhanced by archaeological remains unearthed in the 1960s, which make possible a deeper analysis of internal developments. The frontier between the two great kingdoms of Muḳurra, in the north, with its capital in Dunḳula, and ʿAlwa, in the south, passed between the Fifth and Sixth Nile Cataracts. Succession to the throne was matrilineal, with the son of the previous ruler's sister being next in line.

Muḳurra

In the time of the Fāṭimids, commercial relations between Egypt and Nubia were flourishing, as witness Fāṭimid artistic influence on Nubian manufactures. This was when the *baḳt* took on its classical shape, based on mutual confidence. The king of Nubia was on excellent terms with the patriarch of Alexandria, his protector. The Shīʿite Fāṭimids, isolated in the Muslim world, particularly valued the goodwill of the Nubians who organized offensives timed to coincide with Fāṭimid attempts to conquer Egyptian territory. The Nubians had no hesitation either in handing over runaway slaves and political fugitives to the Fāṭimids. The black recruits from Nubia constituted the solid nucleus of the Fāṭimid forces especially when they enjoyed the protection of al-Mustanṣir's mother, who was black, in the latter half of the eleventh century. Subsequently, the

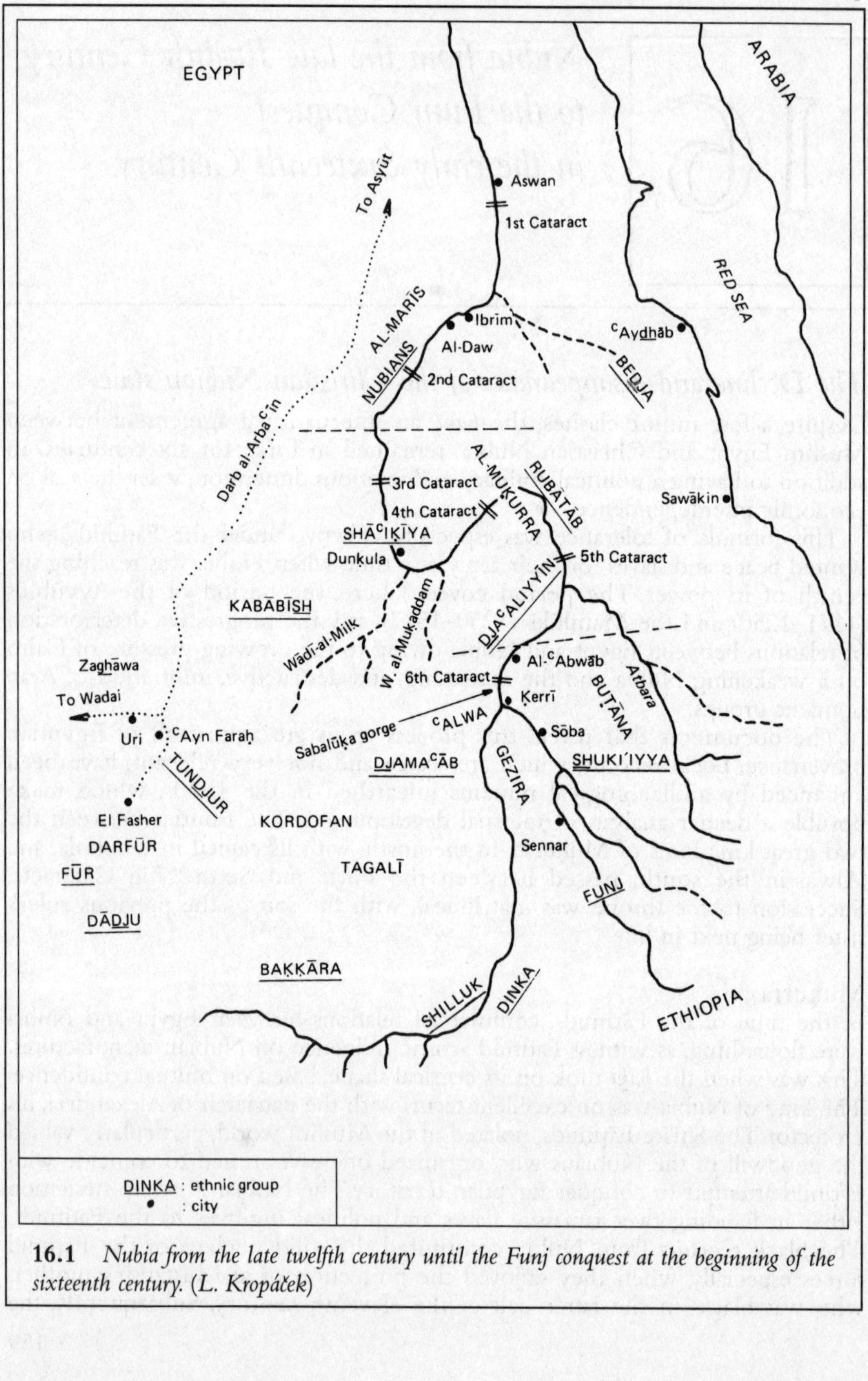

16.1 *Nubia from the late twelfth century until the Funj conquest at the beginning of the sixteenth century.* (*L. Kropáček*)

Nubian soldiers were driven southwards by their Turkish and Berber rivals, but they continued to give staunch support to the Fāṭimid dynasty against the rising power of the Ayyūbids. In dealing with the Arabs, the Fāṭimid hit upon the ingenious solution of sending the Banū Hilāl towards the Maghrib, while quelling the rebellious Banū al-Kanz. In the twelfth century, Kanz al-Dawla, who had sought refuge in Muḳurra, was extradited and handed over to the Egyptians.

Thus, there was coexistence and mutually advantageous exchanges. By the terms of the *baḳt*, traders were protected in their movements in Nubia but could only settle near the northern border of Nubia. Their activities did more for Islamization than the official agents of Fāṭimid Shīʿiism.

The coming to power of the Ayyūbids precipitated a Nubian attack in 1172 which was driven back by the counter-attack of Turanshah, Ṣālaḥ al-Dīn's brother, who took Ḳaṣr Ibrīm. Driving the rebellious Arabs Banū al-Kanz southwards contributed to the Arabization and Islamization of Nubia which included intermarriage with the Banū al-Kanz, who were already a mixture of Arabs and Nubians. Repeated Egyptian campaigns led by the Ayyūbids and the Mamlūks against the *ḳabīla*s of the Beduin nomads drove the latter back, and they sought refuge in the Sudan. But their passage through Nubia, marked by plundering and exactions, was disastrous. Shaken by all these depredations and internal subversion, Muḳurra was no longer a co-operative partner and was slipping towards vassal status which the aggressive interventions by the Mamlūks simply precipitated. Sultan Baybars (1260–77), doubtless motivated by concern for the safety of his empire and by the size of the booty brought back from his campaigns in Nubia and against the *ʿurbān* of Upper Egypt, called on King Dāwūd of Nubia to resume making the deliveries due under the *baḳt*. By way of response, Dāwūd launched an attack which resulted in the conquest of ʿAydhab, an Egyptian port on the Red Sea. Baybars responded with an expedition which dethroned Dāwūd in favour of his cousin Shakanda, who effectively agreed to become a vassal, and the sultan's representative (*naʾib*) with payment of a tribute equivalent to half the country's income. Added to that were the poll tax for non-Arabs, political alignment and the extradition of Arab refugees, not to mention the taking of thousands of slaves carried off by the Egyptians, among them the deposed King Dāwūd for whom the Negus Yekuno Amlāk intervened in correspondence.

Vassalage did not preserve the internal cohesion of Muḳurra, indeed quite the reverse. The Mamlūks, who were soon joined by numerous Arabs, transformed Nubia into raiding country.

King Shamāmūn of Nubia reacted by sacking the Mamlūk garrison left at Dunḳula. Later, in 1290, he thought it necessary to ask Sultan Kalaʿūn for pardon and the latter, engaged against the crusaders, could not but accept. After a period of calm, King Karanbas having omitted to pay the tribute, a punitive expedition set out from Cairo with a new pretender, Sanbū, who was a Muslim. The installation of this latter at Dunkula marks the beginning of the official conversion of Muḳurra to Islam. The old two-storeyed cathedral was transformed into a mosque by Sanbū. But he was soon defeated and killed by Kanz al-Dawla, who had supporters among both the Nubians and the Arabs. The sultan, afraid of this power base, reacted by attempting to restore Karanbas, the Nubian king who had converted to Islam during his captivity in Cairo. He was driven out by Kanz al-Dawla, who was his nephew. Subsequently, the Banū al-Kanz and their allies the Banū al-ʿIkrima clashed frequently with Mamlūk troops sent to take reprisals. Muḳurra was slipping into anarchy. New ethnic patterns were developing without Nubia ever being annexed. But, undermined from within by the infiltration of many groups and many attacks, it lost vigour as an organized state. Intermarriage, which, according to the Nubian principle of succession gave the sons of Arab fathers and Nubian mothers the right to the property of their Nubian maternal uncles, accelerated Arabization and Islamization in the midst of an apparently chaotic situation.

Archaeological work points to the development of insecurity from the middle of the twelfth century particularly through the growth of defensive architecture intended particularly to protect the largest concentrations of Christians.

Numerous vestiges of late Christian communities are situated on islands where the watchtowers look south as if the enemy (probably the nomads) was expected from that direction. Although the Egyptian sources tell of villages burned, waterwheels broken and slaves captured, as well as a scorched earth policy on the part of the Nubians, it seems that the decisive blow against Nubia came from pillaging groups from the desert, Zag̱hāwa Berbers, but mainly Arabs.

ʿAlwa

The history of this kingdom is extremely obscure despite the accounts of Ibn Sulaym (tenth century) and Abū Ṣāliḥ (thirteenth century), who show us a prosperous slave market provided with 400 churches, including the cathedral at Soba. We are told that Adur, the ruler of al-ʿAbwāb, often extradited fugitive Nubian kings in order to ensure the goodwill of the Mamlūk sultans. As in Muḳurra, probably, Arab immigrants who had infiltrated and married locally assumed control over the pastures and ended by undermining central authority by settling near Soba in the latter half of the fifteenth century. On top of that there were attacks by black peoples from the Central and Eastern Sudan as well as the decline of the Church.

The advent of the Funj sultanate of Sennar must not necessarily be seen as being contemporaneous with the fall of ʿAlwa in 1504. One tradition situates the capture of Soba by the Arabs at an earlier date. They are said to have been led by ʿAbdallah Jamma ('the gatherer') against the alleged tyranny (*ẓulm*) of the kings of ʿAlwa. The ʿAbdallāh clan gained supremacy over the nomadic *ḳabila*s and established its centre at Kerri. But from the beginning of the sixteenth century the wave of Funj moving down the Blue Nile occupied the Gezira. These were the communities of traditional religion who, the *Funj*

Chronicle tells us, allied with the Arabs, while other sources mention a battle between ʿAmara Dunkas and ʿAbdallah Jamma. That surely means that after a battle from which the Funj emerged victorious, the ʿAbdallābī Arabs were in a subordinate position in terms of power, which ensured a stability that favoured the Islamization of the country.

The triumph of Islam

The passing away of Christianity

Islam, introduced well before the period we are looking at, was spread by traders, the infiltration of Arabs or the opportunism of some Nubian leaders who, as at Dunḳula, resorted to conversion.

The Christian faith long survived the disappearance of the Nubian kings as is shown by the tomb of a bishop at Ḳaṣr Ibrīm showing that he was in office in 1372. According to a Portuguese priest, Francesco Alvarez, who visited Ethiopia in 1520, among the Nubians, whose country he had visited, there were still 150 churches in old castles. The population, which was neither Christian nor Muslim nor Jewish, was said to want to become Christian. It was said to have sent a delegation to the court of Ethiopia to ask for priests, without success. The area referred to may have been Dunḳula.

In the beginning, the Muslim minorities seem to have lived in peace with their Christian neighbours. Violence against the Christians after the expansion of Islam seems to have consisted of incidental actions rather than systematic exactions: the conversion of churches into mosques, the torture of a bishop and the slaughtering of pigs, for example following the Ayyūbid conquest of Ḳaṣr Ibrīm. Caught between the Egyptian Muslims and the nomadic Muslims who detested each other, the Nubians would have been able to survive for a long time, but for a series of rather chance events.

On the other hand, a number of internal causes help to understand the decline of Nubian Christianity.

In the first place, it seems to have been essentially the religion of an elite without deep popular roots. The Coptic clergy equipped with a foreign culture prayed to saints not one of whom was Nubian. Although the frescoes in churches reveal the faces of autochthonous black bishops, the religion did not become indigenous in the sense that Islam, for example, did. That is why pre-Christian beliefs have survived there with such vigour.

The Nubian church linked to the state was isolated in an Islamic geographical environment. Contacts with Byzantium can be detected in Nubian art but by the thirteenth century the links with the patriarchate of Alexandria had been cut, although a few Nubian pilgrims were still being seen in the Church of the Holy Sepulchre in Jerusalem.

In this context of internal fragility, the external factors had a catastrophic impact; conversion to Islam from top to bottom of the social scale became a new sign of prestige and reintegration.

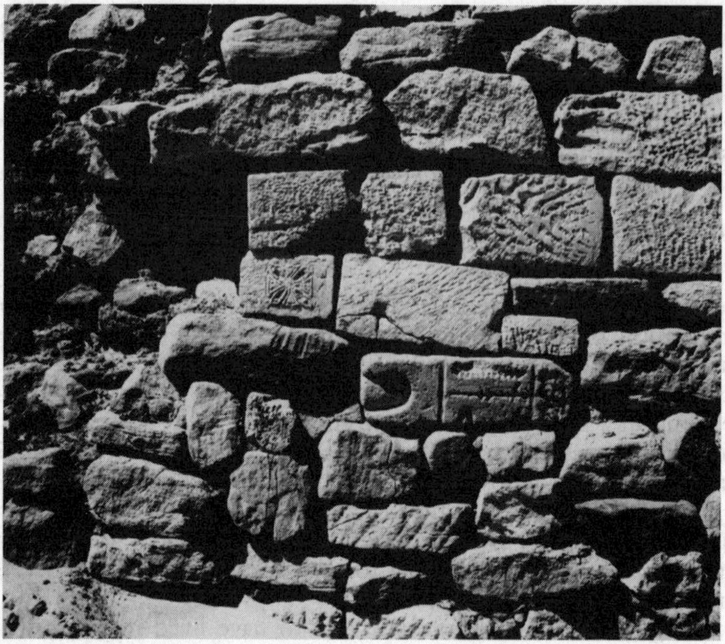

16.2 *The city wall of the Arab citadel of Faras, reconstructed with ancient bricks.* (*K. Michalowski, 1962*)

Arabization

The waves of migration of the Arab *kabīla*s into Nubia and the extensive racial mixing that followed led to the acceptance of Arabic language and culture, an acculturation compensated for by a pronounced Africanization of the racial characteristics of the peoples concerned.

Most of the sources that record this process are the genealogical traditions (*nisba*s) compiled for example in the sixteenth century by the semi-legendary al-Samarkandi. Thee *nisba*s must be used very carefully, as they were generally designed to connect the leading families of the time to prestigious ancestors in order to legitimize them; the ancestor usually invoked were of south Arabian (*Ḳaḥṭānī*) or north Arabian *ʿAdnānī* origin or relative of the Prophet like his uncle al-ʿAbbas. The Funj, on the other hand, claimed ʿUmayyad descent, while the families of religious teachers and jurists in the region formulated similar claims.

The migrations of groups of Arab shepherds going on over several centuries only grew into a massive influx from the twelfth century onwards. The routes taken by these Arab shepherds are partly identifiable.

The suffix -*ʿab* attached to some ethnic names is a loan-word from the Tu-

Bedawie (Bedjawi) clan and indicates a passage through the Bedja country. This area was probably on the earliest route taken by the Arab migrants coming from the Red Sea and Egypt. But the vegetation there was not very suitable for cattle-rearing, so that, despite intermarriage between Arabs and Bedja, most of those arriving had to continue their way toward the middle Nile and the Gezira.

Other Arab groups continued south through the Nile valley to the south of Dunḳula. Others again headed westward probably through the alley of Wādī al-Milk and Wādī al-Muḳaddam or went along the 'forty-day route' (Darb al-Arbaʿīn) into Darfūr.

The Arabic-speaking Nubian groups were mostly connected by their *nisba*s to two comprehensive groups: the D̲jaʿaliyyīn and the D̲juhayna. The D̲jaʿaliyyīn group consisted of sedentary clans such as the D̲jawābra and the D̲jamaʿiyā living in the middle Nile valley and in Kordofan. They claimed descent from a hypothetical common eponymous ancestor, the Abbasid Ibrābīm D̲jaʿal. In fact, the ethnonyms D̲jama Siya and D̲jamāʿab suggest the Arabic verbal root *d̲jamaʿa*, 'to gather'. This semantic indicator refers to abundant and long-standing mixings between Nubians and Arabs who willingly married the daughters of local notables from Nubia to Bornu by way of Darfūr and Wadaī. Thus the Nussabbaʿāt of Kordofan claim D̲jaʿalī ancestry.

The D̲juhayna were more typically Arab. They remained attached to the nomadic way of life, for which they found favourable conditions in the grazing plains of the decaying kingdom of ʿAlwa; but not all the nomads of the region are to be classified as D̲juhayna, in particular the S̲h̲ukriyya, Kināna and Kabābis̲h̲ Arabs, for example. To these various communities must be added the Baḳḳāra situated south of the east–west route across the Sudan, in a zone unsuited to sheep and camels, which led them to specialize in bull-breeding. Their very dark colour is evidence of intensive mixing with the Nubians. Some of them claim that their ancestors came from Tunis and Fezzan. In fact the Baḳḳāra seem to be the result of an amalgamation of Nilotic D̲jud̲h̲ām and groups coming from Fezzan and Chad. The tradition that refers to links between them and the Banū Hilāl also implies that some came from North Africa.

In addition to the Arabs, mention must be made too of the arrival in this region of pure or Arabized Berbers, such as the Howara who from the fourteenth century onwards infiltrated from Egypt into Kordofān and Darfūr.

Social and cultural change

Since antiquity, Nubia has been a meeting-point of tropical and Mediterranean civilizations. The succession of traditional, Christian and Islamic religions simply accentuated this role of crucible which still makes the Sudan today a very specific Arab-African microcosm. The disappearance of the centralized power of the Christian states must have led to insecurity and impoverishment, as the traditions testify, not to mention that archaeology has detected a fall in the level of the Nile, which indicates a climatic deterioration.

It is true that in the twelfth century an Ayyubid envoy described a wretched country growing only sorghum and date palm; but at about the same time an Armenian traveller speaks of a flourishing urban civilization. This is broadly confirmed by the archaeological remains which prove that the painting was of Byzantine inspiration and the pottery in the local Meroitic tradition.

Between the destruction of Dunḳula and the stationing of Ottoman garrisons at the beginning of the sixteenth century there was a dark period for Nubia proper (Muḳurra and Maris). Archaeology and linguistics can help to throw light on it. The key problem is to explain the anomalous difference between the Nubian dialects (*Maḥasī*) spoken by the Maḥa in Middle Nubia and those spoken further north by the Kenūz (Kenzi) and further south by the Danāḳla. However, the general feature of this period is that a large part of the sedentary population turned nomad or semi-nomad. Ibn Khaldūn, who was contemporary with this development, saw in it confirmation of his sociological scheme according to which sedentarization is the decadent stage of the evolutionary cycle of societies; its contrast with the vitality of nearby nomads provokes the intervention of these latter and the beginning of a new cycle.

Speaking of the disintegration of the kingdom by the Beduin *ḳabīla*s, in particular the Djuhayna, Ibn Khaldūn writes: 'And there remains no trace of central authority [*mulk*] in their lands because of the change wrought in them by the influence of Arab beduinization through intermarriage and alliance.' Nevertheless, we must not over-simplify a complex situation and suggest that there was bipolarization and general nomadization.

What is certain is that Arabization led to slow but profound cultural changes, for example the change from matrilineal to patrilineal succession. Similarly, the adoption of Arabic and the search for an Arab identity became general; even though between the Nile and Bornu this Arabization was accompanied by a marked influence of African languages on the Arabic dialects, even if in Nubia proper (from Assouan to Dunḳula) bilingualism was widespread.

Women were ousted from public life and new social customs governed by Islamic laws (*sharīʿa*) were gradually introduced.

While the Christian arts and architecture disappeared, the minor autochthonous arts survived in crafts but, as Ibn Khaldūn observes, the uncouth Beduins who came to power in Nubia did not bring with them any of the technical and artistic refinement which at that time distinguished the central Islamic lands. In this respect, Nubia remained a neglected periphery.

Ibn Khaldūn also mentions that conversion to Islam dispensed the Nubians from tax (*djizya*). But, as already in the time of the *baḳt*, the shortage of slaves had sometimes led to the taking of slaves in Nubia itself, the expansion of Islam pushing the hunting and purchasing grounds further south at the expense of the black peoples living between the Upper Nile and the south of Lake Chad. The decay of the state finally ended in a strengthening of ethnic structures, an impoverishment linked to the preponderance of nomadism and hence to a temporary social regression.

Nubia in Africa

Historians today consider that in the past the northern, or Arab, factor in the history of Nubia was overemphasized, at the expense of both autonomous internal developments and relations with black African cultures. It arose from the imbalance in the sources for this history in favour of written Arab documents, whereas archaeological work, coupled with oral tradition is only just getting underway with, however, interesting results, especially along the east–west axis of the Sudan and even right in the desert of the Bēdja, some of whom, according to Ibn Khaldūn, embraced Christianity. It is important to stress the creative originality of Nubian culture itself in relation to the Coptic communities whose monks sought refuge in Nubia in times of persecution. Nubia, on the other hand, communicated documents found in the Coptic monasteries of Upper Egypt and exported so-called Dunḳula ware.

As for trade via the Red Sea, it flourished until the sixteenth century and the arrival of the Portuguese. Indeed, the Fāṭimids had opted for Nubia as its intermediary with the Indian Ocean through the ports of ʿAydhāo, where Ibn Baṭṭūṭa stayed, and Sawākin. The Arabs and the Bēdja were involved in the traffic through treaties. ʿAydhāb which had owed its extraordinary prosperity to the decline of the Sinai route as a result of the presence of the crusaders in Palestine, declined at the end of the fourteenth century with the rise of Jeddah on the Asian shore; at the beginning of the fifteenth century, its decline was precipitated by Sultan Bārsbāyʿs decision to ruin it as an act of retaliation against the local Arabs and Arabized Bēdja. Sawākin, further south, took over, although it had been attacked by Sultan Baybars before it was recognized by the Mamlūks in return for an annual payment of slaves, camels and ivory. Mamlūk control was tightened in the middle of the fifteenth century.

We shall have to await further evidence before we can say whether relations between Nubia and Christian Ethiopia were closer than is suggested by the scanty evidence that we presently have.

As for relations with the south, they are even more difficult to be sure about. The southernmost point of ʿAlwa was near Wad Medani. Arab authors, who distinguish the Nuba from other blacks, give a few ethnic names: the Kersa and the Bakunna. Ibn ʿAbd al-Zāhir records an attack against ʿAlwa in about 1290; it may have come from ancestors of the Funj, who had reached the Gezira from the south down the Blue Nile. But it may be that the invaders came from Kānem or Darfūr.

To the west, we must be careful not to consider Nubia as the centre for the diffusion of Christianity as far as West Africa through the Central Sudan. Nor must we accept uncritically the thesis of the diffusion of iron-smelting in Africa from Meroe. Not all Christian or Islamic influences must be credited to the countries of the Nile valley, even though the oral traditions of West Africa often mention eastern origins. But such influences, if they existed, must rather have come from medieval Nubia rather than Meroe.

A number of material remains do indeed point to a Nubian cultural impact along the Sudanese routes from Zenkor and Abū Sufyaān in Kordofan to Nguru (Nigeria) through Darfūr and Borno. The pottery from Zenkor resembles that of Soba. At ʿAn Farah in northern Darfūr the ruins of red-brick buildings, identified as a monastery and churches, contain potsherds of Nubian origin from between the eighth and eleventh centuries, decorated with Christian symbols. Of the chain of similar sites, Birnin Gazargamo dates from the sixteenth century at least, while the Chadian sites at Koro Toro and Bochianga, over 1,450 km from the Nile, contain Nubian-style pottery dating from the year 1000 of the Christian era.

The Darfūr region probably played a crucial role in relation to West Africa, but its history is as yet very unclear. It seems that there was a peaceful transfer of hegemony from the Dādju in the south to the Tundjur in the north (in the ninth century?) and finally to the Fūr.

In about 1240, according to Arkell, Darfūr was conquered by Dunama, the great king of Kānem, whose power extended as far as the Nile, in Maris, at the point closest to the so-called route Darb al-Arbaʿin. Borno's influence over Darfār persisted for four centuries, especially under the role of *Mai* Idris in the sixteenth century. In reality Borno cultural hegemony, detectable from the Nile to Hausaland or even to Gao in the administration, the architectural styles and the role of queen-mothers, does not necessarily signify political domination.

According to Arkell, Uri, in northern Darfūr, was a Tundjur and later a Kānem metropolis. It was probably an important emporium at the crossroads of the Darb al-Arbaʿin and the east–west savannah route known as *tariḳ al-Sūdān*. It does not seem to have been used for the pilgrim traffic prior to the sixteenth century. Until then, the normal route from the Sudan to the Holy Places, including for rulers, went by way of the North African coast, Egypt and ʿAydhāb. In the sixteenth century, the Moroccan invasion of Gao and the decline in security that followed had a positive influence, on the one hand, on the far western route along the Atlantic, and, on the other, on the route through the Nile valley, as a result of the destruction of Christian rule in Nubia and the consolidation of Islamic power in Sennar, Darfūr and Wadaī. Moreover, Islam was, initially, above all a court religion under the Tundjur and only penetrated the masses under the Kayra Fūr in the seventeenth century.

Here, as in Nubia, Arabization led in the long run to profound ethnic, cultural, religious, economic, social and political changes. In 1391, Sultan Barḳūḳ in Cairo received a letter from the king of Borno complaining of the exactions of the Djudham and other Arabs, who were taking his subjects captive, even when they were Muslims, as slaves and selling them to dealers from Egypt, Syria and elsewhere. This kind of occurrence indicates an evolution that reaches far beyond the period covered by this volume.

17 The Horn of Africa: The Solomonids in Ethiopia and the States of the Horn of Africa

The political geography of the Horn from the thirteenth to the sixteenth century

The political situation was extremely complex. The most widely known state, in the northern highlands of Ethiopia, was the Christian kingdom which in 1270, passed from the hands of the Zagwe to those of the Solomonid dynasty that claimed descent from King Solomon. This kingdom stretched to Shoa in the south, and to the shores of Lake Tana and the upper Blue Nile in the west. To the north-west lay the kingdom of the Falasha (the so-called 'Jews of Ethiopia') and to the south-west the kingdom of Gojam as well as the powerful state of Damot which represented the traditional faith against the Christian and Muslim principalities and exercised hegemony over the whole region of the Shoa plateau. As for the Muslim emirates, they stretched along the Red Sea coast from the Gulf of Aden and the Indian Ocean by way of Zeila, Berbera, Mogadishu and Merka and also, in the interior, in the eastern foothills of the Ethiopian highlands, Bali, Ifat, ʿAdal etc. These principalities thus enjoyed a strategic position on this vital sector on the route of the international spice trade.

Peoples and languages

The Horn of Africa is a 'museum of peoples'. Several African language groups are represented there, starting with Congo-Kordofian and Afro-Asiatic with the following three branches: Cushitic (Bēdja, Agew, Burgi-Sidamo, Galla and Omotic in the Omo basin etc.); Semitic (Harari in Harar conquered by Muslim princes exiled from Ifat, Amharic, the language of members of the so-called Solomonid dynasty, Gurage and Geʿez). This last-named language had been the literary language of the Ethiopian Church since the fourth century, and as such it has continued down to the present day. As for Tigre and Tigrigna, they are spoken in Eritrea and Tigre. Arabic was the religious and commercial language throughout the eastern part of this region.

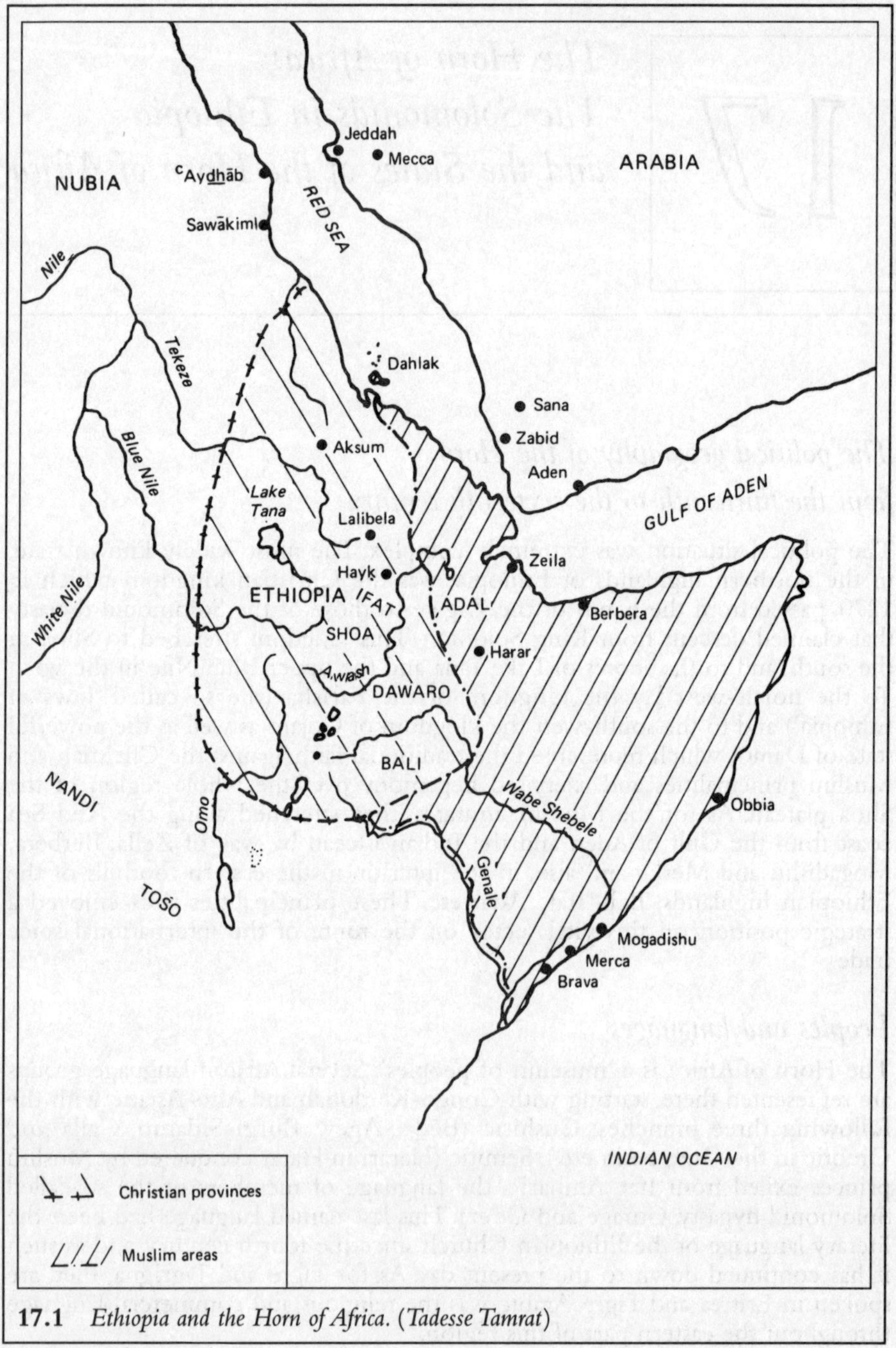

17.1 *Ethiopia and the Horn of Africa. (Tadesse Tamrat)*

The Muslim principalities of the coast

The old African states (Falasha, Gojjam and Damot) are known to us through the chronicles of the Christian and Muslim kingdoms, and even then rather late; and those chronicles only show them when they are being defeated. Only archaeological and linguistic research will make it possible to deepen our historical knowledge of these peoples. On the other hand, the Muslim principalities are much better known.

In the far north, the Dahlak Islands, which, together with the Farasan Islands off the Arabian peninsula, are a bridge between the Yemen and Eritrea and control traffic in the southern sector of the Red Sea. At one time they were controlled by the Yemen, but the archipelago freed itself in the thirteenth century; it was an emirate which was based on trade and piracy and succeeded in preserving its autonomy between the opposing attempts at hegemony by the Mamlūks of Egypt and the Yemeni and Ethiopian rulers.

Further south, at the bottom of the Gulf of Aden, Ibn Baṭṭūṭa, who travelled through the region in the fourteenth century, mentions Zeila, a town inhabited by the black 'Berbera' (Somali) and engaged in camel- and sheep-breeding, fishing and trade.

Maḳdis͟hu (Mogadishu) was also a large commercial centre which, according to Ibn Baṭṭūṭa, exported peerless cloth while growing large quantities of rice, fruits (bananas and mangoes) and vegetables. The town was under the authority of a s͟hayk͟h assisted by viziers. It was dominated by an aristocracy of merchants and lawyers and officials and enjoyed extraordinary international fame for the urbanity and generous hospitality of its inhabitants.

Islam and the teaching of the Koran were highly developed there, but the original African language and the related social and cultural structures remained very much alive.

Arab geographers also tell us about three other trading cities in the region. First, there was Berbera, already mentioned by Ptolemy and in the *Periplus of the Erythraean Sea*; it even gave its name to the Gulf of Aden, which Arab geographers called the Sea or Gulf of Barbara; and they carefully distinguished its inhabitants, the Berābir, from the Berbers, the Swahili and the Abyssinians. They were most likely Somali.

Situated on the southern coast of the Horn, the towns of Merca and Brava were within the orbit and commercial network of Mogadishu, which had a rich and dynamic hinterland.

The Christian and Muslim states in relation to the communities practising traditional African religions

From the tenth century, the extension of coastal trade networks into the hinterland through the expansion of internal routes was the major feature that led to bitter clashes between the principalities of the region. Along these routes travelled numerous cultural and religious influences. From the middle of the thirteenth century even the Christian Zagwe kingdom in northern Ethiopia was using as its outlet not only the sultanate of Dahlak but also the southern port of Zeila. The development of this latter port is probably to be explained by the domination of the Muslim state of Ifat situated between the Gulf and the Shoa plateau; but also by the southward shift of the political centre of Christian Ethiopia and the advent of the Solomonid dynasty.

Yekuno-Amlāk, one of the local leaders in Amhara, is portrayed by the traditions as the man who put an end to the Zagwe dynasty in 1270 and, according to them, restored the ancient Solomonid dynasty of Axum. In reality, for a long time, the Christian settlements in the southern provinces of Ethiopia had been involved in a network of trading relations stretching from the Gulf of Aden to the Shoa plateau, leading, particularly in the Awash basin, to numerous interactions with the Muslims and the followers of traditional religions.

One of the best known rulers of the latter communities is the famous 'king of Damot' mentioned by Ibn Khaldūn. He dominated the region in the thirteenth century and the Christian and Muslim settlements suffered his rule. By the twelfth century, the Christians were already becoming more confident since there is mention of an unsuccessful Zagwe expedition against Damot in which the Zagwe king lost his life. But gradually Zagwe hegemony replaced that of Damot to the point where the Christians of the region considered themselves the subjects of the Zagwe kings; some of them controlled the trading routes between Shoa in the south and Tigre in the north from where they brought back salt which they exchanged for horses and mules. These Christians also engaged in very prosperous mixed farming based on large families and abundant slave labour. Their settlements, which had a strong sense of religious identity, thus moved from paying tribute to the kings of Damot to owing allegiance to the Zagwe, an allegiance compensated for by real economic influence based on their position as commercial middlemen.

The Muslim communities also began by being subjected to traditional African kings. They also had a strong sense of having originally come from Mecca. They competed with one another and were gradually breaking away from Damot. Their principalities sometimes combined to form larger entities such as the 'sultanate of Shoa' or Ifat. They spoke Ethio-Semitic and based their rather comfortable existence, to a much greater extent, on long-distance trade, co-operating when necessary with their Christian neighbours of Shoa and Amhara. The port of Zeila, the trading outlet from central Ethiopia, benefited enormously from this co-operation in a spirit of tolerance, It seems that, before seizing power, Yekuno-Amlāk had made firm alliances with both the Muslim and Christian communities in Shoa. In a letter to Baybars of Egypt (thirteenth century), he expressed pride in having many Muslim horsemen in his army.

Thus, while claiming a glorious past, the Solomonid dynasty rested on an economic and military force in the southern provinces, and it thus shifted the centre of the Ethiopian empire towards Amhara and Shoa.

The kingdom of Ethiopia under the Solomonids

The beginnings of Solomonid rule were difficult both domestically and externally. One of the acute problems to be resolved was that of the succession to the throne. The following solution was adopted: all the kin of Yekuno-Amlāk except his direct descendants were put together on the inaccessible heights of Mount Geshen, which was closely guarded. The princes detained there under house arrest were deprived of all contact with the outside world, but were otherwise well treated. They took up the study of religiously inspired fine arts. And it was only when the ruler died without an heir that one of the exiles was selected as master of the country. This gave rise to the nickname 'mountain of the kings' given to this palace and natural gaol turned into a state institution.

But the external danger was much thornier: this involved relations with the increasingly powerful Muslim principalities between the Gulf of Aden and the Awash valley. But at the time of the accession of Amde-Siyon (1314–44), the grandson of Yekuno-Amlāk, Solomonid power was fragile: reduced essentially to the old Zagwe territory, it had to face up to the agitation of the Jewish (Falasha) and communities of traditional religion communities, not to mention Muslim expansionism. The victorious campaigns conducted by Amde-Siyon against Damot and Gojjam in particular, ended in the annexation of the area north of Lake Tana and control of the termini of the commercial traffic coming from the Gulf of Aden.

This economic and political subjugation substituted resentment and hatred in Muslim circles for the tolerance that had previously existed.

Using as an excuse the capture and enslavement of one of his subjects by prince Aḳˁl Dīn of Ifat, the leading Muslim power in the region, Amde-Siyon sacked Ifat which, after the death of its prince in the battle, became a tributary state of Ethiopia. Other principalities, like Dawāro, had to conclude treaties of friendship. If we add to that the earlier conquest of communities of traditional religions, countries such as Damot and Gojjam, it can be seen that the Ethiopia of Amde-Siyon had accumulated an enormous mass of resources in men and goods. Revolts remained chronic like the one in 1320 that agitated the Christian province of Tigre, and those in 1332 when simultaneous revolts shook Christian power; but it only emerged from them strengthened. The fame of Amde-Siyon's exploits spread far and wide in the Middle East, to such an extent that al-ˁUmari, who was contemporary with these events, wrote of the Ethiopian emperor in these terms: 'It is said that he has ninety-nine kings under him, and that he makes up the hundred.' Although these figures are exaggerated, they are impressive since the Arab historian included among them 'the seven Muslim kingdoms of Ethiopia'.

The Muslim states and Ethiopia

The empire formed by Amde-Siyon remained disparate on the religious, ethnic and linguistic levels. Certainly, as al-ˁUmari stresses, although power was hereditary in the vassal kingdoms, 'none among them has effective authority without being invested by the king of the Amhara'.

This political control of the tributary states made it necessary to maintain a large army to control the provinces and vassal states; troops stationed in one region were recruited in another with a different ethnic group, so as to guarantee the loyalty of the soldiers. This was the price to be paid for maintaining the imperial order, collecting tribute and ensuring the safety of the main trade routes. Reinforcements from neighbouring territories were sent in when needed, and when the situation became critical, as in 1332, the ruler himself would lead the army to put down the rebellion. In fact constant territorial expansion obliged the monarchs to keep the court on a war footing, and do without a fixed residence in a large capital because of the need to show the strength of the government in every region.

The Structure of the Ethiopian empire

The mobile camp of the Solomonid kings was thus the administrative centre and the economic and political focus of the empire and also a melting pot in which the various races and cultures were gradually being merged. It had royal guards and contingents of soldiers, priests assigned to the imperial chapels, and Christian and Muslim traders and craftsmen who found there the demand and the most lucrative market in the empire. In the dry season, the number of people flocking to the court swelled with the influx of vassal princes, governors bearing tribute and subjects who had come seeking decisions from the monarch and his officials. This made it the equivalent of an average town whose mobility was admirably functional since, unlike a permanent settlement, it went out among the rural populations, making for a more dynamic relationship with all the regions and thus promoting cultural assimilation and political integration. That was particularly true for the prisoners recruited in large numbers into the Christian army or assigned to duties in the palace, while princes of the vassal territories were held at the court as guests or hostages, often eventually being appointed to senior positions of responsibility, and developing real devotion to the imperial order.

Nevertheless, it is important not to lose sight either of the repressive aspect of these moves as seen in the massive demands for labour and goods which went with them. In fact, the usual form of political authority in the empire was indirect rule, with local customs remaining in force; in some respects, therefore, the mobility of the court was the expression of a measure of centralization aimed at reducing regional particularisms. That appears above all with the increase in the size of the court and the army in the time of Amde-Siyon. Henceforward, non-payment of tribute was tantamount to an act of high treason. The grant of fiefs to many subjects was a reward for services and at the same time an incentive to supply them. Military control of the hinterland which supplied *ḥabas̱ha* slaves, who were much sought after in the Near East, and were bought and sold by Muslims, brought in more revenues which built up in the form of gold and ivory, the main items of trade in the region. Furthermore, the rich lands of the Ethiopian plateau supplied the coastal towns with cereals and fresh fruits. The Ethiopian rulers benefited considerably from this economic activity in two ways: first, indirectly by taxing merchandise on entering and leaving the country; but, above all, by investing directly in long-distance trade. But, in the long run, the military, political and economic expansion of the Solomonids only ended up provoking as a response the growing organization of the Muslim powers in the area, particularly under the leadership of a break-away branch of ʿUmar Walasma's clan who, working out of the Harar plateau, built up a formidable network of alliances in the area between the Dahlak Islands and the Somali coast on the Indian Ocean. This was the sanctuary of Muslim resistance to Ethiopian power until the *djihād* of 'Imām Gragn' in the sixteenth century.

The revival of the Ethiopian Church

The period from the thirteenth to the sixteenth century also saw a vigorous revival of the Ethiopian Church. In the beginning, the Church was firmly established only in the north, in the ancient provinces of Eritrea, Tigre, Lasta (cradle of the Zagwe and metropolitan see) and Amhara. And even in this last region it was only on the eve of the rise of the Solomonids that an influential monastic school was established by a remarkable monk from Lasta, Iyesus-Moʿa. As the empire expanded southwards, Amhara and Shoa began to provide themselves with a network of major religious establishments, which became centres for the propagation of the Christian faith in all directions. Two major factors explain this considerable diffusion: the internal dynamism within the Church itself and the deliberate policy of the Solomonids, who were more committed to proselytism than the Zagwe kings, and had much greater resources.

Thus the monastery founded by Iyesus-Moʿa in Amhara on an island in Lake Hayḳ was followed by others all over the south of the country. But the rules in these institutions continued the old tradition of the founding fathers of the hermit life, Saint Anthony and Saint Pachomius. At the beginning, the aim of the Ethiopian founders, as of their Egyptian models, was not to spread the faith but to seek personal salvation by abandoning the world to lead a life devoted to meditation and sacrifice in inaccessible places: deserts, mountains, caves, islands etc. But this life of mortification alone or in a community with a few disciples inevitably attracted the attention of the indigenous people who soon began to spread the fame of the hermits and their spiritual exploits.

Gradually, pious persons from ordinary backgrounds or even from princely families came to swell the ranks of the anchorites. Organization became more complex. The community received endowments of land; it would build a church, schools and hospitals, set up a production and distribution system to meet the needs of spirit and body: the poor, the aged and orphans mixed with pilgrims. A hierarchy of democratically elected monks lived by a precise rule

17.2 *Lalibela: St George's Church, a general aerial view of the excavated church.* (*Photo: G. Gerster/Agence Rapho,* Afrique, continent méconnu, *Selection du Reader's Digest, Paris, 1979*)

with some division of labour: calligraphy, religious painting, music and teaching; the country's great monasteries vied among themselves to attract the best specialists who were loaded with honours and money. Brilliant but poor students enjoyed assistance and often entered the religious life either as monks vowed to chastity or as married priests. Nevertheless, the monastic schools were not reserved to future churchmen. With a de facto monopoly of teaching, they attracted all the young men who were ambitious to enter the Christian elite and government of the country. This was particularly true of the princes detained on Mount Geshen.

The Church had this control of teaching from the time of the Christian kingdom of Axum until the fourteenth century and the spread of monasteries in Amhara and Shoa, and it explains the clergy's dominant position in the state apparatus.

Thus the whole of Ethiopia came to be covered with monasteries thanks to the missionary zeal of disciples from the first convents which remained the most prestigious ones: Debre Asbo (later renamed Debre Libanos), founded in Shoa by Tekle-Haymanot (thirteenth century), Debre Gol in Amhara started by Abba Anorewos and Daga on an island in Lake Tana. In the northernmost part of the country, including present-day Eritrea, the monastic revival owed a great deal to the resourceful dynamism of Saint Abba Ewostatewos.

With the agreement of Emperor Amde-Siyon, the Egyptian primate (*abunna*) of the Ethiopian Church, bishop Yakob, systematically organized the monasteries into orders governed by rules and dioceses. The emperor, who was establishing military garrisons all over the country, was anxious to help in the diffusion of monasteries among the Falasha, in Godjam (Gojam) in Damot and even in the Muslim fiefs of Ifat, Bali etc. The rulers, who made generous land grants to them, required that the local people protect them, and they did not hesitate to punish any who failed to harshly, Thus, in the spirit of the peoples who were followers of the traditional or Muslim religions, the image of the Ethiopian Church as inextricably linked with Ethiopian imperialism. Moreover, the over-protected monasteries failed to assert their moral independence. This explains why their actual influence in the countries where they were established was insignificant, and indeed that influence evaporated at the first onset of the Muslim counter-attack in the sixteenth century.

Furthermore, this Church was spiritually dependent on the Coptic patriarch of Alexandria who appointed Egyptian bishops to head the ecclesiastical hierarchy of the empire. Two monastic orders or 'houses' exercised undisputed pre-eminence over the Ethiopian Church. The 'house' of Tekle-Haymanot with its mother house at Debre Libanos was closely associated with the imperial court, which earned it the obedience of most religious communities. As for the house of Ewostatewos, from the fourteenth century it represented a militant minority which established monasteries from Tigre to Eritrea where the great convent of Debre Bizen was established.

It must be noted that this Ethiopian Church was also highly decentralized. The Egyptian episcopate and the emperor did everything they could to reduce this decentralization in order to assert their own authority; they were successful with the secular churches staffed by married priests who were at the mercy of the lay power. The major monasteries, on the other hand, jealously protected their autonomy. Around the Egyptian bishops and at the imperial court, there were moreover ecclesiastical officials, the most prestigious of whom in the monarch's entourage was the *aḳabe-seat* chosen originally from among the monks of the island monastery of Hayḳ, before the abbots of Debre Libanos began to hold this office ex officio.

The period between the thirteenth and the sixteenth century was certainly the most productive in the history of the Ethiopian Church. Despite the frequent rivalries between the orders of Tekle-Haymanot and Ewostatewos, the monastic movement played a decisive role in the expansion of the Church, as well as in the cultural revival, as Guidi and Cerulli have shown for literature. The arts were not left behind during this period, to judge by the illuminated manuscripts, church murals and richly decorated crosses and croziers which have survived for many centuries down to the present day. The emperors were informed patrons since the most remarkable of them, Zera-Yakob (1434–68), is said to have produced a number of theological treatises. The vitality of religious

17.3 *A fifteenth-century Ethiopian manuscript, portraying the Annunciation (Monastery of Yahya Giyorgis).* (*UNESCO/New York Graphic Society,* Ethiopia: illuminated manuscripts, *New York, 1961*)

activity inevitably involved sometimes serious controversies over doctrinal and liturgical issues. In this respect, the instructions of the Egyptian bishops were increasingly challenged by a recalcitrant Ethiopian clergy which, by the end of the fifteenth century, as on the brink of a total break from the patriarchate of Alexandria.

Struggles between Christians and Muslims: The appearance of the Portuguese

The patriarchate of Alexandria may indeed have been a sort of fetter for the Ethiopian Church, but it was also the sole bridge to the Christians of the Holy Land and the rest of Christendom – in other words it was a vital lifeline.

The Ethiopian authorities were well aware of this. That is why the tension with the Coptic Church of Egypt never resulted in open schism. In fact, Ethiopia was caught in a serious contradiction: it wanted both to exploit its identity as a Christian state to establish economic and military relations with Europe, and, at the same time, it was realistically concerned to safeguard peaceful co-existence with its Muslim neighbours living on both sides of the Red Sea, in particular the Yemen. This was all the more so as Mamlūks Egypt which controlled the routes to the Mediterranean and the Indian Ocean held almost all the keys to Ethiopian diplomacy. That helps to understand why the Ethiopian leaders continued to send slaves and gold, and other presents, to the sultan in Cairo whenever they were negotiating the despatch of a new Egyptian bishop or the passage of Ethiopian pilgrims to the Holy Places. But when, with Amde-Siyon, the territorial power of Ethiopia had extended over Muslim areas that were in principle under the protection of the sultan of Egypt, the demands of the Christian emperors became more specific. Thus, Seyfe-Arʿad, Amde-Siyon's immediate successor, led his army as far as the Nile valley in an attempt to reinforce the siege of Alexandria by the king of Cyprus in 1365. Al-Maḳrīzī reports the victories of Dawit I (1380–1412)) over the Arabs in the region of Aswan and the efforts of the Emperor Yishak (1413–30) to form an alliance with Christian Europe in order to end Muslim domination in the Near East. A secret delegation that Yishak sent to Europe was intercepted by the Egyptian authorities on its way back and the head of the delegation hanged. Faced with the persecution of the Copts in Egypt, Zera-Yakob (1434–68) made a strong protest and kept the Egyptian ambassador a prisoner for four years after he had brought back a sarcastic reply from the sultan. It was a far cry from the time when, in the thirteenth century, Yekuno-Amlāk of Ethiopia described himself as 'the most humble of the servants' of Sultan Baybars.

From the fourteenth to the sixteenth century, Ethiopian monks protected by the new power of their princes had formed a chain of small communities reaching as far as Rome, Florence and Venice, by way of the Nile valley, the Holy Land and the islands of Cyprus and Rhodes. Their accounts of the prodigious power of the emperors of their country from the time of Amde-

Siyon led many Europeans to identify these Christian rulers with the legendary 'Prester John', especially as the Mamlūks' decision to cut all communication between Europe and Ethiopia simply incited the latter to send even more missions to the north of the Mediterranean.

In 1450, one of them visited Rome and Naples and brought back a number of European artisans and craftsmen. Some strategists even envisaged the Ethiopians participating in the last crusades.

But in the final analysis, geopolitics was against Ethiopia. Access to the Mediterranean was controlled from all directions by the Mamlūks; and in the person of the patriarch of Alexandria, who controlled the Ethiopian Church, they held a trump card which challenged the very bases of the system of the Ethiopian emperors. These latter were eventually forced to give in to Cairo's demands.

When, in response to the actions of Zera-Yakob, Sultan Jaḳmaḳ had the patriarch of Alexandria beaten and forced him to ask the emperor of Ethiopia to release his imprisoned ambassador, the patriarch himself now had to obtain permission from the sultan to communicate with Ethiopia. The result was that it was 30 years before a new bishop was enthroned – 30 years in which the Ethiopians resumed their usual supplications accompanied by presents to the sultan. Only then 'the priests became many, the Churches were restored, and happiness filled all the land'. (Perruchon, 1894). Thus the position of Ethiopia induced a spiritual dependence and this led to dependency in many other areas.

The Zenith and decline of Ethiopia

At the end of the fifteenth century, after the high point of Christian domination in the reign of Zera-Yakob, decline set in. This emperor had reorganized and purified the Ethiopian Church. He had reconciled the militant monastic order of Ewosatatewos with the other religious 'houses', thus eliminating an extremely serious threat to the overall stability of the system. He had also eradicated the survivals of pre-Christian traditional religious beliefs and practices. Himself a scholarly theologian, he had persecuted dissident monks and established in Debre Berhan (Shoa), a capital equipped with a highly centralized administration. That enabled him to repel the continued attacks by the kingdom of ʿAdal on the eastern provinces and crush the sultan of Hadya's efforts at rebellion. On what is today the Eritrean plateau he founded an outpost of intrepid Maya soldiers transferred from Shoa. This was the zenith, but the price was high. Serious plots were brutally repressed. That is why Zera-Yakob's son and successor, Beide-Maryam (1468–78), began by pardoning many detainees and loosening the vice of centralized power. But this simply led to further explosions of revolt that Beide-Maryam had great difficulty in containing right up to his death. He left two minor sons and hence two groups of supporters who fought one another. It is not surprising that the first serious defeat inflicted on the Ethiopian army by the forces of ʿAdal occurred under Beide-Maryam. The decline continued relentlessly until the final collapse before the d̲jihād of Imām Gragn.

18 The Development of Swahili Civilization

The period from the twelfth to the fifteenth century saw the development on the islands and coast of East Africa of the so-called 'Swahili' people and states which are known from the tenth century. The sudden arrival of the Portuguese conquerors in the sixteenth century marked the great break, the apogee of this Swahili civilization.

In the twelfth century, there was not yet a homogeneous community. Ethnically, the coastal groups saw an influx of people from the interior and from beyond the seas: Arabs, Persians and Indians. Socially, the mass of ordinary free men was dominated by a ruling elite performing traditional functions and by a merchant class wielding economic power. Slaves were not yet numerous enough to merit mention by the chroniclers, whereas by the end of the fifteenth century a Portuguese report describes them as working as farm labourers at Kilwa. There was thus considerable social differentiation about which unfortunately little is known because of the lack of documents.

Economy and commerce

Agriculture and fishing

These accounted for most productive activities. Al-Masʿūdī (tenth century) lists among the food crops: bananas, durra, yams and coconuts. Other authors mention tamarinds and sugar-cane. In the fifteenth century, a Portuguese mentions oranges and lemons, various peas, cotton and cattle at Kilwa. The spindles found in ruins are evidence that spinning and weaving were practised.

Fishing, which al-Idrīsī says was the chief activity of Malindi, is frequently recorded by Arab authors who also mention that pearls, shells and turtle shells were gathered and sold. The shells were used to make necklaces, spoons, plates etc.

The art of navigation developed in two directions: boat-building, either dug-outs (*mtumbwi*) or stitched (*mitepe*) craft equivalent, according to the same anonymous Portuguese, to a 50-tonne caravel. This variety of boats is reflected in the large number of names for them in Kiswahili. Furthermore, study of the astronomical knowledge of the peoples of this region indicates that this knowledge would have had no purpose and been practically impossible to acquire without commercial sailing of the Indian ocean.

Trade and urbanization

Writers report two types of human settlement: villages and towns. The villages were built of mud bricks, bamboo sticks and palm leaves with roofs of leaves and thatch. The villagers hunted for leopards (sometimes rendered harmless by particular rituals) and worked iron. A huge drum played a role in their traditional form of worship. Towns already included stone buildings in which the notables and wealthy traders of Swahili society lived as well as Islamic scholars. Trade there was particularly profitable because of the varying subjective estimates of the value of goods. Thus, imported articles, because of their scarcity, were automatically regarded as luxury objects which were exchanged for gold and ivory which were produced in abundance in the hinterland and thus under-valued.

In the twelfth century, most trade passed via the island of Zanzibar and the Lamu archipelago. But archaeological excavations also show that from the ninth century, the town of Manda on the island of the same name played a major role, and that was the case until the thirteenth century when Kilwa clearly became more important, as the remains excavated reveal; Sassanid-Islamic pottery, Song porcelain from China, masses of cowries, glass beads etc. At Gedi, 'black and yellow' Islamic pottery was imported.

After other Arab sources that already refer to Sofala exporting gold, al-Idrīsī describes the string of coastal and island towns where ships called, such as Brava, Mombasa, Pangani and Ungudja (later Zanzibar). Of Malindi, he states: 'Iron is their main source of revenue and main item of trade.' Moreover, slag has been found. There were also leopard skins and fish.

At the beginning of the thirteenth century, Yāḳūt also writes of Mogadishu with its mixed population, including Arab Muslims; it was one of the finest towns of East Africa, exporting ebony and sandalwood, ivory and ambergris.

Yāḳūt is also the first to identify Kilwa by that name. It was ruled by the so-called S͟hīrāzī dynasty which seems to have been challenged for a time by the Shang people (perhaps from the island of Sanje-ya-Kāti); what was at stake in this rivalry doubtless being control of trade routes. According to the *Kilwa Chronicle*, Kilwa ultimately prevailed, giving rise to the brilliant development of Swahili civilization under the new dynasty of Abū ʿl-Mawāḥib. The quantity of goods imported by Kilwa grew appreciably: sgraffito pottery, porcelain, bottles and flasks for perfumes and kohl. The same types of articles coming principally from Iran and Iraq have been found at Gedi.

It was in the fourteenth century, however, that trade reached its highest level, as Ibn Baṭṭūṭa, who visited the area in 1332, testifies. He tells us that Mogadishu was a major trading centre, where every foreign merchant could find a correspondent or a commercial agent to manage his affairs. The town exported its *makdashi* (Mogadishu cloth), sold as far away as Egypt from where, along with Jerusalem, other textiles came.

Recent excavations have revealed the development at this same period of the town of Pate on the island of the same name. The second half of the fourteenth century saw the first appearance in the region of Muslim green-glazed monochrome ceramics and a large number of pieces of blue Chinese porcelain in the form of small canes.

In the fifteenth century, bluish-white Ming porcelain arrived at Gedi for the first time. However, during the same period, Kilwa seems to have gone through a period of decline associated with clashes between groups engaged in power struggles. Nevertheless, imports continued to increase, and there was twice as much Chinese porcelain as earthenware from the Islamic countries.

Increasingly, added to exports of gold and ivory, rhinoceros horn, ambergris etc. were slaves and cloth, both imported and exported, which circulated between Mombasa, Kilwa and Sofala. According to the *Kilwa Chronicle*, moreover, the island was purchased for a length of cloth equal to the island's total circumference. The ports of East Africa were themselves only staging posts in a multi-continental network linking Asia to the West by way of Madagascar and the Red Sea. In addition to these features were the producing centres of the interior of the continent such as the gold mines near Lake Nyasa, and those in the region of Sofala which, in the fourteenth century, fell under the control of the ruler of Kilwa. Archaeological discoveries like the yellow beads found in excavations in Zimbabwe which are identical to the glassware widespread in India in the thirteenth century show quite clearly the contacts between the coast and the owners of the mines in the hinterland, beginning with those of the Zambezi basin, as is indicated by the cowrie shells exchanged for gold and ivory at Gokomere and Kolomo. At Engaruka too, in present-day Tanzania cowrie shells and glass beads dating from the fifteenth and sixteenth centuries and identical to finds at Kilwa indicate the same type of trade whose mechanism is described by al-Idrīsī (twelfth century): 'Since they have no pack animals, they themselves transport their loads. They carry their goods on their heads or their backs to two towns – Mombasa and Malindi. There they sell and buy.'

As the medium of exchange, in addition to cowrie shells, they used glass beads, china and finally, in major centres such as Kisiwani, Mafia, Zanzibar, Pemba and above all Kilwa after the advent of the Shīrāzī dynasty, copper and silver coins. The presence of coins with a greater exchange value than cowries shows the large scale of business done and the value of the commodities traded. The abundance of gold at Kilwa nevertheless precluded it being used as a medium of payment. But the absence on metallic coins of any indication of place, date and value may indicate that what was important here since the tradition of using cowries existed was the number of units involved.

Trade, the source of great profits, also underlay social and cultural development thanks to the exchanges that it involved with the Arab, Persian, Indian and Chinese worlds. This last moreover only came into play directly from the fifteenth century when a squadron commanded by Cheng-Ho arrived in the region. Until the eleventh century, Chinese trading vessels did not go south or west of Java and Sumatra.

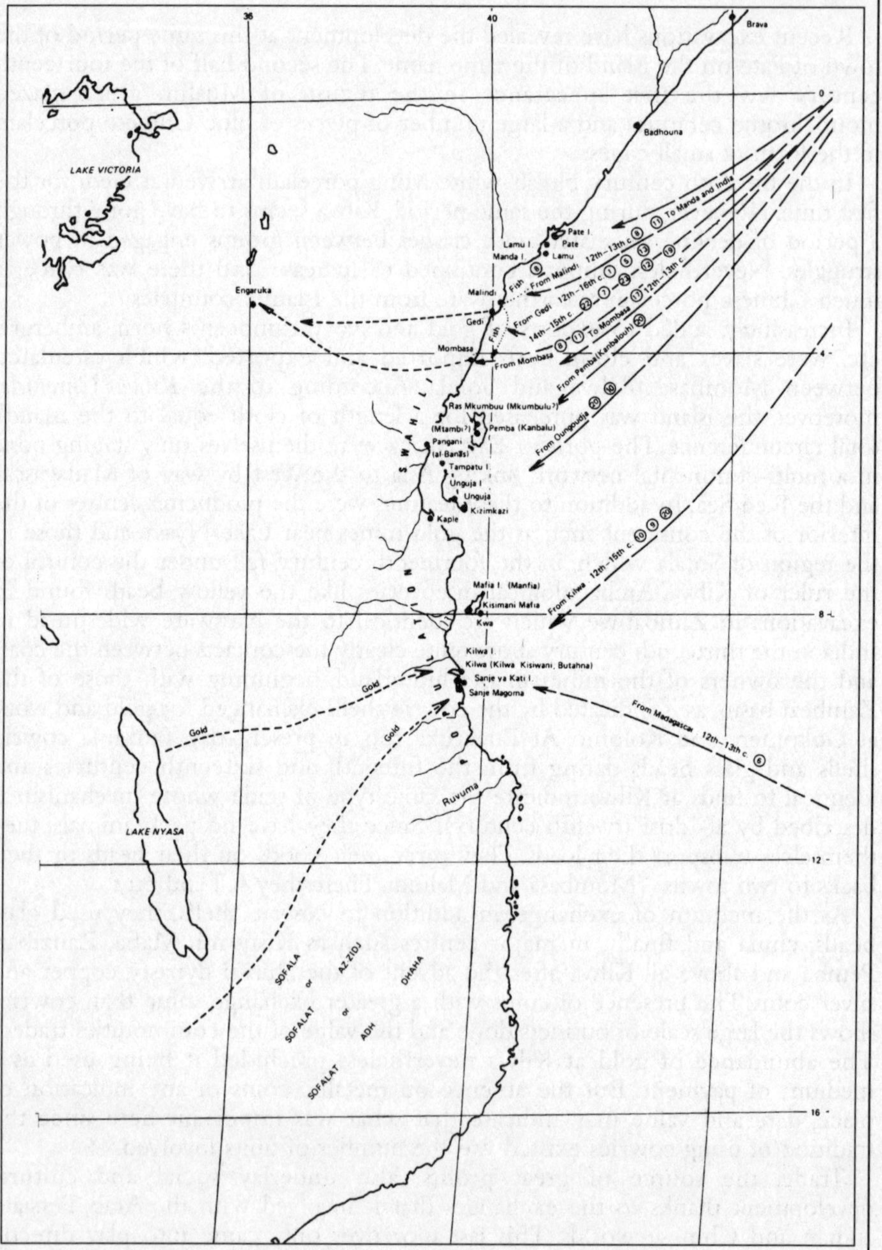

18.1 *Internal and transoceanic trade in the coastal towns of East Africa between the twelfth and fifteenth centuries.* (*V.V. Matveiev*)

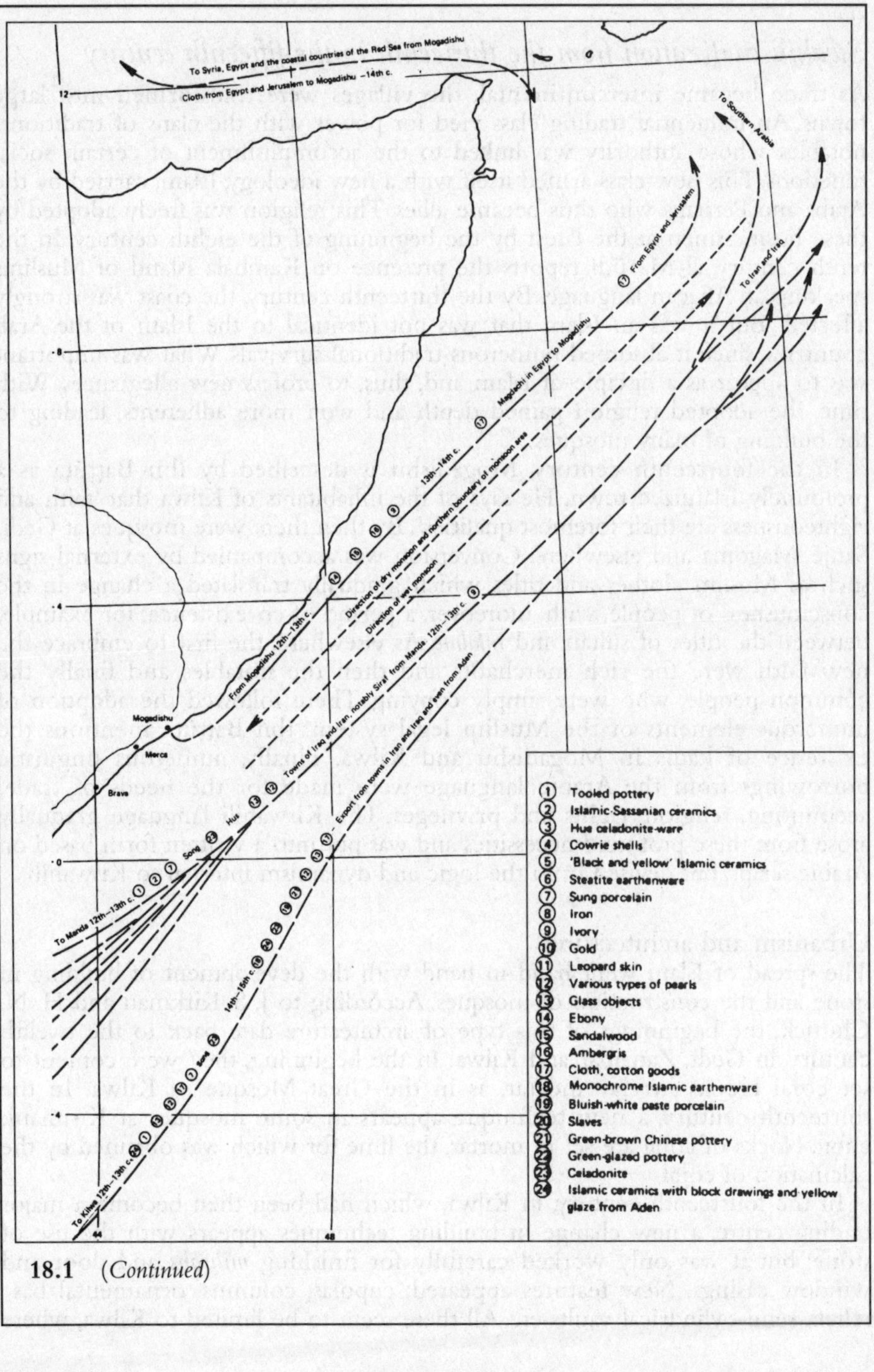
To Syria, Egypt and the coastal countries of the Red Sea from Mogadishu
Cloth from Egypt and Jerusalem to Mogadishu –14th c.
To Southern Arabia
From Egypt and Jerusalem
To Iran and Iraq
Magdechi in Egypt to Mogadishu
13th–14th c.
Direction of dry monsoon and northern boundary of monsoon area
Direction of wet monsoon
From Mogadishu 12th–13th c.
Towns of Iraq and Iran, notably Siraf from Manda 12th–13th c.
Export from towns in Iran and Iraq and even from Aden
Mogadishu
Merca
Brava
Hue
Song
To Manda 12th–13th c.
14th–15th c.
To Kilwa 12th–13th c.
12
8
4
0
4
44
48
1 Tooled pottery
2 Islamic-Sassanian ceramics
3 Hue celadonite-ware
4 Cowrie shells
5 'Black and yellow' Islamic ceramics
6 Steatite earthenware
7 Sung porcelain
8 Iron
9 Ivory
10 Gold
11 Leopard skin
12 Various types of pearls
13 Glass objects
14 Ebony
15 Sandalwood
16 Ambergris
17 Cloth, cotton goods
18 Monochrome Islamic earthenware
19 Bluish-white paste porcelain
20 Slaves
21 Green-brown Chinese pottery
22 Green-glazed pottery
23 Celadonite
24 Islamic ceramics with block drawings and yellow glaze from Aden

18.1 (*Continued*)

Swahili civilization from the thirteenth to the fifteenth century

As trade became intercontinental, the villages were transformed into large towns. An influential trading class vied for power with the clans of traditional notables whose authority was linked to the accomplishment of certain social functions. This new class armed itself with a new ideology, Islam, carried by the Arabs and Persians who thus became allies. This religion was freely adopted by these businessmen at the latest by the beginning of the eighth century. In the tenth century, al-Masʿūdī reports the presence on Kambala Island of Muslims speaking an African language. By the thirteenth century, the coast was strongly affected. But it was an Islam that was not identical to the Islam of the Arab countries, since it absorbed numerous traditional survivals. What was important was to appear as a disciple of Islam and, thus, to profess new allegiances. With time, the adopted religion gained depth and won more adherents, leading to the building of many mosques.

In the fourteenth century, Mogadishu is described by Ibn Baṭṭūṭa as a profoundly Islamized town. He says of the inhabitants of Kilwa that 'faith and righteousness are their foremost qualities'. By then there were mosques at Gedi, Sanje, Magoma and elsewhere. Conversion was accompanied by external signs such as Muslim clothes and titles which gradually translated a change in the consciousness of people, with, moreover, a period of co-existence; for example, between the titles of sultan and *mfalme*. As elsewhere, the first to embrace the new faith were the rich merchants and then the notables and finally the common people, who were simply copying. There followed the adoption of numerous elements of the Muslim legal system. Ibn Baṭṭūṭa mentions the existence of ḳāḍīs in Mogadishu and Kilwa. Finally, numerous linguistic borrowings from the Arabic language were made for the needs of trade, accounting, religion, rights and privileges. The Kiswahili language gradually arose from these profound necessities and was put into a written form based on Arabic script, but devised from the logic and dynamism internal to Kiswahili.

Urbanism and architecture

The spread of Islam went hand in hand with the development of building in stone and the construction of mosques. According to J. S. Kirkman and H. N. Chittick, the beginnings of this type of architecture date back to the twelfth century in Gedi, Zanzibar and Kilwa. In the beginning, they were content to set coral blocks in clay mortar, as in the Great Mosque of Kilwa. In the thirteenth century, a new technique appears in some mosques at Kisimani: cubic blocks of coral are set in mortar, the lime for which was obtained by the calcination of coral.

In the fourteenth century, in Kilwa, which had been then become a major trading centre, a new change in building techniques appears with the use of stone: but it was only worked carefully for finishing *miḥrāb*s and door and window casings. New features appeared: cupolas, columns, ornamental bas-reliefs, semi-cylindrical vaults etc. All these seem to be limited to Kilwa, where the palace fortress and trading centre of Husuni Kubwa stands; it probably dates from the fourteenth century and may have served as a model for the dwellings of notables. These later had a facade giving onto an inner courtyard on which one door to the first room opened. The rooms were long, narrow and parallel, and were almost all dark, as they did not look onto the courtyard. In one corner, at the back of the building were the toilets. Houses like this have been found at Gedi, Kisimani Mafia and Kilwa.

Husuni Kubwa has no parallel and is a masterpiece, although its purpose is not entirely clear. Composed of several dwellings, it contains a space that must have been used as a pool.

In the fourteenth century, Kilwa became a large town with stone houses. The fifteenth century brought further improvements in building methods: from this time, the mortar was poured into casing and rubble was added; even cupolas were built this way. Columns, hitherto monolithic, began to be built with a combination of stone and mortar. Dwellings with one or two floors were built in that way, with vaults and cupolas decorated with porcelain vases from China and Persia set into the body of the construction. The Great Mosque of Kilwa, completed in the reign of Sultan Sulaymān al ʿAḍīl (1412–42) remains one of the masterpieces of Swahili architecture.

Views on the origin of these buildings vary. Some, like G. S. P. Freeman-Grenville, after comparing them with the ordinary mud-walled houses, give them an indigenous origin, whereas others suggest an Arab or Persian origin. Some details in it are incompatible with the stipulations of Islam: for example, the presence in the Gedi mosque of motifs in the form of spearheads. But almost all authors are agreed that 'the architecture of the Swahili coast maintained over the centuries its own traditions distinguishing it from that of Arabia, Persia and any other Muslim land'. At any event, even if there was some resort to external models, there was also rational adaptation, for example to local materials.

According to Portuguese sources, the streets of Kilwa were narrow, bordered by mud-walled houses with roofs of palm fronds, and stone houses with benches along their street front. The palace was the most imposing edifice. The buildings had wooden doors, richly carved and decorated, as can be seen at Bagamoyo and Zanzibar. These buildings were in no way inferior to those of Portugal, say the first European travellers, who were also impressed by the wealth of the inhabitants, the elegance of their clothes made of gold-embroidered silk and cotton cloth. The women wore earrings, bracelets and anklets made of gold, silver and precious stones. Earthenware lamps found in excavations and candles were probably used to light the dark parts of houses, especially for reading, writing or doing accounts.

The furniture included carpets and mats, stools and sumptuous beds inlaid with ivory, mother of pearl, silver and gold. In the houses of notables imported crockery was used: pottery and china from Iran, Iraq, China, Egypt and Syria. The local pottery used above all by the mass of the population included vases with a round or pointed base designed to be placed on the fire, and shallow vessels for serving meals.

18.2 *Mihrab of the Great Mosque at Gedi.* (*S. Unwin*)

Power structures

The Swahili towns were not only centres of trade and Islamization but also the capitals of local Muslim dynasts. Kilwa is typical of them. Its *Chronicle*, which has come down to us in two versions, tells us that the dynasty was of Persian origin and came from Shīrāz. Such myths of origin are numerous on the east coast of Africa and elsewhere on the continent. Examination of them will enable us to settle correctly the problem of the nature of Swahili civilization.

From myth to historical fact

There are two theories on the subject. According to one, it was Persians and Arabs who built towns, introduced Islam and developed a higher culture on the coast, the local Africans being no more than subordinate helpers, as servants, concubines and clients: but this external contribution slowly regressed and, without it, the history of this region would have unfolded in a closed circuit. This interpretation, put forward at the end of the nineteenth century by

J. Strandes, is based on Hegel's thesis which divides the peoples of the world into two categories, those who make history and those who are outside history and passively suffer the action of the first group. This theory still prevails among a number of historians and archaeologists. The other theory, developed by the British archaeologist Chittick and the Soviet one, V. M. Misiugin, corresponds to the views developed by the African historians Joseph Ki-Zerbo and Cheikh Anta Diop, which is that Africans participated actively in their history. Further research is underway demonstrating that the urban dynasties and principalities of this region were in fact of African origin.

The system for the transfer of power

Misiugin's work on the *Pate Chronicle* shows that before the advent of the Nabkhani dynasty there was a state ruled by the Wapate with the royal title of *mfalme*. Moreover, this dynasty retained an organization into groups based on the degree of kinship and also age-sets (*ndugu*). The title of *mfalme* was collectively borne and was transmitted not by an individual, but by the members of the same *ndugu* which might include some members of the Wapate clan. Thus the title of *mfalme* was not given for life; but was transferred from one member of the *ndugu* to another when the latter got married by taking a wife among the girls of the Wapate clan of the same generation. In short, each man in the clan bore the title of *mfalme*, the undivided property of the clan, and performed its functions temporarily, while the women were regarded as the depositaries of this right. It was moreover by marrying a Wapate woman that Sulaymān, the founder of the Nabkhani dynasty, received the title of prince of Pate. He owed this title not to the fact that his wife was the daughter of the *mfalme* of the time but to the fact that she belonged to the next *ndugu* generation. But, nevertheless, that does not mean that Swahili society remained a clan society. According to Misiugin, it means that the Wapate, who were dominant economically, assumed the monopoly of political power based on an existing kinship structure. But Sulaymān was only related to the Wapate royal clan through his wife. Thus for the first time there was a risk that the title of *mfalme* might escape from this clan since according to the customary *ndugu* rule it had to be transmitted to the husband's brothers. The prince's wife was thus the depositary of the abstract right to the title of prince the office of which was discharged by her husband.

Applying this interpretation to the *Kilwa Chronicle*, it has been possible to demonstrate that the *ndugu* system was in force there too for the transfer of power. In the first chapter of that work, it can be seen that the first ruler, Muḥammad, was succeeded by one of his brothers, *Bas<u>kh</u>āt,* then one of the latter's sons. But the latter had only come to power by usurping the right of his paternal uncles. This is a reference to the traditional right of the *ndugu* according to which power should pass to the brothers-in-law of the depositary princess. In chapter three of the *Chronicle*, another episode confirms this interpretation. But the Swahili version of the *Kilwa Chronicle* and the *Pate Chronicle* make the first sultan a Persian who married the daughter of the local chief. This is what happened in many other towns. Thus, the adoption of the local rule for transferring power makes it possible to conclude that the organization of the state was local in origin, despite the apparent and official dominion of Islam and its customs.

Islam and the ideology of power

This influence of Islam probably reflected the emergence of converted sections of Swahili society who had grown rich through trade. In order to counterbalance their impact, the local aristocrats also decided to draw support from Islam, for example by marrying their daughters to rich merchants, who in turn, to make themselves equal to the local aristocrats, invented for themselves illustrious Arab or Persian ancestors. In this way, the Swahili legends of successive waves of immigrant Muslim groups between the seventh and the tenth century into already existing towns, were replaced by tales describing the arrival of founding ancestors coming from Arabia or Persia. Such myths are by no means unique. Did not an Ethiopian dynasty claim to be descended from Solomon and the Queen of Sheba? Peoples of the eastern Sudan claim descent from Arab *ḳabīla* chiefs and the founder of the kingdom of Kānem, Sefe, is identified with the Yemenite king Sayf. The Keita of Mali trace their ancestry back to members of the entourage of the Prophet Muḥammad, and some Yoruba make their genealogical tree go back to the Canaanites of ancient Palestine. Many African dynasties, it is said, were founded by immigrant white strangers. This general trend seems to correspond to the time when a dominant class emerges in a society and seeks to separate its ancestry totally from that of the common people.

Conclusion

Although of African origin, Swahili civilization owed its development to trade, which was both an advantage and a handicap in so far as this civilization was not based on development of the productive forces that had probably remained stationary. Whether for the products of hunting or gold or iron mining, Swahili society did not constitute an internal market; it depended on the outside world for its development, as the story of its fall was to prove.

Some of the circumstances that have been invoked to explain the decline of this civilization (for example, drought or the Zimba invasion) count for little compared to the collapse of maritime trade destroyed by the Europeans. The Portuguese navigators equipped with artillery held up dozens of vessels laden with goods, sank many vessels belonging to Zanzibar's fleet and plundered and destroyed towns that had once teemed with life, notably Kilwa.

19 Between the Coast and the Great Lakes

At the beginning of the twelfth century, the characteristic feature of East Africa from the previous periods seems to have been the close correlation between ecology and ethnicity. The populations, still rather small, despite the great Bantu migrations, were concentrated in the better-watered areas with at least 1,000 mm of rainfall a year. In these areas, the adoption of cereals and some types of livestock had not eliminated the priority previously accorded to the growing of roots and tubers. On the other hand, on the highlands of Kenya and Tanzania, mixed farming, combining grain cultivation and extensive livestock-raising predominated. Here Nilotic-language peoples prevailed, whereas in the south Southern Cushites did.

The hinterland of the East African coast

All along the east coast, it is possible to identify three major clusters of Bantu: the Sabaki-speakers, the Seuta-speakers and the Ruvu.

The Sabaki language

The Sabaki language had three dialects spoken along the Kenyan coast: the ancestral Miji-Kenda, proto-Kipokomo and, on the coast itself, proto-Kiswahili.

These Sabaki communities gave way to peoples with other ways of life, such as the speakers of an early form of Somali and Southern Nilotes. The system of age-grades so typical of Sabaki culture probably came from exchanges between the Bantu and the Southern Nilotes well before 1600. In fact, the pastoralists of the interior and the Bantu along the coast long co-existed with peoples who were still hunter-gatherers, such as the Boni settled north of the River Tana, although they had adopted the language of the Somali pastoralists who were dominant in the region. Similarly, the Southern Cushitic-speaking Dahalo whose vocabulary shows loan-word evidence of continuous interaction with the dominant Pokomo and Swahili peoples.

The Seuta

The Seuta lived south of the Sabaki. By 1100 of the Christian era, the proto-Seuta had already added plants of Indonesian origin such as taro and bananas to

African plants. Over the next 500 years, the original Seuta community branched into three groups: those speaking the Kishamba dialect, the communities speaking proto-Zigula-Ngula and finally, the group using an ancient form of the Bondei language.

The Ruvu Bantu

Finally, south of the Seuta were the Ruvu Bantu settled in the Wami basin. In the twelfth century, they consisted of two communities each with its farming system. The East Ruvu communities, from whom the Wakutu, the Wazaramo and the Wakami derive, settled in the wetter lowland areas and practised a mixed Afro-Indonesian agriculture. The West Ruvu peoples, on the other hand, from whose language modern Kigogo among others derives, settled higher up, and opted above all for grain cultivation and livestock-raising.

From Lake Nyasa to Lake Victoria

In the twelfth century, the second great region of settlement was the area north-east of Lake Nyasa where people speaking proto-Njombe were living. This was the ancestor of modern Kikehe and Kisangu, among others. Further west, there was a group speaking a form of Nyakyusa. Along the highland corridor between Lake Tanganyika and Lake Nyasa were the proto-Wanyiha and the proto-Walapwa, while in the area between Lake Nyasa and the Indian Ocean coast all along the Ruvuma basin were the Wapogoro and the pre-Yao-Makonde.

On both sides of the northern end of Lake Nyasa, large-scale Bantu migrations developed, such as that of the Walapwa west of the lake and the proto-Wasongea west as far as the upper reaches of the Ruvuma. But there were also internal movements within the Njombe zone, with, for example, the first Wakinga encroaching on to former Songea land, and even in the sixteenth century, providing the ruling houses of the Kinyakyusa-speaking Wangonde.

In general, the Bantu migrations, above all from the west and south-west, seem to have disrupted the pre-existing communal systems and thus to have created the conditions for a reordering in the framework of more organized chiefdoms in which the newcomers held the key positions.

At the beginning of the twelfth century, a third area of Bantu settlement could be observed along the shores of Lake Victoria from Mara in the south to the Kavirondo Gulf in the north and south-east of Mount Elgon.

But, despite their contiguity with these Lacustrine Bantu, the societies situated further east remained markedly different; and this difference reflected several centuries of acculturation between Bantu and non-Bantu. Thus, in the twelfth century, the east Victoria Bantu practised both male and female circumcision, two customs unknown to the Lacustrine Bantu, but universally practised by the Nilotes and Cushites who lived next to the east Victoria Bantu. Moreover, this interaction constitutes one of the most remarkable local dynamic historical factors. For example, among the Mara-speaking peoples, the increase in population through the absorption of Southern Nilotes (for example, among the ancestors of the Wakuria) led eventually to the establishment among them of a Southern Nilotic age-grade system superimposed on the pre-existing clan system, Mara remaining the language of the new amalgam.

Furthermore, for the Gusii branch of the Mara sub-group, it was no longer Southern Nilotes but Southern Cushites who had the greatest impact. The Gusii community absorbed the Southern Nilotes in small groups, so that the latters' age-set system was never adopted; on the contrary, by 1600, the Nilotic Kipsigis were adopting Gussi identity and the Bantu type of community organization. There were thus many cultural interactions. Thus the decline of circumcision and non-cyclical age-set systems among the Baluyia can be attributed to the periodic movement, out of the Lacustrine-speaking regions of peoples lacking those ideas. Similarly, the Bantu-speakers were, perhaps from the fourteenth century, engaged in massive settlement of Busoga and Buganda, a movement to which oral tradition refers when it speaks of the Kintu period and which explains the Bantu linguistic influences, as well as the intensification of banana growing in Buganda and Busoga by the Bantu who were already practising it around Mount Elgon.

But in the mosaic of peoples of the north-east of Lake Victoria, Nilotic contacts predominated, leading to the growth in the importance of cattle. Similarly, in the sixteenth century and later, the encounter between Baluyia and Kalenjin Southern Nilotes led to the formation of Bantu-speaking communities organized on a clan basis, but with age-set systems of Kalenjin origin. Later, Luo immigrants into the far south of this area were to bring about major changes.

The inland zones of Kenya and Tanzania

By the eleventh century, some Bantu communities had already settled in drier climates, such as the original proto-Takama nucleus, as linguistic analysis of the distribution of modern Kitakama languages suggests: Kinyamwezi, Kisukuma, Kikimbu etc. The proto-Takama must already have taken up grain cultivation to ensure a more dependable food supply. As regards the rest of the hinterland of Kenya and Tanzania, various Nilotes and Southern Cushites tended towards livestock-raising while keeping grain cultivation for the greater part of their sustenance. Nevertheless, in certain limited regions of irregular rainfall, such as the Maasai steppe and large parts of north-eastern Kenya, it is quite likely that cultivation had been completely or almost completely replaced by stock-raising.

The great difference between settlement of this region in the first millennium compared to present-day conditions was the extent of the settlement of Southern Cushites, such as the East Rift peoples, from Kilimanjaro and the Pare Mountains to the Dodoma region of present-day Tanzania: they herded cattle, sheep and goats and grew bulrush millet, sorghum and, where possible, eleusine. At the beginning of the twelfth century, Nilotic peoples such as the Dadog and the Ongamo came in and disrupted the previous homogeneity of settlement, despite the remarkable resistance of communities such as the Asax, the Kw'adza and the Iringa Southern Cushites.

The aridity of their country continued for several centuries after the twelfth century. The response to this situation was mixed farming which was eventually adopted by the increasing numbers of Bantu communities who were arriving there, such as the Wanjombe, the West Ruvu and the Takama. Despite the lateness of these intrusions, dating from the end of the sixteenth century, the Kw'adza continued to be an important factor in the history of central Tanzania. But the dispersal of the Takama was even more considerable in western Tanzania where it began as early as 1000. Over several centuries this expansion divided the proto-Takama into three communities: the Wembere society and their neighbours, the proto-Wanyamwezi and the Wasukuma on the upper River Wembere. The greater linguistic fragmentation in Usukuma implies that this region was the homeland of the proto-Wanyamwezi-Wasukuma grouping. Furthermore, the majority of words from Southern Cushitic in Kinyamwezi-Kisukuma vocabulary points to the amalgamation of its speakers and Takama-speakers with Cushitic elements.

The expansion of the Wanyamwezi and the Wasukuma was on a far larger scale until, by about 1600, it reached the southern shores of Lake Victoria.

Mountain regions: Kilimanjaro and Kenya

In the north of Maasailand, on the slopes of Mount Kilimanjaro, several East Rift Southern Cushitic communities were using irrigation and manure in basically grain agriculture. This intensive highland agriculture was a major historical event. Bantu groups absorbed Cushitic farming practices and added the Indonesian banana, and this vital innovation seems to have originated with the Bantu communities of Kilimanjaro, Mount Kenya and the Pare Mountains from the eleventh century. The subsequent diffusion of the highland tradition allowed the beginning of the Shambaa settlement in the Usambara range by about 1500.

In the twelfth century, the highland East Rift groups were restricted to the highland zone by the advance of the Ongamo into the Kaputie plains. The Ongamo vocabulary is close to proto-Maasai, which indicates that this people practised stock-raising and grew sorghum and eleusine.

Around 1100, the proto-Chagga were most probably settled on the south-east slopes of Kilimanjaro. The remarkable productivity of intensive agriculture allowed the rapid spread of the Chagga over the next five centuries, absorbing both East Rift and Ongamo communities in the process. In this way the Rombo Wachagga were scattered into several isolated communities along the east of the mountain, while the West Wachagga moved into the forested slopes of Mount Meru.

Even more than that of Kilimanjaro, the history of the Taita Hills between 1100 and 1600 seems to have been dominated by the amalgamation between

East Rift peoples and Bantu. Over the centuries, the former were absorbed by the Bantu.

Among the Sagala, this process was further complicated by the intrusion of Bantu immigrants from the Pare Mountains and Sabaki-speaking groups from the coast in the sixteenth century, Numerous Sabaki loan-words are to be found among the Sagala.

This movement of Sabaki groups into the Taita Hills probably played a major role in the crystallization of the ethnic identity of the Akamba to the north of the Taita Hills in the sixteenth century.

By about 1100, the proto-Thagicu formed a small set of Bantu communities on the south slopes of Mount Kenya. Like the proto-Chagga, they were wedged between the Southern Cushites and Southern Nilotes. But the Maasai only began to influence them after 1600. Before then, the Thagicu considerably extended their agricultural settlement by cutting back the forest, and gave birth to two major ethnic groups: the Kikuyu (in the gap between the Nyandarua range and Mount Kenya) and the Meru, east of Mount Kenya. At the same time the Sabaki immigrants were interacting with the Thagicu of Ukambani, fashioning a mixed group whose language was Thagicu but whose culture resembled that of the Taita or the coastal Bantu. Thus the Akamba replaced the spear with the bow and arrow as their standard weapon and abandoned the age-set system.

To the west of a line running through Mount Kenya and Kilimanjaro lay the one large region in which Bantuization did not take hold in the 1100–1600 period. Dominant in this region until after 1500 were Southern Nilotes, in particular the Kalenjin and Dadog, spreading through the Jasingishu plains and east and south-eastward into the central and southern Rift Valley. This Kalenjin expansion diverged from the common Kalenjin pattern through its incorporation of Bantu people. South-east of Mount Elgon, the Elgon Kalenjin society diverged through incorporating the Bantu. For instance, territorial clans superseded cyclical age-sets and the Elgon Kalenjin began to shift to an agriculture based on bananas.

To the east of the mountain, by 1500, while the ancestral Pokot were coming under the dominance of the Itunga, the proto-Nandian were incorporating Cushites and transmitting to their Kalenjin descendants the typically Cushitic practice of irrigation agriculture which can be observed among Nandian-speaking peoples such as the Keyo. Then, around 1500, the direction of Nandian expansion swung around southward into the forest and the plains of the River Nyando country; from these Nandian settlers the later Nandi and Kipsigi communities would derive.

But the most spectacular expansion was that of the South Kalenjin. Already by no later than 1500, they had reached as far south as the West Ruvu country. In central and northern Maasailand, the South Kalenjin pushed the Dadog aside; and in South Maasai they assimilated or drove out the Kw'adza. In northern Tanzania, they were stopped only by the rift escarpment, for the Dadog continued to control the Loita and Ngorongoro highlands, as well as the

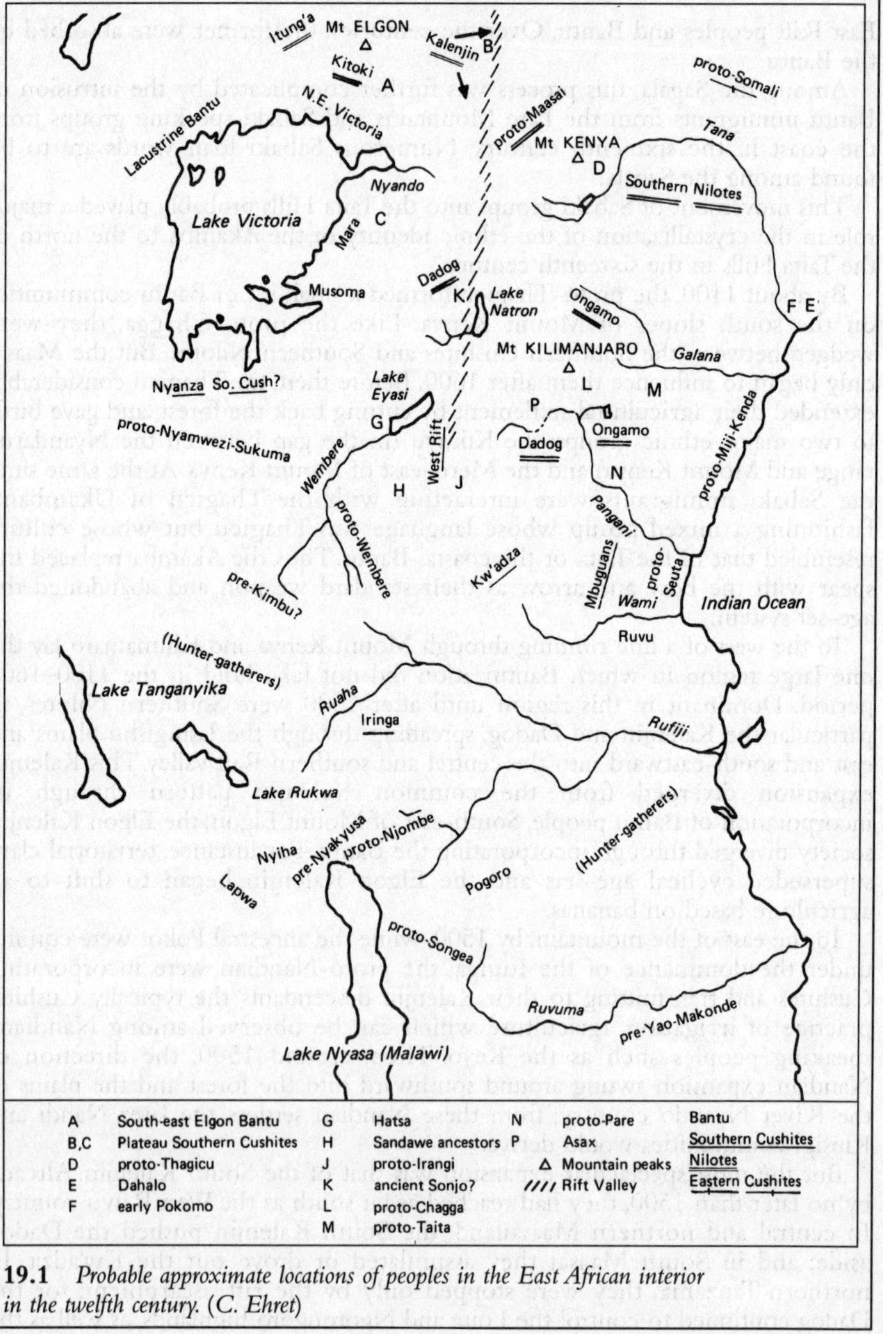

19.1 *Probable approximate locations of peoples in the East African interior in the twelfth century.* (C. Ehret)

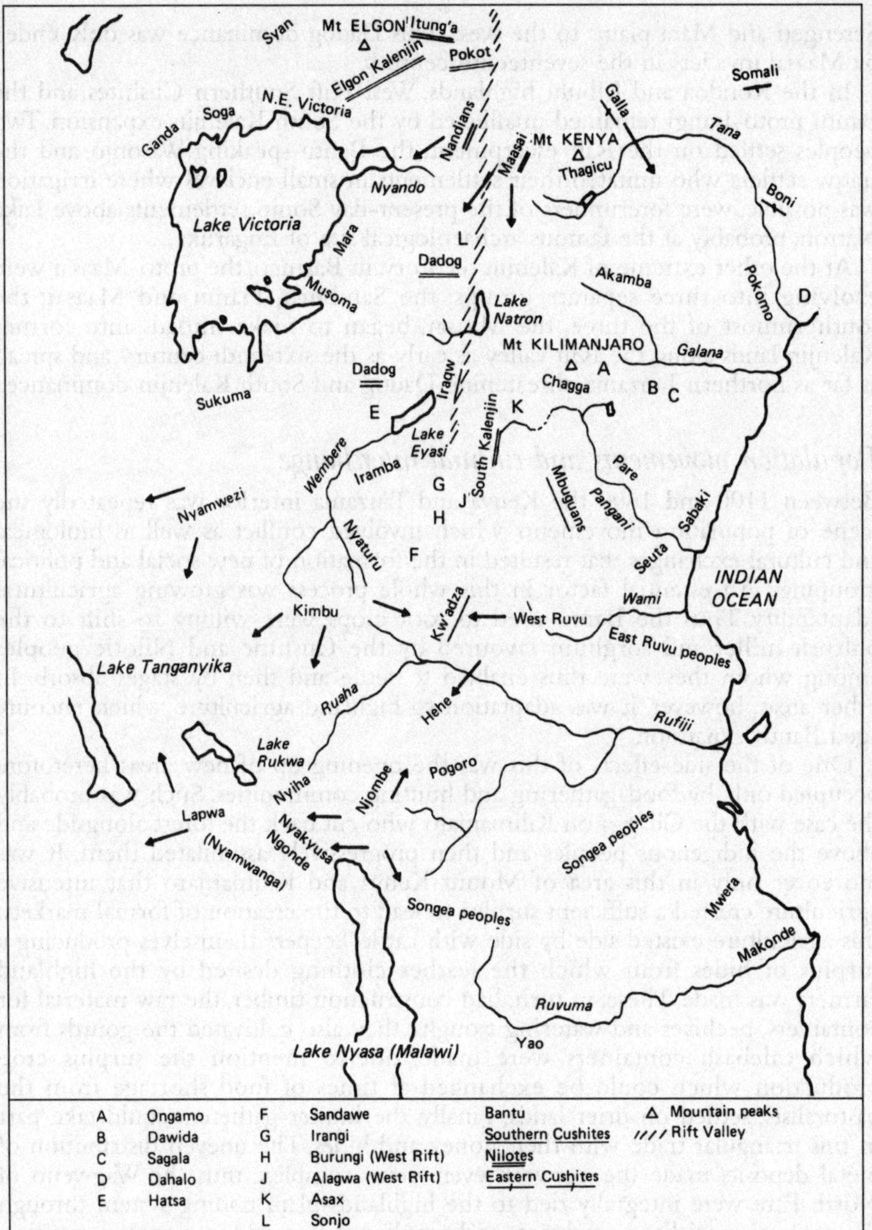

19.2 *Probable approximate locations of peoples in the East African interior in the sixteenth century.* (C. Ehret)

Serengeti and Mara plains to the west. This Dadog dominance was only ended by Maasai invaders in the seventeenth century.

In the Kondoa and Mbulu highlands, West Rift Southern Cushites and the Bantu proto-Irangi remained unaffected by the South Kalenjin expansion. Two peoples settled on the Rift escarpment, the Bantu-speaking Wasonjo and the Iraqw settlers who imitated their settlements in small enclaves where irrigation was possible, were forerunners of the present-day Sonjo settlements above Lake Natron, probably at the famous archaeological site of Engaruka.

At the other extreme of Kalenjin territory, in Baringo, the proto-Maasai were evolving into three separate groups: the Samburu, Tiamu and Maasai; the southernmost of the three, the Maasai, began to make inroads into former Kalenjin lands along the Rift Valley as early as the sixteenth century and spread as far as northern Tanzania, threatening Dadog and South Kalenjin dominance.

Population movements and cultural interchange

Between 1100 and 1600 the Kenya and Tanzania interior was repeatedly the scene of population movements which involved conflict as well as biological and cultural exchanges that resulted in the formation of new social and political groupings. An essential factor in this whole process was growing agricultural adaptability. Thus the Bantu used to root crops were willing to shift to the bulrush millet and sorghum favoured by the Cushitic and Nilotic peoples among whom they were thus enabled to settle and then by stages absorb. In other areas, however, it was adaptation to highland agriculture which encouraged Bantu expansion.

One of the side-effects of this was the opening up of new areas heretofore occupied only by food-gathering and hunting communities. Such was probably the case with the Chagga on Kilimanjaro who cut back the forest alongside and above the indigenous peoples and then progressively assimilated them. It was moreover only in this area of Mount Kenya and Kilimanjaro that intensive agriculture created a sufficient surplus to lead to the creation of formal markets; this agriculture existed side by side with cattle-keepers themselves producing a surplus of hides from which the leather clothing desired by the highland farmers was made. These, in turn, had construction timber, the raw material for containers, beehives and watering troughs: they also cultivated the gourds from which calebash containers were made, not to mention the surplus crop production which could be exchanged at times of food shortage from the pastoralists, settled on drier lands. Finally, the hunter-gatherers could take part in this triangular trade with their honey and hides. The uneven distribution of metal deposits made the network even more complex: thus the Wagweno of North Pare were integrally tied to the highlands-plain trading system through their role as specialized producers and supplies of iron and iron tools, a position occupied by the Thagicu around Mount Kenya.

Elsewhere, markets only really began to appear at this level well after 1600.

20 The Great Lakes Region

A historian of the interlacustrine region is faced with four major problems. First, there is scant oral, linguistic or archaeological data. For example, the traditions portray the founding fathers of clans as the introducers of food crops and cattle. That is why some historians classify them as mythical beings treated, as in the Chwezi myths, as beneficent spirits.

Second, the central theme of the relationships between pastoralists and agriculturalists poses a problem. Many authors portray the pastoralists as civilizing conquerors and the agriculturalists as docile and passive majorities. This bias is expressed for Rwanda by A. Kagame who casts doubt on the contribution of the Hutu to civilization which he sees as being the work of the Tutsi alone. We feel, on the contrary, that state formation among the agriculturalists antedates the advent of the pastoralists who interacted with the indigenous peoples and thus consolidated state structures based on classes and castes. In this connection, the terms 'pastoralists' and 'agriculturalists' are occupational and not ethnic terms; they refer to ways of life; when pastoralists lost their cattle they became agriculturalists, and vice versa.

Another major problem is that of Bantu and Nilotic chronologies. Attempts have been made to reconstruct them using the generational principle, tie-in references and eclipses mentioned in traditions. But serious uncertainties remain. For example, the Bito genealogy in Bunyoro has recently been called into question by D. P. Henige. A. Kagame traces the foundation of the state of Rwanda back to the tenth century, Jan Vansina to the latter part of the fifteenth century. Even if a solution was found for the chronology of each state, these different time-scales would still need to be integrated for the dozens of units over several centuries.

The final problem arises from the fact that, until recently, most of the published histories were court-centred, focussing on the centralized states and paying little attention to large sections of society.

Taking these problems on board, we shall examine successively the following four multi-ethnic groupings: the Kitara complex, the Kintu complex, the Ruhinda complex and the Rwanda complex.

The Kitara complex

This covers Bunyoro, Toro and neighbouring portions of Nkore and Buganda; it is the oldest state system in the interlacustrine region, and its history is marked by the arrival of three groups of invaders: the Batembuzi, the Bachwezi and the Babito. But these three phases which relate to strangers omit the Bantu, mostly indigenous, whose languages dominate the area. Were they mere spectators? According to C. A. Buchanan, the earliest migrations occurred between 722 and 1200. The first arrivals, even before the Bantu, were, according to the linguistic evidence, people from the central Sudan. On the basis of archaeological evidence, that happened before the fourth century. The first Bantu-speaking clans seem to have come from the west of Lake Mobutu (Albert) into the area stretching south of the Nile. They cultivated sorghum and eleusine. They must have arrived in the region in the tenth and eleventh centuries. Some of these clans created small agricultural states, which in that case, owed nothing to pastoralist immigrants but were rather the work of the earliest Bantu-speaking groups. Initially, authors called the Batembuzi period the 'reign of the gods', a mythological rather than a historical period, with, according to Kinyoro or Nkore traditions, respectively 19 and four pioneer kings (*Abakama Abatembuzi*). Buchanan has reconstructed this history by tracing the development of the clans. Thus, the chiefdom of Bugangaizi was established by the Bagabu clan, and its leader, Hangi. The Bayaga, another pre-Bachwezi clan, are associated with the coming of cattle (probably not long-horned) and the salt-work site at Kibiro. A third clan, the Basita clan (identified with the founder, Sitta) figures prominently in the traditions of the states of Nkore, Kiziba and Buhaya as a group deriving its power from knowing how to work iron. The place-name *Mbale* or *Kabale* found in this region is linked to the presence of the Basita.

By about 1250, there was already a number of small Bantu chiefdoms east of the Ruwenzori Mountains, offshoots of the Batembuzi and contemporary, for example, with the first king of Kiziba (1236–63).

The Bukuku clan was named after its founder, who is said to have been a commoner, and was employed in the court of Isaza (c. 1301–28), the last of the 'pioneer kings', whom he is said to have succeeded before adopting Ndahura (c. 1344–71) the great ruler of the Bachwezi period. The totem of the Bukuku clan was the grasshopper and the civet, so important in the history of Busoga. Bukuku, who is also said to have been a potter, shows us that the development of centalized states was not solely due here to alien pastoralists. Nevertheless, Bukuku had to crush a rebellion of chiefs who objected to being ruled by a commoner. But the spread of the uprising enabled Ndahura, founder of the Bachwezi civilization, to seize power.

According to the traditions of Bunyoro and Nkore, this new dynasty had two kings (Ndahura and Wamara) and a regent, Murindwa. Many historians have accepted the historicity of the Bachwezi dynasty: one of them sees them as related to the Sidama of Ethiopia; others identify their kingdom with the

Ganda kingdom of Chwa or with the Bahima. Almost alone, C. Wrigley maintains that the Bachwezi are only a 'collection of named and individualized divinities, imagined as a human kin-group writ large'.

However, in our opinion, it was a real episode in the history of East Africa which took place in the Kitara complex from 1350 to 1500. There are two major theories about these developments. Some, like R. Oliver, argue that the Bachwezi were pastoralist Bahima who had come from the north-east or the south. This latter theory is defended by C. Ehret, who suggests that the modern Tutsi and Bahima derive from Southern Cushites, who themselves he sees as coming from the east, moving into the region from the south in the thirteenth and early fourteenth centuries, to create with their allies amongst the indigenous people an aristocracy and a state over the agricultural population.

Another theory, which is rapidly gaining ground, is that the Bachwezi were local rulers who emerged as a result of economic and demographic changes. What is clear is that the empire of Kitara was created by Ndahura (c. 1344–71) who extended the small chiefdom of Bugangaizi over a vast area which included Bunyoro, Toro, western Buganda, Ankole, Kiziba, Karagwe, the Sese Islands, and part of Rwanda.

In the absence of any military and administrative personnel, Ndahura had to rely on agents appointed in the various areas that provided the economic mainstay of the empire: salt, cattle and iron. He was captured during a battle when an eclipse of the sun caused panic among his troops. He was released but preferred to migrate westward away from his capital at Mwenge. His son Wamara (c. 1371–98) had an even more turbulent reign. He moved his capital to Bwera but had to deal with several immigrant groups including Bantu-speaking clans associated with the Kintu complex, the Jo-Oma, the Bashambo from the south the Luo from the north. The Jo-Oma were probably a Bantu-speaking aristocracy who emerged in western Uganda in the fourteenth and fifteenth centuries. King Wamara had attempted to enlist the support of the immigrants by appointing them to important political posts. For instance, Ruhinda, a Muhima, was placed in charge of the royal herds. Wamara formed a blood brotherhood with Kintu, the leader of the Bantu clans of eastern origin. But these favours were construed by their beneficiaries as appeasement. A great famine, followed by a cattle disease, were all it took to provoke widespread dissatisfaction. Kagoro, the military commander, took advantage of the situation to stage a coup d'état and massacre the Bachwezi aristocracy. On the ruins of their power, two conglomerations of states emerged: the Luo-Babito states of Bunyoro-Kitara and, further south, the Bahinda states. There was thus a struggle between the Luo and the Bahima.

In order to understand the evolution of the Luo states, it is important to emphasize that historical developments in western Uganda cannot simply be explained in terms of the impact of successive waves of pastoralist conquerors as the carriers of civilization. The Luo from the southern Sudan had arrived in the time of Wamara. These were the southern and central Luo who became separated from the northern clans between 670 and 1070 and who themselves split into two between 1170 and 1470. By the end of the fourteenth century, four Luo communities had emerged, one of which lived near Mont Agoro. There they were joined by the Jo-Oma (Bahima). These Luo, hitherto hunters and agriculturalists, learnt about cattle-keeping from the Bahima. Following the outbreak of a cattle disease, they crossed the Nile into the Bachwezi empire during the reign of King Wamara, leaving behind a few groups who, led by Owiny I (1409–36), established the Tekidi kingdom, one of the earliest Luo states. Owiny married a Bahima girl, by whom had a son, Rukidi, who broke away from his father. He was welcomed by Luo who had already migrated to Bachwezi and founded the new Babito dynasty of Kitara. The case of Rukidi shows that there was a great deal of mixing between the Luo and the Bahima, so much so that some writers refer to Luo-speaking Bahima.

Further north, a similar ethnic fusion was taking place in the Bachwezi between the Luo and the Madi. The Nyimur and the Patiko, some of whom later accompanied Rukidi to Kitara to which the Luo-Bakwonga also made their way, emerged from this crucible. Thus it was not a large Luo army that marched into Kitara, but small groups arriving piecemeal, some of which headed towards the Sudan, present-day Zaire or Ethiopia.

From the traditions of Bunyoro, Kiziba, Nkore and Karagwe, it is evident that, although the Babito and the Bahinda who overthrew Wamara had propagated the myth of Bachwezi disappearance, while stressing that they were related to them, they failed to impress their new subjects. Only a mixture of force and guile overcame them. For example, in Kiziba, it took a generation before Kibi (c. 1417–44), a Luo hunter, succeeded in establishing his hegemony through the distribution of game meat and political intrigues. In Bunyoro-Kitara, the struggles lasted even longer. Kagoro, the author of the coup d'état, was unable to maintain the unity of the Bachwezi state which he had destroyed. He ensured, however, that the royal regalia, such as drums, were left behind. Rukidi, who intervened in an area that was as heterogeneous as it was disturbed, had difficulty in finding a capital, and finally settled at Bugangaizi, the centre of the old Batembuzi state. This situation did not stabilize until after 1500 when Bunyoro began to expand towards the Bahinda states and Rwanda.

The Ruhinda complex

The geographical focus of this complex covered parts of Ankole (Uganda), Tanzania, Rwanda and Burundi. The main states involved were Nkore, Karagwe and Buzinza. This complex possessed a high degree of coherence marked by the impact of the Bahima/Batutsi pastoralists, with old clans such as the Basiita, Bazigaba, Bakimbiri and Bashambo among others. Each of these clans represented a chiefdom with a mixed population: Bahima being incorporated into 'Bantu' clans, Bantu into Batwa clans and vice versa. Further evidence is that the dialects used by all of them (Rukiga, Runyankore, Runyarwanda) are closely related.

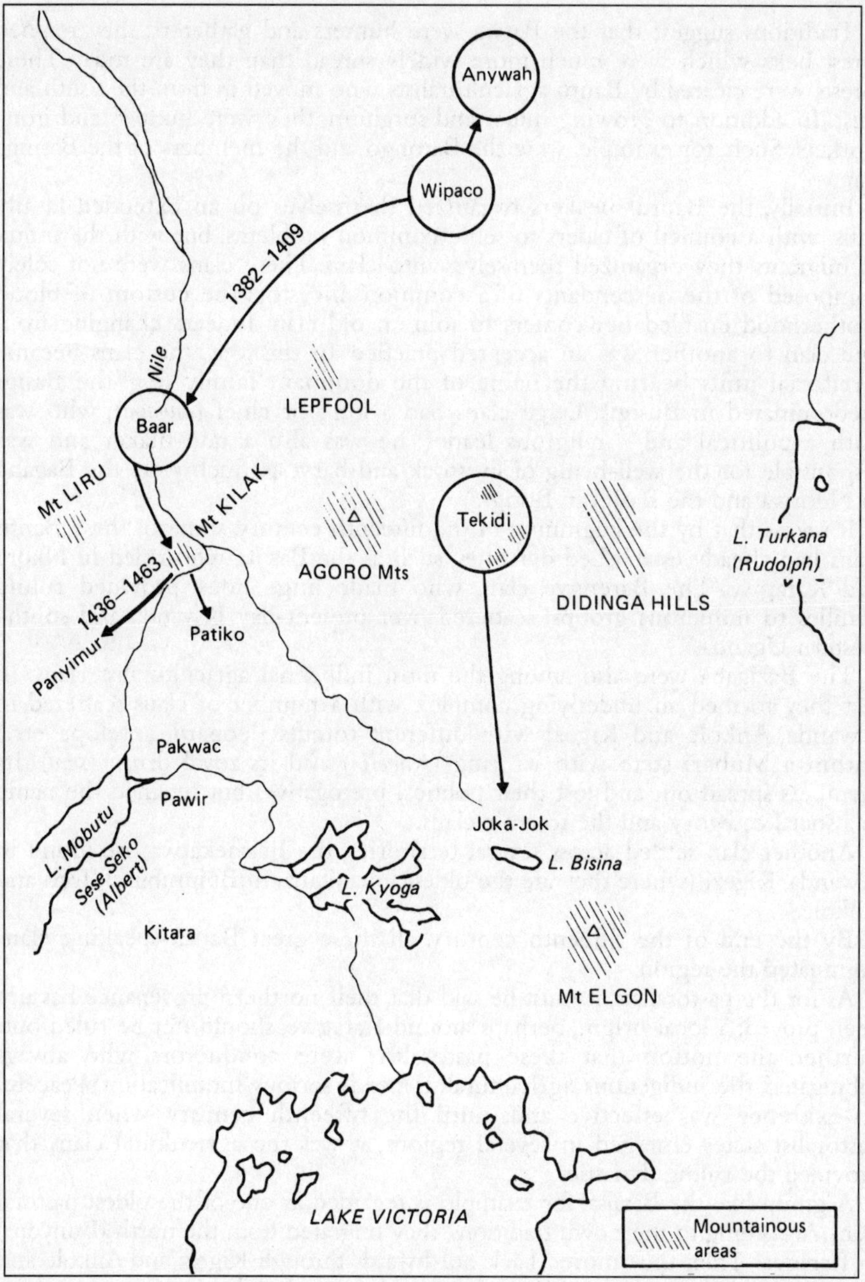

20.1 *Early migrations of the Luo.* (*B. A. Ogot*)

Traditions suggest that the Batwa were hunters and gatherers; they roamed forest belts which were much more widely spread than they are today. These forests were cleared by Bantu agriculturalists who moved in from the south and west. In addition to growing millet and sorghum, they were hunters and iron-workers. Such, for example, were the Barongo and the members of the Basinga clan.

Initially, the Bantu-speakers organized themselves on an extended family basis, with a council of elders to settle common problems, but with the influx of migrants they organized themselves into clans. These clans were not solely composed of the descendants of a common ancestor: the custom of blood brotherhood enabled newcomers to join an old clan. Indeed, changing from one clan to another was an accepted practice. In this way, the clans became territorial units bearing the name of the dominant family (e.g. the Basigi predominated in Busigi). Large clans had a king or chief (*mwami*), who was both a political and a religious leader; he was also a rain-maker and was responsible for the well-being of livestock and harvests. Such were the Bagahe in Ndorwa and the Basigi in Busigi.

It seems that by the beginning of the fifteenth century, some of these Bantu clans had already established dynasties, such as the Basiita who ruled in Nkore and Karagwe. The Barengye clan, who made huge hoes, provided ruling families to numerous groups, scattered over present-day Rwanda and south-western Uganda.

The Bazigaba were also among the most influential agriculturalist clans. In fact they formed an underlying complex with a number of clans scattered in Rwanda, Ankole and Kigezi with different totems (leopard, antelope etc.) within a Mubari state with its king (*Kabeija*) and its royal drum (*sera*). Its members spread out and lost their political prerogatives but retained the name as a social category and the totemic clans.

Another clan settled across several territories, the Baishekatwa, are found in Rwanda, Kigezi (where they are the oldest inhabitants of Bujumbura), Toro and Ankole.

By the end of the fifteenth century, all these great Bantu-speaking clans dominated the region.

As for the pastoralists, it must be said that their northern provenance has not been proved; a local origin, perhaps around Karagwe, should not be ruled out. Further, the notion that these pastoralists were conquerors who always subjugated the indigenous agriculturalists needs serious modification. Peaceful co-existence was effective and, until the fifteenth century when several pastoralist states emerged in several regions, it was the agricultural clans that provided the ruling dynasties.

A group like the Bariisa, for example, is regarded as one of the oldest pastoral clans. According to their own traditions, they migrated from the north (Bunyoro) to Karagwe. Then they moved back northwards through Kigezi and Ankole and then dispersed. A man named Kateizi dropped out and settled in Buhweju, where he married local women, adopted agriculture and founded the sub-clan of the

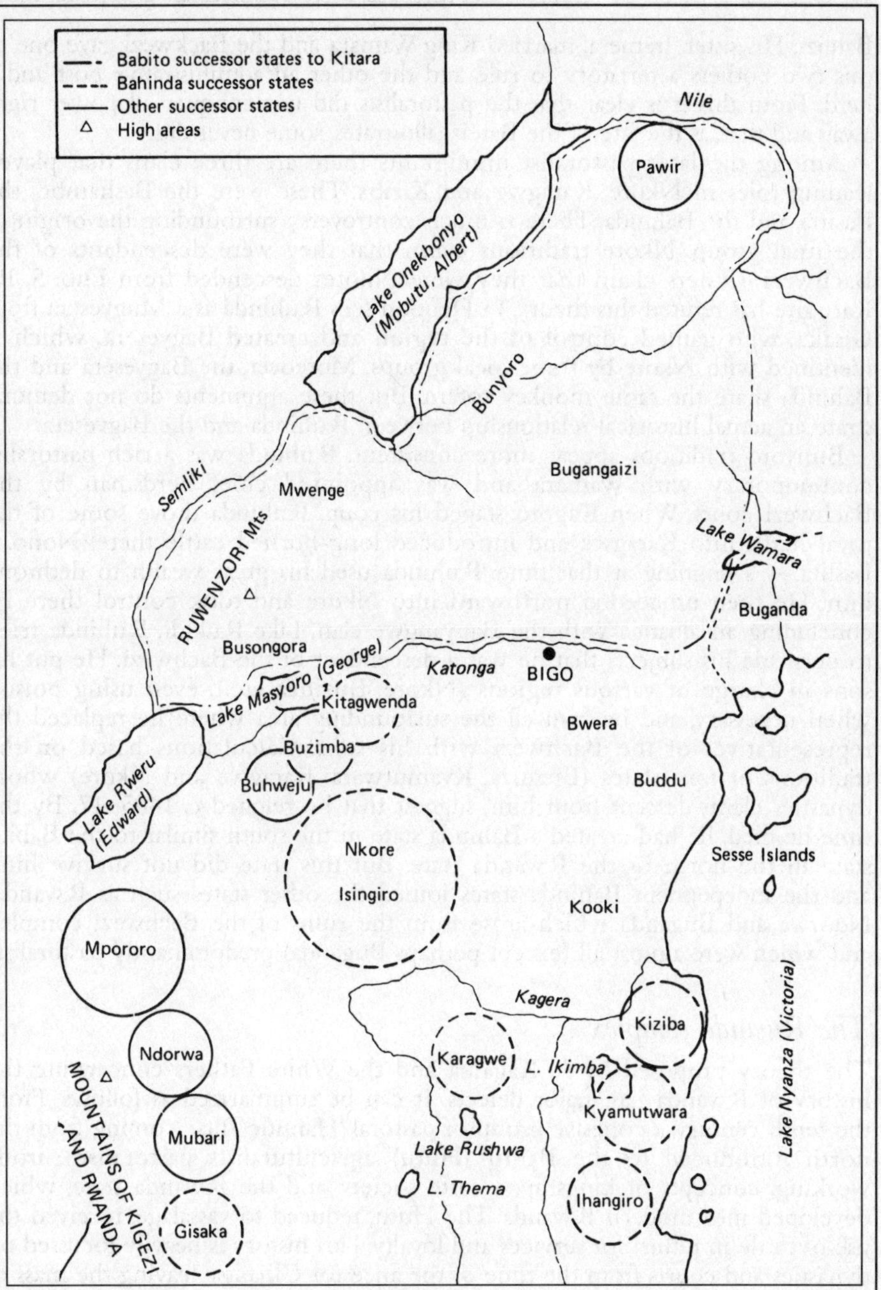

20.2 *The Bachwezi and the immigrants. (B. A. Ogot)*

Bateizi. His sister, Iremera, married King Wamara and the Backwezi gave one of this two bothers a territory to rule and the other an administrative post and a herd. From this it is clear that the pastoralists did not conquer all power right away and that, as the fate of the Bateizi illustrates, some never did.

Among the later pastoralist immigrants there are three clans that played leading roles in Nkore, Karagwe and Kiziba. These were the Bashambo, the Basitta and the Bahinda. There is much controversy surrounding the origin of the final group. Nkore traditions claim that they were descendants of the Bachwezi. Others claim that they were Nilotes descended from Luo. S. R. Karugire has refuted this theory. D. Denoon sees Ruhinda as a Mugyesera from Gisaka, who gained control of the region and created Bagyesera, which is identified with Nkore by some local groups. Moreover, the Bagyesera and the Bahinda share the same monkey totem. But these arguments do not demonstrate an actual historical relationship between Ruhinda and the Bagyesera.

Bunyoro traditions appear more consistent. Ruhinda was a rich pastoralist contemporary with Wamara and was appointed chief herdsman by the Bachwezi court. When Kagoro staged his coup, Ruhinda drove some of the royal herds into Karagwe and introduced long-horned cattle there. Nono, a Basiita, was reigning at that time. Ruhinda used his great wealth to dethrone him. He then proceeded northward into Nkore and took control there by concluding an alliance with the Banyangwe clan. Like Rukidi, Ruhinda tried to persuade his subjects that he was a descendant of the Bachwezi. He put his sons in charge of various regions (Nkore, Buzinza etc.), even using poison when necessary, and overran all the surrounding area where he replaced the representatives of the Bachwezi with his sons. Calculations based on the traditions of four states (Buzinza, Kyamutwara, Karagwe and Nkore) whose dynasties claim descent from him, suggest that he reigned c. 1405–47. By the time he died, he had created a Bahinda state in the south similar to the Babito state in the north or the Rwanda state. But this state did not survive him, and the independent Bahinda states joined the other states such as Rwanda, Ndorwa and Buganda which arose from the ruins of the Bachwezi complex and which were almost all (except perhaps Buganda) predominantly pastoralist.

The Rwanda complex

The theory proposed by A. Kagama and the White Fathers concerning the history of Rwanda has major defects. It can be summarized as follows. From the tenth century, a cohesive group of pastoral 'Hamitic Tutsi' coming from the north introduced to the Bantu (Hutu) agriculturalists pastoralism, iron-working, concepts of kingship, a caste society and the Rwanda state, which developed into modern Rwanda. The Hutu, reduced to vassalage, received the use of cattle in return for services and loyalty. This history is heavily focussed on dynasties and courts from the time of the ancestor Gihanga, leaving the mass of the people out of the picture. J. Vansina and J. K. Rennie have provided a much more balanced and objective history of Rwanda.

We must go back to the pre-Nyiginya states and societies. The first inhabitants were Batwa who were hunters, potters and basket-makers. From Bantu-speaking agriculturalists who arrived after them they received, for example, millet, honey, cattle, iron goods and salt, giving them in return animals skins, meat, baskets etc. By the fifteenth century, many of the Bantu-speakers were organized into small states controlled by the ruling lineage of the chief or king (*mwami*) who was both a land chief and a ritual leader. Some, such as the Singa and Zigaba clans, possessed cattle before the arrival of the Nyiginya clan. The states of the Singa, the Zigaba, the Gesera, the Banda etc. were thus the original owners of the land in Rwanda. According to Tutsi traditions, the oldest of them was established by the Renge lineages of the Singa clan. By the sixteenth century, they had a complex ritual kingship with a body of ritual experts known as Tege. Gihanga, the founder of the Tutsi clans, is supposed to have adopted the idea of the royal drum and the ritual code of royalty from their ancestor Nyabutege. By the middle of the seventeenth century, all the Renge states had been absorbed into the Rwanda state.

In the east of Rwanda was the Mubari state of the Zigaba clan. The Nyiginya clan is first mentioned in the traditions receiving the hill of Gasabo from the Zigaba clan. At this time, the two groups intermarried freely. Even after it had been deprived of its drum by the Rwandan ruler in the late sixteenth century, the dynasty managed to survive until the latter part of the eighteenth century.

Closely related to the Zigaba were the Gesera, who ruled over the powerful state of Gisaka until the end of the nineteenth century. Busigi was not finally incorporated into Rwanda until the early part of the twentieth century. There was thus prolonged co-existence between the endogenous and the alien state systems and the court rituals in Rwanda were politically effective largely because they incorporated agriculturalist and pastoralist rituals, and a number of agriculturalists were given important ritualist positions, thus giving them a vested interest in the system.

Initially probably 'clients' of the agriculturalists, the pastoralists, through the influx of their brothers were transformed after the fifteenth century into dominant clans and in the sixteenth century into masters. The initial peaceful co-existence gave way to clashes. In the fifteenth century, two clans of pastoralists succeeded in establishing independent states: the Hondogo, settled around Lake Mugesera in the south and the Nyiginya, settled at Gasabo in central Rwanda. The institutions of these centralized states incorporated both pastoralists and agriculturalists.

The Buganda, Busoga, Mount Elgon region

Between the twelfth and the sixteenth century, a number of Bantu-speaking clans (in particular the Kintu clans) left the Mount Elgon region to settle on the northern shores of Lake Victoria. Far from having been precipitated by the advance south-eastward of the Luo migrations, this transfer was earlier by at least a century and ended in the foundation of a number of small states, including Buganda. Kintu may have been a mythical figure, but tradition makes him the leader of clans whose totems are the leopard and the lion. They stopped at various places on their way. Other Bantu-speaking clans existed before with a variety of totems such as the *manis* and the reedbuck. This last clan ruled by the Abaiseigulu lineage and based on a large pottery industry around an important shrine, had created the chiefdom of Bugulu in Busoga. They belonged to the indigenous *banansagwa* clans or 'those found in the place'. The lungfish clan was also one of these; they were important fishermen and iron-workers. A section of them led by Walumbe met the Kintu group in the south of Busoga and sealed an alliance with him by giving him his daughter in marriage. Kintu moved westwards to Buswikira where they were soon joined by a group of his in-laws led by Walumbe. A dispute over the distribution of lands followed and Walumbe moved further west to Buyanirwa.

From Busoga, Kintu moved westwards into a territory where, with a number of allied clans (the elephant and duiker clans), they could face Bemba, the ruler of the large kingdom of Buddu, who was defeated and killed. Kintu then established the nucleus of what was to become the state of Buganda.

Thus in Buganda, Busoga, eastern Uganda and western Kenya, Bantu-speaking agriculturalists had created several small states while the activities of the pastoralists remained peripheral until the fourteenth century. Among the indigenous peoples, class structures and caste systems began to emerge.

After the death of Kantu, a leader from the east, by Lake Wamara, various clans fell back into the equatorial forests north of Lake Victoria. This was the origin of the Kimera complex. Kimera is said to have reigned from c. 1344 to 1374. One tradition suggests that the totem of his clan indicates he was of Luo origin. Others link him to a different clan and argue that he was a member of the Basonga dynasty who had arrived before the appearance of the first Babito rulers in Bunyoro. What is important is that, in order to escape Ndahura's expeditions, human groups fled the Bachwezi empire to settle in the equatorial forests while others moved into Nkore and Buganda. According to the traditions of this latter country, the Kimera complex included the following clans: buffalo, bushbuck, grasshopper, squirrel etc. Depending on the clan being examined, it will give Kimera a Luo or a Bahima ancestry.

As these people were fleeing from various regimes, their ideologies were understandably anti-Bachwezi, anti-Babito and anti-Bahima. That is why the traditions linking Buganda to any of the three groups have been suppressed, even where the evidence is overwhelming. What actually happened can be discovered by comparing traditions.

Although they arrived in Buganda in successive waves, many of those who claim to have been part of the Kimera migration because he was successful, became absorbed into the 35 clans led by the new dynasty that he founded. Each clan, anxious to participate in the monarchy and give itself a chance of one day giving the ruler a successor from its ranks, rushed to present wives to the *Kabaka*.

21 *The Zambezi and Limpopo Basins* 1100–1500

Cultures and societies of the Iron Age around the year 1000

By the end of the first millennium of the Christian era, two types of human groups were living in the vast savannah woodland between the Zambezi and Limpopo rivers from the Kalahari to the Indian Ocean. The first was composed of agriculturalists growing sorghum and millet combined with stock-raising, with hunting and gathering supplementing the food supply. These peoples had mastered iron-working. Pockets of later Stone Age hunting populations living essentially by hunting and gathering still survived among these peoples principally in the steppes of the Kalahari.

There is evidence of Iron Age settlement in South Central Africa as early as 200 of the Christian era, and slowly growing early agricultural populations were widely scattered in areas free from the tsetse fly, with extremely low population densities. The distribution of tsetse belts was affected by the pattern of agriculture which in turn affected population growth and distribution. But forest clearance was limited by the state of technology which was initially very rudimentary. There was simple but well-made pottery, and copper-working to make ornaments and later wire, in a framework of self-sufficiency with trade reduced to barter or local trade. These earliest cultural traditions whose development has been traced by looking at pottery style and radiocarbon dating persisted well into the second millennium with agricultural techniques based on the iron hoe and their social and political organization in small villages.

The so-called Kalomo culture marks the beginning of the Iron Age in the upper Zambezi valley on the Batoka plateau where the savannah woodlands gave way to grazing lands free of the tsetse fly and thus suitable for stock-raising. There, at Isamu Pati, the remains of a culture marked by a new pottery after the first centuries of an occupation that had begun in the seventh century have been uncovered. A village abandoned in the thirteenth century consisted of huts built around a central cattle enclosure. Cereal agriculture and the making of simple iron implements or weapons were the principal activities. But signs have also been found of local or long-distance bartering: copper strips and beads from mines several hundred kilometres away, and glass beads and cowrie shells imported from the east coast. But these infrequent exchanges were not

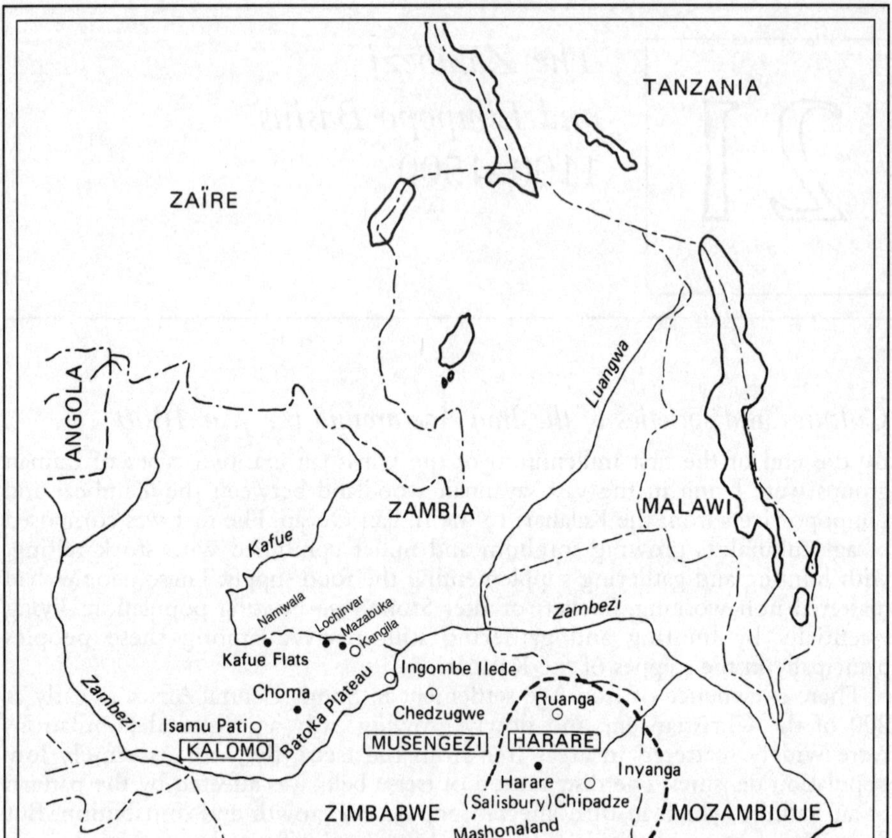

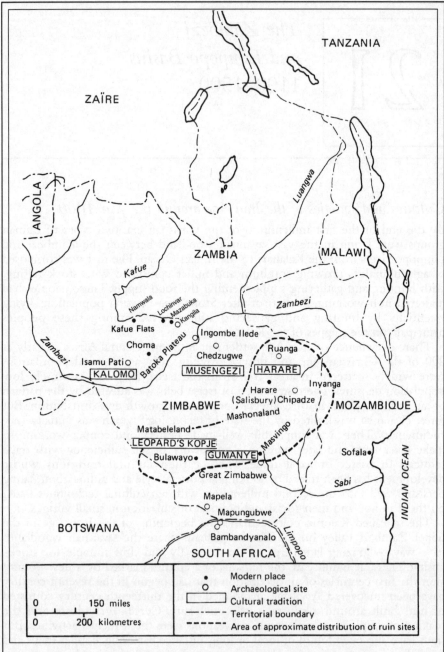

21.1 *Sites and archaeological traditions mentioned in the text.* (*B. M. Fagan*)

enough to produce major changes in the social structure: there was village fission from time to time to reduce pressure on agricultural and grazing land. In this way, the Kalomo culture appears to have survived as late as 1450 but never reached the northern parts of the Batoka plateau.

Other sites, such as the ones at Sebanzi on the edge of the Kafue Flats and at Kangila seem to prefigure the modern Ila-Tonga culture who are one of the oldest ethnic groups north of the Zambezi.

Later history is overlain by intensive population movements and social and political mixing marked by contributions from the Zaire basin. As regards pottery, Early Iron Age traditions gave way to two major pottery styles identified by D. W. Phillipson: the Luangwa tradition in central and eastern Zambia and extending into Malawi; and the Lungwebungu style in western Zambia.

Economic and social transformations in the eleventh and twelfth centuries

The prototype of the new societies that appeared in this region during the eleventh and twelfth centuries is the so-called Leopard's Kopje tradition, which extends from the Limpopo valley northwards into the Bulawayo region and the central parts of the Limpopo-Zambezi watershed. Here the villages are smaller than the settlements of the previous period; whereas cattle herds seem to have been larger. Ox figurines and other remains showing a marked break with earlier traditions suggest that the Leopard's Kopje peoples were immigrants although the cultivation of millet and sorghum as well as hunting continued during this period.

In the twelfth century, the population expanded and began to till the more fertile but heavier soils of the Matabeleland gold belt. Villages were occupied for much longer, which may have coincided with the first mining and working of gold. The sites also became much larger.

At Mapela Hill, for example, a hill was terraced with roughly piled-up stones, which indicates a substantial and disciplined community. Moreover, a group of huts at the top of the hill was much larger and more substantial than those lower down. They were probably the houses of important personages. There was thus social differentiation and a social hierarchy. Glass beads and other imports are more common, too, as if the tempo of long-distance trade had increased significantly. This development continued, as the later sites of this culture show: power and wealth became more concentrated as is most clearly demonstrated by the ruins at Mapungubwe, where in the fifteenth century a small group of wealthy rulers occupied the summit of a hill overlooking the Limpopo valley, literally dominating a large village. Gold beads and sheets show that these notables, whose authority was as much religious as political, had grown rich on the abundant copper deposits of the Limpopo valley.

Elsewhere, other sites, such as those at Musengezi on the right bank of the Zambezi valley, are more characteristically situated in the Leopard's Kopje tradition but at a more elaborate level. The same is true in the Inyanga region.

In fact, the Leopard's Kopje tradition had separated into northern and southern branches, and the latter, improved, survived into the nineteenth century. How can this pattern be correlated with the present ethno-linguistic map of the region?

Shona, with its dialect clusters (Karanga, Manyika, Korekore etc.), is far and away the largest indigenous linguistic family. Other languages that had come from outside the area, such as Ndebele, Tonga and Venda, were introduced in the nineteenth century. The cultural traditions that we have just described are thus clearly part of the evolution of Shona-speaking peoples.

Origins of Zimbabwe culture

The famous Great Zimbabwe ruins near the modern town of Masvingo have fuelled the sometimes extravagant imagination of writers who sought its origin outside Africa. The reality is that it was an essentially African development, built of local raw materials and according to age-old architectural principles. But the ultimate causes of the emergence of the economic, social and political organization that lay behind this achievement and other similar ones are still much debated by historians.

Archaeological discoveries and the oldest settlement

The lowermost levels, dated to the fourth century, of the long cultural sequence on the so-called Acropolis Hill overlooking the Great Enclosure of Zimbabwe as well as a few scatters of pottery in the valley below are Early Iron Age.

At that time, the site was probably not very large: cultivation and hunting were the principal activities. It was not until the tenth century that later Iron Age peoples settled at Great Zimbabwe. Little of their intermediate culture, between Leopard's Kopje and Great Zimbabwe cultures, is as yet known. This Gumanye culture is earlier than the building of the great walls.

By the twelfth century a decisive change had occurred: the pottery became better finished, clay human figurines were made, many more glass beads and other imported articles appear, as do local objects made of copper, bronze and gold. Mud-and-pole buildings became more solid and stone buildings came into use. Elsewhere, including in Leopard's Kopje sites such as that at Mapela, the same sort of developments can be detected right across a region where there are signs of a common culture probably underpinned by Shona. Manifestly, economic accumulation and the concomitant increased social specialization were underway. But where did the initial impetus come from? There are two major hypotheses:

Donald Abraham sees the Shona as immigrants at the end of the first millennium who introduced certain techniques, particularly mining techniques, but also ancestor cults. They created shrines, the principal of which was built on a hill named *Dzimba dzemabwe* (houses of stone). He believes that by astute manoeuvring the Shona established ascendancy over a loose existing confederacy, whose chiefs they transformed into vassals for whom they performed complex sacrifices to the ancestors and the *Mwari* (cult) in exchange for which the local chiefs paid them tribute in ivory and gold dust. These commodities attracted the Arab traders from the East African coast; and thus trade expanded. This first so-called religious hypothesis makes the cultural factor the motive force in the overall dynamism.

The hypothesis of intensified trading activity, on the contrary, assumes that in a lineage society, the chief is the most wealthy person, but his wealth is recycled in the performance of numerous social functions. On the other hand, as trading contacts are intensified, wealth and power are concentrated in the hands of a few who can soon conscript the population to undertake state works, as the Lozi of Zambia did. This is what happened in the case of the great walls of Great Zimbabwe and the origin of the Karanga state where, in the fourteenth century, trade was at its peak with the presence of Syrian glass, Persian faience and Chinese celadon paid for in gold and copper objects which also proliferate in Great Zimbabwe.

This was also the time when Kilwa was at its apogee associated with gold and ivory of the Sofala region, the coastal entrepôt of Central Africa. According to Ibn Baṭṭūṭa, who visited Kilwa in 1331, the gold of Sofala came from 'Yufi in the land of the Limis', one month's journey into the interior. The trade hypothesis is strong in some respects, but is less so when it assumes that economic power automatically equals political authority, or again when it assumes that enormous labour forces were needed to build stone walls, which may not have been the case.

Political and economic power in the formation of the Great Zimbabwe state

Both the hypotheses discussed take little account of the realities of subsistence agriculture and of the complex decision-making mechanisms. Certainly, by the thirteenth century both the Leopard's Kopje and the Gumanye traditions were showing signs of considerable development of trade and centralized political authority. Furthermore, population growth and improvements in agricultural methods may have permitted longer intervals between fallowing. But most of the basically self-sufficient people remained scattered in villages and were only drawn to long-distance trade by powerful religious or economic motivations. And even then it required a higher authority to regulate such trade in order to make it viable. But the demand for raw and processed materials alone was not enough to stimulate the appearance of such an authority. What was required was, on the one hand, that a group take the required political and/or religious initiative, and, on the other, that a considerable number of villages (which after all had other alternatives) accept a new hierarchy compensated for by an increase in opportunities.

Here as elsewhere, the religious or commercial motive alone is not enough to explain the rise of the state.

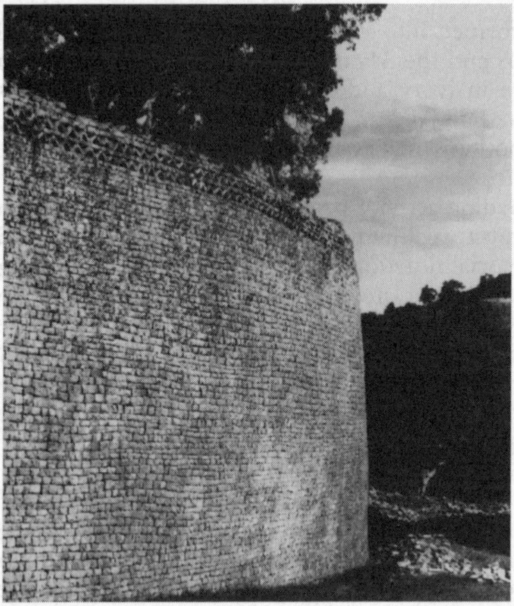

21.2 *The wall of the Great Enclosure at Great Zimbabwe.* (*P. S. Garlake, 1973*)

21.3 *Soapstone sculpture of a bird on a monolith found in the Philip's ruins in the valley of Great Zimbabwe.* (*P. S. Garlake, 1973*)

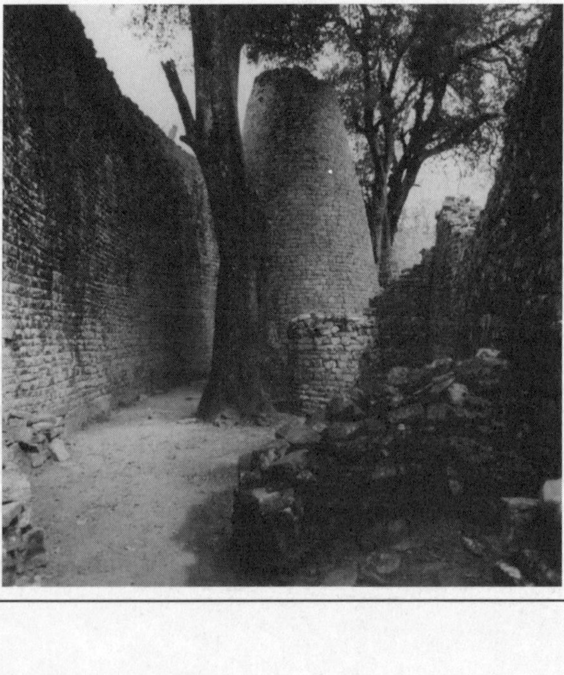

21.4 *The conical tower of Great Zimbabwe.* (*Department of Information, Zimbabwe*)

In short, Great Zimbabwe is a most impressive monument dominated by the Acropolis which is covered with enormous boulders linked together by walls built over the centuries and thus marking off enclosures the largest of which is the westernmost one. Stratigraphy has made it possible to trace a development in three stages at least.

Intensive occupation began only in the eleventh century, but no stone walls were built until the thirteenth century, when the small huts were replaced by more substantial mud houses. The wall for the western enclosure also coincided with the influx of imports. The final stage was when the first buildings were constructed in the valley below. The Great Enclosure was built over about a century; the vast enclosing wall has an average height of 7.3 m, and is 5.5 m thick at the base and between 1.3 m and 3.6 m at the top. It encloses another enclosure wall. Between these two walls a defile leads to a skilfully constructed conical tower. From its very structure, the Great Enclosure must have been the dwelling place of the rulers of Great Zimbabwe.

In the upper levels of the Acropolis and in the Great Enclosure many gold and copper ornaments, fine soapstone bowls and carvings, large quantities of imported glass beads, Chinese, Persian and Arab china dating back to the fourteenth century have been found. This was the period of Ibn Baṭṭūṭa's stay in East Africa and also the time of great trade of which the rulers doubtless had a monopoly, which suited them and ensured security and maximum profit for the traders from the coast as well as a political guarantee. This was especially so as the gold and ivory that they sought were creamed off by the rulers through religion and tribute. There is nothing to indicate whether the Arabs from the coast exercised any political or technological influence so far into the interior at this period. Comparisons between the conical tower and the mosques of East Africa are pure fantasy. The reality is that the architecture of Great Zimbabwe is the logical culmination of the large enclosures and chiefs' quarters which were formerly built of grass and mud and now in stone because new means made it possible, society was organized to be able to do it and the abundant granite was exfoliated in natural layers about 50–100 cm thick, and obtaining blocks was an operation that could be accelerated with the use of fire and water. With the exception of the mysterious conical tower, there is nothing in Great Zimbabwe which is alien to African practice. In particular, unmistakable Arab influence is impossible to detect.

Such an intimate aspect of culture as the habitat could not be transformed by the sort of sporadic long-distance trade undertaken by the handful of Arabs or commercial agents who may have resided within the frontiers of Great Zimbabwe.

Great Zimbabwe's expansion and its regional supremacy

Great Zimbabwe is a unique site only on account of its scale compared to the 150 similar ruins scattered over the granite country that forms the Zambezi-Limpopo watershed, which occasionally contain gold or copper objects and glass beads. Chronologically, they span the period from the fourteenth to the fifteenth century. Their structure indicates the important place that cattle sometimes played, and they are usually small, which indicates that they had minimal populations and were not viable economically, even though they possibly received tribute and labour contributions from surrounding villages devoted to shifting agriculture.

At Nhunguza ruins there was only a single building, very large but divided into three rooms: one was very large (for audiences), the second contained a single seat and the third was completely secluded and must have contained objects of value or religious objects. What we have here once again is the pattern of religious or political authority, which alone could be the cement that held together such a community. The borders of the Great Zimbabwe state, even in the fourteenth century, are ill-defined, but its heartland was in central Mashonaland. Some ruins in an identical style in what is now Matabeleland stand out as outposts of the influence of Great Zimbabwe in Leopard's Kopje territory.

Commercial ties with the East African coast

We must not be misled by the small volume of the commodities exchanged between the centres in the interior of Africa and the East African coast: the commodities were valuable items. If Ibn Baṭṭūṭa could write in the fourteenth century that Kilwa was one of the most beautiful cities in the world, the town owed it largely to the gold trade of Sofala. Similarly, the wealth of the rulers of Great Zimbabwe was linked to the prosperity of the coastal trade, the sole unimpeded outlet for gold, copper and ivory – which the Africans seemed to be able to supply in limitless quantities. But the trade began to decline from the late fifteenth century, and by the time the Portuguese arrived it was already but a shadow of its former self.

The looting of ruins in this area makes it difficult to reconstruct the mechanics and terms of the trade with the east coast. But, in the far north-west of Mashonaland and the middle Zambezi valley, sites such as that at Chedzugwe, spread out over 24 hectares of fine grassland, show, by the abundance of cattle and game bones, the importance of pastoralism and hunting. In addition, iron- and copper-working were both prosperous, copper being made into standardized ingots of two fixed weights. Wire bracelets made from copper and tin alloys were commonplace. Textiles and extremely fine pottery with a fine finish and delicate decoration complete the picture of an economy that was exceptionally well organized for the period.

Archaeology and the limits of Zimbabwe's influence

Chedzugwe was in touch not only with Great Zimbabwe but also, as the presence of fine copper ingots and delicate pottery shows, with the isolated site of Ingombe Ilede on the summit of a hill where 11 richly decorated burials surrounded by an array of the finest domestic and imported goods were found. One of the skeletons wore a necklace of sea-shells, traditionally associated with

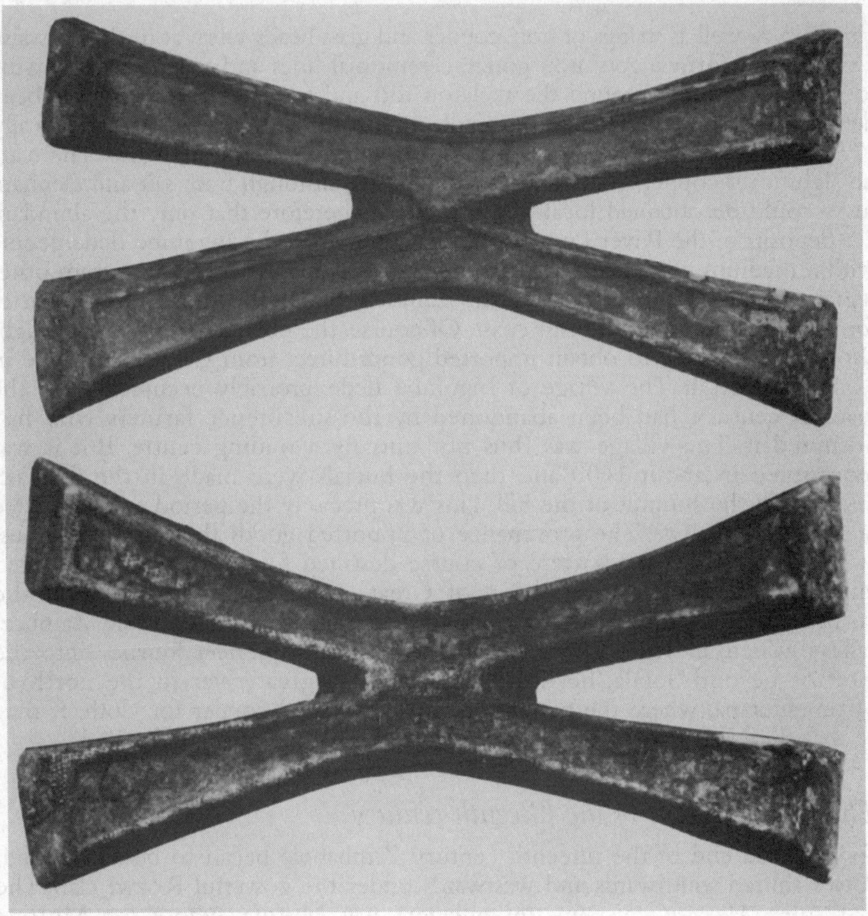

21.5 *Two copper cruciform ingots from Ingombe Ilede, Zambia (post-eleventh century).* (*B. M. Fagan*)

chiefship, as well as strings of iron, copper and glass beads worn at neck and waist. Copper cruciform ingots, iron gongs, ceremonial hoes and sets of wire-drawing tools were arranged around the skeleton too and traces of garments have been detected as well as the remains of spindle whorls showing they were made locally.

Almost all these objects come from long-distance trading networks. There are no significant copper, gold or iron-ore deposits, although both salt and elephant tusks could be obtained locally. It is thought therefore that only the abundant salt deposits of the River Lusitu could have provided the Ingombe Ilede people with a medium of exchange to acquire the precious metals coming from other regions to the north and south of the Zambezi, which they in turn could barter for luxury goods from the east coast. Of course, the notables of Ingombe might also have been able to obtain imported goods direct from Great Zimbabwe in exchange for salt. The village of Ingombe Ilede, probably occupied since the seventh century, had been abandoned by the subsistence farmers who had occupied it. The village was thus not initially a trading centre. But it was reoccupied in about 1400 and then the burials were made in the fine ash midden on the summit of the hill. This was precisely the period of the apogee of Great Zimbabwe. The provenance of imported goods thus seems obvious; but such precious goods were of course destined for only a tiny privileged minority. The social stratification of Great Zimbabwe is thus here at the northernmost frontier of trading activity between the Limpopo and Zambezi valleys. When, in 1514, Valentim Fernandes made a pioneer journey into the interior beyond Sofala, he heard tales about a great river to the north of Mwenemutapa, where the people of 'Mobara' traded copper for cloth. It may be that the Mbara are to be identified with the people of Ingombe Ilede.

The turning-point of the fifteenth century

Towards the end of the fifteenth century Zimbabwe began to be abandoned. Power shifted southwards and westwards under the powerful Rozwi clan. The first ruler, *Mwenemutapa* (master pillager), was Mutota, whose son Mutope expanded the kingdom, moving his capital northwards away from Great Zimbabwe. In about 1490, the southern portions of the empire broke away under Changamire. The Mwenemutapa, his power reduced, fell fatally under Portuguese control in the sixteenth and seventeenth centuries.

But the question of why Great Zimbabwe was abandoned still remains. The surrounding countryside may no longer have been able to support the villages, still less the costly superstructure of Great Zimbabwe. In the absence of artificial fertilization or irrigation, which was impracticable here, the exhaustion of the land forced the people to move to new tracts of woodland.

Despite his sacred and immovable character, the Mwenemutapa had to move. The political upheavals of the late fifteenth century may thus well have been due to ecological and economic reasons. Once the two pillars of prosperity, a vigorous agriculture and an active trade network, were exhausted, Great Zimbabwe and its successor (the Rozwi state) were shaken to their foundations.

22 Equatorial Africa and Angola: Migrations and the Emergence of the First States

The present state of knowledge

Between 1100 and 1500, this region is barely touched on by contemporary written sources which deal almost wholly with the single kingdom of Kongo. Excavations in the Shaba and Bas-Zaïre provinces do not yet give a complete enough chronological picture. Oral traditions thus constitute an essential source, until such time as linguistic data have been fully exploited for the study of the proto-Bantu society, the differentiation of languages and the processes of state formation. Only then will it be possible to exploit the anthropological data. But the stumbling-block remains the absence of a sufficiently reliable absolute chronology.

In these circumstances, the only possible approach is to try and embrace this period in a context of archaeological and linguistic data and oral tradition from the preceding period to the period after 1500; thus obtaining a picture in which the earliest and the most recent threads are joined. But the picture that emerges consists essentially of hypotheses.

If the expansion of the Bantu languages reflects the great migrations, these ended well before 1100. It is true – according to R. Oliver and M. Guthrie – that the original core of the Bantu peoples originated in Shaba. It is there that their typical way of life based on the use of iron and cereal-growing took shape, leading to population growth and migrations along the rivers, the coast and even the forests where, in about 1000, remnants of hunter-gatherer groups were still living (pygmies and pre-Bantu agriculturalists). These moreover still remained after 1500 by which time the movements of Bantu peoples had ended.

This theory is rejected by many linguists who follow J. H. Greenberg in placing the original home of Bantu expansion between the Rivers Benue and Cross (Nigeria). Bantu-speakers are said to have spread out from there towards equatorial Africa along the corridors of the Sanaga and the Ogowe, on the one hand, and along the Ubangi-M'Bomu, on the other. In a second stage, there was a language 'explosion' from Shaba or the Great Lakes area. All these developments had in any event come to an end before the year 1000.

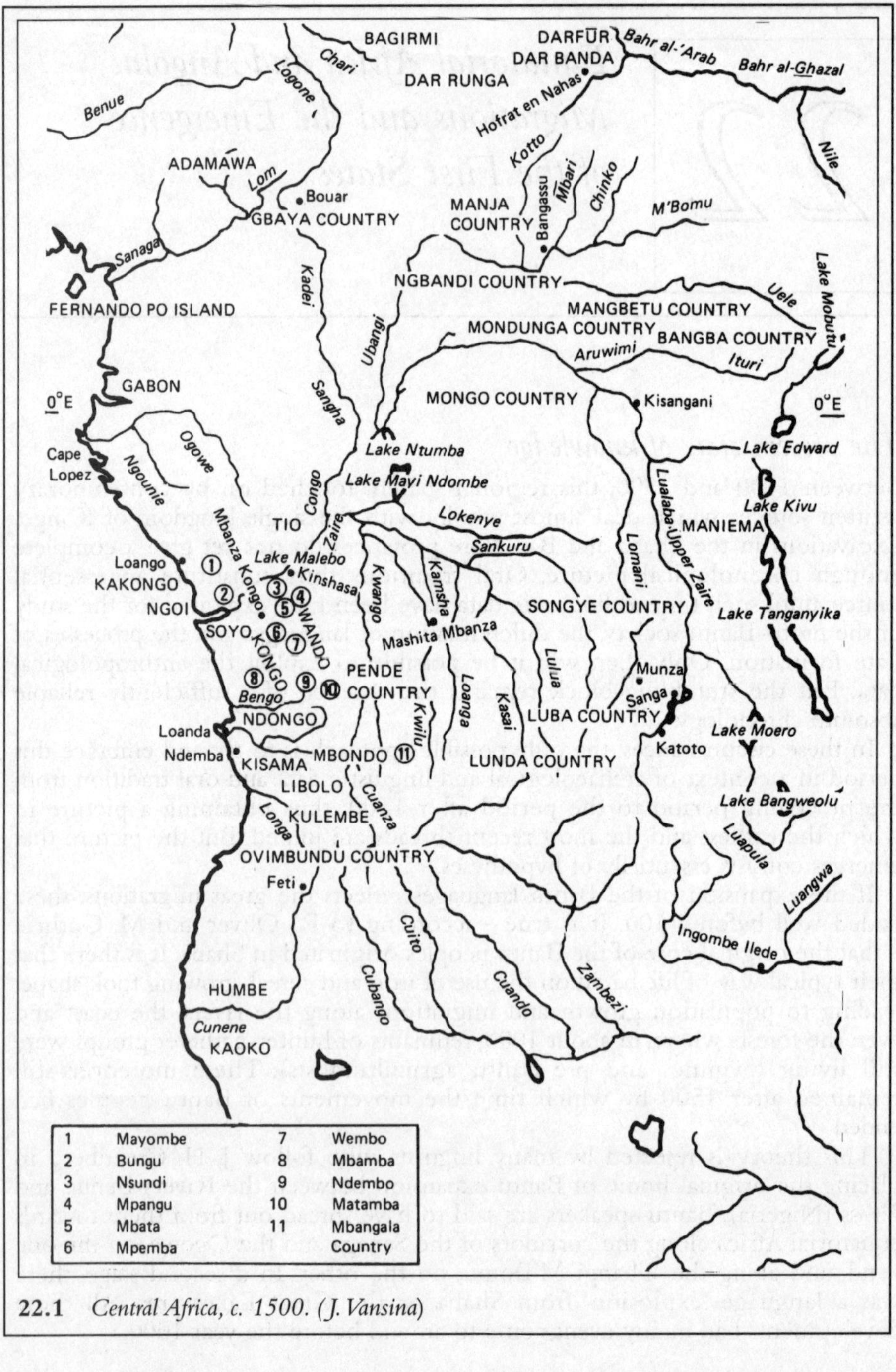

22.1 *Central Africa, c. 1500. (J. Vansina)*

In the Ubangi basin, an area of confrontation between languages and ethnic groups, the oldest languages belonging to the eastern group of East Adamawa were eroded by Bantu or Sudanese languages which were themselves locked in a conflict whose outcome was undecided for centuries.

Elsewhere, the Bantu had secured the adoption of their languages, not without having borrowed other cultural traits from the indigenous peoples, thus constituting rich and varied civilizations.

Well before 1500, the broad outlines of the map of the early ethnic groups were already in place, as is shown by the case of the Imbangala who were a mixture of Luba, Lunda, Ovimbundu and Ambundu. The mixing also resulted from the division of labour between agriculturalists, hunters and fishermen and the necessary complementarity between them.

Exchanges within the central basin explain in particular why the Mongo languages remained so uniform. Conversely, in an area such as the Maniema, the forest and the mountainous terrain preserved local particularities; but even there, two large groups, the Lega and the Komo became dominant.

The interaction in the vital area between the Zaïre and the Ubangi-M'bomu is still the object of hypotheses. For Ehret, a linguist, the central Sudanese occupied not only the north-east but all the country east of the Lualaba where they were already divided into separate language groups before the arrival of the Bantu-speakers. But it must be remembered that the picture of the establishment of peoples was profoundly blurred by the subsequent great migrations from the seventeenth to the nineteenth century. Thus, the Banda immigration from the southern Sudan fleeing slave raiding swept aside the Sabanga who only survived in the form of islands in the great mass of the Banda. Only the powerful Nzakara kingdom resisted and survived this drive whereas in the west raids from Adamawa drove the Gbaya groups eastwards.

History and civilization

Agriculture

The ecological and archaeological data indicate that even before 1100 agriculture was practised everywhere, except in southern Angola close to the Kalahari desert and in some forest areas. Red sorghum and millet (especially in the savannah), yams, cocoyams, bananas and sugar-cane of Asian origin (especially in the forest), as well as groundnuts and various beans were widely cultivated with iron implements. Fishing, hunting and the gathering of caterpillars and grubs combined with the keeping of small stock (including pigs and horned cattle in the lower part of the river) helped to maintain an adequate diet. Nor should we forget the natural intercalary savannahs interspersed in the forest. And it is precisely on the edges of such savannahs, on the edges of the forest, that human groups enjoying the advantages of two different environments could increase more rapidly. It was the same with the wooded galleries along the numerous rivers teeming with fish.

Crafts and trade

By 1100, craft techniques that foreign travellers would admire at the end of the period were already known: pottery, basket-making, raffia weaving, cooperage, the production of rock and sea-salt, the extraction of salt from plants and salt marshes, and metal-working, as shown by excavations at Bouar, Sanga and, perhaps, Munza (Shaba).

The first indicators of the circulation of cruciform copper ingots as money appear in the copperbelt around the year 1000, and can be found from the Zambezi to the Lualaba before 1450. As other currency units of account, use was made of shells (*nzimbu*), raffia squares and rock-salt from Kisama. The first transporters were probably fishermen on navigable reaches of rivers and traders bartering iron, copper and salt, particularly with the forest producers of game.

Society and the organization of power

The groups lived in compact villages, and the lineages were patrilineal. But there is a matrilineal belt stretching from Namibia to the Zambezi and from the Ogowe to Lake Tanganyika. G. P. Murdock argues that the same was true of all the forest peoples west of the Lualaba. What is certain is that in the fifteenth century, except for the Luba of Kasai and Shaba, who in any case were to change after 1500, all the forest peoples were patrilineal. Evolution worked in favour of this system. In fact, in the Bantu matrilineal system, the principle that men possessed authority over women was recognized, leading, for example, to virilocal residence. This resulted in the weakening of matrilineal lineages in favour above all of territorial, and therefore political, authority in the village. Chieftaincy thus existed from the beginning.

Among the patrilineal non-Bantu-speakers, the situation varied. In the north, some were divided into scattered hamlets without chiefs, whereas along the Ubangi and the Chari, there were large hamlets with lineages under the authority of chiefs.

In the southern savannah, masters of the land who were also priests of the spirits of the land enjoyed what was in effect political authority over a group of villages, that were embryonic kingdoms. In reality, the patriarches of the largest and richest lineages became lords of the land, and then kings by absorbing others lineages or by force. The production of surpluses freed the chiefs and their counsellors from manual labour, thus creating an embryonic state power. This was happening in a territorial framework in which everyone recognized a single authority. In the beginning, that authority retained its religious attributes, which explains its sacred character. Later, the growth of the surpluses made it possible to make a selective redistribution which enlarged and structured the system of counsellors, judges etc. Clientelism developed, notably through the distribution of palm wine or beer. The ritual of the king's drink gave concrete expression to this process. To meet the demand which grew with the size of the clientele, and in the absence of significant technical advances, more hands were needed. The emergence of domestic slavery met this need, the first slaves probably being prisoners of war or criminals whose death sentence has been commuted. They were added to an essentially female labour force. More frequent wars associated with the growth of states amply fuelled such a system.

Nevertheless, despite favourable economic conditions, some lineage groups were hostile to state-building. Devotion to equality and the need to build up strength were two contradictory demands that were reconciled by the growth of lineage confederations based on ritualized associations. Such were the Ngbandi who still provided lineages of rulers elsewhere. Such were the Gbaya who were still neighbours of the Mbum who were organized into states. Finally, the Sara helped to form the Bagirmi kingdom, but retained their lineages for themselves.

On the religious level, there was great homogeneity, with magic, divination, fertility and healing rituals, as well as cults of the ancestors and local spirits. All forms of authority including that of the head of the family had a superhuman aspect which has been rather hastily christened 'sacred kingship' and attempts made to find a single origin for it in time and space. But there are crucial differences in patterns, for example in the Luba kingdoms or on the Atlantic coast, which militate against treating the phenomenon as a uniform one.

The northern savannahs

The oral tradition of the patrilineal Ngbandi, who came from the present-day Republic of the Sudan south of the Baḥr al-ʿArab, makes it possible to say that they were probably driven out of their homeland by nomadic Baḳḳara Arabs in about 1300. The myths speak of whites armed with spears, bows and arrows, knives darts and even guns, who precipitated a migration that continued for two centuries and took the Ngbandi in about 1500 to an area between Kotto and Dar Runga, then occupied by the Manja-Ngbaka in the west and the Bantu-speakers in the east. The peoples of the central Sudan were already divided into at least two blocs, one of which included the Sara and the future Bagirmi.

In the sixteenth century, a Ngbandi lineage founded the Nzakara kingdom whose subjects spoke Zande, while other Ngbandi formed great lineages under lords. Probably this was simply one case among others of an extremely complex movement of ethnic and linguistic groups which moved not in waves but rather by infiltration, with acculturation of some traits. Thus pygmies, for example, adopted the languages of the central Sudanese. What archaeologists observe here is the long survival of Stone Age implements alongside iron ones, as in ancient Egypt. The stone involved is haematite containing a higher proportion of iron, such that the slightly greater efficiency of iron tools did not justify the considerable extra work to process the haematite.

The great equatorial forest

The forest was not an impenetrable green barrier, but rather a filter crossed by at least two routes: one along the coastal and one from the Kadei Sangha, by

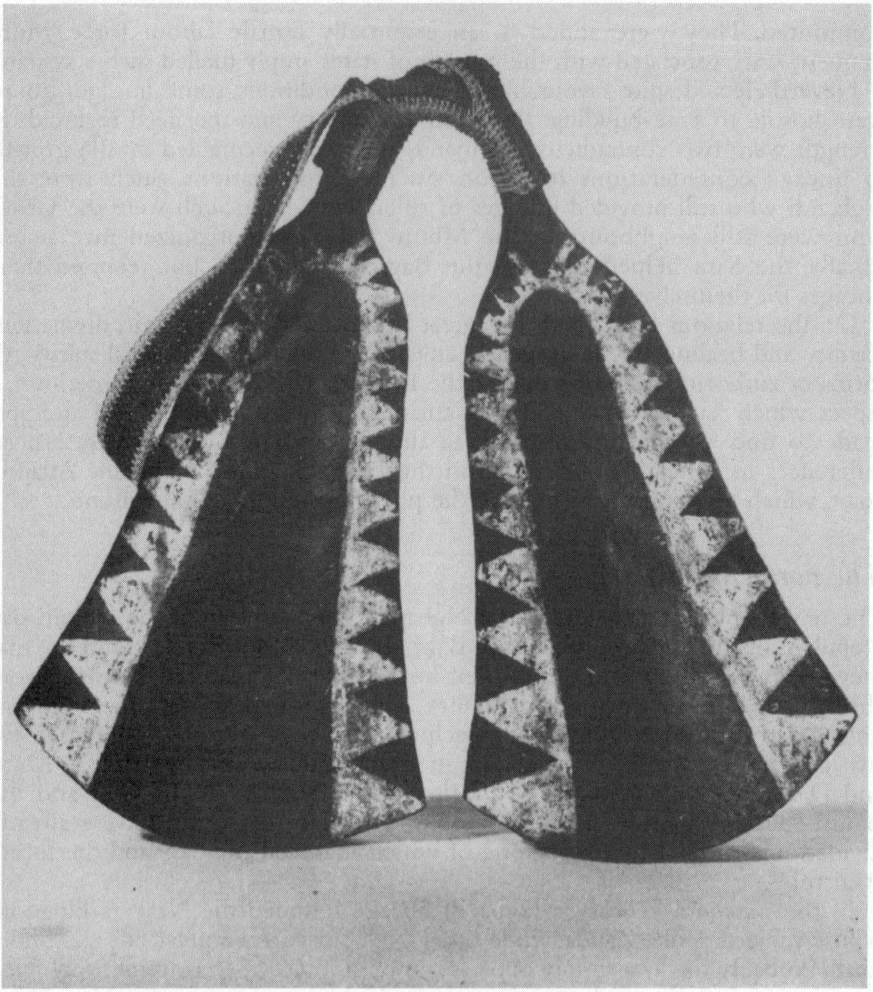

22.2 *Double iron bell from Mangbetu (Zaïre). (Musée Royale de l'Afrique Centrale)*

way of the Ubangi and the Congo/Zaïre as far as Lake Malebo. Sea voyages were undertaken before the year 1000, as demonstrated by the presence of the Bubi people of Fernando Po and the production of polychrome wooden statuary from Yorubaland to Loango.

Finally, the confluence of the Ubangi, Sangha and Zaïre/Congo formed a vast marshy area of flooded forest frequented only by fishermen who could thus cross the forest.

Thus the single clapperless bell and later the double bell crossed the forest from north to south, moving from Ife in its great period to Zimbabwe by the fifteenth century. These bells involve a knowledge of sheet-iron working and of soldering. Furthermore, the double bells were used to reproduce the tones of the spoken language (in this case Bantu languages), apart from the function of such bells as symbols of political power, from Nigeria to Zambia. In the same way, throwing knives and small signalling drums also came from the north (confirming the above-mentioned theory of Bantu expansion). Clearly, with these objects, ideas and customs could also travel. Among these notions was the key idea of the political chief. The Mongo languages, for example, distinguish the right of blood relationship expressed by the term *mpifo* from the right of the first occupier, lord of the land, *okofo*. It was the first lords who, through the process of clientelism mentioned above, were to become first paramount chiefs and then kings.

Social organization in the forest and the clearings

Before 1500 there was a slow but massive expansion of people speaking Mongo-type languages in the far south-west of Sankuru and Kasai. The small chiefdoms or *nkumu* established in the course of this movement were marked by the following features: the village had two spokesmen, one for each of the two quarters on either side of the main street. Relations with the pygmies were ambivalent: sometimes they lived in symbiosis, sometimes they fought each other. Authority went with age in a 'gerontocracy'. In the south of the region, matrimonial alliances reinforced territorial power. What is remarkable here is the forest people's ability to work in iron. The Songye acknowledge that the Luba, who came from the forest, taught them how to smelt iron. By burning trees of very hard wood, the forest peoples were able to produce very high temperatures and they had even discovered how to make steel.

Very little is known about the history of the forest from Gabon to the Republic of the Congo at this time. The Pahwin migration was a gradual drift which started before 1500, probably with structures of the *nkumu* type. In the Maniema, the ancestors of the Lega peoples were probably already living with the socio-political associations known as *bwami*, with their complex hierarchy of grades in which the highest constituted a collective moral and political authority. It is believed that it was on the basis of the *bwami* that the peoples west of Lakes Kivu and Tanganyika developed the concepts of chiefship and kingship.

The same process probably lay behind the development of elective 'lordships' among the Songye in the south. In short, paradoxically, the forest was the source of considerable technical and socio-political advances.

The savannahs of Shaba

A clear distinction must be made between an eastern tradition (subdivided into a Luba complex and an upper Kasai/upper Shaba complex) and a western tradition on the Atlantic coast. In this respect, the stories of the origin of the Luba and Lunda empires cannot be considered were myths.

The principal site in terms of metal-working techniques is the one at Sanga. In connection with these advances, social differentiation must have arisen in the region between the middle Zambezi and the Limpopo. Furthermore, this region was linked to the Lualuba lakes by sustained trade in copper crosses. Part of a trade network that extended as far as the Indian Ocean.

The Luba and Lunda kingdoms

Oral tradition speaks of 'Luba' chiefs in Malawi and Zambia. A Lunda state is known to have existed from before 1450. In reality, all the conditions were present for an early development of powerful chiefdoms: the Shaba copper mines, fertile soils and the ease of movement through the savannah all stimulated trade.

The Luba kingdom was probably founded before 1500 by a certain Kongolo, near Kalongo, by the fusion of several patrilineal clans. Each clan headed by a chief or *kiloto*, the 'owner of slaves', recognized the king's authority. The king was surrounded by at least two dignitaries, the guardian of emblems, called *inabanza*, and the military chief or *twite*. The 'sacredness' or *bulopwe* of kingship was inherent in the blood which flowed in the veins of the reigning lineage on the principle of *mpifo*.

The resources of salt, metals and copper, the mixing of populations and trade could not fail to stimulate the emergence of large towns, the growth of surpluses and the development of political institutions. On this last point, the Songye differ markedly from the Luba in having an elective kingship in which the criterion of wealth counted for a great deal: it was often a royalty limited in time and dependent upon the advice of a secret society, the *bukinshi*.

The matrilineal eastern Luba government was based on such esoteric associations.

As for the Lunda, from the upper Kwango to the upper Kasai and the borders of Zambia, they were developing on the ideological and political principle of perpetual kingship. This system denied the passage of time in order to ensure the unbroken cohesion of the dynasty and considered that the successor actually 'became' his predecessor, adopting his name, his relations of kinship, his duties and prerogatives, thus perpetuating the network of 'fraternal' agreements, alliances and federations. This was the ideological tool that the vast Lunda empire forged after 1500.

The west of this region was rather poor but had salt-mines and copper deposits between the Lualaba and the Luapula. The Lozi state, which was to appear in the upper Zambezi valley, was probably prompted by the Lunda model.

Angola

The basin of the Lui, a tributary of the Kwango, saw the early development of chiefdoms ruled by the Pende. At the beginning of the sixteenth century, south of Libolo, a Kulembe state appeared based on a military initiation association, the *kilombo*. It was perhaps one of the first Ovimbundu states whose characteristic feature was stone tombs. The Ovimbundu, who speak a south-west Bantu language, were responsible for the foundation of Humbe, in the south of Angola, based on the *kilombo*, which may have been introduced here by the Imbangala. Some of the 14 Ovimbundu states, which are socially and culturally linked to southern Angola, seem to have come into being before the sixteenth century.

The Bantu speakers of southern Angola and Namibia were divided into three main branches: the Nyanyeka-Humbe, the Ambo and the Herero. Among the first group, only Humbe formed a powerful chiefdom, whereas by the nineteenth century the Ambo had organized a dozen states with well fortified capitals, matrilineal succession and power symbolized by a sacred fire and an economic structure based on possession of cattle. The Herero were cattle-keeping nomads, hunters and gatherers, like their Khoi neighbours in Namibia.

The Nyanyeka-Humbe claimed to be autochthonous. The other branches seem to have come from the Zambezi area, to the east. All these groups seem to have absorbed large numbers of Twa hunters.

It appears that the Bantu-speaking peoples who occupied the central plateau of Angola and the valleys of eastern Angola were surrounded by black hunters with a San culture in the coastal zone and by Khoi and San in the south in the land between the rivers.

In the north, which was better watered, groups belonging linguistically to the Lunda-Guangella-Cokwe groups were practising an Iron Age agriculture.

The savannahs of the south-west

When they arrived, the Portuguese found three kingdoms, from north to south: Great Makoko or the Tio/Bateke kingdom inland, Loango and Kongo, founded one after the other in the thirteenth and fourteenth centuries. It is possible, if they did indeed have a common origin in the north, that the original society on the edge of the forest of Mayombe may have existed around the year 1000. They adapted first to the savannah or the Bateke high plateau. Then the Kongo spread southwards, the Vili of Loango along the coast, while the Bateke occupied the southern high plateaus and the woodlands of Gabon.

The same pattern of evolution can be postulated here as in the forest: large matrilineal villages with politico-religious chiefs and counsellors; alliances and federations, ancestor and spirit cults and social diversification leading to the creation of aristocrats and captives devoted to agricultural work and trade based on an elaborate monetary system.

The kingdom of Kongo before 1500

Thanks to Portuguese accounts, this is easily the best known kingdom.

It was Lukeni Nimi who set out from Mayombe, crossed the river and founded, by conquering, the Ambundu chiefdom of Mbanza Kongo. Subsequently, the newcomers mixed with the indigenous peoples. According to F. Pigafetta and D. Lopes (1591):

> The Kingdom is divided into six provinces: Bamba, Sogno, Sundi, Pango, Batla and Pemba. Bamba, the largest and richest, is governed by Dom Sebastiaõ Mani Mamba, a cousin of King Dom Alvaro, who died recently . . . there are many dependent lords . . . The word *mani* means 'Lord' and the second part of the names denotes the country. Thus, for example, Mani Bamba means 'Lord of the region of Bamba' . . . Bamba . . . is the key to the kingdom, its shield and its sword . . . its inhabitants are courageous and always ready to take up arms, to drive back the enemies from Angola . . . in case of need an army of four hundred thousand warriors can be mustered.

This last figure is surely exaggerated but it gives an idea of the considerable population of the country.

The king of Kongo, while not an absolute ruler, enjoyed great authority. He nominated governors, except for the governor of Mbata, 'elected by the people and the dignitaries of the Nsaku family, with royal confirmation'. In the province of Soyo, its governor was hereditary. It seems moreover that, before 1500, the Kongo kingdom was even larger since it continued to lay claim to sovereignty over, for example, Kakongo, Loango and the kingdom of Teke.

The governors collected taxes and tributes paid in kind: millet, palm wine, cattle, ivory, leopard skins, but above all raffia squares and shells (*nzimbu*, used as money). Leopard and lion skins had a symbolic value as attributes of chiefship.

The central administration, which was subject to dismissal, was made up of a chief of the palace, who acted as viceroy, a supreme judge, a receiver of taxes together with his assistants, a chief of police, a messenger service etc.

The lord *kabunga*, a descendant of the autochthonous people, acted here as elsewhere in Africa as high priest and master of the land. The governors were close relatives of the king who entrusted Nsundi and Mpangu to his favourite sons. They thus had a strong base from which to contest the succession. The governors appointed lesser lords who in turn ruled over the *nkuluntu*, the hereditary village chiefs. The tombs of the ancestors, close to the capital, were the object of a cult. Though the king was called *nzambi mpungu* or 'superior spirit', his person was not sacred: only power was sacred. By committing incest with his sister, the ruler put himself outside the ordinary run of men and, by becoming 'family-less', could rule equitably over all families. By this act and by a special initiation, he acquired great power over charms thanks to a magical power. His insignia included a head-dress, a drum, a copper or ivory bracelet and a carved wooden stool; he was surrounded by an almost religious code of etiquette which the Portuguese described quite well, as they did the capital and court life in the fifteenth century.

Banza (which means 'residence of the king or lord') was a fortified capital with stone walls, from which aid could be sent rapidly to every region of the kingdom, and it was also a major commercial metropolis, and the meeting place for main roads, which the Portuguese renamed San Salvador.

A college of nine or 12 members was supposed to choose the king's successor and advise. him. The governor of Mbata, who was ineligible to succeed, was an ex-officio member, and the lord *kabunga*, the chief of the land, had a right of veto. These counsellors/electors, chosen from outside the royal family, often simply registered the existing balance of power by choosing the most powerful. In addition, during the reign, the council of state including among others the holders of the great offices, had the right to oversee the ruler especially in such matters as war, the appointment or dismissal of governors, and trade (opening routes).

The state supervised the output of *nzimbu* and the payment of salaries. Trade went on in iron objects, pottery, mats and baskets and salt, but also basic items such as copper or ivory trinkets, fabrics etc. There was no full-time specialization in any one craft, and iron-smelting and raffia-weaving were reserved for the nobility.

The *nzimbu* arrived by the route from Loanda, sea-salt, fish, pottery and wickerwork from Bas-Zaïre, copper by the route from Mbamba etc. Little is known of the vast majority of society. The matrilineal structure is not clearly demonstrated. For example, the name of the first king included a name connecting him to his father and another connecting him to his mother's father. The society was divided into three orders: the endogamous aristocracy, freemen and slaves. Marriages sealed alliances between clans. The former masters of the land (*kitomi*) were an integral part of the aristocracy.

Conclusion

The first major feature that emerges from this survey of the history of equatorial Africa from the twelfth to the sixteenth century is the key role of the forest in the development of technology (iron-working) and social systems including state systems, the two things moreover being linked. Although this role was not exclusive (we are thinking for example of the pioneer place of the earliest Luba centre), it has too long been misunderstood for it not to be stressed today.

But there still remain considerable dark areas that further linguistic and archaeological research will elucidate.

23 Southern Africa: Its Peoples and Social Structures

*The writing of history and the problem of sources**

Apartheid in contemporary South Africa has hindered objective knowledge of the African past. History, like all material and social values, is also reserved for the white minority.

> The tendency to concentrate on the past of the dominant white minority has been accentuated by the rigid positions adopted by South African universities and South African publishers in general who refuse to accept the validity of non-written sources for historical reconstruction. (UNESCO, 1980)

Sciences such as archaeology, anthropology and linguistics are rejected as historical sources, and only the past of the whites, available in written sources, merits attention. Again, the Portuguese sources have been studiously neglected. Oral traditions are ignored, and even some written sources are excluded in the name of apartheid. In short, African peoples are excluded from white history which projects into the past the ideology of its domination. Nevertheless, the independence of Angola and Mozambique as well as that of Zimbabwe in 1980 has opened a wide field for research.

The state of knowledge

Two problems dominate historical inquiry: first, the dates when the various peoples settled there, i.e. the migrations, and, second, the power structures. In the first place, we must stress how long ago the Khoikhoi settled in the region. The Early Iron Age, which ended towards 1100, began about a century before the Christian era between the Zambezi and the Limpopo. At Lydenburg, in the Transvaal, pottery heads have been uncovered along with evidence of the existence of farming.

Towards 1100, the Middle Iron Age began. A group of researchers with the linguist C. Ehret used a corpus of 90 words to study the correlations between two groups of languages in the region: The Shona dialects and the Sotho,

*UNESCO Note: This text was written before the end of Apartheid and does not take into account changes which might have occurred in South African historiography since 1994.

Nguni, Venda and other dialects. The Shona-speakers are said to have settled in what is now Zimbabwe, while the peoples in the second group occupied an area farther south.

There, between 1000 and 1500, crucial developments occurred: the Khoikhoi became pastoralists and expanded over a huge area. The specific traditions took shape that are so characteristic by about 1500 of the Sotho, Tswana and Nguni Bantu-speaking peoples.

These changes deeply influenced the lives of the coastal fishing communities along the Atlantic coast and the shepherds near the Cape. Since written or oral evidence for this period is extremely scare it is important to mobilize as much as possible and collate sources such as archaeology, comparative anthropology and linguistics. In particular, we need to reconstruct early Nguni and early Sotho vocabulary and study Khoisan loan-words in Bantu languages and vice versa.

The evolution of the southern Bantu languages

The latest linguistic research has shown that Shona and the south-east Bantu dialects form distinct sub-groups of the same language group. The strongest correlation is between Venda and Shona (55 per cent), then between Tsonga and Shona (41 per cent), followed by Chopi (38 per cent), Sotho (37 per cent) and Nguni (35 per cent).

Shona, on the one hand, and the other languages, on the other, formed two distinct centres from which the Bantu language spread rapidly through the south-east; the Sotho, Chopi and Tsonga languages, for example, occupying the lower valley of the Limpopo, while Nguni and Sotho-Tswana are widely diffused on both slopes of the Drakensberg. The differentiation between the Sotho and the Nguni language groups is much more recent than the others. These differentiations, which reflect or induce particular patterns of settlement, had already developed between 1500 and 1600, which would be consonant with the oral traditions that record genealogies going back to the fifteenth or sixteenth century.

A very widely accepted theory equated the Bantu expansion to that of agriculture and iron-working at the beginning of the Christian era. In fact, it is not certain that everywhere the Bantu brought with them qualitatively new farming techniques and tools, but rather improvements which favoured economic and demographic growth as well as new forms of settlement. There was thus no massive revolutionary historical upheaval but rather successive infiltrations.

The Shona, Venda and Tsonga peoples and languages seem to have lived for a long time side by side in the region between the Zambezi and the Limpopo; this could explain the considerable resemblance in social habits (patrilineal inheritance, circumcision and polygamy). Furthermore, the Nguni are the only ones not to have clan totems.

North of Ukhahlamba

At Olefantspoort, at Melville Koppies and at Platberg teeth of cattle, sheep and goats, iron tools and millet seeds belonging to the Middle Iron Age complex were found and almost certainly belonged to the Sotho-Tswana. The only site where the stages in the evolution within the Early Iron Age is clearly apparent is at Eiland in the central Transvaal, where salt was worked throughout the period. From the eleventh century Early Iron Age pottery gave way to Mapungubwe ware and, later, Phalaborwa pottery.

This site constitutes one of the major centres of copper production in the Transvaal at that time. It lies near a tributary of the Limpopo, the Olifants river – which Vasco da Gama called 'the river of copper' in 1498. Mining had gone on there at least since the eighth century. The style of the pottery is similar to that of the Lobedu, some distance to the north; the Lobedu became differentiated notably by their rain queens.

Through the changes in this region, continuity seems to have been provided by the indigenous miners and potters, who were also the traders; perhaps they were Songha who had to face the Venda conquerors.

In short, between 1100 and 1500, on the Transvaal low veld, agricultural settlements must have traded among themselves and exchanged their craft products. The Phalaborwa mines were a source of iron objects, within a radius of a few dozen kilometres, and a source of copper over much greater distances, as far away as the Limpopo and the coast. Metal-working and trade may have been responsible for the first large chiefdoms which clashed with neighbouring chiefdoms and roaming bands of hunters until the seventeenth century, when they were absorbed into a single kingdom by the Venda.

North of the Vaal, near Johannesburg, traces have been found of villages whose round houses had platforms and plastered floors, whereas the walls were of perishable materials, all the houses being located around an oval or circular space which presumably was the cattle kraal.

This type of settlement immediately preceded building in stone which dates from the fifteenth or sixteenth centuries. Sites of this latter type (called 'N' type) north and south along the upper Vaal river as far as the Drakensberg, in an area that enjoys good rainfall and rich grasslands with houses, granaries and byres with a wall surrounding the whole settlement, is evidence of a mixed economy of agriculture and stock-raising.

Whether the pre-stone and stone settlements can be identified with the Sotho way of life, as has been suggested, and some pottery styles in these villages with distinct Tswana groups must remain a subject for future research.

The origin of stone buildings may be either local, for example in areas where grazing is good but wood scarce, or adapted from buildings erected by rulers in the Zambezi region.

The settlement sites north of the Drakensberg show dramatic changes after 1100, with an increase in the size of settlements and the growing role of cattle-

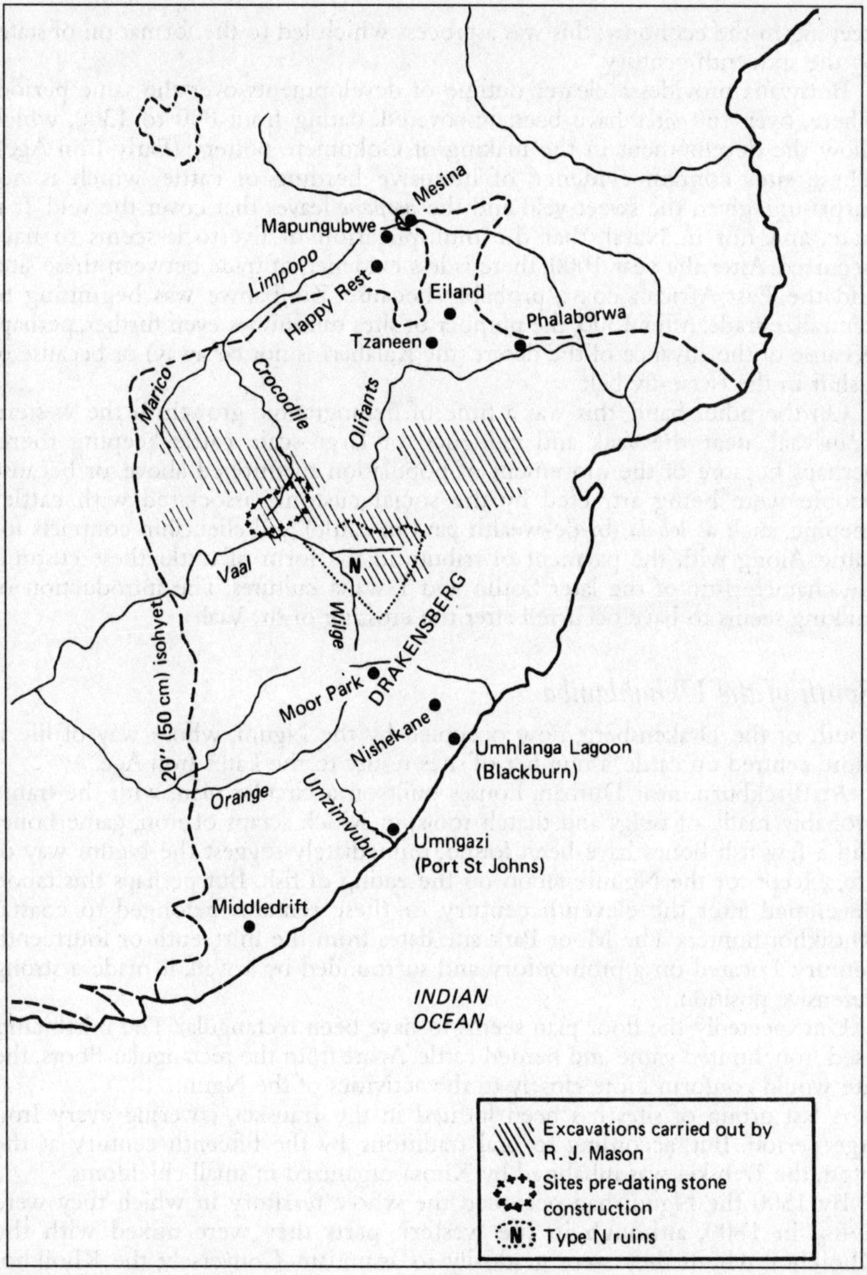

23.1 *Archaeological sites of southern Africa, 1100–1500. (J. Vansina)*

keeping in the economy; this was a process which led to the formation of states by the sixteenth century.

Botswana provides a clearer outline of developments over the same period. There, over 150 sites have been uncovered, dating from 800 to 1300, which show the development in the making of Gokomere pottery (Early Iron Age). These sites contain evidence of intensive herding of cattle, which is not surprising, given the sweet veld and the *mopane* leaves that cover the veld. It is here, and not in Natal, that the multiplication of livestock seems to have occurred. After the year 1000, there is less evidence of trade between these sites and the East African coast, probably because Zimbabwe was beginning to centralize trade. After 1300, the number of sites diminishes even further, perhaps because of the advance of the desert (the Kalahari is not far away) or because of a shift in the tsetse-fly belt.

On the other hand, this was a time of demographic growth in the western Transvaal, near the Vaal, and evidence of large-scale cattle-keeping there; perhaps because of the movement of population mentioned above, or because people were being attracted by the social customs associated with cattle-keeping, such as *lobola* (bride-wealth paid in cattle) and clientship contracts for cattle. Along with the payment of tribute in the form of cattle, these customs are characteristic of the later Sotho and Tswana cultures. The introduction of milking seems to have occurred after the crossing of the Vaal.

South of the Ukhahlamba

South of the Drakensberg, now occupied by the Nguni, whose way of life is more centred on cattle, a number of sites testify to the Later Iron Age.

At Blackburn, near Durban, houses built on a circular plan, with the frame probably made of twigs and thatch roofs, in which scraps of iron, game bones and a few fish bones have been found, immediately suggest the Nguni way of life, except for the Nguni's taboo on the eating of fish. But perhaps this taboo developed after the eleventh century, or these remains belonged to coastal Khoikhoi hunters. The Moor Park site dates from the thirteenth or fourteenth century. Located on a promontory and surrounded by a wall, it made a strong defensive position.

Unexpectedly, the floor plan seems to have been rectangular. The inhabitants used iron, hunted game and herded cattle. Apart from the rectangular floors, the site would conform more closely to the activities of the Nguni.

A last group of sites has been located in the Transkei, covering every Iron Age period. But, according to oral traditions, by the fifteenth century at the latest, the Transkei was inhabited by Xhosa organized in small chiefdoms.

By 1500 the Nguni had occupied the whole territory in which they were living in 1800, although in the western parts they were mixed with the Khoikhoi, whom they were gradually to assimilate. Conversely, the Khoikhoi left a deep imprint on both the eastern and the western Nguni languages, although this influence was late, after 1600, i.e. after the Xhosa and Zulu language clusters had begun to separate. With Khoikhoi influence on Zulu and Xhosa amounting to about 14 per cent and 20 per cent of the vocabulary respectively, Khoikhoi influence transformed the Xhosa phonetic system. The Khoikhoi must have occupied tracts of land deep into Natal, since even the easternmost Nguni tongues were affected.

The preponderance of pastoralism over agriculture among the Nguni was also a result of Khoikhoi influence, although the Sanga cattle of the Nguni was different from the South African breeds of the Khoikhoi; these latter also taught several peoples to milk animals and taught the Xhosa to use pack oxen. Finally, the Khoikhoi also influenced the Xhosa in religious matters, the pattern of residence and the practice of lopping off a portion of the little finger.

The Nguni today represent a cross between the 'Negro' and Khoikhoi. This presence of a majority of common genes appears also between the Khoikhoi and the Tswana. Taking the linguistic evidence and the biological evidence together, one must reach the conclusion either that at one time many Khoikhoi were in close contact with the Nguni in Natal, or perhaps even before their migration into this region. In short, the impact of the Khoikhoi on the history of the peoples of southern Africa was much greater than historians have allowed for up to now.

The Khoikhoi

The personality of the Khoikhoi stood out from the very first contact with the Portuguese expeditions led by Bartolomew Dias in 1488 and Vasco da Gama in 1497. In 1510, they killed sixty Portuguese (including Dom Francis d'Almeida, the Viceroy of India) in a skirmish at Table Bay, despite the fact that the Portuguese had firearms. A century and a half later the Dutch, anxious to secure the Cape region for themselves, began to exterminate the indigenous people.

Khoikhoi, in its various dialects, was one of the most widely spoken languages in the region from northern Namibia to the Cape and eastwards at some periods as far as Natal. This linguistic homogeneity indicates a quite recent and rapid dispersal of the Khoikhoi. They kept cattle and fat-tailed sheep, and rode cattle which were also loaded with their belongings and poles for their houses. This gave them a high degree of mobility, which explains the diffusion of their language. This language belongs to the 'Khoisan' group[1] to which they also belong in terms of their physical type, despite a few differences due to having milk in their diet. When the Portuguese arrived, they were already in the Cape area. They had acquired cattle in large numbers in northern Botswana, partially abandoned hunting and gathering there and learned to forge metals but not to smelt them. The decrease in the population in Botswana after 1300 seems to coincide with the exodus not only of Bantu-speakers but also of the Khoikhoi.

Following the valleys as much as possible, the Khoikhoi moved southwards as far as the confluence of the Vaal and the Orange. From there, one branch

1. Khoisan corresponds to the two groups called Hottentot and Bushman

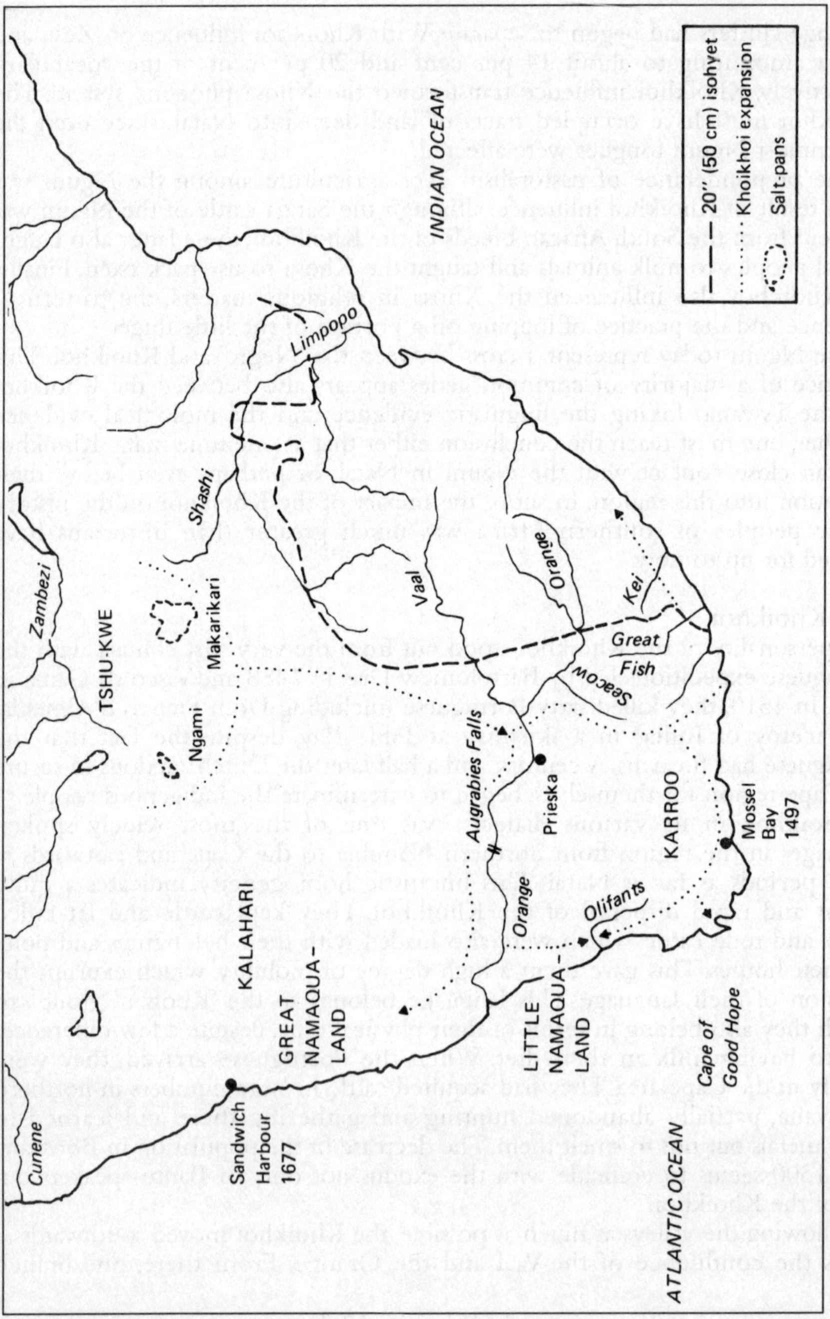

23.2 *Khoikhoi expansion.* (*J. Vansina*)

headed westwards into Namibia, and the other continued southwards and split into two branches, one heading eastwards into Natal and the other westwards into the superb pastures of the Cape area. It is true that eleventh century remains have been found at Middledrift, with the remains of domestic cattle, pottery and stone tools, but no trace of iron. If Middledrift is a Khoikhoi site, the migration hypothesis outlined above would no longer be valid. But these remains may equally well come from older hunters who had acquired cattle.

The Khoikoi expansion deeply affected the life of all the inhabitants of southern Africa. The idea that the Nguni found no Khoikhoi in Natal is false. It seems on the contrary that the Khoikhoi subjugated the agriculturalists whom they found in the Transkei and Natal. It was later that the balance of power was reversed in favour of the Xhosa, especially in the sixteenth century. In the west too, the Herero settled further north, while not adopting the language of the Khoikhoi, borrowed their pastoral way of life and their clan organization. When the cattle stock waxed, they formed larger political units, under the leadership of hereditary chiefs with systems of tribute, at least by the seventeenth century. A certain dynamism of changes affected Khoikhoi society. For example, while political leadership was associated with individual wealth, the system of inheritance and the matrilineal system gave only part of the heritage to the descendants. Reversals of fortune could thus occur; in the event of impoverishment, some reverted to a hunting and gathering life. But a coalition of poor people could seize large herds and secure social leadership. In periods of plenty, the balance was more stable, but in the event of drought or epidemic, thieving of cattle and strife increased. Thus, while the Khoikhoi initially had an advantage over the agriculturalists, thanks to their mobility and organization, in the long run, fluctuations of climate and internal contradictions worked in favour of the agriculturalists, at least in the eastern regions. The presence of the Khoikhoi also led to upheavals for the aboriginal hunters and sheep-herders who were competing for the same resources. The sheep-herders were dispossessed by the Khoikhoi or reduced to clientage. The same happened to the coastal hunters. But the hunters in the interior who looked upon the Khoikhoi as poachers, while they themselves were seen as robbers, put up a long resistance. They were subordinated in normal times, but they regained some advantage whenever the environmental conditions became adverse, which led to their ranks being swollen with Khoikhoi reduced to being hunters. But the Khoikhoi way of life was gradually gaining the upper hand, and by the seventeenth century their language had become the *lingua franca* of the whole Cape area.

Conclusion

Two major facts stand out: the diffusion of the Bantu language and the expansion of the Khoikhoi from Botswana.

Starting from Zimbabwe and in the high veld, proto-Sotho and Tswana agriculturalists established chiefdoms north of the Drakensberg. As the Nguni came into contact with the Khoikhoi they specialized further in cattle-herding. But when they separated from the Sotho and crossed the Limpopo remains a mystery for the time being. It is also difficult to know why, between about 800 and 1300, the pastoral way of life became established in northern Botswana. This development does not seem to have been the work of Bantu-speakers, as their languages are poor in cattle-keeping terms, or of hypothetical immigrants from the central Sudan. It is more natural to think of the ancestors of the Khoikhoi themselves, who, over five centuries, perfected their civilization without wholly abandoning their nomadic and hunting traditions.

24 Madagascar and the Neighbouring Islands from the Twelfth to the Sixteenth Century

The essential constituents of the population of Madagascar were present by the end of the twelfth century, even though further waves of migration occurred until the sixteenth century. These events occurred in the general framework of 'historical relations across the Indian Ocean'. The chief problem during the period covered in this chapter is the slow and complex biological and socio-cultural interaction among Africans, Arabs and Indonesians which, by the sixteenth century, had produced the original identity of the Great Island. The wars recorded in the traditions between the newcomers and the *Vazimba* probably simply refer to the clashes between immigrants such as the Merina and the indigenous peoples who were probably African by descent and were therefore called 'ancestors' (*Vazimba*).

On the Arab migrations there are documents written in the Antemoro language but in Arabic characters known as the *sorabe*.

But by what process were the kingdoms formed that the Portuguese found already established when they arrived in the sixteenth century? Although the later Indonesian arrivals contributed to organizing them more firmly, it is quite clear that when they arrived the island was already organized into large chieftaincies probably by its oldest inhabitants, Africans and Arabs.

The origins of the kingdoms

The traditions concerning the *Vazimba* have been misinterpreted as pitting foreign conquerors and civilizers from across the ocean against unorganized autochthonous peoples, especially as the Betsileo report that they only appointed chiefs in time of war.

The hypotheses on the origins are various and contradictory. P. Ottino stresses the Indonesian contribution which was associated with a cultural one. The popular contribution derived from Malay-Polynesian immigrants and traditions, while the aristocratic and state traits were brought in the twelfth century by Indonesian Hinduism, as can be seen by comparing the dynastic festivals of Imerina with those of Hinduized regions of Insulindia (Indonesia). J. Lombard however, attributes the formation of large political units in this region to Arabized groups arriving in the south and west.

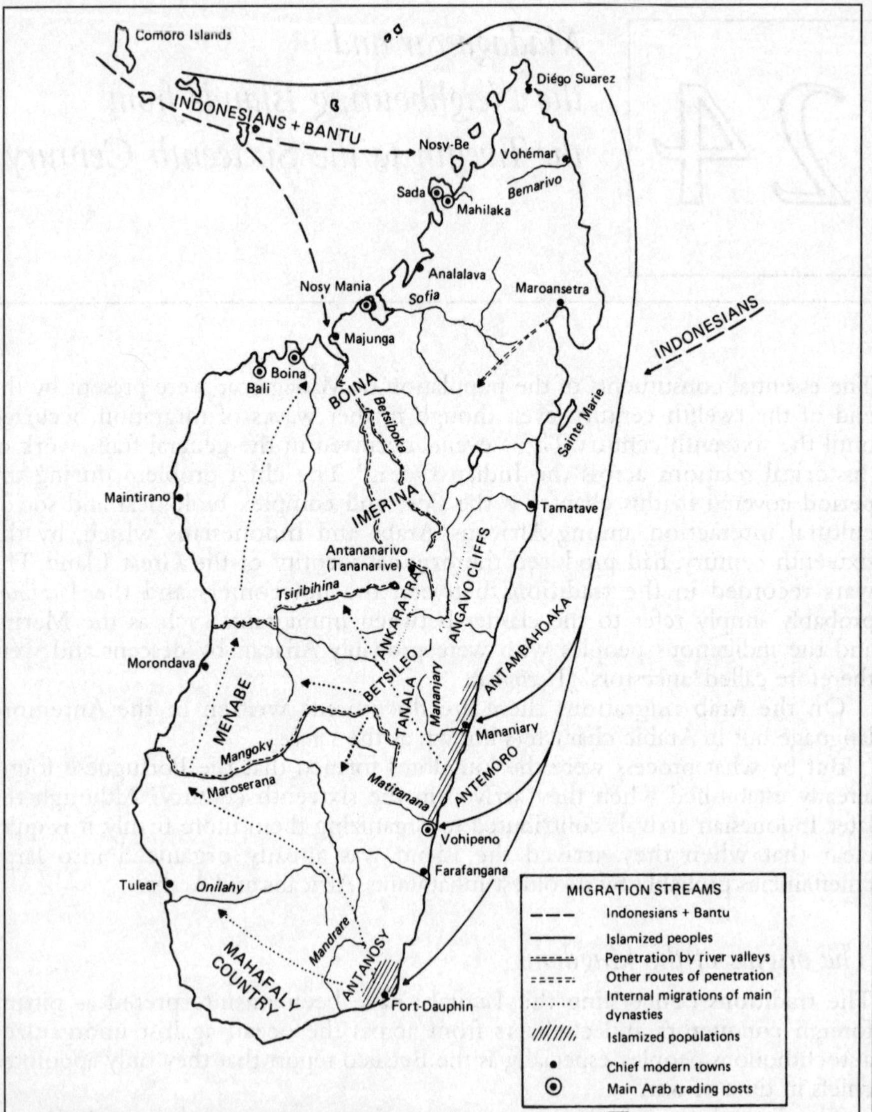

24.1 *Madagascar: migration streams and peopling.*
Source: F. Esoavelomandroso with the collaboration of T. Rajaona, using elements from the Atlas de Madagascar by S. Ayache (pl. 20 and 20 bis) and the Atlas du peuplement de Madagascar *by F. Ramiandrasoa*
Notes: The last migratory waves of Indonesians came between the twelfth and thirteenth centuries. The Islamized peoples (Swahili and Arabs) had their main base in the Comoros from where they circumnavigated the island by the north

In other words, how the biological and cultural as well as political symbiosis which appears in the Muslim influence on the institutions of Imerina evolved does not emerge very clearly.

J. P. Domenichini, for his part, stresses the African contribution. If, for example, one analyses the magic charms or *sampy* mastered by the kings to exercise their domination, it can be observed that only a very small minority (three out of 14) come from the south-east, the main area of Muslim influence. Ottino also recognizes the existence of small kingdoms without clearly established rules of succession before the arrival of the Maroserana. Moreover, he distinguishes between the pre-Sakalava kingdoms that were the work of the first immigrant agriculturalists, who were 'matrilineal Bantu', and the Sakalava kingdoms formed by the patrilineal Bantu pastoralists: in fact, the island must have felt the impact of early political organization that was proceeding on the continent nearby.

What is important above all is to unravel and follow over time the various contributions which ended up forming the Malagasy personality, which is undeniably a mixture. This calls for reasoning in terms of cultural traditions rather than of individual peoples. For example, Raminia, the founder of the Islamized kingdom of the south-east, must have come from south-west India; and the Maroserana and Andrevola dynasties were probably of Indo-Arabic origin. The kingdoms strictly so-called seem to date from after the twelfth century, even though earlier, clearly hierarchical federations of clans already formed large chiefdoms.

Nevertheless the tangle of internal migration makes it even more difficult to define the respective roles to be assigned to the various human groups involved. (On this subject, see Volume III of the *General History of Africa*.)

Birth of the Merina kingdom

The highlands are occupied today by the Merina, the Betsileo and the Bezanozano, who may all have the same origin; but the Merina form the aristocratic group, whose ancestor Andriantomaza is said to have landed at the Bay of Antongil, either directly from South-East Asia, or after stays on the African continent and in the Comoro Islands. The slow advance of these groups up into the highlands, pushed on by the arrival of small groups of Asians over several centuries was completed by the fifteenth century. These various routes are punctuated by sites which have now been identified.

The Arab and Portuguese documents confirm the late arrival of these migrations which the Betsileo traditions also mention, with the rise of their dynastic ancestors the Iarivo from the coast towards the sources of the Mahatasiatra.

In fact, there was not a conquering wave. There was a long period during which they lived side by side which brought the two communities concerned together. It was only after two reigns, including that of Andriamanelo, that the newcomers unleashed a war against their hosts.

The low population density over vast forested areas favoured good neighbourliness without clashes and inter-marriages, so much so that stories continue without a break from a genealogy of the so-called *Vazimba* kings (which has a Bantu ring to it) to the genealogy of the Merina kings. As a result, these latter were able to present themselves as the legitimate successors of the former. It is thus possible that the newcomers found a state framework with which they initially collaborated and which they ten took over and transformed. The later conflicts between the masters of the land or *tampon-tany* and the newcomers over the allocation of the best lands were very bitter. King Andriamanelo is said to have won because his soldiers had iron weapons, and the 'masters of land' did not know the use of this metal. In fact, iron was almost certainly introduced into Madagascar before the end of the first millennium of the Christian era. So what happened was that the victors simply ideologically appropriated this earlier invention.

For J. C. Hébert, between these latter and the indigenous Sakalava, joking relations (*ziva*) were established, which assume solidarity, the exchange of goods and the gratuitous insult, such as exist in many parts of Africa between indigenous people and immigrants. *Manazimba* means 'to insult', a reference to this institution bringing to mind the indigenous *Vazimba* who were of African origin or a mixed black and Indonesian population.

The Merina and Betsileo traditions speak of the vanquished fleeing westwards as far as the Menabe region. After being driven out of the highlands, their Sakalava descendants still remember this episode (for example, among the Mikea in the Tulear region). But there was no total replacement of populations: the autochthonous people did not simply flee leaving the venerated tombs of the indigenous peoples. In fact, the presence in the heart of Imerina of the Antehiroka clan, who claim to be descendants of the *Vazimba*, contradicts any such idea. Most of the autochthonous inhabitants remained; and the Merina in whose interests it was to come to an understanding with the 'masters of the land' so as to win the favours of the earth gods, increased the number of marriage alliances with the indigenous peoples, who saw in it a way of being associated with the new power. Thus, in the west, the alliance between the immigrants and the *tampon-tany* group of the Andrambe gave rise to the first historical figure in the Andriambolamena dynasty. This was the Menabe kingdom. Others were created in similar circumstances by the Merina, the Betsileo and others. In addition, there were the contributions of the Muslims present in the region from as early as the ninth century.

Islam in Madagascar and the Comoro Islands

With the rise of Swahili seafaring culture on the East African coast (see Chapter 18) relations intensified between the two sides of the Mozambique Channel. Muslim 'colonies' settled in the Comoro archipelago. Thus the north-west of Madagascar, closer to the influence of these Muslim groups, acquired a Swahili and Comoran type of identity, through the customs and traditions of seafarers, whereas the south-east of the island, furthest removed from such influences, remained unaffected by them. As elsewhere, the usual traditions of origin, highly ideological in content, are to be found here. Thus the Antemoro *sorabe* recount the arrival in the fifteenth century of the ancestor Ralitavaratra, the custodian of the sacred relics, bequeathed by Moses and coveted by the Sultan of Mecca. After many adventures, he found the 'promised land' on the banks of the River Matitanana. The Antanosy also speak of the arrival from Mecca of their ancestor, Raminia. A Comoran tradition recounts the arrival in Anjouan in the fourteenth century of a group of Sunni Muslims who had been forced to flee Persia. Even though the religious motives for this influx are important, they were later replaced by the commercial attraction of the Swahili world which it is important to place in the framework of voyages in the western Indian Ocean, thereby disseminating men, things and values between the African coast, the Comoro Islands and Madagascar.

The staging posts of the Swahili world

Intense, long-established commercial activity linked the towns and islands from Madagascar to Sofala since antiquity. The Swahili ports look seaward and they became increasingly prosperous from the twelfth century onwards, and they acted as staging posts between Arabia and India on the one hand, and the Comoro Islands and Madagascar on the other.

Many Muslims who made landfall in the Great Island were strongly marked by Swahili culture and were often black Muslims. African influence was thus considerable, since archaeology has shown that many cities on the north-west coast were founded by Africans, not by Arabs.

There is in fact a family resemblance between these trading posts and the Comoran and Swahili towns with their fortifications, their mosques and their richly carved gates doorways such as at Anjouan, Mutsamudu, Domoni, Sima, Mahilaka, Nosy Boina and Langany. The Portuguese have left a description of this last-named post which stresses that 'their mosques and most of their houses were built of limestone, with balconies after the style of Kilwa and Mombasa' (quoted by Poirier, 1954). The dhows were loaded on the coast of Madagascar with rice and soapstone funeral vessels from Iharana; they brought to the Great Island Indian pearls, fabrics, Chinese ceramics and objects that are also found in the Swahili towns. This business continued after the sixteenth century despite competition from the European newcomers.

Although the Comoros, and the island of Anjouan in particular, probably received Bantu and Indonesian immigrants, they were swamped by Islamized groups from the east coast of Africa, each group of whom arrived with a programme of religious reforms and renewal. In the north-west of Madagascar, immigrant groups formed the Antalaotse group, a commercial bourgeoisie that controlled economic and religious power in the staging posts.

Malagasy civilization from the twelfth to the sixteenth century

In addition to the oral traditions and writings, much may be expected from the archaeologists, whose work is only just beginning.

Material culture

The cultivation of rice, bananas and cocoa spread through the island after the twelfth century. Domestic animals (cattle and poultry) and yams were of African origin. Indeed, African influence was predominant in the south, west and part of the north-east. On the other hand, the outrigger canoe, which ensured mastery of the sea, and paddy-rice growing are of Indonesian origin. As for political and religious models, they were doubtless the result of interaction between the African patterns and Asian and Islamic contributions.

The clans (*foko, troki* or *firazana*), organized around elders or a patriarch, experienced many clashes, which resulted in the spread of the victorious clans and political polarization.

In the Comoros, the *beja* had already given way to the first Islamized chiefs, the *fani*. On the Great Island, the dynasties of the west and south (Sakalava, Mahalafy, Zafimanara of the Androy region) and those of the south-east (Zafiraminia of the Anosy region) seem to have been related. The tradition mentions east–west migrations which set out from Antemoro country and from the Anosy region and ended, for example, in the Menabe.

Although it is difficult to untangle the African and Indonesian influences, not to mention the indigenous dynamics, it is almost certain that the cult surrounding the relics of dead kings (the *dady* in Sakalava country) comes from contacts between the kingdom of the Maroserana Volamena and the famous empire of Mwenemutapa. Dismissing the 'myth of the white kings' of Asian origin, R. K. Kent even puts forward the hypothesis that the Andriana Merina were of very mixed origin, the biological counterpart of the socio-political synthesis of the autochthonous 'masters of the land' (*tampon-tany*) of African origin, and Arabized, Indonesian and other immigrants. What is certain too is that, after the fourteenth century, new concepts were introduced, such as the organization of the kingdom into homogeneous territorial units.

Religion

Here too there is an obvious synthesis between the African, Indonesian and Islamic elements. In the pantheon, first place is reserved to the principal god of Indonesian origin: Zanahary or Andriananitra (perfumed lord). He created the world, formed society and bestowed customs. But, according to African thought, this god is too distant, whence the all-pervasive presence of spirits or *djinns* of the waters, the forest, the ancestors, the *Vazimba*. Sacrifices of buffaloes or cows were frequently made to them. If the word for magician or 'sorcerer' is of Asian origin (*inpamosary*), reality is very close to African practices. Double funerals are reminiscent of Indonesia; and among the Betsileo, the pallbearers dance as if possessed, moving in a zigzag fashion.

In conclusion, the period from the twelfth to the sixteenth century was an essential phase in the formation of the Malagasy people as it is today. The UNESCO colloquium on historical relations across the Indian Ocean in Port Louis (1974) made it possible to throw light on a number of aspects of this complex evolution of Madagascar, in which Africa, Arabia, India and Indonesia have come together, offering the world a striking example of biological and cultural intermixture, – the offspring of whom are so handsome.

25 Relationships and Exchanges among the Different Regions

Introduction

Between 1100 and 1500 Africa was a privileged partner in inter-continental relations with the Old World. Across both the Mediterranean and the Indian Ocean, Europe and Asia were linked with Africa by an active trade, usually conducted by Muslims. It was in many respects a high point economically and commercially before the opening of the Western slave trade.

Great currents of cultural exchange necessarily accompanied these cross-currents of trade affecting every region without exception: neither forests nor deserts presented impassable barriers.

The Sahara and the Sahel: a privileged space in external relations

Authors long sought the so-called 'technological backwardness' of Africa in the existence of the Sahara seen as a major obstacle to the spread of knowledge and goods. In fact, the period we are looking at saw the golden age of trans-Saharan trade. Like a sandy Mediterranean, the Sahara united the countries bordering it with southern 'ports' like Timbuktu, Tichīt, Walāta, Gao and northern 'ports' like Sdjilmāsa, Tlemcen, Wargla and Ghadāmes. The dromedary, the sole ship of the desert, assumed vital importance, as did the pastures that it needed to survive and over which the nomads fought violently.

Through the 'ports' just mentioned, trans-Saharan trade extended much further into Europe and the Middle East on the one hand, and the Gulf of Guinea on the other.

The nomads living in the heart of this traffic profited greatly from it, receiving cloth, gold, cereals, ivory and slaves in exchange for salt and other minerals as well as meat and guides for hire. Ibn Baṭṭūṭa left a striking and valuable description of this trade on its long journey across the desert where the caravan chief 'was in command of everyone like a ship's captain'. From Sidjilmāsa to Walāta, a two months' journey with a stop-over at Teghāzza, where ten days' rest were necessary before setting off again. Specialized Massūfa guides were paid very well to assure safe passage for the caravans, a great number of which were, however, swallowed up by the desert, as is shown by the masses of cowries, copper bars and scraps of cloth found by T. Monod in Mauritania in 1964.

From Walāta it took 24 more days to reach Niani, the capital of Mali, on a route so safe that it was possible to travel alone. In short, the human vagaries were at least as important as natural constraints, to make the desert a filter of transactions. So long as a strong authority controlled the routes, traffic flowed easily. As soon as that authority weakened, the wells marking the route became blocked, insecurity prevailed and the nomads fled the desert and came to prowl around the cities.

The gold mines

In the tenth century, the king of Ghana, according to Ibn Ḥawḳal, was 'the richest sovereign on earth' because of the reserves of gold that his dynasty had built up from the royal monopoly over gold nuggets. These gold-mines at Galam, Bure and Bambuk were so important that access to them was forbidden to Berber Arab traders. During his pilgrimage, *Mansa* Kankū Mūsā I was very laconic on this strategic question about the gold-mines. Nevertheless, shortly after this pilgrimage, the king of Mali appears in a Majorcan atlas holding a large gold nugget. In addition to the mines previously mentioned, gold from the Volta, Lobi country and Akan country also passed through the big cities of the Sudan to the north of the Sahara and the Muslim world or Europe. But the bulk of the reserves were hoarded, as gold was an almost sacred product whose exploitation was governed by almost religious rituals.

Other merchandise

Salt was the main item here, and the rulers of the Sudan were concerned to lower its price although the taxes on this produce represented a large proportion of crown revenues. Thus, salt from Tegh̲āzza which sold at 10 *mith̲ḳāl* a load in Walāta could cost four times that in Niani, the capital of Mali.

Salt from the Senegalese coast at Awlīl had lower transport costs; but when it arrived among the peoples of the forest, it was bought by the weight of gold, and, sold in pieces, was used as currency to purchase kola nuts, slaves, ivory etc. In the event of shortage, the Africans fell back on substitutes, extracted for example from certain vegetable ashes.

Copper was also an important item in commercial transactions, as *mansa* Kankū Mūsā I stressed, mentioning the red copper mine at Takedda, imported in bars to Niani, and exported to the countries in the south (Worodugu) 'where we sell it at a rate based on the weight of a *mith̲ḳāl* of gold'. The profits from this were enormous. According to Ibn Baṭṭūṭa, Takedda was a great trading centre where gold was shaped into both thick and thin bars, and sold wholesale; in the deepest Sudan, this copper in smaller pieces also served as a currency, while exporting it to Egypt made it possible to bring back manufactured goods including fine fabrics.

A third item that was, unfortunately, very profitable was male and female slaves. When Ibn Baṭṭūṭa crossed the Sahara from the Sudan to Tuat, in the fourteenth century, he travelled in a caravan with 600 female slaves. These slaves were highly sought after in the courts of the Arab and Berber princes and were used as servants, soldiers, concubines and courtesans, and were sometimes very influential, especially when they were well-educated or extremely beautiful.

From the fifteenth century, these slaves were increasingly used as agricultural labour in the Middle East, for example, but above all in Mediterranean Europe. It is true that the black rulers also took slaves from the north, but as symbols. When the *mansa* sat on his throne in the public square 'behind him stand some thirty Turkish (Mamlūk) or other mercenaries, purchased for him in Cairo. One of them holds a silk parasol, surmounted by a cupola and a gold bird representing a sparrow-hawk', writes al'Umarī. Some authors have perhaps exaggerated the demographic loss resulting from this slave trade by the Berber Arabs. Raymond Mauny has estimated it at 20,000 a year or 2 million for the century. For example, by the terms of the *baḳt* the king of Nubia had to send 442 slaves to Cairo annually. In reality this tribute was exacted essentially from the communities practising traditional religion in the south.

Other products exchanged included ivory, as the tusks of the African elephant were softer and more easily carved than those of Indian elephants. The Sudan also exported skins, oryx hides, cereals and fabrics. In the fourteenth century, the most heavily used route was the one taken by Ibn Baṭṭūṭa, but there was also one from Timbuktu to Kayrawan, via Wargla. North of the Sahara, there were dynasties of rich traders, true privateers, who loaded up and financed caravans. Such were the al-Makkari brothers: accredited to the rulers of Mali, they had a complex business network which, in addition to the mother house in Tlemcen, had branches in Sidjilmāsa and the Sudan.

South of the desert, powerful corporations of Dioula or Hausa traders were no less knowledgeable in business than their counterparts in the north. Jewish communities also participated in these transactions, for example at Tuat as early as the eighth century, and perhaps right into the heart of the Sudan. From the fifteenth century, with the Spanish *reconquista*, and the search to circumvent the Islamic world, Europeans risked travelling as far as Tuat, in the person of the Genoese Antonio Malfante and perhaps as far as Timbuktu in the person of Benedetto Dei.

The scale of this trans-Saharan trade should not be downplayed: ordinary caravans had a thousand camels. But Ibn Khaldūn speaks of caravans of 12,000 camels between the Sudan and Egypt.

The spread of ideas and techniques

The mixing of Berber Arabs with the peoples of the Sahel, at least in the towns, inevitably led to two-way flows of techniques, ideas and values.

For example, was the patrilineal system introduced by Islam? It seems not, although the period from the twelfth to the sixteenth century saw a clear shift from the matrilineal to the patrilineal system, for example in the kingdom of Ghana and the empire of Gao, including Mali which offers an intermediate system (frequent fraternal succession) that is full of contradictions.

But, on the other hand, there are matrilineal Muslim Berbers and Sudanese peoples such as the Bambara. Furthermore, the patrilineal peoples in the Congo had no contact with Islam. Islam at this time was not propagated by violence. It was above all proselytizing by Berber Arab traders, Wangara and Hausa, who peacefully carried the new religion further south. Indeed, for a long time, this Islam tolerated certain ancient practices despite the exhortations of the reformer al-Maghhīlī. The piety of the Sudanese was prodigious, according to what Ibn Baṭṭūṭa observed; but he also noted anomalies of behaviour typical of the tolerance of the Sudanese.

In the towns, the Arabic language became the language of scholars and the court: Mansa Mūsā spoke it correctly. An African literature in Arabic came into being, but bore its finest fruit in the sixteenth century. There were scholarly exchanges between universities across the Sahara on a footing of equality. The rulers of the Sudan were surrounded by counsellors, jurists and imāms who were for the most part followers of the Mālikite rite.

Relations between Chad and the Mediterranean

Trans-Saharan exchanges in this region are less well documented than in the western Sudan. But the central Sudan also had age-old relations with Egypt, Libya and the Maghrib.

In the fourteenth century, the kingdom of Kānem stretched as far as the Fezzān in the north and Wadai in the east. One main route ran from Kānem to Egypt by way of the Kawār salt-pans, Zawīla in the Fezzān, the Libyan oases and the Mediterranean coast. A second route linked the lake to Cairo by way of Tibesti and Aswan. A third went to Tunis and Tripoli through Ghadāmes. These routes were most active at the time of the rise of the Hausa states. But Arab slaving activities in the Darfūr region killed the eastern route to the Nile.

The central Sudan exported leather, slaves and ivory. The Hausa here acted as middlemen between the north of Africa and the forest (Ifẹ, Ọyọ, Benin, Igbo-Ukwu) on the one hand; and between the great empires of the western Sudan and the countries of the Nile, on the other.

The savannah and the forest

African businessmen in the Sahel remained very discreet when attempts were made to get information out of them on the countries of the forest. In fact, they were trying to keep it secret and retain the monopoly on relations with this zone that was complementary to the savannah with its precious products: gold, kola nuts, spices etc. exchanged for beads, salt, iron tools, ironmongery, fabrics and dried fish from the middle Niger. Kola nuts in particular were the object of long-distance trade organized from the Guro, Bete or Asante country by dynamic groups of well organized traders.

In fact, among many peoples, this fruit, which is found as far away as the Congo, enjoyed an irreplaceable role in diet and social life. In their quest for

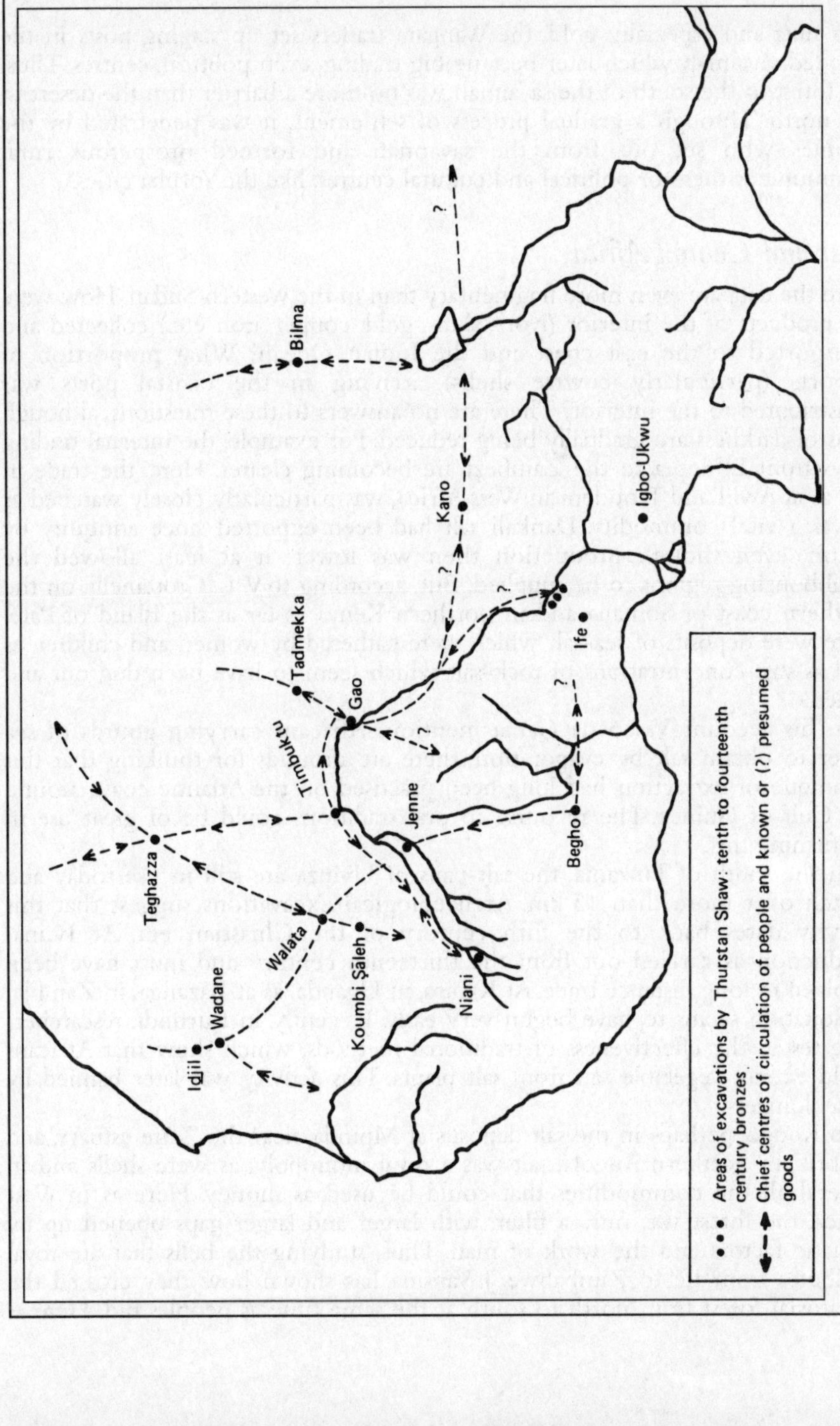

25.1 *Circulation of men and techniques in West Africa (J. Devisse)*

kola nuts and especially gold, the Wangara traders set up staging posts in the wooded savannah which later became big trading, even political, centres. Thus, the forest to the south of the savannah was no more a barrier than the desert to the north. Through a gradual process of settlement, it was penetrated by the peoples who set out from the savannah and formed prosperous rural communities there or political and cultural centres, like the Yoruba cities.

East and Central Africa

Here the data are even more fragmentary than in the western Sudan. How were the products of the interior (ivory, skins, gold, copper, iron etc.) collected and transported to the east coast and the Indian Ocean? What proportion of imports (particularly cowrie shells) arriving in the coastal ports was redistributed to the interior? There are no answers to these questions, although areas of darkness are gradually being reduced. For example, the internal trading flows from Ethiopia to the Zambezi are becoming clearer. Here, the trade in salt, as at Awlīl and Taoudeni in West Africa, was particularly closely watched as it was a vital commodity. Dankali salt had been exported since antiquity by Axum, even though production then was lower; it at least allowed the neighbouring regions to be supplied. But, according to V. L. Grottanelli, on the southern coast of Somalia and in northern Kenya as far as the island of Pate, there were deposits of sea-salt which were gathered by women and children as well as vast concentrations of rock-salt which seem to have been dug out and traded.

In his account, Vasco da Gama mentions Africans carrying gourds of sea water to obtain salt by evaporation; there are grounds for thinking that this technique of extraction had long been practised on the Atlantic coast, around the Gulf of Guinea. The recourse to oral traditions could be of great use in confirming this.

In the south of Tanzania, the salt-pans of Uvinza are still in use today and stretch over more than 15 km. Archaeological excavations suggest that this activity dates back to the fifth century of the Christian era. At Ivuna, production as carried out from the thirteenth century and must have been involved in long distance trade. At Kabiro, in Uganda, as at Bazanga, in Zambia, exploitation seems to have begun very early. Recently, in Burundi, researchers have tested the effectiveness of traditional methods, which show that Africans could extract vegetable salt from salt plants. This activity was later banned by the colonizers.

In Kongo, perhaps in the salt deposits at Mpinda, near the Zaïre estuary, and Ambriz, in northern Angola, salt was a royal monopoly; as were shells and in general all the commodities that could be used as money. Here as in West Africa, the forest was only a filter, with larger and larger gaps opened up by climatic factors and the work of man. Thus, studying the bells that are royal attributes from Ife to Zimbabwe, J. Vansina has shown how they crossed the equatorial forest from north to south at the same time as peoples did. Here as

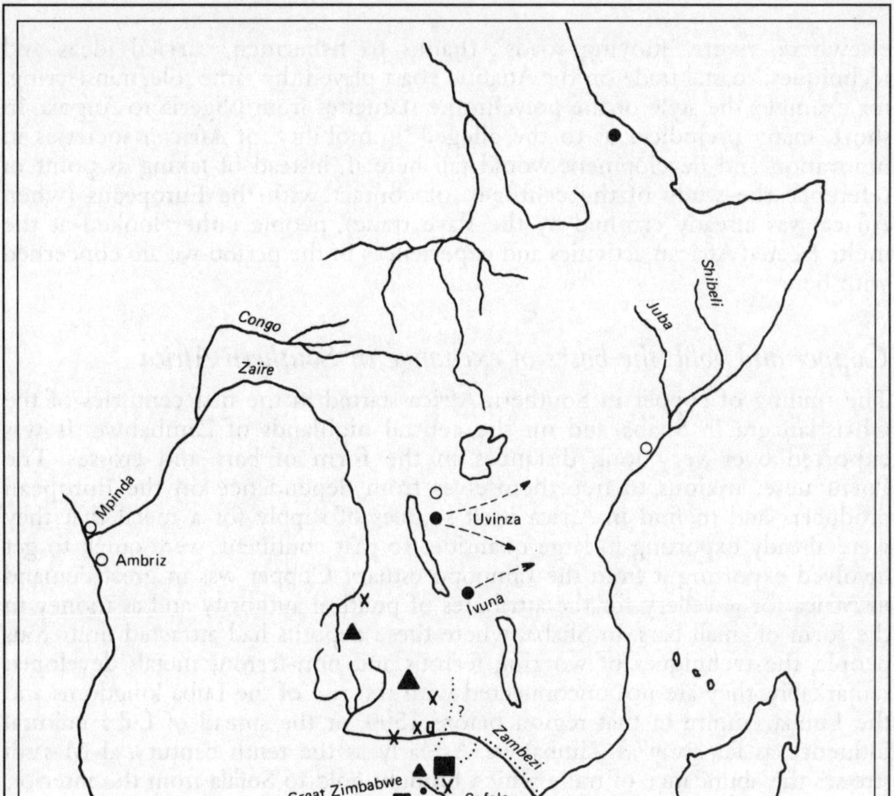

25.2 *Central, East and Southern Africa, eleventh to fifteenth centuries.* (*J. Devisse*)

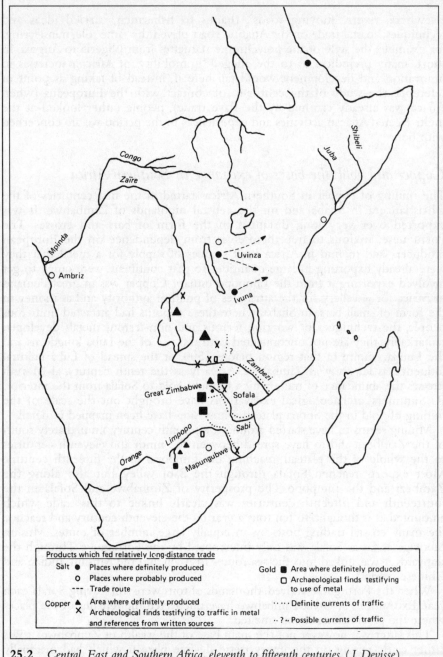

elsewhere, rivers, 'moving roads', thanks to fishermen, carried ideas and techniques; coastal trade on the Atlantic coast played the same role, transferring, for example, the style of the polychrome statuettes from Nigeria to Angola. In short, many prejudices as to the alleged 'immobility' of African societies in innovation and development would fall here if, instead of taking as point of reference the study of the centuries of contact with the Europeans (when Africa was already crushed by the slave trade), people rather looked at the multi-faceted African activities and experiences in the period we are concerned with here.

Copper and gold: the bases of exchange in Southern Africa

The mining of copper in Southern Africa started in the first centuries of the Christian era in Shaba and on the central highlands of Zimbabwe. It was exported over very long distances in the form of bars and crosses. The Portuguese, anxious to free themselves from dependence on the European producers and to find in Africa itself sources of supply for a metal that they were already exporting in large quantities to that continent, were quick to get involved exporting it from the Limpopo estuary. Copper was in great demand in Africa for jewellery, for the attributes of political authority and as money in the form of small bars. In Shaba, where these deposits had attracted numerous people, the techniques of working ferrous and non-ferrous metals developed remarkably; they are not unconnected with the rise of the Luba kingdoms and the Lunda empire in that region before 1500, or the spread of Luba cultural influence as far away as Zimbabwe. As early as the tenth century, al-Masʿudi stresses the abundance of trade which brought gold to Sofala from the interior. R. Summers' archaeological excavations have brought out the scale of the mining of gold in the Shona plateau whose sites have been mapped in detail.

Mining seems to have started around the seventh century, immediately south of the Zambezi, and to have spread between the ninth and eleventh centuries to the whole of the plateau, reaching the Limpopo in the fifteenth century. Most exports reached Sofala through the Sabi valley, but also along the Zambezi and the Limpopo. The prosperity of Zimbabwe and Sofala in the fourteenth and fifteenth centuries was clearly linked to this trade which amounted, it is thought, to ten tons a year by the eleventh century and reached the many coastal trading posts by an equally large number of routes. Muslim cabotage as far as Sofala was only interrupted by the Portuguese. Through the shipyards it was linked into the sea routes to Aden and the Muslim, Indian and Chinese worlds.

When the Portuguese arrived, thousands of tons were still leaving Sofala each year. Excavations at Great Zimbabwe have uncovered the remains of the places where the precious metal was smelted.

This latter was however not the main base of the wealth of Zimbabwe. it was rather cattle-raising on the grassy tsetse fly-free plateau which had originally made the masters of Zimbabwe sacrificial kings. The 'miners' and 'builders' later grafted their impressive achievements onto the achievements of the 'cattle-raisers'. These groups were probably the ancestors of the present-day Sotho and Shona. The racist South African state[1] prevents objective research into the past of southern Africa, seeking to abolish the memory of the great social, economic, political and cultural achievements of the blacks, before the arrival of the whites.

Finally, it is important not to minimize in this region the very busy maritime contacts between the continent, Madagascar, the Comoro Islands and other neighbouring islands. For thousands of years, these contacts carried ideas, techniques and organizational models in both directions (as the import of Malagasy stone vases by the Africans shows).

1. See UNESCO Note on p.230.

26 Africa in Inter-Continental Relations

The image of Africa in the world

It is difficult to tell how Africans who made contact with the world through their merchants, their rulers and their scholars perceived the world. At least we know, for example, that the Wangara had a structured perception of space. For them, the north was the land of salt, *Kogodugu*, the south the land of the kola nut, *Worodugu*, or *TuKoro*, (forest). The 'clear country' (*Gbe Kan*) stretching from east to west was open land that was good for trade. It was a geography based on concrete experience.

But this perception of the world, this *imago mundi*, extended to include North Africa and the Near East, as a result of the pilgrimages, trade and embassies from the black rulers south of the Sahara. It was the same with the Zandj and Swahili with regard to the countries bordering or beyond the Indian Ocean.

In the high schools of Timbuktu, a more speculative geography was probably taught which gave rulers like Kankū Mūsā quite a clear idea of the international 'system' and Mali's place in it.

What did others think of Africa?

The Muslims knew Africa and their knowledge of the continent made a qualitative leap forward in the fourteenth century thanks to in-depth exploration. But their knowledge was still dependent on the archaic hypotheses of Ptolemy or al-Idrīsī on whom Ibn Khaldūn still relied.

The equatorial regions and those further south were considered to be uninhabited and uncivilized. Apart from the Mediterranean basin, 'the cradle of civilization, according to Ibn Khaldūn, because of the optimal climatic conditions, the equatorial regions, like those in the north, were uncultured because their climates were extreme. In the far west the Canary Islands were the boundary of humanity. Thus, in a Mediterranean-centred conception of a world surrounded by a boundless ocean, peripheral countries like black Africa were regarded as the homes of men 'nearer to animals than to reasonable beings', a situation due to their distance from the temperate zone, which 'means that their nature becomes closer to that of the brute beasts'. But, gradually, on the spot travels between the tenth and the fourteenth century transformed this approach. Thanks to al-ʿUmari and Ibn Baṭṭūṭa, and despite the measures to protect their civilization taken by the black rulers, a deeper and more nuanced knowledge began to replace the stereotypes of bookish learning: and this was true of the whole area from Mauritania and the shores of the Red Sea and the Indian Ocean. The forest remained rather inaccessible until the arrival of the Europeans in the sixteenth century.

In the West, for a long time Africa interested traders, rulers and religious zealots only in relation to the Muslim worlds which they wanted to circumvent and defeat. The efforts of the cartographers were vital in opening up these perspectives. The mention of a 'Rex Melli' on Angelino Dulcert's map in 1339 foreshadowed the visit by the Genoese Malfante to Tuat a century later. This was a reconnaissance trip to the 'mysterious continent', access to which was solidly blocked in the west by Morocco and in the east by the power of Cairo. But from the thirteen century, the College of Miramar in the Balearic Islands and the European *Studia Arabica* aimed at converting the infidels, provided further information. The papacy, through diplomatic conventions, aimed above all at preserving the small Christian enclaves on the southern shore of the Mediterranean.

Until the fifteenth century, Asia, despite the Persian and Indonesian migrations, did not pay much attention to the African continent. It was in this framework that the sudden arrival of the Portuguese south of the Tropics marked a decisive upheaval in information and strategies.

From Mediterranean diplomacy to Afro-European exchanges

The Muslim states on the southern shore of the Mediterranean, including al-Andalus, did not pursue a more consistent and united policy than the Christian countries. Despite religious interests, Genoa constantly upheld the interests of Granada against Castile; while Egypt, a client of Castile and Aragon, baulked at supporting Granada. The Venetians and the Genoese fought over markets among the Mamlūks and Ottomans, while the Ḥafṣids of Tunis, the Marinids of Morocco and the rulers of Tlemcen clashed with one another and fought a series of wars or made bilateral or triangular alliances.

The reality is that the strategic framework of these contradictory relations lies elsewhere. The Muslims, the masters of trade between Asia and Europe, brought the Sahel economy into world trade and through it the gold of the Sudan which fuelled the Arab monetary system and later that of the West. In short, the Muslim world drew the maximum advantage from its midway position between Europe and deepest Africa. But its two partners did everything they could to break this monopoly. The Sudanese empires organized a careful system for controlling exports and taxing imports, and diversified routes and customers, intervening through active diplomacy in Arab–African relations and using economics to influence the fate of the Marinid, Waṭṭāsid and Saʿdian dynasties.

The Christian empires attempted to shake up the status quo through commercial treaties which simply sharpened competition between them and, gradually, through political and religious strategies. Venice, for example, focussed on Egypt and the eastern Mediterranean basin, where it specialized in the purchase of Asian spices and the monopoly of sugar from the East, Cyprus and Crete. Occasionally, it exchanged its glass and cloths in Tunis and Tripoli for gold from the Sudan. The Genoese specialized in the fourteenth century in wheat, slaves and English woollens.

The Ottoman conquest drove them out of the eastern Mediterranean basin, and they fell back on North Africa, dumping sugar on the market to compete with the Venetians. This led them to want to control the sugar-producing areas by associating with the Spaniards who were beginning to produce it, supporting the Portuguese policy of discoveries and the sugar plantations on the islands in the Atlantic (Madeira, Canaries). This brought the Italians into the Atlantic and the world of Africa and the Americas beyond it, and the explosion of shipbuilding adapted to a new 'heroic and brutal dream'. The Catalans also hired their ships to Muslims and attempted to corner a share of the traffic, but they counted for little compared to Venice and Genoa, the two giants of the period.

In this economic confrontation, Africa's contribution was chiefly the articles that drained it to fuel the economy of the North – gold and slaves. In the eleventh and twelfth centuries, African gold contributed to the excellence of the Fāṭimid, ʿUmayyad, Almoravid, Almohad and Ḥafṣid coinages. Until the fifteenth century, this flow contributed to the economic well-being, the flowering of civilization and the luxury of courts, described by the Arab writers.

Gradually, from the twelfth century onwards, the Christian countries, through their trade with North Africa, captured part of the gold of the Sudan on the markets of Cairo, Tunis, Bidjiya, Tlemcen etc. With the increase in the tonnage of ships, profits grew. For the fifteenth century, the annual revenue from Catalan trade with the Maghrib is reckoned to have been in the region of 120,000 dinars. In this way, the use of gold as money, abandoned in the West for centuries, resumed in the second half of the thirteenth century, and this was due, partly, beyond all doubt, to African gold. But the thirst for the 'fabled metal' in the West continued to grow; this led to the pioneering enterprises of merchants such as Malfante and others in search of the gold routes beyond the Sahara.

In addition to the commercial profits, rulers were enriched by the tributes imposed on Muslims after Christian victories. In the twelfth century, the kings of Tunis paid 33,000 gold bezants a year to Sicily. The sultans of Granada, who received some of the African gold, transmitted between 10,000 and 40,000 dinars annually to Castile. At the end of the thirteenth century, Tlemcen paid over to the king of Aragon between 2,000 and 6,000 dinars a year. The chartering of ships, the building costs of which could have been amortized in four months, or the hiring of mercenaries by the Christians (to Morocco, for example) was one method of securing the precious metal. By these various means the crown of Aragon secured revenues amounting to 10 per cent of its annual resources. But the North African kingdoms too had an interest, at least in the short run, in this unequal trade because of the customs duties (10 per cent) levied on European imports. In the fifteenth century, the Ḥafṣid custom-house produced an annual revenue of 150,000 dinars. The more clear-sighted of the rulers of the Maghrib saw the deleterious long-term effects of this commercial colonization.

Since the seventh century, clashes between Muslims and Christians had ended in the taking of slaves among the defeated. In the tenth and eleventh centuries, this 'market' was favourable to the Muslims. The trend was reversed, from the twelfth century onwards, with the pressure of the Christian *reconquista*. More and more too, blacks appeared among the batches of slaves previously imported from the Sudan or Nubia. There were 'blackamoors' in the armies of Muslim Spain which fought the Christians. In the fourteenth and fifteenth centuries, traders controlled the market. In Naples, in the second half of the fifteenth century, 83 per cent of slaves were black. There were also many blacks in Sicily. This labour force was something new, especially as it was increasingly made up of slaves from 'Guinea'. From the end of the fifteenth century, the Portuguese were raiding the coast of Mauritania for them. The market at Valencia was well supplied with slaves from 1494 onwards, some of whom were of Senegalese origin. The consequences of this influx were that prices collapsed. Black slaves became the cheapest, condemned to the hardest agricultural or mining work. The attitude of contempt towards blacks in Mediterranean societies dates from this time. It was at this time that the economic growth recorded by the African continent in the fourteenth century was seriously jeopardized. With, on the one hand, in the east, the struggle for control of the Indian Ocean and Ottoman expansion, and, on the other, in the west, the foundation of European slave trading posts on the Atlantic coast, Africa was caught up for several centuries in a vice which was to interrupt the burgeoning growth of the fourteenth century.

Africa, Asia and the Indian Ocean

Major trade routes, by land and sea, carried the rich produce of Asia to western Asia. The Muslims had controlled them since the seventh century. But there was fierce competition between the route terminating on the Arab/Persian Gulf, which fed Mesopotamian and Syrian trade, and the route ending at the Red Sea, which led, through the Nile, to the development of the delta ports – two rival terminal points. In the period with which are concerned, upheavals in Asia and the collapse of Muslim domination in Mesopotamia left the field open for Egypt from the time of the Fāṭimids and the Mamlūks: Cairo was at its zenith.

The Mediterranean was, in effect, abandoned to the Christians after 1100, but their military and commercial efforts to reach the route to the Red Sea via Egypt remained fruitless. The Egyptians themselves were dependent on Aden, the hub of this trade. There, the Kārimī traders controlled the trade in spices, gold, precious stones, ivory etc. between Asia, East Africa and Egypt. Their opulent prosperity rebounded on Alexandria where westerners came to buy what they wanted.

In the thirteenth century, ʿAydhāb became one of the busiest ports in the world. But no power could ensure control of every branch of this trade. The Kārimī were unavoidable intermediaries, and were covered by diplomatic immunity to negotiate agreements between Egyptians and Asians. The Mamlūks seized control of the ports on the west coast of the Red Sea: Sawākin, Massawa and Assab. But Egypt's thirst for gold in the twelfth century, before the influx of gold from the Sudan, whetted the Fāṭimids' interest in the gold of Sofala and the route leading there. But it was from there that African iron of exceptional quality mentioned by al-Idrīsī also left for India, as well as ivory, animal skins, wood etc. It has been estimated that ten tonnes of fine gold of Sofala a year was marketed in Kilwa, an amount equal to West African exports of gold. The Africans received new plants, glass beads, cowrie shells and cloths. In the thirteenth century, 60 per cent of customs duties levied at Kilwa came from imported cotton, which reached the mysterious 'land's end' of Africa beyond Sofala through the Mozambique Channel.

From the shipyards of Mombasa and Malindi ships set out for Asia. Navigation by the stars and use of the compass, both borrowed from the Chinese, the knowledge of winds, currents, marine flora and fauna all constituted a valuable addition to the store of science and technology. Trading posts and settlements proliferated in India, Africa and southern Arabia. From Cape Gardafui to Sofala, over 50 towns were prospering even before the arrival of the Arabs. In these towns, a new aristocratic and bourgeois class came into being, in what was the ethnic, cultural and Islamic crucible of Swahili civilization. Archaeology has yielded marvellous remains of it: beautiful stone mosques and palaces, magnificent glassware imported from Persia, ceramics from China and precious faience from India, copper jewellery and carpets from the Middle East. This affluence contrasted with the harsh life of the indigenous people, who were sometimes carried off into slavery.

In Kilwa, 'one of the most beautiful towns in the world', Chinese sources describe four- or five-storey houses in the fifteenth century. That was when the Chinese arrived in great numbers in this region, although there is mention of Africans in China as early as the seventh century. But, in 1402, a Korean map gave a non-Ptolemaic outline of southern Africa. In the fifteenth century, enormous ships, five times bigger than the Portuguese vessels, headed by Cheng Ho, carried the most sought after African products to China: gold, ivory, amber, slaves. From Malindi, Cheng Ho brought back a delegation which presented a giraffe to the court at Beijing. Then quite suddenly, these brilliant Chinese explorations ended, for domestic reasons.

At this time, in 1488, Bartholomew Diaz rounded the southernmost tip of Africa and discovered a geographical shape different from that on Ptolemy's 'map'. Europe had at least broken into the Indian Ocean; in 1498, Vasco da Gama had a glimpse of the splendours of the African states on the Zambezi plateaus and admired the quality of the clothes of the Swahili 'bourgeois'. He was well treated by the sultan of Mombasa, and set off at once for India, guided by an Arab compiler of a sea chart, Ibn Masdjid. It was the dawn of a new era.

The mastery of the Atlantic and its consequences for Africa

Arabs and Europeans knew very little of Madeira, the Azores and the Canary Islands. In the eleventh century, al-Bakrī speaks of the production of amber on the Atlantic coast of Ghana, and al-Idrīsī mentions the salt trade between Awlīl and Senegal. The real reasons for the European conquest of the Atlantic do not lie in technical superiority. In the twelfth century, the Almohad war fleet had such a reputation that Ṣalāḥ al-Dīn sought its support against the Christian vessels. But by the end of the thirteenth century, after the victories of the Europeans in the battle for Gibraltar and the seizure by them of the principal areas producing ship timber for the shipyards, the balance of power shifted. The promoters who financed shipbuilding were private capitalists who profited from the economic upturn from 1200 to 1600; the Genoese and, later, the Venetian fleets linked mercantile Italy with industrial Flanders and England. The Muslims did not respond to this challenge, either because of the weakness of the kingdoms of the Maghrib or because the caravans already brought them back far more gold than the caravels ever would. The Arabs thus lacked motivation, which enabled the Europeans, at the cost of persistent efforts and untold failures, to advance towards Cape Bojador on the coast of western Sahara. What attracted them more than the gold of the Sudan was new lands warm enough for the large-scale production of wheat, vines and sugar-cane. As early as the thirteenth century, Morocco was exporting sugar to Flanders and Venice. But investment and sales organization did not follow, and, after a great boom, Saʿdian Morocco failed to develop. The indigenous people of the Canary Islands were enslaved by the Europeans, who gradually replaced Morocco.

South of Cape Bojador

Here was the Atlantic of the trade winds and anticyclones. Efforts to move south beyond this point encountered numerous setbacks and failures. From there, it took 50 years to reach the Congo. Without claiming absolutely that, beyond Cape Bojador, it was impossible for ships to return, we must note the many attempts that ended in disaster and the numerous sacrifices that marked this advance. Scientific and technical research, often based on Arab achievements, was necessary to perfect smaller and more manoeuvrable ships of the caravel type before they were replaced by heavy galleons. The Portuguese, disappointed at not discovering the pot of gold that they had dreamed of, reduced the continent to the unhappy role of supplier of 'black manpower' carried off to the Americas which were felt to be more promising. Asia too eclipsed Africa at this time.

According to al-ʿUmari, Mansa Kankū Mūsā, the ruler of Mali, reported that his predecessor did not believe that the ocean was impossible to cross. He therefore fitted out 200 vessels. It was a disaster in which he himself eventually disappeared. Can we conclude from this that in the fourteenth century Malians had discovered the Americas before Columbus? Probably not, although this thesis has been argued and Africans had mastered a certain area of the sea, if only for coastal trade. But the very size of the continent, and the nature of the coastal relief did not turn Africans to the sea. The main centres of power were inland, except for North Africa, the east coast and, perhaps, Kongo. It is then all the more important to note this concern of the Malian ruler, which reflects a scientific concern, contemporary with the European endeavours, but which was not sustained by the same logistics and the same traditions.

Expansion, disappointment, exploitation

Once they had mastered the techniques of returning by the Azores, the Portuguese took 54 years to reach the Cape which they named 'of Good Hope', round it and then sail into the Indian Ocean. Brutality, pillage and slave raids marked the early stages, but expansion later became organized around trading posts dealing in gum, leather and amber. Then royal control made a place for private concessions, not without challenging the competition of other European countries.

Disappointments piled up: small numbers of small ships from a small country could not amass large profits. The attempts to penetrate deeply into the continent foundered at the Felou rapids on the River Senegal, the Yelada rapids on the Zaïre or the intractable hostility of the indigenous peoples, as at Wadane, or again in the face of already existing commercial organizations as at Cantor, on the Gambia, faced with the Dyula traders. As for the quest for gold, it was disappointing. The caravels took about a fifth and perhaps only a seventh of the gold that the dromedaries continued to carry across the Sahara. Malaguetta and black pepper from Benin were soon in competition with Asian pepper. Only the sale of silver, textiles, horses and copper kept the balance of trade even.

Furthermore, on the political and religious level, the Portuguese sought in vain for Prester John, thinking that they had found him first in Mossi, then in Kongo . . . But there was no trace of the Christian power until distant Ethiopia.

On the other hand, on the scientific level, the harvest was considerable thanks to the observations of navigators, traders or missionaries concerning the summer rains, the pattern of winds, in particular the trade winds, and the first ethnographic and anthropological observations, sometimes spontaneous and valuable, as in Kongo, sometimes steeped in prejudice, for example about the so-called 'fetish'.

Agriculturally, the hopes of founding colonies with the transfer of men, techniques and plants to be acclimatized, ran up against the reality of a climate that killed men and inspired fear. It was only on São Tomé, occupied in 1472, that the idea arose of 'making sugar' and to do so to transfer black slaves there who were soon being carried to the other islands of the 'Atlantic Mediterranean'.

From 1440 onwards, Zurara, in his *Chronicle of the Discovery and Conquest of Guinea*, invoked the curse of Noah on his son Ham, from whom the blacks were alleged to be descended; but as these blacks, despite everything, had a soul and were not Muslims, 'it should be easier to guide them on the path to salvation'. In short, there were two reasons to embark on the slave trade with a clear conscience.

In 1444, a company was set up in Lagos, Portugal, to exploit the slave trade and establish a staging post at Arguin, which immediately began supplying several hundred slaves a year. After 1460, some 1,000 slaves a year were taken from the land between Cape Verde and Sine Salum (Senegal). It was the beginning of an infernal cycle. At this time Castile recognized Portugal's monopoly on the trade. But by the end of the fifteenth century the organization of the trade was stabilized, as were the prices: six slaves for one horse, which was gradually replaced by copper bars. For several centuries, the African slave trade, which replaced the gold that had been dreamed of, became the most profitable trade of the Europeans in Africa.

During the fifteenth century as a whole, Africa withdrew into itself away from the slave trading posts where local African agents, locally called 'kings', officiated. There were many forms of rejection of this trade: contact with the *mansa* of Mali remained impossible; relations with King Nkuwu of Kongo remained very ambiguous until his apostasy after having for a time received a few carpenters, masons and stock-breeders. The traditional religion put up a remarkable resistance.

Nevertheless, the harmful impact of the trade in human beings had a long-term effect on the economic, social and political structures of Africa. For example, up till then in Senegambia, Mali, by placing an embargo on iron, ensured for itself control of the coast of the Gambia and the Casamance, leaving the region further north under the authority of Jolof. But the massive sale of iron to Jolof by the Portuguese altered this balance. Conversely, the *Burba* of Jolof recognized by Cajor and Baol turned away from the internal trade which had hitherto sustained him and bought horses on the coast in exchange for men. But, on this ground, Cajor and Baol had a geographical advantage which they hastened to exploit to throw off the authority of Jolof.

Socially, the slave trade led to a simplification and an aggravation of the cleavages previously laboriously balanced. Power became autocratic, even slave-based, whereas previously the captives produced by wars, debts and famines, had been absorbed in a non-slave based mode of production. State power, formerly sacred in character, was socially and morally discredited. That is what explains, for example in Senegambia, the adherence to Islam of the masses, as a means to challenge powers that had lost their way, powers that would soon be fighting each other in slave wars.

27 Conclusion

This volume ends with the beginnings of European expansion and predominance in the world, opening a new chapter in history. New techniques were opening up the vast Atlantic Ocean to European dynamism, thanks to the exploitation of the African continent. History appeared to turn its back on the Mediterranean, an ancient lake situated in the heart of the Old World. The Italians, who were timidly trying to reach the Sudan across the desert, were replaced by their compatriots who, with the Spaniards and the Portuguese, 'discovered' America and got round Africa to reach Asia. It was not by chance that these discoverers were precisely the ones who inherited Antiquity's scientific heritage, built upon by the Berber Arabs and transmitted across Africa to Europe as it awakened.

From the twelfth to the sixteenth century, Africa played a leading part in the world economy. With the discovery of America, it was pushed aside and utilized as an instrument. During the period covered by this volume, three major facets need to be stressed.

Religious and political aspects

During this period, black Africa demonstrated a great personality. First, in relation to the religions and political systems that were spreading there. Islam only became popular by adapting, otherwise it would have remained a thin veneer reserved for royal courts, scholars and merchants. Similarly, Christianity was Africanized as in Ethiopia, where it met resistance as in Kongo. In the nineteenth century, Islamic holy wars and Christian expansionism were still at work. The traditional religion was able to remain a living force, pervading even the institutions and rituals of power at Koumbi as at Niani, and in Yatenga, Kānem and Mwenemutapa. But tolerance was the rule, enabling Mali and Ethiopia to mix a variety of peoples belonging to different religions.

This same principle was valid for the political structures federating clans and castes or orders in an equilibrium that may have been unstable but was institutionalized. In North Africa, even the kingdoms were only collections of *ḳabīla*s around the *ḳabīla* of the ruler. Similarly, in Mali, Mossi and Rwanda,

Africa reconciled extensive diversity with integration over large areas. It was in the seventeenth century above all that centrifugal processes and kingdoms based on ethnic identity emerged. This process was, in this particular case, further advanced in North Africa after the vast attempt at unity by the Almohads. Moreover, during this period, Islam, formerly all-conquering, fell back on to the defensive before the Christian *reconquista*. The Christians got a foothold south of the Mediterranean, and went on to circumvent the Islamic bloc by the Atlantic and burst into the Indian Ocean, access to which had previously been blocked by the Ayyubids and the Mamlūks. Nubia, it is true, is a case where Christianity was eradicated after a long struggle. But that was essentially because it was the religion of the elite associated with a Coptic clergy and a foreign culture without indigenous saints or martyrs, although the frescoes in churches show the black faces of Nubian bishops. But the centuries-long resistance of traditional rituals was a historical reality here too. Finally, the often one-sided character of the Arabic written sources for the Nilotic Sudan has led to an over-emphasis on the northern factor at the expense of indigenous developments within the black African substratum. Even in the deserts or the virgin forests, the highly individualized clans and groups were living in symbiosis with other ethnic groups in an exchange which might indeed be unequal, as with the Tuaregs, the Pygmies, the Khoikhoi and the San.

Thus, before 1600, Africa was deploying the whole range of political formations, from clans to empires, which implies a range of political experiences of tremendous richness.

In central Africa and even southern, where the policy of apartheid[1] hinders knowledge of the African past, archaeological and linguistic evidence throw light on it. The great necropolises of Sanga and Katoto just south of the Luba empire are evidence of a political organization, the tangible remains of a highly elaborate political organism. And they date from before the year 1000. This antiquity of the state system, in the very heart of the continent, removed from all extra-African influences, is witnessed in the Great Lakes region in the Bantu-speaking groups. It is only the reflection of the unique antiquity of the human experience in Africa. It is the antiquity of states like Luba that doubtless accounts for the vast spread of the languages of this group from eastern Kasai as far as Zambia. Despite the looting of the royal tombs of the Zimbabwe-Mapungubwe civilization, their authentically endogenous mighty stone buildings are similar to those at Manykemi in Mozambique or those of the ancient Transvaal. Moreover, Mapungubwe achieved a synthesis of Bantu culture and the previously little known one of the Khoikhoi. The diffusion of iron was completed here long before the tenth century and perhaps even before the Christian era, and the Mapungubwe civilization flourished until the fifteenth century when it suffered the disastrous and eventually fatal impact of the slave trade.

1. See UNESCO Note on p. 230.

Economic and cultural aspects

The African economy during this period was far from being autarkic and enclosed in 'subsistence'. On the contrary, one is struck by the density of trade networks overcoming every natural obstacle. They were virtually the beginnings of several great sub-regional markets in the north, west, north-east, east and centre-south of the vast continent; and that was due to Arab, Persian, Berber, Swahili, Mandingo, Hausa and Kongo merchants and many other middlemen. The African rulers who bore the eloquent title of *Kaya Maghan* ('king of gold'), Mwenemutapa ('lord of metals') etc. were perfectly well aware of the economic role of the metals, even if they did not fully understand the terms of trade. They made carefully devised arrangements to control information, the movement of men, customs duties and exploitation, up to and including monopoly. They knew how to use the lure of gold to secure foreign technical assistance, as, for example, did Mūsā I of Mali who brought back architects, scholars and religious experts from Cairo.

From this point of view, North Africa's duty to act as intermediary between the whole continent and the East as far as Turkey greatly benefited the Maghrib and Egypt, which explains the bitter rivalry between their political leaders and their mercantile bourgeoisies to control the routes across the Sudan, as the analyst Ibn Khaldūn perceptively describes.

The east coast of Africa alone had and has the privilege of direct contact with the world of the East, both near and far: the result, here as in Madagascar and the neighbouring islands, was an Afro-Arab and Asian symbiosis of a unique quality, from the exchange of plants to languages and religion, including socio-political systems.

Never before in Africa had cultural exchanges been so important. The book trade was one of the most flourishing lines in the cities of the Niger bend. The kingdoms of Abyssinia, Borno, Hausaland, Songhay and Mali developed an original literature in which theology and history stood out. Pilgrimages and business amplified the trade of the mind. At the time when Vasco da Gama rounded the Cape in 1498, the African societies of southern Africa, including the Bantu, had already organized hierarchical and complex societies.

The racist thesis of an uninhabited land at the time of the arrival of the whites, who then went on to fight to seize the lands and later the mines from the indigenous peoples, is thus an imposture. The importance of precious metals with which foreigners identified the lands of the blacks must not be allowed to obscure, even for Great Zimbabwe, the predominance of agriculture during the period we are studying. Agriculture was based on the family farm and scattered royal or notable estates where slaves, serfs or even peasants providing forced labour worked without being the victims of a purely slave regime.

Stock-raising was present throughout Africa but it had already become a specialization of numerous societies all over the continent as discussion of the Fulbe, the Nilotes and the Khoikhoi shows.

Trades, sometimes powerfully organized as in Hausaland, were, in the Sudanese zone, often organized into endogamous 'castes', but so far with no form of exclusion, indeed quite the contrary in the case of *griots*, jewellers and smiths.

In normal times, the patriarchal mode of production which underpinned the state structures with the concept of the king–father, subject to custom, assured respect for a minimum of rights for all. In the Maghrib, revolts by the *ḳabīla*s against the sultan's tax collectors were common.

The presence of corporations of traders evolving towards a 'bourgeois' status in the context of growing urbanization created islands that foreshadowed another society which the slave trade often either prevented from developing or distorted.

The dynamism of Africa

All the processes that have been described in this volume show abundantly that in every aspect of human activity, African and Malagasy societies had developed essentially from internal wellsprings, towards increasingly complex forms of production, consumption, exchange, invention and self-management. Without denying the external influences, we must reject one-sided explanations. It is not possible, for example, to explain every historical development south of the Sahara solely by Islam; or to claim that southern Africa was historically immobile before the European impact made itself felt. Even in the case of an external impact, the cultural identity of the peoples was never eradicated by this irruption, as the vitality of Berber cultures shows. In the case of the Almoravid movement, on the contrary, we see that the Berber and black peoples, having adopted Islam, became eminent protagonists of it and took the initiative as actors in history: there followed the break-up of the empire of Ghana and the striking conquests as far as the banks of the Ebro. The Islam of Mali had, as Ibn Baṭṭūṭa testifies, become a distinct form of Islam, and Sudanese doctors were in demand north of the Sahara as active contributors to Islamic learning. It was the same with Christianity in Nubia and Ethiopia.

Theoretically, there has been much controversy on the theme of the 'African mode of production'. But is it possible to characterize the mode of production of countries of whose history nothing is known, even the broad outlines?

Let us simply stress the basic and overwhelming fact: private ownership of land was not the basis of social and economic evolution in the same way as in Europe. The land was regarded as an undivided good of the various communities, even though, at the end of the period, atypical and contradictory forms of land rights were already appearing.

Agricultural techniques developed too towards intensive forms with use of the hoe and animal manure in horticulture, as along the middle Niger valley. Large estates using the labour of whole villages subject to corvée assured mass production for the needs of the court or trade. But the slaves, especially the slaves of the crown, were not purely passive. In North Africa, when they were freed, and south of the Sahara, they sometimes played a leading military or political role. Moreover, to counter-balance the pressures of the turbulent urban aristocracy, the king often entrusted important posts to slaves, who were his men, even his creatures.

Africa was not an under-populated continent before the sixteenth century. It was high population densities that justified and made possible architectural achievements such as the great mosques of Fez, Cairo or Kayrawan and the gigantic edifices of Great Zimbabwe. The reports of the earliest Arab and Portuguese travellers south of the Sahara are categorical on this point: there were hundreds of villages and people, and the cities of the Sudan were comparable to the large European cities of the time.

If we are to believe Maḥmud Ka'tī, Mali had 400 towns or large population centres. The emperor of Gao is said to have had a standing army of 100,000 men. It can be estimated that the urban population constituted ten per cent of the total population of Africa, which is estimated to have been some 200 million at this time.

This population was very unevenly distributed, but it was soon to be even more so with the growth of the overseas slave trade. Traditional African slavery as part of a *sui generis* pre-capitalist mode of production was not of the same nature as slavery in the service of burgeoning capitalism.

In the period from the twelfth to the sixteenth century there is still much that is not yet known, and only through long-term methodological investigation will it be possible to reduce the gaps in our knowledge, in particular through the systematic collection of traditions. The exemplary work of the late Mūsā Galaal in Somalia on popular knowledge of the constellations (*xiddigo*), the calendar, and their social impact, should be recalled here. Work of the same kind among the Dogon in Mali provides a mine of information that interests not only historians but also botanists, zoologists, jurists, philosophers, doctors and pharmacists.

The esotericism of many African knowledge systems which dates back a long way militates against the kind of patient research that is respectful of cultures. In this context, making those involved in participant research aware of their responsibilities is the royal road to exhuming the past.

In the area of traditions, particular stress must be put on the artistic documents whose many different expressions (music, crafts, statuary, architecture etc.) constitute so many history handbooks whose keys and codes need to be understood.

Muslim art in the Maghrib and Egypt gave this period some of its most prestigious masterpieces. And the first navigators arriving on the shores of Senegambia, the Gold Coast or Benin met there a fabulous world of masks, statues of ancestors, and symbols of power, which implied peoples that had reached an aesthetic and spiritual level of a high quality.

Selected Bibliography

The publishers wish to point out that, although every effort has been made to ensure that the details in this Bibliography are correct, some errors may occur as a result of the complexity and the international nature of the work.

Abraham D. P. (1961) 'Maramuca: an exercise in the combined use of Portuguese records and oral tradition', *Journal of African History*, London, **2**, 2, pp. 211–25.

Adamu, M. (1978) *The Hausa factor in West African History* (Zaria: Ahmadu Bello University Press and Oxford University Press).

Adamu, M. (1979) 'Distribution of trading centres in the central Sudan in the eighteenth and nineteenth centuries', in Y. B. Usman (ed.), *Studies in the history of the Sokoto caliphate: the Sokoto Seminar Papers* (Zaria: Ahmadu Bello University Department of History for the Sokoto Caliphate Bureau), pp. 59–104.

Alvares, F. (16th century) 1881 ed. and English trans. Lord Stanley of Alderley, *Narrative of the Portuguese embassy to Abyssinia during the years 1520–1527* (London: Hakluyt Society).

Alvares d'Almada, A. (1594) *Tratado Breve dos Rios de Guiné*; 1946 Portuguese ed. L. Silveira (Lisbon); 1842 French trans. V. de Santaren (no further details available).

Anonymous (IInd or IIIrd century of our era) *Periplus Maris Erythreae (Periplus of the Erythraean Sea).*

Arkell, A. J. (1963) 'The influence of Christian Nubia in the Chad area between AD 800–1200' *Kush*, **II**, pp. 315–19.

Ashtor, E. (1971) *Les métaux précieux et la balance des paiements du Proche-Orient à la basse époque* (Paris: SEVPEN).

Baikie, W. B. (1856) *Narrative of an exploring voyage up the rivers Kwora and Binue* (London: Murray).

al-Bakrī (1968) 'Routier de l'Afrique blanche et noire du nord-ouest' French trans. V. Monteil, Bulletin de l'Institut fondamental d'Afrique noire (BIFAN), B, 30, **I**, pp. 39–116.

Barros, J. de (1552) *Decadas da Asia*, Vol. I; 1937 partial English trans. in G. R. Crone, q.v.

Barth, H. (1857, 1858) German edn, *Sammlung und Bearbeitung*, (including Centralafrikanischer Vokabularien), 3 parts in 2 (Gotha: Perthes); English edn, *Travels and discoveries in North and Central Africa; being a journal of an exploration undertaken under the auspices of HBM's government in the years 1849–1855*, 5 vols (London: Longman); 1965 English reprint, 3 vols (London: Cass).

Bautier, H. R. (1955) 'Les relations commerciales entre l'Europe et l'Afrique du Nord et l'équilibre économique méditerranéen de 12e au 14e siècle', *Bulletin philosophique et historique*, pp. 399–416.

Bedaux, R. M. A. (1972) 'Tellem: reconnaissances archéologiques d'une culture de l'Ouest africain au Moyen Age: recherches architectoniques', *Journal de la Société des africanistes*, **42**, 2, pp. 103–85.

Bedaux, R. M. A. (1977) 'Tellem', *Afrika Museum* (Groesbeck, Netherlands).

Bello, M. (n.d.) *Infāk al-Maysūr, 1922 ed. and trans. E. J. Arnett,* The rise of the Sokoto Fulani (Kano: Emirate Printing Department).

Béraud-Villars, J. M. E. (1942) *L'empire de Gao: un état soudanais aux 15e et 16e siècles* (Paris: Plon).

Bernus, S. and Gouletquer, P. (1976) 'Du cuivre au sel: recherches ethno-archéologiques sur la région d'Azelik (campagne 1973–1975);, *Journal de la Société des africanistes*, **46**, 1–2, pp. 7–68.

Boahen, A. A. (1974) 'Who are the Akan?' in Bonduku Seminar Papers (Bonduku: University of Abidjan).

Bonduku Seminar Papers (1974) 'Colloque inter-universitaire Ghana – Côte-d'Ivoire: Les Populations communes de la Côte-d'Ivoire et du Ghana' (Bonduku: University of Abidjan).

Boulègue, J. (1968) 'La Sénégambie du milieu du 15e siècle au début du 17e siècle' (doctoral dissertation, University of Dakar).

Boulnois, J. and Hama, B. (1954) *Empire de Gâo: histoire, coutumes et magie des Sonrai* (Paris: Maisonneuve).

Buchanan, C. A. (1974) *The Kitara complex: the historical tradition of western Uganda to the sixteenth century* (doctoral dissertation, University of Indiana, Bloomington).

Bovill, E. W. (1993) *Caravans of the old Sahara; an introduction to the history of the western Sudan* (London: Oxford University Press for IIALC); revised edn 1968, *The golden trade of the Moors* (London: Oxford University Press).

Brasseur, G. (1968) *Les Etablissements humains au Mali* (Dakar: *Institut fondamental d'Afrique noire*; Mémoires, 83).

Braudel, F. (1946) 'Monnaies et civilisations: de l'or du Soudan à l'argent d'Amérique: un drame méditerranéen', *Annales – Economie, Sociétés, Civilisations*, Paris, **I**, pp. 9–22.

Ca da Mosto, A. da (15th century) 1895 French trans., *Relations des voyages à la côte occidentale de l'Afrique d'Alvise da Ca da Mosto, 1455–1457* (Paris: Leroux); 1937 ed. and English trans. G. R. Crone (q.v.); 1948 Italian text with Portuguese trans., *Viagens de Luis de Cadamosto e de Pedro de Sintra* (Lisbon: Academia portuguesa da história.

Carbou, H. (1912) *La région du Tchad et du Oüadai*, 2 vols (Paris: Leroux; University of Algiers Faculté des lettres et des sciences humaines, 47–8).

Chapelle, J. (1957) *Nomades noirs du Sahara* (Paris: Plon).

Chaunu, P. (1969) *L'expansion européenne du 13e au 15e siècle* (Paris: Presses Universitaires de France).

Chittick, H. N. (1963) 'Kilwa and the Arab settlement of the East African coast', *Journal of African History*, **4**, 2, pp. 179–90.

Chittick, N. H. (1974) *Kilwa: an Islamic trading city on the East African coast*, 2 vols (Nairobi: British Institute in Eastern Africa, Memoirs, 5; London: distrib. by Thames and Hudson).

Cissoko, S. M. (1966) *Histoire de l'Afrique occidentale, Moyen Age et temps modernes 7e siècle–1850* (Paris: Présence Africaine).

Cissoko, S. M. (1968) 'Famines et épidémies à Tombouctou, et dans la boucle du Niger du 16e au 18e siècle', *Bulletin de l'Institut fondamental d'Afrique noire*, Dakar **30**, 3, pp. 806–21.

Cissoko, S. M. (1972) paper presented at Mandingo conference, London.

Cissoko, S. M. (1975) *Tombouctou et l'empire Songhay: épanouissement du Soudan nigérien aux 15e–16e siècles* (Dakar, Nouvelle Editions Africaines)

Cissoko, S. M. (1981) 'De l'organisation politique du Kabu'; and (1981) 'Introduction à l'histoire des Mandingues de l'Ouest'; both in *Colloque international sur les traditions orales du Gabu* (Dakar: Ethiopiques, special issue, October 1981), pp. 73–92, 195–206.

Cortesão, J. (1958, 1961) *Os descrobimentos portuguêses*, 2 vols (Lisbon: Arcadia).

Crone, G. R. (ed. and English trans.) (1937) *The voyages of Cadamosto, and other documents on Western Africa in the second half of the fifteenth century* (London: Hakluyt Society).

Cuoq, J. M. (ed. and French trans.) (1975) *Recueil des sources arabes concernant l'Afrique occidentale du 8e au 16e siècle (Bilād al-Sūdān)* (Paris: Centre national de la recherche scientifique, Sources d'historie médiévale, 3).

Curtin, P. D. (1969) *The Atlantic slave trade: a census* (Madison: University of Wisconsin Press).

Daniel, F. de F. (1940) *History of Katsina* (London: Colonial Office Library).

Dapper, O. (1668) *Naukeurige Beschrijvinge der Africaenshe gewesten van Egypten, Barbaryen, Libyen, Biledulgerid* . . . (Amsterdam: Van Meurs); 1970 English trans. and adaptation, J. Ogilby, *Africa: being an accurate description of the regions of Aegypt, Barbary Lybia, etc.* (London); 1670 German trans. *Beschreibung von Afrika* . . . (Amsterdam: Van Meurs); 1686 French trans., *Description de l'Afrique* . . . (Amsterdam: Wolfgang Waesberge et al.).

Davidson, B. (1959) *Old Africa rediscovered* (London: Gollancz).

Davidson, B. (1964) *The African past: chronicles from antiquity to modern times* (London: Longman; Boston: Little, Brown).

Davidson, B. and Bush, F. K. (1965, 1967), *The growth of African civilization: a history of West Africa 1000–1800* (London: Gollancz).

Davis, R. W. (1970) 'The problems of possible pre-Colombian contacts between Africa and the Americas: a summary of the evidence', *Ghana Notes and Queries*, Legon. **6**, 2, pp. 1–7.

Delafosse, M. (1912) *Le Haut Sénégal-Niger*, 3 vols; 1972 ed. M. F. J. Clozel (Paris: Maisonneuve and Larose).

Delafosse, M. (1913) 'Traditions historiques et légendaires du Soudan occidental, traduites d'un manuscrit arabe inédit', *Afrique française: renseignements coloniaux et documeuts*, Paris, August, pp. 293–306; September, pp. 325–9, 355–69.

Delafosse, M. (1922, 1941) *Les Noirs de l'Afrique* (Paris: Payot); English trans. F. Fligelman. *The Negroes of Africa* (Port Washington: Kennikat Press).

Delafosse, M. (1924) 'Les relations du Maroc avec le Soudan à travers les âges'. *Hespéris*. **4,** pp. 153–74.

Denoon, D. (1972) 'Migrations and settlement in south-west Uganda', Makerere Seminar Papers.

Deschamps, H. J. (ed.) (1970–71) *Histoire générale de l'Afrique noire*. 2 vols (Paris: Presses universitaires de France).

Devisse, J. (1972) 'Routes de commerce et échanges en Afrique occidentale en relation avec la Méditerranée: un essai sur le commerce africain médiéval du IIème au 16e siècle', *Revue d'historie économique et sociale*, Paris **50,** pp. 42–73, 357–97.

Diabaté H. (1974) 'A propos de la reine-mère dans les sociétés akan', in Bonduku Seminar Papers, q.v.

Diagne, P. (1965) 'Royaumes sérères: les institutions traditionnelles du Sine Saloum', *Présence africaines **54,*** pp. 142–72.

Diop, C. A. (1955, 1965) *Nations nègres et cultures* (Paris: Présence Africaine).

Diop, C. A. (1960) *L'Afrique noire précoloniale: étude comparée des systèmes politiques et sociaux* . . . (Paris: Présence Africaine).

Domenichini, J. P. (1971) *Histoire des palladium d'Imérina d'après des manuscrits anciens* (Tananarive: Travaux et documents du musée d'art et archéologie de l'Université, 8).

Dramani-Issifou, Z. (1975) 'Les relations entre le Maroc et l'empire songhai dans la seconde moitié du 16e siècle' (Doctoral dissertation, University of Paris).

Dupuis, J. (1974) 'La diffusion du maïs dans l'ancien monde et hypothèses de voyages arabes en Amérique précolombienne', *Comptes rendus trimestriels des séances de l'Académie des sciences d'outre-mer,* Paris.

Duyvendak, J. J. L. (1949) *China's discovery of Africa* (London: Probsthain).

Ehret, C. (1973) 'Patterns of Bantu and central Sudanic settlement in Central and Southern Africa (*ca* 100 BC to 500 AD)', *Transafrican Journal of History,* Nairobi, **3,** I, pp. 1–71.

Ehret, C. (1974) 'Lacustrine history and linguistic evidence: preliminary considerations' (Los Angeles: UCLA Seminar Paper).

L'Empire du Mali (1959), *Notes africaines*, Dakar: Institut fondamental d'Afrique noire, **82**, pp. 1–63; 83, pp. 64–70.

Fage, J. D. (1964) 'Reflexions on the early history of the Mosi-Dagomba group of states', in *The historian in tropical Africa* (London: International African Institute proceedings, fourth international African seminar, Dakar, 1961), pp. 177–91.

Fage, J. D. (1964) 'Some thoughts on state formation in the western Sudan before the seventeenth century', (Boston: University papers in African history, 1). pp. 17–34.

Fagg, B. E. B. (1977) *Nok Terracotas* (Lagos: Nigerian Museum; London: Ethnographica).

Fagg, W. B. (1963) *Nigerian images* (London: Humphries; New York: Praeger); French trans. *Les merveilles de l'art nigérien* (Paris: Editions du Chêne).

Fernandes, V. (n.d) 1951 eds T. Monod, A. Teixeira da Mota, R. Mauny, French trans. P. de Cenival and T. Monod, *Description de la côte occidentale d'Afrique (Sénégal du Cap de Monte, Archipels)* (Bissau: Publicaçaões do contro da Guiné portuguesa, 11).

Filipowiak, W. (1979) *Etudes archéologiques sur la capitale du Mali* (Stettin: Museum Narodin).

Fisher, A. G. B. and Fisher, H. J. K. (1970) *Slavery and Muslim society in Africa: the institution in Saharan and Sudanic Africa and the Trans-Saharan trade* (London: Hurst).

Forman, W., Forman, B. and Dark, P. (1960) *Benin art* (London: Hamlyn).

Fortes, M. (1940) 'The political system of the Tallensi of the Northern Territories of the Gold Coast', in M. Fortes and E. E. Evans-Prichard (eds), *African political systems* (London: International African Institute), pp. 239–71.

Franco Silva, A. (1979) *La esclavitud en Sevilla y su tierra a fines de la Edad Media* (Seville: Diputación Provincial de Seville).

Freeman-Grenville, G. S. P. (1962) *The medieval history of the coast of Tanganyika* (London/New York: Oxford University Press).

Frobenius, L. (1925) *Dichten und Denken im Sudan* (Jena: Diederichs).

Fuglestad, F. (1978) 'A reconsideration of Hausa history before the Jihad', *Journal of African History* ***19,*** 3, pp. 319–39.

Galaal, Musa H. I. (n.d.) 'Stars, seasons and weather' (unpublished).

Garlake, P. S. (1973) *Great Zimbabwe* (London: Thames and Hudson).

Godinho, V. de Magalhães (1969) *L'économie de l'empire portugais aux 15e et 16e siècles* (Paris: SEVPEN).

Goitein, S. D. F. (1967–78) *A Mediterranean society: the Jewish communities of the Arab world as portrayed in the documents of the Cairo Geniza,* 3 vols (Berkeley: University of California Press).

Goes, D. de, et al. (15th century) 1749 ed. R. Boache (Lisbon); 1926 ed. J. M. Teixeira de Carvalho and D. Lopes (Coimbra: Scriptorum Rerum Lusitanorum); (n.d.) ed. and French trans. in V. de Castro e Almeida, *Les Grands Navigateurs et colons portugais du 15e et du 16e siècles* (Brussels: Desmet-Verteneuil), **4**, pp. 191ff.

Goytom, W. M. (1970) *An atlas of Africa* (Addis Ababa No further details available).

Gray, J. (1963) 'The solar eclipse in Ankole in 1492', *Uganda Journal,* Kampala **27,** 2, pp. 217–221.

Gray, R. and Birmingham, D. (1970) *Precolonial African trade: essays on trade in Central and Eastern Africa before 1800* (London/New York: Oxford University Press).

Gray, W. (1826) *Voyage dans l'Afrique occidentale pendant les années 1818, 1819, 1820, 1821 depuis la rivière Gambie jusqu'au Niger* (Paris: Gastel).

Grebenart, D. Paper presented to 1979 seminar on the 'History of the Central Sudan before 1804'.

Greenberg, J. H. (1955) *Studies in African linguistic classification* (Bradford: Compass Publications).

Greenberg, J. H. (1963) 'The languages of Africa', *Journal of African Languages,* London **29,** 1, (Part 2); republished as Publication of the Bloomington Research Center in Anthropology, Folklore and Linguistics, **25**.

Griaule, M. (1938) *Masques dogons* (Paris: Institut d'ethnographie).

Griaule, M. (1966) *Dieu d'eau: entretien avec M. Ogotemmêli* (Paris: Fayard).

Grottanelli, V. L. (1965) *Prescatori dell'Oceano Indiano; saggio etnologico preliminare sui Bagiuni, Bantu costieri dell'Oltregiuba* (Rome: Cremonese).

de Grunne, B. (1980) *Terres cuites anciennes de l'Ouest African,* Publications d'Histoire, de l'Art et d'Archaéologie de l'Université Catholique de Louvain, **22**.

Guthrie, M. (1967–71) *Comparative bantu . . .* 4 vols (Farnborough: Gregg International).

Guthrie, M. (1962) 'Bantu origin: a tentative new hypothesis', *Journal of the Anthropological Institute* London.**I**, pp. 9–21.

Hair, P. E. H. (1967) 'Ethnolinguistic continuity on the Guinea coast', *Journal of African History,* **8,** 2, pp. 24–68.

Hama, B. (1966) *Enquête sur les fondements et la genèse de l'unité africaine* (Paris: Présence Africaine), including 'Un manuscrit inédit de Abkal Aould Aoudar', pp. 205–15.

Hama, B. (1967) *Histoire du Gobir et du Sokoto* (Paris: Présence Africaine).

Hama, B. (1968) *Histoire des Songhay* (Paris: Présence Africaine).

Hamani, D. (1975) *Contribution à l'étude de l'histoire des états hausa: l'Adar précolonial (République du Niger)* (Niamey: Institut de recherche en sciences humaines).

Hamidullah, M. (1958). 'L'Afrique découvre l'Amérique avant Christophe Colomb', *Présence Africaine,* Dakar, 18–19, pp. 173–83.

Harris, M. F. (1974) Paper presented at Bonduku Seminar (no further details available).

Hasan, Y. F. (1967) *The Arabs and the Sudan: from the seventh to the early sixteenth century* (Edinburgh: Edinburgh University Press).

Hasan, Y. F. (1971) *Sudan in Africa: studies presented to the first international conference sponsored by the Sudan Research Unit, February 1968* (Khartoum: Khartoum University Press).

Hazard, H. W. (1952) *The numismatic history of late medieval North Africa* (New York: American Numismatic Society).

Hébert, J. C. (1958) 'La parenté à plaisanterie à Madagascar', *Bulletin de Madagascar,* (Antananarivo) **142,** pp. 175–216; 143, pp. 268–336.

Heers, J. (1966) 'Le rôle des capitaux internationaux dans les voyages de découverte aux 15e et 16e siècles' in *Les Aspects internationaux de la découverte océanique aux 15e et 16e siècles: Actes du cinquième colloque international d'histoire maritime 1960* (Paris: SEVPEN), pp. 273–94.

Henige, D. P. (1974) 'Reflections on early interlacustrine chronology: an essay in source criticism', *Journal of African History*, **15**, I, pp. 27–46.

Heusch, L. de (1972) *Le roi ivre, ou l'origine de l'état: mythes et rites bantous* (Paris: Gallimard).

Hiernaux, J. and Maquet, E. (1968) *L'Age du fer à Kibiro (Uganda)* (Tervuren: Musée royal de l'Afrique centrale; Annales: série in octavo: sciences humaines, 63).

Hugot, H. J. and Bruggman, M. (1976) *Sahara: dix mille ans d'art et d'histoire* (Paris: Bibliothèque des arts).

Hunwick, J. O. (1964) 'A new source for the biography of Ahmad Baba al-Tinbukti (1556–1627)' *Bulletin of the School of Oriental and African Studies*, London.

Ibn Baṭṭūṭa (1357) *Tuhfat al-nuẓẓār fig̲h̲arā, ib al-amṣār wa'ad̲j̲ā'ib al-asfar*, 1853–9, 1922–49 ed. and French trans. C. Defremy and B. R. Sanguinetti, *Voyages d'Ibn Batoutah*. 4 vols (Paris: Imprimerie impériale; Collection d'ouvrages orientaux publiée par la Société asiatique); 1960 edn (Beirut); 1958, 1962, 1971, English trans. H. A. R. Gibb, *The travels of Ibn Battuta*, 3 vols, in progress (Cambridge: Hakluyt Society); 1966 partial French trans. R. Mauny et al., *Textes et documents relatifs à l'histoire de l'Afrique: extraits tirés d'Ibn Baṭṭūṭa* (Dakar University: Publications de la section d'histoire de la faculté des lettres et sciences humaines, 9); 1975 partial French trans. in J. M. Cuoq (ed.), 1975 (q.v.), pp. 289–323.

Ibn Furṭwa, Aḥmad (16th century) *Ta,rik̲h̲ mai Idrīs wa g̲h̲azawātihi lil Imām Ahmad Burnuwī* 1932 ed. H. R. Palmer (Kano: Amir's Press); 1926 English trans. H. R. Palmer *History of the first twelve years of the reign of Mai Idris Alooma of Bornu (1571–1583), by his Imam* (together with the 'Diwān of the sultans of Bornu') (Lagos: Government Printer).

Ibn K̲h̲aldūn, Walī al-Dīn ʿAbd al-Raḥmān b. Muhammad (14th century) *al-Mukaddima*; 1858 ed. E. Quatremère, 3 vols (Paris: Duprat); 1863–8 French trans. M.W. de Slane, *Les Prolégomènes d'Ibn Khaldoun*; 3 vols (Paris: Imprimerie nationale); 1934–8 reprint (Paris: Geuthner); 1958 English trans. F. Rosenthal, *Prolegomena* 3 vols (New York: Pantheon; Bollinger Series, 43); 1967–8 French trans. V. Monteil, *Discours sur l'histoire universelle*, 3 vols (Beirut: Commission internationale pour la traduction des chefs d'oeuvre); 1975 partial French trans. in J. Cuoq (q.v.), pp. 328–63.

Ibn K̲h̲aldūn . . . (14th century) *Kitāb al-ʿIbār wa-diwan al-mubtada wa'l-Khabar* ('Universal History 1868 edn, 7 vols (Būlāk); 1852–6, partial French trans. M. W. de Slane, *Histoire des Berbères et des dynasties musulmanes de l'Afrique septentrionale*, 4 vols (Algiers: Imprimerie du gouvernement); 1925–6 reprint (Paris: Geuthner); 1956–9, complete French trans., 7 vols (Beirut: Commission internationale pour la traduction des chefs d'oeuvre); 1975 partial French trans. in J. Cuoq (q.v.), pp. 328–63.

al-Idrisī Abū ʿAbd Allāh (1154) Kitāb Nuzhat al-mus̲h̲tāk fī 'k̲h̲tirāḳ al-āfāḳ (also known as the 'Book of Roger' after its royal patron, Roger II of Sicily); 1866 partial edn and French trans. R. Dozy and M. J. de Goeje, *Description de l'Afrique et l'Espagne* (Leiden-Brill); 1970ff., complete edn in progress, ed. E. Cerulli et al., *Opus geographicum, sive Liber ad eorem delectationem qui terras peragrare studeant* (Rome: Instituto Italiano per il Medio e l'Estremo Oriente); 1836–40, French trans. P. A. Jaubert, *Géographie d'Edrisi*, 3 vols (Paris: Imprimerie royale): 1975 partial French trans. in J. Cuoq (q.v.), pp. 126–65.

Innes, G. (ed.) (1974) *Sunjata: three Mandinka versions* (London: School of Central and African Studies).

Izard, M. (1973) 'Remarques sur le vocabulaire politique mossi', *L'Homme*, **13,** 1–2, pp. 193–230.

Jeffreys, M. D. W. (1953) 'Precolombian maize in Africa', *Nature*, **172**, 4386, pp. 963–6.

Jeffreys M. D. W. (1963) 'How ancient is West African maize?', *Africa*, London, **33,** pp. 116–18.

Jeffreys, M. D. W. (1971) 'Maize and the Mande myth', *Current Anthropology*, Chicago. **12,** 3, pp. 291–320.

de Jonghe, E. and Vanhove, J. (1949) 'Les formes d'asservissement dans les sociétés indigènes du Congo belge', *Bulletin de l'Académie royale des sciences d'outre-mer*, Brussels, Section des sciences morales et politiques, **19,** pp. 483–95.

Kagame, A. (1955) 'La structure de quinze clans du Rwanda', *Annales Lateraniensis*, Vatican City, **18,** pp. 103–17.

Kake, I. B. (1980) *Les armées traditionnelles de l'Afrique* (Paris/ Libreville: Lion).

Kake, I. B. (1981) 'Les Portugais et le Gabu: 15e, 19e siècles', in Colloque international sur les traditions orales du Gabu (unpublished communication).

Kalck, P. (1974) *Histoire de la République centrafricaine; des origines préhistoriques à nos jours* (Paris: Berger-Levrault).

Karugire, S. R. (1971) *A history of the kingdom of Nkore in Western Uganda to 1896* (Oxford: Clarendon Press).

Kaʿti, Maḥmud b.al-Hadjdj al-Mutawakkil (before 1593), completed (1654–5) by grandson, called Ibn al-Mukhtār by N. Levtzion (1971) who attributes whole work to him, *Ta'rīkh al-fattāsh 1913–14* (revised 1964) ed. and French trans. O. Houdas and M. Delafosse (Paris: Publications de l'Ecole des langues orientales vivantes, 5e série, 10); 1981 Unesco reprint of 1913–14 edn and trans. (Paris: Maisonneuve; Librairie d'Amérique et d'orient).

Kawada, J. (1979) *Genèse et évolution du système politique des Mosi méridionaux: Haute-Volta* (Tokyo: Asia Africa gengo bunla kenkyûzyo).

Keech, S. and McIntosh, R. J. (1980) 'Jenne-Jeno: ancient African city', *Times*, 1 September, p. 18.

Kent, R. K. (1970) *Early kingdoms in Madagascar: 1500–1700* (New York: Rinehart and Winston).

Kirkman, J. S. (1954) *The Arab city of Gedi: excavations at the great mosque, architecture and finds* (London: Oxford University Press).

Ki-Zerbo, J. (1972) *Histoire de l'Afrique noire d'hier à demain* 2nd edn (Paris: Hatier).

Köhler, O. (1958) 'Zur Territorial-Geschichte des Nizerbogens', *Baessler Archiv* (Berlin) **61,** 2, pp. 229–61.

Labatut, F. and Raharinarivonirina, R. (1969) *Madagascar: étude historique* (Paris: Nathan).

Laburthe-Tolra, P. (1977) *Minlaaba: histoire et société traditionelle chez les Béti du sud Cameroun*, 3 vols (Lille: University of Lille II; Paris: Champion).

Lambert (Captain) (1907) 'Le pays mossi et sa population: étude historique, économique et géographique suivie d'un essai d'ethnographie comparée' (Dakar: Archives du Sénégal, unpublished monograph).

Lange, D. (1977) *Le Diwān des sultans du (Kanem)-Bornu: chronologie et histoire d'un royaume africain de la fin du 10e siècle jusqu'à 1808* (Wiesbaden: Steiner; Studien zur Kulturkunde, 42).

Lange, D. (1978) 'Progrès de l'Islam et changement politique du Kanem du 11e siècle au 13e siècle', *Journal of African History*, **19**, 4, pp. 495–513.

la Roncière, C. de (1924–7) *La découverte de l'Afrique au Moyen Age, cartographes et explorateurs*, 3 vols (Cairo: Mémoires de la Société royale de géographie d'Egypte, 5, 6, 13).

Laroui, A. (1970) *L'histoire du Maghreb: un essai de synthèse*, 2 vols (Paris: Maspero); 1977 English trans. R. Manheim, *The History of the Maghrib: an interpretative essay* (Princeton: Princeton University Press).

Last, M. in Adamu, M. (forthcoming) *History: essays in honour of Professor Abdullahi Smith* (Zaria: Ahmadu Bello University Press).

Lavergne de Tressan, M. de (1953) *Inventaire linguistique de l'Afrique occidentale française et du Togo* (Dakar: Mémoire de L'IFAN, 30); 1972 reprint (Amsterdam: Swets and Zeitlinger).

Lebeuf, A. M. D. (1969) *Les Principautés kotoko: essai sur le caractère sacré de l'autorité* (Paris: CNRS).

Lebeuf, J. P. and Mason-Detourbet, A. (1950) *La civilisation du Tchad* (Paris: Payot).

Le Moal, G. (1963) 'Commentaire des cartes ethniques', in G. Brasseur (ed.), *Cartes ethno-démographiques de l'Afrique occidentale française* (Dakar: Institut fondamental d'Afrique noire), pp. 9–21.

Leo Africanus (1550) 'Descrittione dell 'Africa', in G. B. Ramusio, *Navigationi e viaggi* (Venice), Vol. I; 1956 French trans. A. Epaulard, *Description de l'Afrique* (Paris: Maisonneuve).

Le Tourneau, R. (1969) *The Almohad movement in North Africa in the twelfth and thirteenth centuries* (Princeton: Princeton University Press).

Levtzion, N. (1968) *Muslims and chiefs in West Africa: a study of Islam in the Middle Volta Basin in the pre-colonial period* (Oxford: Clarendon Press).

Levtzion, N. (1971) 'A seventeenth century chronicle by Ibn al-Mukhtār: a critical study of Taʿrīkh al-Fattāsh', *Bulletin of the School of Oriental and African Studies*, London, **34,** 3, pp. 571–93.

Lewicki, T. (1974) *Arabic external sources for the history of Africa to the south of Sahara* (London: Curzon Press), 2nd edn.

Livingstone, F. B. (1962) 'Anthropological implications of sickle-cell gene distribution in West Africa', in A. Montagu (ed.), *Culture and the evolution of man* (New York: Oxford University Press).

Lombard, J. (1973) 'La Royauté sakalava: formation, développement et effondrement du 17e au 20e siècle: essai d'analyse d'un système politique' (unpublished).

Lopez, R. S. (1974) *La rèvolution commerciale dans l'Europe médiévale* (Paris: Aubier-Montaigne).

Lovejoy, P. E. (1978) 'The role of the Wangara in the economic transformation of the central Sudan in the fifteenth and sixteenth centuries', *Journal of African History*, **19**, 2, pp. 173–93.

Ly-Tall, M. (1977) *Contribution à l'histoire de l'empire du Mali, (13e–16e siècles): limites, principales provinces, institutions politiques* (Dakar: Nouvelles éditions africaines).

Ly-Tall, M. (1981) 'Quelques précisions sur les relations entre l'empire du Mali et du Gabu', in *Colloque international sur les traditions orales du Gabu,* 1980 (*Ethiopiques*, special issue, October 1981), pp. 124–8.

McIntosh, R. J. and McIntosh, S. K. (1981) 'The inland Niger delta before the empire of Mali: evidence from Jenne-Jeno', *Journal of African History*, **22**, 1, pp. 1–22.

al-Maghīli, Muḥammad b. ʿAbd al-Karīm (c. 1490), untitled treatise written for Askiya Muḥammad of Gao; 1932 English trans. T. H. Baldwin, *The obligations of princes: an essay of Moslem kingship* (Beirut: Imprimerie catholique); 1975 partial French trans. in J. Cuoq, pp. 398–432.

al Maghribī Ibn Saʿīd (13th century). *Mukhtaṣar Djughrāfiyā*, sometimes called *Kitāb baṣṭ al-arḍ fi tūlihū waʾl-ard; 1970 ed. I. al-Arabī* (Beirut); partial French trans. in J. M. Cuoq (q.v.), pp. 201–19.

al-Maḳrīzī, Abu ,Abbās Aḥmad b. ʿAlī (before 1442) MS (b) 'al-Khbar an adjnas al-Sudan' (MSS, Cod. Or 372a, folio 339v–340r) Leiden: Rijksuniversität Bibliothek); 1820 ed. and Latin trans. H. A. Hamaker, *Specimen catalgoi codicum Mss. orientalium bibliothecae Academiae lugduno-batavae* (Leiden: Luchtmans); 1979 French trans. D. Lange, 'Un texte de Makrīzī sur les "races du Soudan" ', *Annales islamologiques,* **15,** pp. 187–209.

Malowist, M. (1970) 'Quelques observations sur le commerce de l'or dans le monde occidental au Moyen Age', *Annales – Economie, Sociétés, Civilisations*, Paris, **25**, pp. 1630–6.

Mané, M. (1978) 'Contribution à l'histoire du Kaabu, des origines au 19e siècle', *Bulletin de l'Institut fondamental d'Afrique noire*, Dakar, **40**, 1, pp. 87–159.

Manessy, G. (1963) 'Rapport sur les langues voltaïques', in *Actes du 2e Colloque international de linguistique négro-africaine, Dakar, 1962*, pp. 239–66 (no further details available).

Maquet, J. J. P. (1961) *The premise of inequality in Ruanda: a study of political relations in a central African Kingdom* (London: Oxford University Press for International African Institute).

Marçais, G. (1913) *Les Arabes en Berbérie du 11e au 14e siècle* (Constantine/Paris: Leroux).

al-Masʿūdī, Abu 'l-Hassan ʿAlī b. al-Husayn B. ʿalī (10th century) *Murūdj al-dhahab; 1861*–77 ed. and French transl. C. Barbier de Meynard and J. Pavet de Courteille, *Les Prairies d' or,* 9 vols (Paris: Imprimerie impériale); 1962–71, French trans. C. Pellat, *Les Prairies d' or* (Paris: Société asiatique); partial French trans. in J. Cuoq (q.v.), pp. 59–62.

Mauny, R. (1961) *Tableau géographique de l'Ouest africain au Moyen Age d'après les sources écrites, la tradition orale et l'archéologie* (Dakar: Institut fondamental d'Afrique noire, Mémoires, 61).

Mauny, R. 'Hypotheèses concernant les relations pré-colombiennes entre l'Afrique et l'Amérique', *Anuario de estudios atlanticos*, Madrid **17,** pp. 369–84.

M'Baye, E. H. R. (1972) 'Un apeȩçu de l'islam ou: réponses d'al-Magili aux questions posées par Askia El-Hadj Muhammad, empereur de Gâo', *Bulletin de l'Institut fondamental d'Afrique noire*, B, **34,** 1–2, pp. 237–67.

Médeiros, F. de (1973) 'Recherches sur l'image des Noirs dans l'occident médiéval, 13–15e siècles', (doctoral dissertation, University of Paris).

Meillassoux, C. (ed.) (1975) *Esclavage en Afrique précoloniale* (Paris: Maspero).

Meillassoux, C., Doucouré, L. and Simagha, D. (eds) (1967) *Légendes de la dispersion des Kusa (épopée soninké)* (Dakar: Institut fondamental d'Afrique noire; *Initiations et études africaines*, 22).

Michalowski, K. (1962) *Faras, fouilles polonaises* (Warsaw: University of Warsaw).

Mieli, A. (1966) *La Science arabe et son rôle dans l'évolution scientifique mondiale* (Leiden: Brill).

Miers, S. and Kopytoff, I. (eds) (1977) *Slavery in Africa: historical and anthropological perspectives* (Madison: University of Wisconsin Press).

Miracle, M. P. (1965) 'The introduction and spread of maize in Africa', *Journal of African History,* **6,** 1, pp. 39–55.

Misiugin, V. M. (1966) 'Suakhiliiskaia khronika srednevekovnogo gosudarstva Pate: La Chronique swahili de l'état médiéval du Paté', in *Africana. Kul'tura i iazyki narodov Afriki* (Moscow: Akademiia nauk SSR. Trudy Institua etnograffii im. N. N. Miklukho-Maklaia. n.s., **90**, Afrikanskii etnograficheskii sbornik, **6**), pp. 52–83.

Monteil, V. (1966) *Esquisses sénégalaises: Wâlo. Kavor Dyolof, Mourides, un visionnaire* (Dakar: Institute fondamental d'Afrique noire; *Initiations et études africaines,* 21).

Monteil, V. (1968) 'Al-Bakri (Cordoue, 1068). Routier de l'Afrique blanche et noire du Nord-Ouest', *Bulletin de l'Institut fondamental d'Afrique noire* **30**, 1, 39–116.

Murdock, G. P. (1959) *Africa: its peoples and their culture history* (New York: McGraw-Hill).

Mworoha, E. (1977) *Peuples et rois de l'Afrique des lacs au 19e siècle: le Burundi et les royaumes voisins* (Abidjan, Nouvelles éditions africaines).

Nachtigal, G. (1879, 1881, 1889) *Sahara und Sudan: Ergebnisse sechsiahriger Reisen in Afrika,* vols 1 and 2 (Berlin: Weidmann). vol. 3 (Leipzig: Brockhaus); 1967 reprint (Graz: Akademie Drüker); 1971, 1974 English trans. A. G. B. and J. J. Fisher (London).

Nadel, S. F. (1942) *A black byzantium: the kingdom of Nupe in Nigeria* (London, New York: Oxford University Press for the Institute of African Languages and Cultures).

Niane, D. T. (1960); 2nd edn 1971) *Soundjata ou l'épopée mandingue* (Paris: Présence Africaine).

Oliver, R. (1953) 'A question about the Bachwezi', *Uganda Journal,* Kampala, **17,** 2, pp. 135–7.

Oliver, R. (1966) 'The problem of the Bantu expansion', *Journal of African History*, **7**, 3, pp. 361–76.

Oliver, R. and Mathew, G. (eds) (1963–76) *History of East Africa*, 3 vols (Oxford: Clarendon Press).

Ottino, P. (1975) *Le Moyen Age de l'Océan indien et le peuplement de Madagascar* (Ile de la Réunion).

Pacheco Pereira, D. (1505–6) *Esmeraldo de situ orbis*; 1905 ed. A. Epiphanio da Silva Dias (Lisbon: Typografia Universal); 1937 ed. and English trans. G. H. T. Kimble (London: Hakluyt Society); 1954 ed. D. Peres (Lisbon: Typografia Universal); 1956 French trans. R. Mauny (Bissau: Publicaçaões do Centro de estudos da Guiné portuguêsa, 19).

Pageard, R. (1962) 'Contribution critique à la chronologie historique de l'ouest africain suivie d'une traduction des tables chronologiques de Barth', *Journal de la Société des africanistes*, Paris, **32**, 1, pp. 91–117.

Pageard, R. (1962) 'Réflexions sur l'histoire des Mossi', *L'Homme*, a, **1**, pp. 111–15.

Pageard, R. (1963) 'Recherches sur les Nioniossés', *Etudes voltaïques,* Ouagadougou.

Palmer, H. R. (ed.) (1909) 'The Kano Chronicle', *Journal of the Anthropological Institute,* London, **38,** pp. 58–98; reprinted in H. R. Palmer, (1928), q.v., vol. 3, pp. 97–132.

Palmer, H. R. (1927) 'History of Katsina', *Journal of the African Society,* London, **26**, pp. 216–36.

Palmer, H. R. (1928) *Sudanese memoirs: being mainly translations of a number of Arabic manuscripts relating to the Central and Western Sudan,* 3 vols (Lagos: Government Printer); 1967 edn (London: Cass).

Palmer, H. R. (1936) *The Bornu, Sahara and Sudan* (London: Murray).

Papadopoulos, T. (1966) *Africanabyzantina: Byzantine influences on negro-Sudanese cultures* (Athens: Grapheion Demosieymaton Akademias Athenon; Pragmateiai tēs Akademias Athenon, 27).

Perrot, C. (1974) 'Ano Asema: mythe et histoire' *Journal of African History*, **15**, 2, pp. 199–222.

Perruchon, J. (1894) 'Histoire d'Eskender, d'Amda-Seyou II et de Na'od rois d'Ethiopie', *Journal asiatique,* Paris, serie 9.

Person, Y, 1962) 'Le Moyen Niger au 15e siècle d'après les documents européens', *Notes africaines,* Dakar, **78,** pp. 45–57.

Pigafetta, F. and Lopes, D. (1591); 1881 English trans. M. Hutchinson, *A report of the kingdom of Congo and the surrounding countries* (London: Murray), 1970 reprint (London: Cass); 1963, rev edn 1965, French trans. W. Bal, *Description du royaume de Congo* (Léopoldville/Kinshasa: University of Lovanium; Publication du Centre d'études des littératures romanes d'inspiration africaine, 4).

Phillipson, D. W. (1968) 'The Early Iron Age in Zambia: regional variants and some tentative conclusions', *Journal of African History*, **9,** 2, pp. 191–212.

Phillipson, D. W. (1974) 'Iron Age history and archaeology in Zambia', *Journal of African History,* **15,** I, pp. 1–25.

Poirier, C. (1954) 'Terre d'Islam en mer malgache: (îlot Nosy Langany ou Nosy Manja)', *Bulletin de l'Académie malgach,* no. spécial du cinquantenaire, pp. 71–116.

Posnansky, M. (1974) 'Archaeology and Alean civilization' in Bonduku Seminar Papers, (Bonduku: Univesity of Abijan).

Premier colloque international de Bamako (1975) Actes du Colloque, *L'empire du Mali, histoire et tradition orale* (Paris: Fondation de la Société commerciale de l'Ouest africain pour la recherche scientifique en Afrique noire, Projet Boucle du Niger).

Ptolemaeus, Claudius (Ptolemy, Claudius) *The Geography,* trans. E. L. Stevenson (1932) (New York).

Quatremère, E. M. (1811) *Mémoires géographiques et historiques sur l'Egypte et sur les contrées voisines*, 2 vols (Paris: Schoell).

Raffenel, A. (1846) *Voyage dans l'Afrique occidentale exécuté en 1843–1844* (Paris: Bertrand)

Randall-MacIver, D. and Mace, A. C. (1902) *El Amrah and Abydos*, pts 1–2 (London/Boston: Egypt Exploration Fund).

Randles, W. G. L. (1968) *L'ancien royaume du Congo, des origines à la fin du 19e siècle* (Paris: Mouton; *Civilisations et Sociétés*, 14).

Randles, W. G. L. (1975) *L'Empire du Monomotapa du 15e au 19e siècle* (Paris: Mouton; *Civilisations et Sociétés*, 46).

Rattray, R. S. (1929) *Ashanti law and constitution* (Oxford: Clarendon Press).

Rattray, R. S. (1932) *Tribes of the Ashanti hinterland*, 2 vols (Oxford: Clarendon Press).

Renan, E. (1866, 1925) *Averroes et l'averroisme: essai historique* (Paris: Calman-Levy).

Rennie, J. K. (1972) 'The precolonial kingdom of Rwanda: a reinterpretation', *Transafrican Journal of History*, Nairobi, **2**, 2, pp. 11–64.

Riley, C. L. (ed.) (1971) *Man across the sea: problems of pre-Colombian contacts* (Austin: University of Texas Press).

Robert, D., Robert, S. and Devisse, J. (1970) *Tegdaoust* (Paris: Arts et métiers graphiques).

Rodney, W. (1970) *A history of Upper Guinea coast: 1545–1800* (Oxford: Clarendon Press).

Rouch, J. (1954) *Les Songhay* (Paris: Presses universitaires de France).

Rouch, J. (1960) *La religion et la magie des Songhay* (Paris: Presses universitaires de France).

al-Saʿdī, ʿAbd al-Raḥmān b. ʿAbd Allāh (1656) **Ta,rīkh al-Sūdān**; 1898 ed. O. Houdas and E. Benoist with 1900 French trans. O. Houdas, 2 vols (Paris: Leroux); 1964 revised trans. (Paris: Maisonneuve et Larose).

Saidi, A. (1963) 'Contribution à l'histoire almohade: une première expérience d'unité maghrébine' (doctoral dissertation, University of Lyon).

Sarton, G. (1927–48) *Introduction to the history of science*, 3 vols (Baltimore: Carnegie Institute).

Shaw, T. (1970) *Igbo-Ukwu, an account of archeological discoveries in eastern Nigeria*, 2 vols (London: Faber and Faber for the Institute of African Studies, Ibadan).

Shinnie, P. L. (1971) 'The culture of Medieval Nubia and its impact on Africa', in Y. F. Hasan (ed.), *Sudan in Africa* (Khartoum: Khartoum University Press), pp. 42–50.

Skinner, N. (1968) 'The origin of the name Hausa', *Africa*, London, **38**, 3, pp. 253–7.

Smith, H. F. C. (Abdullahi) (1971) 'The early states of Central Sudan;, in J. F. A. Ajayi and M. Crowder (eds), *History of West Africa* (London: Longman), vol. 1, pp. 158–201.

Smith, M. G. (1959) 'The Hausa system of social status', *Africa*, London, **29**, 3, pp. 239–52.

Smith, M. G. (1960) Government in Zazzau, 1800–1950 (London: Oxford University Press for the International African Institute).

Strandes, J. (1899) *Die Portugiesenzeit von Deutsch- und Englisch Östafrika* (Berlin: Reimer); 1961 English trans. J. F. Wallwork, *The Portuguese period in East Africa* (Nairobi: East African Literature Bureau).

Summers, R. (1969) 'Ancient mining in Rhodesia', Memoirs of the National Museums and Monuments of Rhodesia (present Zimbabwe), Salisbury (present Harare).

Sutton, J. E. G. (1979) 'Towards a less orthodox history of Hausaland', *Journal of African History*, **20**, 2, pp. 179–201.

Tamakloe, E. F. (1931) *A brief history of the Dagomba people* (Accra: Government Printer)

Tauxier, L. (1917) *Le noir du Yatenga; Mossis, Nioniossés, Samos, Yarsés, Silmi-Moissis, Peuls* (Paris: Larose).

Tauxier, L. (1924) *Nouvelles notes sur le Mossi et le Gourounsi* (Paris: Larose).

Teixeira da Mota, A. (1954) *Guiné portuguêsa*, 2 vols (Lisbon: Agência geral do Ultramar).

Terrasse, H. (1949–50) *Histoire du Maroc des origines à l'établissement du protectorat français*, 2 vols (Casablanca: Atlantides).

Tiendrebeogo, Y. (1964) *Histoire et coutumes royales des Mossi de Ouagadougou* (Ouagadougou: Naba).

Trimingham, J. S. (1962) *A history of islam in West Africa* (London: Oxford University Press).

al-ʿUmarī in Cuoq, J. M. (ed.) and French trans. (1975) *Recueil des sources arabes concernant l'Afrique occidentale du 8e au 16e siècle (Bilād al-Sūdān)* (Paris: Centre national de la recherche scientific, Sources d'histoire médiévale, 3).

al-ʿUmarī, Ibn Faḍl allāh (14th century) *Masālik al-absār fi Mamālik al-amsar,* 1924 edition (Cairo); 1927 trans., Gaudefroy-Demombynes, *L'Afrique moins l'Egypte* (Paris: Geuthner; Bibliothèque des géographes arabes, 2).

UNESCO (1980) *The Historiography of Southern Africa: proceedings of the meeting of experts, Gaborone, 1977;* The General History of Africa – Studies and Documents, no. 4 (Paris: UNESCO)

Urvoy, Y. (1949) *Histoire de l'empire de Bornou* (Dakar: Institut fondamental d'Afrique noire; Mémoires, **7**; Paris: Larose); 1968 edition (Amsterdam: Swets and Zeitlinger).

Vansina, J. (1960) *L'évolution du royaume Rwanda des origines à 1900* (Brussels: Mémoires de l'Académie des sciences d'outre-mer, classe des sciences morales et politiques, n.s. **26**, 2).

Vansina, J. (1969) 'The bells of kings', *Journal of African History,* **10**, 2, pp. 187–97.

Westermann, D. and Bryan, M. A. (1970) *Languages of West Africa* (Folkestone: Dawsons; Handbook of African languages, pt 2).

Wiener, L. (1920–2) *Africa and the discovery of America,* 3 vols (Philadelphia: Innes).

Wiet, G. and L. Hautecoeur (1932) *Les mosquées de Caire* (Paris: E. Leroux).

Willcox, A. R. (1975) 'Pre-Colombian intercourse between the old world and the new: consideration from Africa', *South African Archaeological Bulletin,* Cape Town, **30**, pp. 19–28.

Willett, F. (1962) 'The introduction of maize into West Africa; an assessment of recent evidence', *Africa,* London, **32**, 1, pp. 1–13.

Wondji, C. (1974) 'Conclusion in Bonduku Seminar Papers (Bonduku: University of Abidjan)

Wriglev, C. (1973) 'The story of Rukidi', *Africa,* London, **43**, 3, pp. 219–31.

Wylie, K. C. (1977) *The political kingdoms of the Temne: Temne government in Sierra Leone 1825–1910* (London/New York: Africana Publications).

Yāḳūt b. ʿAbd Allāh al-Hamawī (13th century). *Mu'djam al-Buldān; 1866–73* ed. J. F. Wüstenfeld, Jacut's geographisches Wörterbuch, 6 vols (Leipzig: Brockhaus), **5**, pp. 75–6, 302–699.

Young, M. W. (1966) 'The divine kingship of the Junkun: a re-evaluation of some theories', *Africa,* London, **36**, 2, pp. 135–53.

Zouber, M. (1977) *Ahmad Baba de Tombouctou, 1556–1627: sa vie, son oeuvre* (Paris: Maisonneuve et Larose; Publications de département d'islamologie de l'Université de Paris-Sorbonne, 3).

Zurara, G. E. de (1896, 1899) *Cronica dos feitos de Guiné; The chronicle of the discovery and conquest of Guinea,* ed. and English trans. C. R. Beazley and E. Prestage, 2 vols (London: Hakluyt Society); 1949 edition, *Cronica dos feitos de Guiné* (Lisbon: Divisao de publicações et biblioteca, agencia geral das colonias); 1960 French trans. L. Bourdon, *Gomes Eanes de Zuraga, Chronique de Guinée* (Dakar: Institut fondamental d'Afrique noire Mémoires, 1).

Index